Before European Hegemony

BEFORE
EUROPEAN
HEGEMONY

The World System A.D. 1250–1350

JANET L. ABU-LUGHOD

New York   Oxford

OXFORD UNIVERSITY PRESS

Oxford University Press

Oxford   New York   Toronto
Delhi   Bombay   Calcutta   Madras   Karachi
Petaling Jaya   Singapore   Hong Kong   Tokyo
Nairobi   Dar es Salaam   Cape Town
Melbourne   Auckland

and associated companies in
Berlin   Ibadan

First published in 1989 by Oxford University Press, Inc.,

198 Madison Avenue, New York, New York 10016-4314

First issued as an Oxford University Press paperback, 1991

Oxford is a registered trademark of Oxford University Press

Library of Congress Cataloging-in-Publication Data
Abu-lughod, Janet L.
Before European hegemony: the world system A.D. 1250–1350
Janet L. Abu-lughod.
p.   cm.   Bibliography: p.   Includes index.
ISBN 0-19-505886-0
ISBN 0-19-506774-6 (pbk)
1. Economic history—Medieval, 500–1500.
2. International trade—History.
3. Cities and towns, Medieval.
I. Title.
HC41.A28 1989   330.94'017—dc19   88-25580

15   17   19   20   18   16   14
Printed in the United States of America
on acid-free paper

To the memory of my parents
who encouraged in me
an insatiable curiosity

Preface

In his *The Structure of Scientific Revolutions*, Thomas Kuhn suggests that one of the major ways in which theoretical paradigms about the world change is through the accumulation of anomalies—that is, observations and pieces of data that do not "fit into" existing theories and generalizations or cannot be accounted for by existing paradigms. The Kuhnian position, however, stresses discoveries in the "real world" that force a rethinking of approaches. This reveals the basic positivism of his assumptions; such a position can be taken only if one believes in some Platonic ideal of "real truth."

This book begins from a somewhat different premise. Particularly in the social and cultural sciences, anomalous findings can arise from *what is in the observer*, as well as what is to be observed. This more relativistic view assumes that scientific knowledge is socially constructed. If knowledge is not some disembodied product isomorphic with the world but rather is produced through collective definition, that is, it represents a transient human "consensus about the world," then it follows that not only new pieces of information but new vantage points from which to observe existing ones can produce paradigmatic revolutions.

Several recent transformations in sociohistorical work have forced reformulations of prior knowledge. Some have arisen from new facts, but most have been made possible by changes in the identities of knowers or have derived from changes in ways of knowing. Let me single out a few.

First, certainly not unprecedented but always productive are works that cut across disciplines—combining economics, politics, sociology, and history. Each discipline has its own traditional perspective, which means that observers from various disciplines view the same "real world" somewhat differently. Original insights are often possible when scholars risk crossing disciplinary lines: one thinks, inter alia, of the incursions of anthropologist Eric Wolf and sociologists such as Immanuel Wallerstein and Christopher Chase-Dunn into history, of historians such as Fernand Braudel and Philip Curtin into economics, or of the interdisciplinary blending so evident in the work of Charles Tilly, Perry Anderson, and Eric Hobsbawm. Granted, this is perilous, and yet there may be no gain without risk.

My own background straddles many disciplines, because I have accumulated disciplines as I found them interesting. I began as an American urban sociologist/demographer/planner, studied economic and "development" planning, did work that was later defined as geography, was impelled to learn Middle Eastern history and culture when I lived and worked in Egypt, and, in time, expanded those interests to other parts of the Third World. Each disciplinary and geographic shift increased my understanding, albeit at the cost of becoming marginal to mainstream American sociology whose parochial boundaries have only recently expanded to encourage a broader, more historical and comparative perspective.

A second new way of viewing has come from the revisionist work being done in many fields of history and social science by scholars from outside the western world. There is no part of the so-called "Third World" in which the received wisdom of ethnocentric western scholarship has not been called into question by "subalterns" (as they are called in Indian historiography) who find in their own histories not the stasis of tradition but the dynamics of orthogenic change, not the backwardness vis-à-vis the west, assumed so off-handedly in much western scholarship, but the development of underdevelopment through subordination. It is no small challenge to cross the battlefields that now lie between received wisdom and subaltern challenge, and yet some new "truth" may come from a perspective that incorporates the interpretations of victims as well as victors. In this book I have tried to draw upon both to present a more balanced image.

There is perhaps a third way in which knowledge changes, namely, by changing the distance from which "facts" are observed and thereby changing the scale of what falls within the purview. Only rarely have historians risked looking globally. Arnold Toynbee and William McNeill are among the few whose reputations have survived attacks by scholars specializing in narrower limits of time and place. The social organization of historians is a remarkable phenomenon. In the historians' matrix, constituted vertically by time, horizontally by space, and third dimensionally by focus, there are only a few specialists situated at each of the thousands of unique intersections; there they dig long and deep. The skills they must bring to their tasks, not only linguistic but cumulatively contextual, require lifetimes to develop. Their work is the basis on which all generalists must depend. And yet the cost of such concentration is often a loss of peripheral vision.

This book, by contrast, suffers from the opposite problem. However, I am hopeful that the insights I obtained by looking at the *connections between* geographic entities that are usually treated by separate sets of specialists may yield enough to compensate for the *hubris* of taking so global a view. While writing this book I often felt as if I were a clumsy high-wire walker, teetering across world voids. My sole net has been the forebearance and generosity of many of the best specialists I could find, situated at their own points in the history matrix.

And finally, some changes in view occur by the idiosyncratic accumulation, within the mind of a scholar, of diverse bits of information that resist reconciliation. To some extent, the present study grew, even before I was aware of its need, out of my discomfort over discrepancies between "received" wisdom and, at least at first, some fairly accidental accretions of anomalous information.

My work on the history of Cairo had convinced me that the Eurocentric view of the Dark Ages was ill-conceived. If the lights went out in Europe, they were certainly still shining brightly in the Middle East. Visiting and studying most of the other major cities in that region of the world reassured me that Cairo was only one apex in a highly developed system of urban civilization. This led me to reject both the widely acclaimed work of Henri Pirenne on the revival of European *Medieval Cities* and the similarly well-regarded essay by Max Weber on *The City*, which makes a sharp distinction between the medieval city of the occident (which Weber defines as the *true* city) and the presumably spurious city of the orient.

Somewhat later, when preparing a collection of readings on *Third World Urbanization*, which focused largely on contemporary urban problems, I sought an excerpt to demonstrate that although the Third World now lags sadly behind the West, this had not always been so. It was at that point that I first read Gernet's study of thirteenth-century Hangchow, then the largest and most advanced city in the world.

Still later, while living in Paris, I had the opportunity to spend some time in Bruges—one of the world's most lovingly preserved and restored medieval cities—and began to read its history. Then, in good company, I fell victim to the romance of Venice and, shortly thereafter, quite by chance, came upon the Gies' small gem, *Life in a Medieval City*, which describes Troyes in the thirteenth century. Indeed, long before the idea for this book materialized out of the miasma of random interests, it was being formed subliminally from these experiences.

Intrigued by the connections I found among these places (and others as well), I searched the works of historians for a book that systematically explicated what I had begun to see as a global system. Two thousand bibliography cards later, I had still not found that source, although I had grown increasingly dissatisfied with much of the literature I had found.

By that time, the first two volumes of Wallerstein's *The Modern World-System* had appeared. I read them both with great interest but with a gnawing sense of Kuhnian anomaly, since they tended to treat the European-dominated world system that formed in the long sixteenth century as if it had appeared de novo. This heightened the "dis-ease" I had long felt about the works of the great German historical sociologist, Max Weber, and even about Marx's treatment of the origins of capitalism.

In 1984, despairing that I would ever find a book that answered my questions, I began to formulate the research agenda for a study

I really wanted to *read*, not write. Here is the outcome of that study, albeit with warts and with more questions raised than answered. Hopefully, it will generate additional anomalies, thus stimulating those more versed in the necessary languages, better trained in history, and with deeper understanding of given areas to revise the picture I have tried to draw.

So many persons and institutions have contributed to this work that it is impossible to list them all. The scholar whose early encouragement meant most to me was William McNeill, who, after reading a very preliminary application for a grant, written when the project was still only vaguely delimited, took the initiative to contact me. His kind letter, saying he thought I was onto something significant, sustained me when, with good reason, I was periodically overwhelmed by the enormity of what I had undertaken.

As I searched the literature it became clear that whereas scholars, many with great diligence and skill, had investigated parts of the puzzle, few had attempted to piece together in systematic fashion the connections among them. Reading widely in the separate histories of the various regions, I came to value the work of certain specialists and determined that the only way to protect myself from gross errors of fact, albeit not necessarily interpretation, was to throw myself on the mercy of those who had devoted lifetimes to learning in depth what I could only know most superficially. A great many of the specialists to whom I wrote or spoke gave wise guidance to sources and/or critiqued drafts of chapters in their own "areas." Thus, in addition to the published sources listed in the bibliography, I learned a great deal personally from John Benton, Robert Lerner, David Nicholas, Ravi Palat, Paul Wheatley, Immanuel Wallerstein, David Ludden, Robert Hartwell, Carl Petry, and K. N. Chaudhuri. Among the many who suggested additional sources were Andre Gunder Frank and Robert Wicks.

Two respected colleagues, Arthur Stinchcombe at Northwestern University and Charles Tilly at the New School for Social Research, read and commented on the entire manuscript, asking hard questions but at the same time encouraging me by their interest.

I am also grateful to Jay Weinstein and Nanda Shrestha, co-editors of *Studies in Comparative International Development*, for inviting me (much too prematurely!) to contribute an article on the world system in the thirteenth century to their special twentieth anniversary series, thus forcing me to focus my ideas. They solicited commentaries on it from William McNeill, Alastair Taylor, Andre Gunder Frank, J. M. Blaut, and Anthony de Souza, whose reactions to the project stimulated clarifications and refinements in my work.

New School graduate students enrolled in my experimental course on Change in Global Context in the fall of 1987 served as faithful substitutes for "the general reader" and offered important corrections to the text. Another New School graduate student, Richard Ganis, performed the exacting task of verifying, where possible, the numerous bibliographic references. (Residual errors have undoubtedly crept in for sources I examined in foreign libraries but which could not subsequently be verified in the United States.)

Time and money were indispensable to this book. Northwestern University in general, at which I taught sociology for twenty years, and its Center for Urban Affairs and Policy Research in particular, with which I was affiliated for a decade, generously supported this study by granting me a reduced teaching load for the three-year period during which most of the manuscript was researched and written. Typing and endless corrections were done by two secretaries in the Sociology Department at Northwestern; the contributions of Leyla Gungor and Barbara Williamson may go unnoticed by readers but are deeply appreciated by me.

Travel funds were also crucial. Northwestern contributed a small sum that helped me spend a summer in Europe, gathering materials and consulting libraries in Belgium, France, and Italy. A short consulting stint with the United Nations Habitat office in Nairobi, with suitable ticket downgrading, facilitated work in East Africa and even got me as far as Pakistan and the People's Republic of China. An invitation from the Social Research Centre of the American University in Cairo to be a Visiting Distinguished Professor in the spring of 1986 made it possible for me to gather materials for the Middle East portion of the study. An earlier trip to India had been made possible through a Fulbright short-term fellowship, and as a result of a grant from the Social Science Research Council, I was also able to travel to Southeast Asia to conduct research there. My husband's calm travel know-how greatly enhanced my capacity to get much done on the trips to Europe, China, and

Southeast Asia, and I am appreciative not only of his help but his good company. The only region covered in the book that I was never able to visit, much to my regret, was Central Asia, but one must leave something to look forward to.

At Oxford University Press two individuals contributed in important ways. I am grateful to editor Valerie Aubry, who was both my most enthusiastic reader and trenchant critic, and Andrew Mudryk, whose erudition and artistic skills yielded maps that truly illustrate the adage that one picture equals a thousand words!

I say goodbye to this book with reluctance, not only because it remains imperfect but also because I have never enjoyed any project as much. I shall miss my obsession.

New York   J.A.L.
August 1988

Contents

Introduction

Part I: The European Subsystem

Part II: The Mideast Heartland

Part III: Asia

Conclusion

List of Illustrations and Maps

"You take delight not in a city's seven or seventy wonders, but in the answers it gives to a question of yours."

"Or the question it asks you, forcing you to answer, like Thebes through the mouth of the Sphinx."

ITALO CALVINO
Invisible Cities

Before European Hegemony

CHAPTER

1

Studying a System in Formation

The second half of the thirteenth century was a remarkable moment in world history. Never before had so many regions of the Old World come in contact with one another—albeit still only superficially. At the beginning of the Christian era, the Roman and Chinese empires had been in indirect contact, but the connections between them declined when both empires fragmented. In the seventh and eighth centuries, Islam unified many parts of the central region that lay between the European and Chinese extremities, reaching out in both directions, but the peripheral areas of this reviving world economy still remained relatively isolated from one another. By the eleventh and, even more, twelfth century, many parts of the Old World began to become integrated into a system of exchange from which all apparently benefited. The apogee of this cycle came between the end of the thirteenth and the first decades of the fourteenth century, by which time even Europe and China had established direct, if decidedly limited, contact with each other.

The thirteenth century was remarkable in another way. In region after region there was an efflorescence of cultural and artistic achievement. Never before had so many parts of the Old World simultaneously reached cultural maturity. In China, the most glorious pottery ever produced, Sung celadonware, was being created, and in Persia glowing turquoise-glazed bowls constituted the only serious rival. In Mamluk Egypt, craftsmen were fashioning elaborate furniture inlaid with complex arabesques of silver and gold, and in western Europe, cathedral building reached its apex. The gem-like stained glass window-adorned Saint Chapelle of Paris was built in mid-thirteenth century, just before St. Louis departed on crusade. The great Hindu temple complexes of south India climaxed at this same time. Almost everywhere there was evidence of a surfeit of wealth being devoted to ornamentation and symbolic display. The era was equally productive intellectually, suggesting that the surplus was used not only to produce things but to support scholars as well.

These two qualities of the thirteenth century, increased economic integration and cultural efflorescence, were not unrelated. Technological and social innovations produced surpluses, which were, in turn, traded internationally to further intensify development. Parallel advances in navigation and statecraft facilitated contact among distant societies, which generated even more surpluses. In all areas, prosperity—at least at the top—yielded high culture, and Europe, hitherto the least developed region, perhaps had the most to gain from the new links being forged.

In this book we explore the thirteenth century "world economy" which facilitated such pandemic prosperity for its rulers, and examine how it was forged. We also examine why this promising start faltered by the middle of the fourteenth century. How much of it remained when, in the sixteenth century, Europe took the lead in forging what Wallerstein (1974) has termed the "modern world-system"? In *that* world system, which has persisted for some five hundred years, the West was clearly hegemonic. But to understand its roots it is necessary to examine the period *before* European hegemony. That is the descriptive task of this book.

There is an analytic task as well. The world economy of the thirteenth century is not only fascinating in itself but, because it contained no single hegemonic power, provides an important con-

Pair of doors inlaid with carved ivory. Mamluk Egypt, late thirteenth to early fourteenth century. Courtesy of the Metropolitan Museum of Art; bequest of Edward Seymour, 1891 (91.1.2064).

Celadon vase, Chinese, late thirteenth century to early fourteenth
century. Courtesy of the Metropolitan Museum of Art; anonymous
gift, 1965 (65.82.3).

trast to the world system that grew out of it: the one Europe
reshaped to its own ends and dominated for so long. This contrast
suggests that the characteristics of world systems are not invariant.
There is no unique way for the parts to be organized. Furthermore,
world systems are not static. They evolve and change. At this
moment in time, the particular world system that originated in the
sixteenth century is in the throes of change. Understanding the
system that preceded it may help in better comprehending what

Stained glass window, Troyes cathedral, France, late twelfth century. Courtesy of the Metropolitan Museum of Art; gift of Ella Brummer, in memory of her husband, Ernest Brummer, 1977 (1977.346.1).

Brass bowl inlaid with silver, Mongol Iran, mid-fourteenth century. Courtesy of the Metropolitan Museum of Art, Rogers Fund, 1935 (35.64.2).

lies ahead. We return to these themes at the end of this book, but first we need to know much more about the thirteenth century itself.

The Thirteenth Century: A World System?

Between A.D. 1250 and 1350 an international trade economy was developing that stretched all the way from northwestern Europe to China; it involved merchants and producers in an extensive (worldwide) if narrow network of exchange. Although primary products (including but not confined to specialty agricultural items, mostly spices) constituted a significant proportion of all items traded, particularly over short distances, manufactured goods were surprisingly central to the system, which probably could not have been sustained over long distances without them. The production of these goods had to be sufficient to meet domestic needs as well as those of export. Thus, all the units in the system were producing surpluses, impossible unless the methods of mobilizing labor and organizing the work process were quite advanced.

Furthermore, the trade involved a wide variety of merchant communities at various points on the globe. These merchants did not necessarily speak or write the same languages, although Arabic covered a wide area, as did Greek and the vernaculars of Latin, and Mandarin Chinese was a lingua franca for the many nationalities in the far east. Nor were their local currencies the same. Silver was highly valued in Europe, gold was used in the Middle East, whereas copper coins were the preferred specie in China. Distances, as measured by time, were calculated in weeks and months at best, but it took years to traverse the entire circuit. And yet, goods were transferred, prices set, exchange rates agreed upon, contracts entered into, credit—on funds or on goods located elsewhere—extended, partnerships formed, and, obviously, records kept and agreements honored. I hope to show how advanced this system was in the thirteenth century—although whether it was "modern capitalism" and whether this could be called a "world system" remain to be established.

In this book I have no intention of engaging in a fruitless argument concerning the "origins" of "true" or "modern" capitalism.[1] Nor do I intend to engage world system theorists in a similarly unproductive debate about the precise moment in history at which one moves from world empires to a more global system, much less to determine when "traditional world-economies" metamorphosize into a modern world system. Wallerstein (1974) distinguishes multiple and ordinary "world-economies" and empires from *the* "modern world system." Although he acknowledges the existence of world empires before the sixteenth century, he still treats the modern world system as if it were the first.[2] But he is simply one of the more recent to enter the fray (see also Ekholm, 1980; Mann, 1986; Schneider, 1977; Chase-Dunn, 1989).

Historians have traditionally disagreed about the dating of the capitalist (as opposed to the classical) world economy. Even Marx was ambivalent, at one time tracing capitalism back to the thirteenth century, but later changing his mind and opting for the sixteenth century. Students of the thirteenth-century textile industry of Flanders (see Chapter 3 for Espinas, 1923; Laurent, 1935) argue forcefully, on the basis of the mode of production and the growing opposition between owners and workers (a class conflict that reached its peak in the latter part of the century), that industrialization had already occurred there, and that this industrial system was inextricably linked to an already established "world market."[3] Braudel (1984) acknowledges that the commercial revolution of the thirteenth century clearly initiated a European "world-economy" that, although it may have temporarily aborted in the trough of the mid-fourteenth century, nevertheless foreshadowed the system that was to come. And Eric Wolf (1982), in his book that begins with 1400, also stresses that the Eurocentered world system that developed after that date was built on the base of an existing system not previously dominated by Europe. These debates, in the last analysis, are over definitional niceties rather than empirical realities. It seems more important to examine the seamless web of the latter than to fight over the precise boundaries between historic epochs.

One empirical basis for distinguishing between the "traditional" and "modern" periods might be to differentiate societies organized for production for the market that *do not separate* ownership of capital from ownership of labor power from those societies that do. But upon closer inspection, this distinction does not hold up, for free labor and monetization of exchange long predate "modern industrial production,"[4] slave labor and barter persist far into the modern era, and there probably never was an urban society in which "owners" were not leisured.

Another distinction often made is between the "commercial revolution" and the "industrial revolution," but to draw the line between the two would often be too arbitrary and, indeed, too late. Industrialism developed at different times in different places. The level of development of Chinese metallurgy in the twelfth century would not be achieved in Europe until the sixteenth century (Hartwell, 1966, 1967), and China's paper making and printing technology would not be duplicated in the West for several centuries (Carter, 1955; Needham, 1954–85, 1981). Although we know less about the processes of production in the Middle East and Asia than we do about those in Europe, the fact that large quantities of cloth were produced (cotton and linen in the Arab region, cotton and silk in India, and silk in China) suggests that the techniques used for production must have been equal to those in other places (such as Flanders) for which we do have information.

Nor will scale allow us to differentiate the thirteenth from the sixteenth century. One must acknowledge that the scale of production and trade in the thirteenth century was less than what prevailed in the sixteenth century, although it was higher than in the fifteenth. But that is hardly a fair measure. In comparison with the scale of international commerce today, the exchanges of the sixteenth century are miniscule. The important comparison is not with the future but with the past. Did a significant increase in trade occur in the thirteenth century? And did it unite many developing areas? Most medievalists claim that it did. The comments by Lopez (1976: 93–94) are quite relevant:

> At first glance, if we compare the patterns of trade in the Commercial Revolution to those in the Industrial Revolution, certain differences will strike us . . . [A]ll proportions are almost unbelievably smaller. Luxury products . . . tend to play a more important role than commodities for mass consumption. Many . . . business men show greater interest in enlarging profit margins . . . than in enlarging the number of sales. . . . Still the volume of exchanges . . . [by the thirteenth century was] impressive . . . [T]he sea trade of Genoa in 1293 was three times

as large as the entire revenue of the Kingdom of France in the same year. . . .

The same radical increase in the scale of international trade was observed in Sung China. Mark Elvin (1973: 171–172) describes the thirteenth-century expansion of China's international trade, noting that by then China was exporting

> copper and iron goods, porcelain, silks, linens, chemicals, sugar, rice and books, and receiving in exchange spices and other exotic items. Parts of the Chinese rural economy became directly linked to production for the overseas market.

Relatively speaking, then, the scale in the Middle Ages did not differ very much from that in the early "modern capitalist" age, particularly if we recognize that technology had not changed drastically by the sixteenth century. If we are not to come to a technologically determined resolution of this problem, claiming that the "industrial" period appears when inanimate energy is substituted for animate,[5] we had best abandon the a priori attempt to define world system, modernity, capitalism, etc. until we use these terms—duly separated and empirically loaded—to analyze concrete moments in history in concrete places.

Of all the comments I have read, those of Fernand Braudel seem to be the most sensible.[6] He acknowledges that world-economies existed in various parts of the world long before the thirteenth century and that certainly a European world-economy had taken shape before the sixteenth century, singled out as so crucial by Wallerstein and in certain writings by Marx.[7] He argues that thirteenth-century Italy had all the capitalist institutions and even the industrial production, using free wage labor, that would be required to classify it as a capitalist world-economy (Braudel, 1984: 79, 91).

But even the wisdom of Braudel cannot protect him from an unconscious Eurocentric slip. Although he readily acknowledges that "the first world-economy ever to take shape in Europe [was born] between the eleventh and thirteenth centuries" (1984: 92) and that "several world-economies have succeeded . . . each other in the geographical expression that is Europe," or rather, the "European world-economy has changed shape several times since the thirteenth century" (1984: 70), he fails to make what to me is the essential point. Before Europe became *one* of the world-economies in the twelfth and thirteenth centuries, when it joined the long distance trade system that stretched through the Mediterranean into the Red Sea and Persian Gulf and on into the Indian Ocean and through the Strait of Malacca to reach China, there were numerous preexistent world-economies. Without them, when Europe gradually "reached out," it would have grasped empty space rather than riches. My plan is to examine this world system as a whole, treating Europe at that time as it should be seen, as an upstart peripheral to an ongoing operation.

This book is less interested in identifying origins and more in examining a crucial moment in history. It takes the position that in terms of time, the century between A.D. 1250 and 1350 constituted a fulcrum or critical "turning point" in world history, and in terms of space, the Middle East heartland region, linking the eastern Mediterranean with the Indian Ocean, constituted a geographic fulcrum on which West and East were then roughly balanced. The thesis of this book is that there was no *inherent historical necessity* that shifted the system to favor the West rather than the East, nor was there any inherent historical necessity that would have prevented cultures in the eastern region from becoming the progenitors of a modern world system. This thesis seems at least as compelling as its opposite. The usual approach is to examine ex post facto the outcome—that is, the economic and political hegemony of the West in modern times—and then to reason backward, to rationalize why this supremacy *had* to be. I want to avoid this.

It is not that I do not recognize that the outcome determines the narrative constructed to "lead inexorably" to it. This indeed is the real methodological problem of historiography. I am struck with the incisive comment of Germaine Tillion, written in a somewhat different context:

> [A]s we all know, events must run their course before becoming history, so that *all* true history exists only by virtue of its conclusion, and begins its historical career from there.[8]

If this is indeed correct, then beginning with a different outcome at a different moment in time will lead to a different account of the sequence and a different set of items to be explained. Rather than taking the outcome of the industrial revolution for granted and then trying to explain its "causes," I therefore start from an earlier vantage point. While my story is no more true (nor more false) than the conventional one, it does illuminate areas and issues that the story of Europe's hegemony conceals.

I examine the system of world trade circa 1300 A.D. to see how and to what extent the world was linked into a common commercial network of production and exchange. Since such production and exchange were relatively unimportant to the subsistence economies of all participating regions, the question is not one of defending an unrealistic vision of a tightly entailed international system of interdependence and exchange. This was also true in the sixteenth century, however. Thus, if it is possible to argue that a world system began in that century, it is equally plausible to argue that it existed much earlier.

To some extent, it depends upon which part of the system is used to determine when volume is enough to be "counted" as part of such a system. Certainly, considering Europe, which at mid-thirteenth century was still very much part of the periphery, long-distance trade was not making a significant contribution to the internal economies, still heavily agrarian and oriented to subsistence. However, even in Europe there were major variations between the "city-states" of Italy and Flanders and the more peripheral subregions, such as Germany or England. Lopez (1976: 93) points out that "the difference between Italy north of the Tiber and the most retarded parts of Europe during the Commercial Revolution was as significant as that between England or the United States and India or China during the Industrial Revolution." And once one moved away from the city centers that maintained links to the outside, one was clearly in the shadowy world of subsistence. Braudel (1984: 30) adopts Richard Haëpke's felicitous phrase, "an archipelago of towns," to describe the spottiness of development. This seems a particularly sensitive way to capture the fact that, within the same general region, a variety of social formations coexisted: from the monetized trading centers, already profiting from foreign exchange and already beginning to shape production in their hinterlands for export, to outpockets in the most depressed mountain ridges and valleys, untouched by the changes taking place. It is because of this that I have chosen to focus on cities rather than countries, since I want to trace the connections among the highpoints of the archipelagos themselves.[9] But it must be stressed that they were, then even more than now, surrounded by a vast sea of encapsulated rural regions.

Not only were there great variations in the European periphery, but there were also substantial differences within the countries in the Old World core—in the Middle East, India, and China (at that time the leading contender for hegemony). Although the Middle East was generally more developed than Europe, it contained large areas relatively unintegrated with the central places that controlled empires. Cairo and Baghdad stand out as dual imperial centers, but their linkages through overland and sea routes tied them selectively to an "archipelago" of hinterlands. Antioch, Aleppo, and Acre connected Baghdad to the Mediterranean, whereas Basra connected Baghdad to the Indian Ocean and the trade of the east. Northeastward across the desert was Baghdad's overland link to the east, the same route the Mongols used to invade her in the second half of the thirteenth century. Cairo was connected to the Mediterranean world through Alexandria, whereas the Nile linked her to the Sudan and desert roads led across North Africa; the sea trade along the Red Sea made a port call at Jiddah or at Upper Egypt before transiting via Aden to the east.

Nor was China a simple and unchanging monolith. That vast zone was differentiated on at least three axes: north and south, coast and interior, and along rivers or off their pathways. In general, times of expanding prosperity were associated with movements of population from north to south, from interior to coast, and from alluvial valleys to more peripheral places (see the careful work of Hartwell, 1982).

The Indian subcontinent was similarly complex and divided into subregions subject to very different imperatives. Northern India prospered when links to the Muslim world were strong and when the land routes to Russia on the north and to China on the east were open. The condition of south India, on the other hand, was contingent more upon the sea trade through the Indian Ocean, and there was often a clear differentiation between coastal and interior zones.

Similarities

One of the striking findings of the research was that similarities between trading partners in the thirteenth century far outweighed differences, and, wherever differences appeared, the West lagged behind. This seemed to contradict the usual assumptions. Furthermore, in spite of the tendency of western scholars dealing with the "Rise of the West"[10] to stress the *unique* characteristics of western capitalism, comparative examination of economic institutions reveals enormous similarities and parallels between Asian, Arab, *and* Western forms of capitalism. This finding is particularly intriguing because, as we all know, variations cannot be explained by constants. The chief areas of similarity are these:

THE INVENTION OF MONEY AND CREDIT

In all three culture areas recognized currencies were a *sine qua non* of international trade, with developments in western Europe coming much later and, if our contention is correct, derivatively (the Italian merchants borrowing existing mechanisms from their Muslim counterparts in the Middle East who had been using them for centuries).[11] In all three regions states played an important role in minting, printing, and/or guaranteeing such currencies. Indeed, the preferred specie for international transactions before the thirteenth century, in Europe as well as the Middle East and even India, were the gold coins struck first by Byzantium and then Egypt. It was not until after the middle of the thirteenth century that some Italian cities (Florence and Genoa) began to mint their own gold coins, but these were used to supplement rather than supplant the Middle Eastern coins already in circulation.

In China, money followed a somewhat different line of development. Because of the strong state (and a preference for copper rather than gold), the fictive connection between worth and the coin that represented it seems to us more transparent. The currency had value because it was backed (and later controlled) by the state. This clear connection made possible the introduction of paper money in China as early as T'ang times (ninth century) and its further expansion during the Sung and Yuan dynasties, even though paper money did not appear in Europe until centuries later.

Credit, of course, is the intermediate step between "hard" (i.e., metallic) money and paper as legal tender. It is important to note that credit instruments (essentially promises to pay later and in some other place) were also highly developed in the Middle East and China long before they became critical to business transactions at the fairs of western Europe.

Similarly, the social role of "banker" was found in the Orient long before it appeared in the form of the "benches" or "banco's" of the Italian merchants who set them up at the trade fairs of Champagne. Occasionally, western scholars point out that letters of credit elsewhere were usually between "owners" and their agents or factors abroad and that, at least in the case of major Middle Eastern and Indian traders, including Jews, these were connected through family ties. But it is important to recall that in the beginning, and for quite a long time afterward, the ties that bound transactions in Europe were also those of blood. Family firms were the original form of credit banking and, throughout the Middle Ages and beyond, banking houses (of which the later Medicis of Florence were to become the most famous example) were "family" houses. This institution continued down through the nineteenth century, with the "houses" of Rothschild and even Rockefeller running banks involved in international finance.

MECHANISMS FOR POOLING CAPITAL AND DISTRIBUTING RISK

For long distance trade in particular, large amounts of initial capital were required to purchase the goods that were to be shipped for later sale. During the long voyages, this "capital" was "tied up" in goods that might or might not reach their destinations. Six months was not an unusual duration for transit and, of the ships that sailed out filled with items of high value, some would sink and others would be captured, with their value either lost entirely or reduced by the sums needed to ransom them.[12]

In the Middle East there were elaborate techniques for pooling capital through partnerships or for apportioning profit on the basis of formulas that returned a certain percentage to the merchant advancing the goods (or the financier putting up the money to buy the goods) and another percentage to the partner who accompanied the goods and saw to their disposition at the point of sale (Udovitch, 1970a). Here again, partnerships were often within families or, in the case of Jews (and later Indian and even oversea Chinese), with coreligionists or conationals. This was also true in Europe. Byrne (1930) described the elaborate system for long-distance shipping that was in place in twelfth and thirteenth century Genoa. It bears some resemblance to the institutions already used by the Arabs to conduct their shipping trade. Furthermore, the father and uncle of the illustrious Marco Polo, who preceded him to the eastern capital of the Khans, constituted just such a family firm.

In thirteenth-century China the state, because it was stronger, played a more central role in trade (an invisible partner, as it were, to the merchants) and wielded a heavier regulatory hand. Furthermore, slavery may have been more important in recruiting the labor force used to produce goods for foreign trade in the royal/state production centers, and slaves were often used as agents for major merchants. This was also true in Mamluk-ruled Egypt. Nevertheless, guilds of independent merchants were powerful in both places (Kato, 1936, for China; Fischel, 1958, and others for Egypt). This introduces a third area of similarity.

MERCHANT WEALTH

It is conventional to celebrate the "laissez-faire" character of western capitalism and to differentiate the European economic system from the "Asiatic" mode by stressing the greater interference of the state in the Orient. The ideology is that European merchants were independent of the state whereas Asian and Arab merchants were dependent upon and under the control of rulers who had other interests. Neither of these stereotypes is entirely correct.

In all three culture areas, merchant wealth, independent of the state, was an important factor. Merchants had a certain latitude to accumulate capital, even though they were in the last analysis at the mercy of the ruling apparatus that often "borrowed" their capital, with no necessary requirement to repay, or imposed heavy forced "contributions" to the public coffers when the state faced economic difficulties. This financier function of the major merchants was common to all three regions.

Furthermore, although in European city-states there was theoretically a government by "burghers," this did not mean autonomy. In the case of the Champagne fairs, the Count, a supraurban au-

thority, played a significant controlling role, and in the cases of
the textile towns of Flanders or the city-states of Italy, relatively
small and dictatorial "patriciates," comprised of large land owners
and capitalists, formulated the policies of the "state" in their own
interests, which were not necessarily those of the rest of the inhabitants (Lestocquoy, 1952a; van Werveke, 1944, 1946).

To explain Europe's subsequent hegemony, then, it is necessary
to look beyond her internal inventiveness and the virtues of her
"unique" entrepreneurial spirit. During the thirteenth century the
other world powers had as promising a level of business acumen
as, and an even more sophisticated set of economic institutions
than, the Europeans, who by the thirteenth century had entered
their world system.

Differences

What, then, distinguished the two regions—Europe and the Orient? The difference was that in the thirteenth century Europe
lagged behind the Orient whereas by the sixteenth century she had
pulled considerably ahead. The question to be asked is why, particularly if one rejects the facile answer that Europe had unique
qualities that allowed her to. My contention is that the context—
geographic, political, and demographic—in which development occurred was far more significant and determining than any internal
psychological or institutional factors. Europe pulled ahead because
the "Orient" was temporarily in disarray.

Although the full answer to this question will be presented in
the rest of this book, some of the findings might be previewed
here. First, there was progressive fragmentation of the intervening
overland trade route regions that had been unified by Genghis
Khan during the first half of the thirteenth century but, by the end
of the century, had been subdivided among his successors. These
warring factions shattered the relative calm that existed even as
late as the reign of Kubilai Khan (under whose safe conduct the
Polos were able to traverse all of central Asia). Arab Asia survived
the Crusaders and the capture of Baghdad by the Mongols (1258),
but it seems not to have survived the depredations of Tamerlane
around 1400. Egypt's prosperity and role in world trade outlived

Baghdad's; Cairo's prosperity reached a peak in the third decade of the fourteenth century (Abu-Lughod, 1971).

Second, the Black Death, which spread from China all the way to Europe in the "calamitous" mid-century between 1348 and 1351, decimated most of the cities along the great sea route of world trade, disturbing customary behavior, changing the terms of exchange because of differential demographic losses, and creating a fluidity in world conditions that facilitated radical transformations, benefiting some and harming others (Gottfried, 1983; McNeill, 1976).

This could be seen in Europe, where England, previously part of the periphery, began to play a more central role after the Plague, since her "die-off" rate was lower than on the continent, and also on the Italian peninsula which had been hit hardest because her trade and traffic with the Middle East were so intense. And although Renaissance Italy recovered her strength, with the Italian towns remaining prosperous and vital until the beginning of the sixteenth century and continuing to dominate Mediterranean trade even afterwards, the Mediterranean had ceased to be the primary highway, in part because the eastern Mediterranean had ceased to offer a unique gateway to the East.

Interestingly enough, it was the galleys of the Italian city-states that, by the end of the thirteenth century, opened the North Atlantic to traffic. This delivered the coup de grâce to a world system that had existed for centuries. By the end of the fifteenth century the Portuguese, strategically sited on that ocean, had "discovered" the sea route to India, sailing down the Atlantic coast of Africa and then up the eastern coast to enter the gateway to the all important Indian Ocean, still under the control (but not for long) of Arab and Indian fleets. This was scarcely a "discovery," for Arab navigation manuals had charted these waters long before (Tibbetts, 1981), and the coastline, albeit in the reverse order from east to west (!), is described in such detail in the manuals that one cannot doubt the prior circumnavigation of Africa by Arab/Persian sailors.

Nevertheless, Arab and Indian vessels proved no match for the Portuguese "men-of-war" that appeared in their waters in the early 1500s. By the end of the opening decade of the sixteenth century,

Portugal held important African ports of call, had defeated the Egyptian fleet guarding the entrances to the Red Sea and the Persian Gulf, had moved on to establish beachheads on the west coast of India, and had taken over the key point of Malacca that guarded the crucial strait through which, like an eye of a needle, all ships bound for China had to pass. Note that all of this occurred long before the Venetians defeated the Ottoman Turks at the battle of Lepanto (1571), the point at which Braudel (1972) claims European power was assured, and before 1559, the turning point Wallerstein singles out.

The failure to begin the story early enough has resulted, therefore, in a truncated and distorted causal explanation for the rise of the west. I hope to correct this by beginning at an earlier point when the outcome was far from determined. The time between the thirteenth and sixteenth centuries marked the transition, and geopolitical factors within the rest of the world system created an opportunity without which Europe's rise would have been unlikely. This is explored in the chapters that follow.

But before moving on to this story we make two digressions. The first contrasts Europe in the thirteenth and sixteenth centuries to demonstrate how dramatically she had shifted to center stage. The second discusses sources, methodological issues, and the unavoidable problems involved in preparing a work of this ambitious scope.

European Exemplars of the Thirteenth and Sixteenth Centuries

One way to illustrate the change in Europe's relationship to the East between the thirteenth and sixteenth centuries is to contrast the lives and preoccupations (as well as fates) of two quintessential scholar/statesmen of their ages: Roger Bacon who lived in the earlier century, and Francis Bacon who lived in the later. The differences in their lives clearly exemplify two central changes: the reversed positions of east and west, and the changing relationship between church and state in Europe.

Roger Bacon, English philosopher, scientist, and educational reformer, was born in c. 1220 A.D. and lived until c. 1292; the peak of his intellectual productivity came between 1247 and 1257, when he was exploring new branches of knowledge—mathematics, optics, astronomy, and, interestingly enough, alchemy. He was particularly interested in languages and advocated the study of oriental living languages, inter alia, as a way of gaining knowledge from the Muslims of Spain and the Middle East. He hoped to reform European education by incorporating the knowledge that was available in these "higher" civilizations.

Sir Richard W. Southern (1962, third printing in 1980) distinguishes three phases in Europe's attitude toward the Middle East. Phase I, termed "The Age of Ignorance," stretched from about A.D. 700 to 1100 and was based upon religious myths and deductions from the scriptures. The second phase began with the First Crusade (1099), which introduced more elaborate fictions about the Muslim world. During the first half of the twelfth century there was an efflorescence of writings about the "Saracens," about Muhammad, and about the high culture and brave opponents faced in the Crusades. Southern refers to this phase as the "Century of Reason and Hope." By the middle of the twelfth century, mythology was beginning to be supplanted by greater knowledge, particularly after the Qur'an was finally translated into a western language in 1143.[13] "With this translation, the West had for the first time an instrument for the serious study of Islam" (Southern, 1980: 37).

During the next century, Europeans hoped that the peoples contacted in the Crusades would convert to Christianity and that Christian culture would be strengthened by the knowledge held by or transmitted through Islamic cultures. It is in this context that Roger Bacon's interest in "living oriental languages" and St. Thomas Aquinas' (ca. 1225–1274) dependence on Arabic transmitters for Aristotle's works on ethics must be seen. Just before the middle of the thirteenth century, Aristotle's natural, metaphysical, and then moral and political philosophies were gradually recovered. Aquinas' consummate reconciliation between Christian theology and Aristotelian philosophy resolved matters until the reformation of the sixteenth century.

However, by 1250 and particularly after Europe's "discovery" of the Mongols, the benign hope of converting the world to Christianity began to fade as Europeans gained a better sense of the geographic size and population of the non-Christian world. In Southern's words (1980: 42–43):

> The effects of [Europe's encounter with the Mongols] . . . on the outlook for Western Christendom were many and various. . . . [T]he Mongols greatly enlarged the geographical horizon and increased many times the number of people known to exist in the world. . . . Peter the Venerable [estimated] that Islam contained a third, or possibly even a half of the people of the world. . . . By the middle of the thirteenth century . . . it was seen that this picture . . . was . . . far too optimistic. There were ten, or possibly a hundred, unbelievers for every Christian. Nobody knew; and the estimate grew with each access of knowledge.
>
> One consequence of this was to make the Crusade seem either quite impossible, or in need of a drastic reassessment of its aims and methods. For the rest of the Middle Ages the Western world was divided into one or other of these two camps: either no Crusading was called for, or very much more and better Crusading.

Roger Bacon lived during the peak of this shift in Western knowledge of and attitudes toward the rest of the world.

In 1257, not atypical for the times, he entered a religious order, withdrawing from the "secular" life of Oxford. He wrote to Pope Clement IV, appealing to him to set up a grand project—an encyclopedia of new knowledge in the natural sciences. The impact of translations from Arabic on his thinking cannot be ignored. As Southern notes (1980: 53), the change in Western philosophy

> was very largely the result of the work of a small body of devoted translators at work in Toledo in the third quarter of the twelfth century. These men introduced the works of the great Moslem philosophers Al-Kindi, Al-Farabi, Avicenna, and others to the West, and to a great extent they put the West for the first time in possession of the tradition of Greek philosophical and scientific thought. . . . A large body of this work was accessible in Latin by the end of the twelfth century; but it was not until about the year 1230—when Roger Bacon was of an age to begin his university career [sic]—that the ideas and terminology of these writings made their way into Latin theology. . . . It would have startled the theologians of an earlier generation to see the name of Avicenna quoted beside that of Augustine; but this is what happened with astonishing rapidity, and modern scholars are finding increasingly

extensive traces of the influences of Moslem writers in thirteen century theology.

Roger Bacon was fully aware of this literature and in his letters to the Pope he stressed the need to supplant wars and crusades by teaching and preaching. For that, greater knowledge was needed of the languages and systems of belief of those who were to receive the preaching. Bacon's outpourings of ideas continued even after the Pope died. Between 1268 and 1278, he produced an enormous quantity of writings, for which his reward from his fellow theologians was condemnation and imprisonment.

What religion had been to thirteenth century Roger Bacon, politics was to sixteenth century Francis Bacon—testimony to the supplanting of religious orders by the absolutist state in Europe (see Anderson, 1974a). Francis Bacon, English philosopher, man of letters, and sometime Lord Chancellor of England, was born in 1561 and died in 1626; his life thus straddled the period of Islamic eclipse and Europe's long sixteenth century ascent to the apex of the evolving world system.

Roger Bacon's hopeful but unrequited relationship to the Pope is paralleled by Francis Bacon's more secular relation to the monarchy. In 1584 he became a Member of Parliament and a political adviser to Queen Elizabeth. In 1597 he published his first *Essays*, along with other works, but his partisan connections with Lord Essex, condemned in 1600, led him to fall out of favor with the Queen. After the accession of King James I in 1603, Bacon was gradually restored to favor, dedicating his 1605 *Advancement of Learning* to the new king. This was a plan to reorganize the study of the natural sciences, but by then such sciences were indigenous. In 1618 he was appointed Lord Chancellor and in 1620 he published his *Novum Organum*. In 1621, accused of having taken bribes, he was imprisoned in the Tower of London; although the king later reduced his punishment, he never again sat in Parliament and instead spent his final years in quiet scholarly activities.

Note both the parallels and the differences. The primary parallels are a commitment to the natural sciences, appeals to authorities to back their schemes, and eventual disgrace. The differences are in many ways more interesting. Whereas Roger Bacon's orientation was toward the sacred, Francis Bacon was squarely in a more secular world. Whereas Roger hoped to convince the Pope, Francis appealed to the monarch. The most telling difference, however, was in their attitudes toward learning. For Roger, knowledge lay in the east, hence his concern with oriental languages and Islam. Francis believed little could be gained from others; he assumed that knowledge would be new and indigenously achieved. Perhaps nothing reveals so clearly how the relative positions of East and West had changed in the three intervening centuries.

Some Historiographic Methodological Problems

Although it is possible to use metaphors, such as the Baconian one, to indicate broad sweeps of change, it is somewhat more difficult to make the details clear and comparable. For that we need to evaluate disparate sources of information and build a credible composite picture of the world system as it existed in the later thirteenth and early fourteenth centuries. Judgments are inextricably linked backward to uneven types of data and forward to the synthetic story that is not self-explanatory but must be constructed out of bits and remnants of pieces, some more veracious than others. This problem turned out to be a greater obstacle to producing this book than I had foreseen. Two difficulties were particularly intractable.

First, cultures at that time varied greatly in terms of what was considered significant to record, where it was preserved (and on what, since clay tablets last much longer than palm fronds), and how much detail was recorded and with what accuracy. In a comparative work such as this, in which one would ideally like to have uniform and equally reliable data, it is frustrating to find valuable documents in one place that have no parallels elsewhere, or, even worse, to find that virtually no data have survived (as in the case of Malaysia). I call this the "problem of data."

Second, even when we have data, we must use them with great caution. Some of the most tantalizing primary material at our disposal for reconstructing the world of the past consists of accounts written by individuals who lived at the time. The gap between such documents and the "real world" (comparable to what exists in survey research) I call the "problem of testimony." The major methodological challenge—once hope is abandoned that testimony tells the truth—is to use the selective and distorted testimony as yet another way to "read" what was going on. I have called this the "problem of perspective." My strategy has been to shift viewpoints, noting how each society viewed itself while also trying to gain a more "objective" perspective by comparing different views of the same fact.

The Problem of Data

Any comparative analysis immediately confronts the dilemma of getting comparable data. It is perhaps here that the primacy of culture makes itself most frustratingly obvious. Some societies have been preoccupied with enumeration and the counting and recording of events, persons, and transactions. In contrast, the written records of others do not evidence the same preoccupations, although they may have meticulously enumerated items that later social historians find less than interesting; or such records may have vanished almost totally.

In this study I was unable to obtain comparable data for each of the several societies becoming more intimately connected during the thirteenth century. At one extreme were Genoa and China with almost compulsive approaches to recording and enumerating. The thousands of notarized documents produced by Genoese traders, not only at home but in trading emporia abroad, offer the student interested in tracing business transactions an embarrassment of riches that can never be fully integrated. (Those dealing with Flanders alone have been compiled in the three-volume work by Doehaerd, 1941 and *seq*.) The Chinese, also, seem to have preserved in written form not only the world's oldest demographic records but also primary documents, written by officials, that detail if not how much was traded and for what, at least what the bureaucratic procedures were for conducting foreign trade.[14]

At the opposite extreme were three crucial participants in the trade of the thirteenth century—the Mongols of Central Asia, the principalities along the Strait of Malacca, and, to a much lesser extent, the Islamic region. The Mongols left only a modest primary record that is focused largely on campaigns, dynastic successions, and conquests. Only the secondary accounts of Marco Polo and other travelers give us information on items central to the present study.

For the principalities along the Strait of Malacca, the nature of the terrain (tropical rain forest), the absence of compelling harbors (which led to migrating emporia rather than solidly built and preserved cities with permanent records), and perhaps other factors as well, resulted, according to Paul Wheatley, in the virtual absence of all evidence other than epigraphic.

And finally, in the Muslim world, a tendency for the literate 'ulema to remain "above" crass commerce meant that there was a discrepancy between what was recorded for posterity (primarily religious tracts, *fiqh*, legal decisions, chronicles of kings and nobles) and what a contemporary economic historian would like to find preserved. The following quotation illustrates what appears to be an almost gratuitous dismissal of the purposes of this study.

> My Illustrious Friend and Joy of my Liver: The thing you ask of me is both difficult and useless. Although I have passed all my days in this place, I have neither counted the houses nor have I inquired into the number of inhabitants; and as to what one person loads on his mules and the other stows away in the bottom of his ship, that is no business of mine. But, above all, as to the previous history of this city, God only knows the amount of dirt and confusion that the infidels may have eaten before the coming of the sword of Islam. It were unprofitable for us to inquire into it. O my soul! O my lamb! Seek not after the things which concern thee not.[15]

Such a cultural attitude toward the mundane poses an almost insuperable obstacle to a contemporary researcher. Fortunately, the records of worldly matters, such as what persons loaded on their mules or stored in the holds of their ships, have come down to us in fragmentary fashion—albeit via a highly skewed sample. In Old Cairo, one area of concentration of the Egyptian Jewish community during medieval times, there was a repository into which Jews threw all papers with writing on them, for fear that if the papers were destroyed, the name of God might inadvertently be destroyed as well. This repository, the Geniza, contained records of just those matters of daily transactions so eschewed by the official chronicles and so disdained by the writer quoted above. From laborious study of these snippets of paper, Goitein (see Chapter 7) meticulously reconstructed many aspects of Jewish life in eleventh and twelfth century Cairo and obtained information on their trade with Spain, North Africa, the Levant, and even India. He was also able to expand his view to Muslim inhabitants, since the scarcity of paper in those days forced it to be used and reused many times. Thus, on the back of a sheet containing a Jewish marriage/dowry list, for example, there might be a Muslim bill of sale or a rental agreement.

Scholars of the Middle East have also been able to reconstruct economic life through documents drawn up for entirely different purposes. Thus, *waqf* documents deeding properties in trust for a family or for a religious institution such as a school or mosque can be used to compile lists of wealthy families or the location of public facilities, as Lapidus has done for Aleppo and Damascus in the fourteenth century (1967). Chronicles and necrologies can be used to identify important wholesale merchant families, as Wiet did for the Egyptian "karimi" merchants (1955), or to trace the interplay between 'ulema scholars and their origins and travels, as Petry did for fifteenth century personages (1981). Even coins—their diffusion, debasement, or acceptance—can supply indirect evidence of prosperity and decline. In addition, gross changes in the size or extent of individual settlements can be employed as indirect measures of the expansion and contraction of population. (See Figure 15 in Chapter 11.)

In summary, lack of comparable data has made it difficult to trace the levels of living within and the relationships between the areas selected for study. Judgments have often had to substitute for what social scientists call "hard data." However, this is probably no less foolhardy than blind acceptance of figures, just because they appear to be "scientific." It is wise to remember the classic statement made by Sir Josiah Stamp, statistician with the English Department of Inland Revenue between 1896 and 1919, who reflected:

> The government is very keen on amassing statistics. They collect them, add them, raise them to the nth power, take the cube root and prepare wonderful diagrams. But, you must never forget that every one of

these figures comes in the first instance from the village watchman, who just puts down what he damn pleases.

I believe that as much judgment has to be exercised in interpreting numbers presented in documents as is necessary to exercise when they are absent. Neither data nor testimony, as we shall see, is a transparent reflector of the world.

The Problems of Testimony and Perspective

The story of Europe's Commercial Revolution in the thirteenth century is constructed largely through European (mostly Italian) documents, either trade accounts, wills and *commenda* documents, or travel accounts. Southern European material is quite explicit about that region's direct relations across the Mediterranean. But relations with the world beyond—namely India and China and intervening points—remain unclear. Intermediary agents in Middle Eastern ports and trading centers are acknowledged as being involved in the transshipping of objects from farther east (i.e., spices, porcelains, etc.), but the regions with which *they* trade remain *terrae incognitae* until considerably later. Therefore, European documents cannot be expected to describe the crucial trade links between the Muslim intermediaries and the Indian and Chinese urban centers with which they traded because (1) the latter were relatively unknown, and (2) even when they were seen, they were not attended.

The "Story of Marco Polo" is in many ways a perfect example of the motes in European eyes that have so distorted our image of the thirteenth-century world system. Eileen Power (reprinted 1963: 43) sets a Eurocentered scene of Venice's involvement in the world system around the time Marco Polo set out for China.

Life was a fair and splendid thing for those merchant princes, who held the gorgeous East in fee [sic] in the year of grace 1268. In that year traders in great stone counting-houses, lapped by the waters of the canals, were checking, book in hand, their sacks of cloves, mace and nutmegs, cinnamon and ginger from the Indies, ebony chessmen from Indo China, ambergris from Madagascar and musk from Tibet. In that year the dealers in jewels were setting prices upon diamonds from Golconda, rubies and lapis lazuli from Badakhshan, and pearls from the fisheries of Ceylon; and the silk merchants were stacking up bales of silk and muslin and brocade from Baghdad and Yezd and Malabar and China. In that year young gallants on the Rialto . . . rubbed elbows with men of all [sic] nations, heard travellers' tales of all lands, and at dawn slipped along the canals in gondolas . . . ; and the red-haired ladies of Venice whom centuries later Titian loved to paint, went trailing up and down the marble steps of their palaces, with all the brocades of Persia on their backs and all the perfumes of Arabia to sweeten their little hands.

Marco Polo's father and uncle had left Venice in 1260 and returned nine years later with fabulous tales of their lives in the court of Kubilai Khan, the Cathay-based head of the Mongol eastern empire. They had been sent back to Italy with a message from the Khan to the Pope. Two years later they left again for the east, this time taking young Marco with them. Many years later, after several decades of sojourn in the east, Marco was imprisoned by the Genoese. To pass the time, he told his travel adventures cum "geography" to a cellmate who wrote them down. Marco Polo's fame as the "first" to discover the Orient is spurious. As we shall see, he was not the first European to have contact with the East (see de Rachewiltz, 1971, and Dawson, 1980, for earlier travelers); he is simply the one whose memoirs, due to chance, were recorded.

But what is this source, so crucial to European knowledge of the Orient? The tale is a jumbled one, told not in chronological but in geographic atlas form. It describes his various itineraries, town-by-town, desert-by-desert. What he reports reflects not only what he experienced but what he chose to "notice." Reading the text not as an "original document" giving the "true picture" but as a selective account of what did or did not interest him and of what documents he accidentally obtained gives the historical investigator a very different interpretation than that generally obtained from historical accounts.

For example, there is Marco Polo's preoccupation with textiles. Over and over again he refers to cities in the Far East as being engaged in much trade and commerce, and yet the only manufactured goods he specifies in detail are textiles. Is this because his family traded in cloth and Venice was chiefly preoccupied with importing cloth or because he takes all other industries for granted? Second, there is his preoccupation with spices and where they are grown. This is somewhat more understandable, given the fact that spices were still the chief import to Europe from the Far East. But he seems truly outraged that certain spices, so highly valued in Europe and in short supply, are abundant elsewhere. Precious stones constitute the third object of his interest. A recurring theme in his discussion of precious stones, pearls, etc. is that eastern political rulers are forever "restraining trade" by limiting the amount that can be mined or put into circulation, often through a royal monopoly. Gold also figures in his accounts. From this it is clear that Marco Polo describes only those parts of Far Eastern agriculture and industry of direct concern to a European trader, ever aware of the "value" of these objects at home.

As interesting as the attention paid to certain items is his selective inattention to others. Conspicuous in Marco Polo's account of Chinese, Malay, Indonesian, and Indian ports are his passing references to foreign merchants (identified variously as "worshippers of Mohammet," "Saracens," and "idolators") who often maintained their own quarters or streets in these cities. But who are they? In what are they trading? Do they stay in the ports or travel back and forth with their goods? What is their relation to the host country? From what "home bases" do they come? Such matters are of no interest to Marco Polo. He does not inquire about these traders; he never interacts with them, and thus his account supplies no information about the active trade occurring between the Near and Far East.

I raise this point to suggest that accounts by Europeans, including Marco Polo's, are responsible for a distorted definition of the thirteenth century as a period of Commercial Revolution [for whom?] and have been perpetuated by historians of medieval Europe who have depended almost exclusively upon documents generated in the West.

Closely linked to the problem of testimony, therefore, is that of perspective. History is inevitably "distorted" by the vantage point of the historian. This results because questions are framed in terms of what is problematic in the historian's culture and because the indigenous sources report not what happened or what was there but what someone chose to mention and what someone knew as "true," whether indeed it was or not.

This can be illustrated by two examples—one with respect to

evaluation and the second with respect to "real facts." First, it is possible to examine the views of the "other" as they appear in the primary sources of the Middle Ages. A case in point is East and West viewing each other across the divide of the Crusades. Contrast Krey's edited book, *The First Crusade, the Accounts of Eye-Witnesses and Participants* (1921, reprint 1958) with Maalouf's recently translated *The Crusades through Arab Eyes* (1984). Or contrast the admiration of the East expressed by Marco Polo with the subtitle of a description of "foreign lands and peoples" written in the thirteenth century by Chau Ju-Kua, a Chinese port official. He calls his book a description of "barbarous" peoples, referring chiefly to Arabs since he had not even met any Europeans (English translation 1911). Or read the Chinese and Mongol travelers and historians translated in E. Bretschneider's two volume work, *Mediaeval Researches from Eastern Asiatic Sources* (1875–1876) to obtain an oriental "view of the world."

On matters of fact the case is even clearer, yet no less biased. When Chau Ju-Kua reports that certain goods were imported to China from specific places, it is obvious that his information is wrong. It is clear to an outsider that the foreign traders he interviewed were often reluctant to divulge their sources of supply, lest the Chinese bypass their middlemen and deal directly with the places from which their goods came. It is a relatively simple matter to identify the correct provenance today, for these various spices and goods were also traded in other places where their origin was not concealed.

Lack of information, in itself, can be used as a sensitive indicator of world perspective, particularly when it is presented in good faith. It is possible, for example, to use gross inaccuracies in the accounts of Arab geographers or European travelers in the Middle Ages to draw a relatively accurate map of the world they knew, either personally or through the eyes of informants with first-hand experience. Fabulous tales of dog-faced peoples (Idrisi on the Andaman Islands, for example) or mythological humanoids, called Chin-Chin, covered with hair but having no knees (whose blood was reported by Friar William of Rubruck to be the source of the red dye used in Chinese textiles), clearly indicate that the zones described lie beyond the experience of contemporaries. So also, Chinese accounts of water sheep that grow cotton instead of wool, or western accounts of special Chinese trees whose leaves are covered with silk floss, suggest that although each had knowledge of the other's products because they imported them, neither had even seen the raw material.

Therefore, we intend to use materials reflecting perspective as additional data—but only after evaluating their significance either for reflecting the "world" or for reflecting a distortion in its perception.

Plan of the Book

No world system is *global*, in the sense that all parts articulate evenly with one another, regardless of whether the role they play is central or peripheral. Even today, the world, more globally integrated than ever before in history, is broken up into important subspheres or subsystems, such as the northern Atlantic system (western Europe and the United States–Canada), the Pacific rim (Japan, Taiwan, Korea, Indonesia, Malaysia, etc.), the socialist "bloc," China, still a system unto itself, and the North African–western Asia Arab world. Each of these subsystems may have its own core, containing a hegemonic state whose economy sets the terms of trade for its "satellites." What Friedmann and Wolff have called "world cities" (1982) exist within these dominant places or, as in the cases of Hong Kong and Singapore, even stand alone. Such metropoles drain their own hinterlands, drawing surplus not only from rural areas but even from the capital cities of their satellites.

But over and above these regional subsystems there is an overarching world system that works through world cities whose "transactions" are increasingly with one another. Significantly, Friedmann and Wolff mapped their "world cities" using a base map provided by the Japan Airlines. The polar projection eliminates the usual east or west bias of the Mercatur projection, and the air routes demonstrate accurately just how "central" certain world cities are.

In the thirteenth century, also, there were subsystems (defined by language, religion, empire) dominated by imperial or core cities as well as mediated by essentially hinterlandless trading enclaves. Their interactions with one another, although hardly as intense as today, defined the contours of the larger system. Instead of airlines, these cities were bound together by sea lanes, rivers, and great overland routes, some of which had been in use since antiquity. Ports and oases served the same function as air terminals, bringing goods and people together from long distances.

Given the primitive technologies of transport that existed during the earlier time, however, few world cities at opposite ends of the system did business directly with one another. The journey had to be broken geographically, with centers between flanking places serving as "break-in-bulk" and exchange points for goods destined for more distant markets. Nor was the world the "global village" of today, sharing common consumer goals and assembly-line work in a vast international division of labor. It was rare then, although not unknown, for products partially produced in one place to be finished or assembled in another. The subsystems in the thirteenth century were more self-sufficient than they are today and therefore less vitally dependent upon one another for common survival. What is remarkable is that, in spite of the hardships and handicaps that long-distance trade then entailed, so much of it went on.

There were some eight interlinked subsystems involved, which, in turn, can be grouped into three larger circuits—the western European, the Middle Eastern, and the Far Eastern. (See Figure 1 for the rough "shapes" of these subsystems and the locations of cities that played key roles in them.) These, taken successively, organize the text. I begin in Part I with the European subsystem and then move eastward, even though this order cannot be defended on conceptual grounds. However, since I wish to refute the image of Europe as inherently superior, it is important at the outset to establish the relatively primitive level of its development during medieval times.

By the middle of the thirteenth century, three European nodes were forming into a single circuit of exchange: east-central France, which hosted the fairs of Champagne in four towns—the trading and production centers of Troyes and Provins and the smaller market centers of Bar-sur-Aube and Lagny (discussed in Chapter 2); the textile-producing region of Flanders, in which Bruges was the most important commercial and financial center and Ghent the

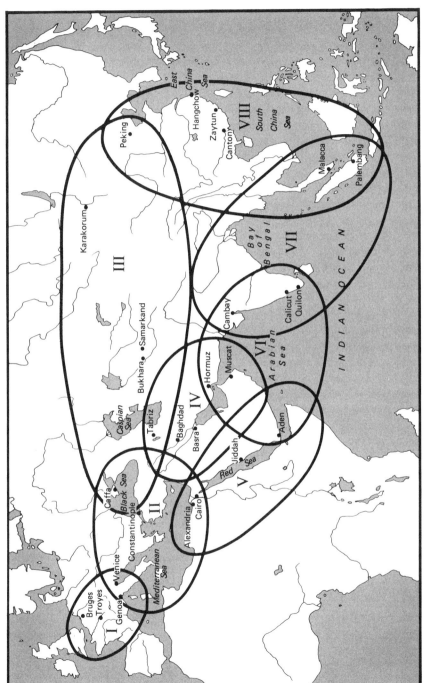

FIGURE 1. The eight circuits of the thirteenth-century world system.

chief industrial town (covered in Chapter 3); and the international trading ports on opposite sides of the Italian peninsula–Genoa facing west and Venice facing east (treated in Chapter 4).

Admittedly, these three nodes were scarcely the only participants in the evolving European "world-economy," as the lists of "foreign" traders who frequented them clearly reveal. I have selected these communities because each was the meeting ground for merchants coming from many directions, and because the non-local trade that formed the basis for their prosperity *circulated* among them. Other parts of the system at that time might be thought of as satellites or spurs, linked to the core circuit to be sure but by thinner and more linear strands. If one conceptualizes a trading circuit as a network, the Champagne fair towns, the cities of Flanders, and the ports of Italy formed a core because their linkages were dense and multistranded and because they had a wider reach.

Because of this wider reach, it does not make sense to treat the European (first) subsystem in isolation from the trans-Mediterranean (second) subsystem that linked the Italian ports to West Asia. When we discuss Middle Eastern trade, as we do in Part II, we cannot leave the Italians behind. They had established three critical beachheads in the Middle East.

One beachhead lay on the Black Sea where a third subsystem linking Constantinople to China began. This overland circuit, whose reticulation in the thirteenth century owed much to the unification of Central Asia achieved under the Mongols and, indeed, to their conquest of China itself, is treated in Chapter 5.

A second beachhead lay along the coast of Palestine where the temporary implant of the Crusader kingdoms put Europe in touch with a fourth subsystem that passed overland to Baghdad before it split into two branches, one that set out northeastward to join the Central Asian caravan circuit, and the other that went southward to the Indian Ocean via the Persian Gulf. Included in this latter circuit of trade were the multiple ports that flanked the Gulf (e.g., Hormuz, Siraf) or that lay along the southern shores of the Arabian peninsula (such as Aden). Chapter 6 describes this subsystem.

Europeans had tried hard to establish a third beachhead—on the North African coast at Egypt. However, after the disastrous failure of St. Louis' 1250 Crusade, they were forced to content themselves with a highly constrained trading partnership controlled by the rulers of Egypt. This gave the Italians limited and only indirect access to the fifth subsystem that connected Egypt with the Indian Ocean via the Red Sea.

For the same reason that I ignore Spain, Germany, Baltic Russia, Dalmatia, and Africa south of the Sahara in Part I, even though they contributed important resources to the circuit, I reluctantly omit East Africa from Part II. Without any doubt, the coastal zones of current-day Ethiopia, Kenya, Tanzania, and of insular Madagascar were integrated in trade with Egypt, Aden, Basra, Hormuz, and even Gujarat on the Indian subcontinent. Contact among these places was intense. But Africa's geographic reach was relatively limited. African merchants were largely local and African goods seldom made their way to China or Europe. (The evidence to the contrary, namely the Chinese pottery shards that litter the East African coast, turn out to be mainly ballast brought in Arab and Gujarati ships.)

Part III of the book addresses the key actors in the Asian circuit (and indeed in the entire world system, as we shall show) but, as was true with respect to the Italians in the Mediterranean, we cannot leave the Arabs and Persians behind when we examine trade in the Indian Ocean. Three interwoven subsystems were involved: the westernmost circuit that linked the Arab world to western Indian (subsystem six, introduced briefly in Chapters 6 and 7 but discussed in greater detail in Chapter 8); the central circuit that linked southeast India to the zone flanking the Strait of Malacca (subsystem seven, covered in part in Chapter 8 and more in Chapter 9); and the easternmost circuit between the straits and China (the eighth subsystem, described in Chapter 9).

But Chinese merchants were present in Srivijaya (at the Strait), and Muslim traders—Arab, Persian, and Indian—were present in what might be termed the Chinese "treaty ports" (an older version of what came later). The Chinese traders, linking the China Sea to the south (subsystem 8) with the great heartland of the Asian steppes to the north and west, are treated in Chapter 10 of the book. It was they who closed the circle by connecting China with subsystem 3 that doubled back through Russia (Samarkand), Persia, and Asia Minor to rejoin the outposts Genoa maintained on the shores of the Black Sea.

As can be seen, although this was not a global or worldwide system (the Baltic was just beginning to be drawn in, only the eastern coast of Africa was involved, the New World was still isolated, Japan was a borderland outreach, and the Pacific islands, including Australia, were unconnected to it), it covered a significant proportion of the central land mass of Europe and Asia and contained most of the population that existed at that time, since the peripheral regions were only sparsely populated.

This book explores, through a set of empirical case studies, the processes by which international connections were forged, expanded, and strengthened during the course of the thirteenth century, and describes the roles—cooperative, conflictual, or symbiotic—the varied participants played in the ongoing commercial exchanges. Each gained from the system but not to the detriment of others. When the system reached its zenith in the opening decades of the fourteenth century, no single power could be said to be hegemonic; the participation of all was required for its perpetuation.

In spite of these promising beginnings, however, during the middle decades of the fourteenth century the system fragmented and many parts went into simultaneous decline. By the end of that century, what had previously been a circulation system with many alternate routes had been reduced to a narrower set of links and numerous gaps had appeared. The economic difficulties experienced almost universally during the second half of the fourteenth century symptomized the break up of the system. Much of it was already gone by the time Portugal, a new player, entered the Indian Ocean at the beginning of the sixteenth century to set in motion the next phase of world integration.

One of the major questions this book seeks to answer is why the thirteenth-century system unraveled. The answer will not be a simple one; there are no monocausal explanations. No single overwhelming factor accounted, like some deus ex machina, for the fraying of the complex net of interrelationships among these various subsystems or for their transformation into a new balance, as world hegemony shifted westward. Rather, the cumulative effects of more modest alterations within and between subsystems undoubtedly contributed to a new weighting of the whole. If the fulcrum tipped its balance, it was because many of the subsystems were simultaneously but cumulatively shifting in the same direction.[16]

Notes

1. *Viz.* the not very useful debate between a Weberian definition (original 1904–1905) of modern capitalism with its attendant "psychological" attitude (and what a tortured argument Weber must make to draw his distinction between the modern capitalism generated by the Protestant Ethic and the old-style greed of earlier and other capitalists) and a Tawney (1926) definition of modern capitalism based upon the existence of such "modern" institutions as credit and rational bookkeeping. Even Weber (1981 reprint) did not fully agree with his own distinction because, in his *General Economic History*, the distinction is clearly based more upon institutional and cultural criteria. At least two not necessarily entailed elements may be used to define capitalism: the existence of "private ownership of property and the transaction of social relations through the market," and the existence of classes "in the sense of distinctive groups or categories defined by their relation to the means of production." Capitalism in the first sense can be found in classical Rome (Runciman, 1983: 157) as well as in most parts of the thirteenth century world. Capitalism in the latter sense comes only sporadically and later. Wallerstein (1983), as well as later Marx and the Marxist historian, Maurice Dobb (1947, reprinted 1984), argue that only the second form is "real capitalism."

2. In Volume I (1974) Wallerstein traces only the first phase of the "modern world-system" (ca. 1450–1640 +) which he considers "still only a European world-system" (Wallerstein, 1974: 10). His definition of world system, however, remains distressingly imprecise. He apparently defines it as a system "larger than any juridically-defined political unit" (Wallerstein, 1974: 15), which distinguishes it only from a centralized nation-state or empire. As we show later, the world-system economy in the thirteenth century was just as extensive (except of course for the "new world") and contained about the same mixture of free, semifree, and slave labor as in the sixteenth century. It was, however, organized according to very different principles. The term "world system," as it is currently used, has unfortunately been conflated with the *particular hierarchical structure of organization* that developed from the sixteenth century onward. This makes debates over world systems less than fruitful. It is important to remember that a system is simply "a whole composed of parts in orderly arrangement *according to some scheme*" (Oxford Dictionary). The scheme itself is not specified. We shall be exploring a quite different system in this book, one which no single hegemon dominated.

3. For example, Henri Laurent (1935: 206), a specialist on the textile industry in Flanders in the Middle Ages, is quite explicit that the urban medieval textile

economy "largely merited, by force of expansion which carried its fame to the limits of the then-known world, to be considered as a participant in a *world-economy*."

4. See, for example, Bruges in the thirteenth century or the Italian city-states which provided the first European bankers.

5. Gideon Sjoberg (1960) takes this position, but this distinction ignores the entire period before "steam," during which water power was harnessed.

6. See in particular Braudel's discussion in Chapter I of *The Perspective of the World*, Vol. 3 of *Civilization & Capitalism, 15–18th Century* (1984).

7. Braudel calls our attention to Marx's own ambivalence on this matter. In answer to Wallerstein, Braudel writes: "Is the problem [i.e., when to date the beginning of the capitalist world economy] that perplexes him [Wallerstein] not in the end the same one that was raised by Marx? Let me quote again the famous sentence, 'The life-history of capital begins in the sixteenth century.' For Wallerstein, the European world-economy was the matrix of capitalism. . . . I am therefore in agreement with the Marx who wrote (though he later went back on this) that European capitalism—indeed he even says capitalist *production*—began in thirteenth-century Italy. This debate is anything but academic" (Braudel, 1984: 57).

8. Germaine Tillion (1983: 20). In more scholarly fashion the same point is made, inter alia, by Sidney Packard (1962) and even more cogently by the Dutch scholar, J. C. van Leur (1955). See the compilation and translation of van Leur's earlier writings (1955), particularly Chapter 1 in which he stresses how Eurocentric history distorts and deforms other histories. Charles Tilly makes a similar point in his *As Sociology Meets History* (1981).

9. My decision to focus on cities as nodal points in a larger system can be defended on the grounds that they were the *only* comparable units in a system that included everything from city-states to loose confederations to extensive empires. This decision, however, was not without its costs. It was easiest, within this framework, to deal with the city-states themselves—found primarily in Europe, the Persian Gulf–Arabian Sea zone, and at the Strait of Malacca. It proved a far less useful framework for handling vast imperial domains. Although I include some discussion of the major centers of these empires, primarily to give the flavor of urban life and to illustrate how imperial vicissitudes were reflected in the "rise" and "decline" of specific places, my expositions of Mamluk Egypt and Syria, of the Mongol confederations of Central Asia, and particularly of China, of necessity, go beyond the urban framework. I see this dilemma as unavoidable, given the diversity of participants in a common system. Had I taken "empire" as my unit of analysis, I would have had even greater trouble placing the city-states within that framework.

10. That term is a favorite of American scholars, being the title of both McNeill's early and famous text (1963) and of a recent article by Chirot (1985). The latter, following Max Weber, claims that the unique qualities of the West were largely responsible for its "rise." But he does so on the basis of western secondary sources, not recognizing the effects of the methodological problem of historiography we have noted. Jones (1981) suffers from the same defect. On the other hand, McNeill acknowledges the remarkable strengths of the Muslim, Mongol, and Far Eastern worlds that were coalescing in the thirteenth century (see in particular McNeill,

1963: 479, 485, 525–526) and is aware of many of the exogenous factors that eventually undermined them. Other exceptions to western ethnocentrism are Philip Curtin's *Cross-Cultural Trade in World History* (1984) and Eric Wolf's *Europe and the People without History* (1982). The latter follows an approach whose premises are closest to my own. Wolf boldly acknowledges that history written from a western point of view leaves most of the world's people "without a history," like the "anthropologist's 'primitive contemporaries'," and that the eastern accomplishments in empire building and long-distance trade "shaped a world that Europe would soon reorganize to answer requirements of its own" (quoted from Wolf, 1982: 25). This is a breath of fresh air in an otherwise self-centered literature.

11. A large body of literature exists to demonstrate that the instruments of credit used by the Italians were actually borrowed from the East. See, for example, the collection of documents in Lopez and Raymond's *Medieval Trade in the Mediterranean World* (1967), as well as the work of Udovitch (1967, 1970a) and Rodinson (English translation 1974).

12. Hence the perennial complaints about piracy on the high seas—with the "pirates" usually nationals of a rival city or state who may have viewed their activities as a form of warfare.

13. See Southern (1980: 37), who in turn cites what he calls the "epoch-making study" by Mlle. M. T. d'Alverny, "Deux traductions latines du Coran au Moyen Age," *Archives d'Histoire Doctrinale et Littéraire du Moyen Age* XVI, 1948, 69–131. He also cites James Kritzeck's review of the findings in "Robert of Ketton's Translation of the Qur'an," *Islamic Quarterly* II, 1955, pp. 309–312.

14. *Chu-Fan-Chi* by Chau Ju-Kua (English translation 1911); and P'u Shou-keng (see Kuwabara, 1928 and 1935).

15. It appeared in Austen H. Layard's *Discoveries among the Ruins of Nineveh and Babylon* (London, 1853: 663), as quoted in Jacques Barzun and Henry Graff (1957: 3).

16. There are intriguing parallels with the new science of "chaos." See James Gleick, *Chaos: Making a New Science* (1987).

PART
I
✠✠✠✠✠

The European Subsystem

Emergence from Old Empires

In the second century A.D. the Roman empire covered a vast territory that included all regions abutting the Mediterranean Sea. The empire extended northward to encompass England and all of western Europe except Germany, eastward to encompass Greece, Anatolia, and the Fertile Crescent, and southward across the entire stretch of littoral North Africa. Rome's southern and eastern peripheral areas were in contact, both overland and by sea, with sizable portions of the rest of the "Old World" as far away as India and China. By that time, the first nascent world system had come into existence, although it would not survive the "fall of Rome."

It is important to note, however, that what is referred to as the "fall of Rome" was a complex process that took several centuries, during which disorder increased on the peripheries and finally at the center. Furthermore, the "fall" did not have an equal impact on all portions of the former empire. In northwestern Europe it had far more devastating effects than it had along the Mediterranean coast or in the eastern basin of the Mediterranean. The "Dark Ages," then, refers exclusively to northwestern Europe.

In that zone, internal weakening eventually made it possible for Germanic tribes occupying zones north and east of the Italian core—tribes that had formerly been blocked at the frontiers but had traditionally served as a fertile source of the captured slaves who worked the large agricultural estates of the empire—to break through Roman lines. The first waves of invasions occurred in the third century but were soon spent without lasting results. Successive ones were not so easily repelled. Throughout the fifth century there was a series of more successful invasions that culminated toward the end of that century in the demise of unified Roman rule and the fragmentation of the western portion of the empire among the Gauls, the Vandals, the Visigoths, and, later, the Lombards.

On the European continent these successive conquests "led to a regression in the level of sophistication and performance of the successor States" (Anderson, 1974b, 1978 reprint: 125–126) as Roman and Germanic traditions of law and personal status were melded into an uneasy amalgam in highly decentralized and diverse attempts to organize a subsistence economy in the absence of empire or trade. In the eighth century Charlemagne attempted a reorganization of this inchoate system under his control, assuming the title of Emperor of the West in 800 and utilizing the Church, the only institution that had retained any unity, to legitimate his pretensions. It was then that western Europe began to emerge from the fragmented and isolated position to which she had sunk after the collapse of the Roman empire.

And yet, the ascent was slow. After Charlemagne's death the precarious empire again fragmented and came under attack from Magyars and Vikings. By the end of the ninth century a defensive system of protofeudalism had been established in northwestern Europe, based upon an amalgam of Roman and Germanic antecedents.[1] A century later the social formation called feudalism had actually become institutionalized, particularly in France and the Low Countries. By then, in Perry Anderson's words (1974b, 1978 reprint: 142; but see also Pirenne, 1925: 50–51),

> the countryside of France, in particular, became criss-crossed with private castles and fortifications, erected by rural seigneurs without any imperial permission, to withstand the new barbarian attacks, and dig in their local power. The new castellar landscape was both a protection, and a prison, for the rural population. The peasantry, already falling into increasing subjugation in the last . . . years of Charlemagne's rule, were now finally thrust down to generalized serfdom. . . . [F]eudalism . . . slowly solidified across [northwestern] Europe in the next two centuries.

It solidified away from the coasts. Small trading centers grew up or were eventually revived around the castles of the war lords or within the protected radii of monasteries, where goods could be exchanged by merchants who obtained special dispensations and protection from the local lords in return for their commercial services. Some of these settlements, particularly those located at points where important overland or river routes crossed, eventually served as sites for periodic fairs or as exchanges for the miniscule amount of "international trade" that reached the interior.

By the end of the tenth century, however, the Vikings had either been turned back or absorbed (as in the case of England). Towns were then able to expand beyond the tiny walled enclaves to which fear had hitherto confined them. In the eleventh century, northwestern Europe, although still fragmented into relatively self-sufficient feudal territories, was gaining greater integration and the ability to produce a larger surplus for exchange. The number of towns multiplied and some were even established closer to the coastline. In the next two centuries there would be a virtual explosion of urbanization on the continent (Hohenberg and Lees, 1985, for details).

This internal explosion of population and urbanization was not unrelated to the external explosion that forever broke the isolation to which the fall of Rome had consigned the continent. At the close of the eleventh century, the counts of northwestern Europe launched their First Crusade against the Islamized "Holy Land," marching overland to Constantinople and then down to Palestine. Nothing could convey more explicitly the bifurcation that still existed on the continent between northern Europe and the Mediterranean coast than their avoidance of the sea route to the Levant via the Mediterranean. And nothing could indicate with greater clarity the changed relationship between the two subregions of Europe than the fact that in all subsequent crusades, the north transported their troops on Italian ships.

In this part of the book we trace the creation of the European system that developed from a coalescence of post-Dark Ages northwestern Europe with a prospering southern Europe that had never undergone the same process of detachment and then reconnection to the world. If the lights went out in northwest Europe during the Dark Ages, they remained on in Italy, albeit sometimes flickering and for a time dimmed.

When the Lombards occupied the Italian peninsula in the sixth century, some of the inhabitants on the northeast coast sought refuge in the lagoons offshore, founding the city of Venice. These seamen—for they had little other choice—retained their links to the truncated eastern portion of the Roman Empire, the Byzantine Christian state that ruled a much reduced area from its capital at Constantinople. Venice thus served as a crucial link across the Mediterranean, keeping alive contacts and knowledge, even though intense interactions across that sea waned.

During the seventh century, much of the eastern region outside Asia Minor was absorbed into the expanding Muslim empire. Islam spread across North Africa, reaching Morocco within the first century of its growth and then crossing the Strait of Gibraltar into southern Spain. Eastward, the Islamic *Umma* spread into Persia, Afghanistan, and eventually into northern India and western China, creating a new world economy that would serve as the nucleus for an enlarged system, once Europe joined it. The Venetians, the Genoese, and other Italian coastal city-states as well, would serve eventually to link northwestern Europe with the Middle Eastern system.

The most disturbing development in this expansion of Islam, insofar as Christendom was concerned, was the conversion to Islam of the population of the Fertile Crescent—which meant that control of the Holy Land passed into the hands of "unbelieving Saracens." Byzantium was forced to withdraw from this region but the ambition remained for a reconquest, an ambition the Crusades were designed to fulfill. Once Europe's economy had sufficiently recovered in the eleventh century, it could afford to sublimate some of the warrior energy of military feudalism into a "reconquest" of Palestine.

Between the beginning of the twelfth century and the end of the thirteenth—signaled by the recapture of Palestine from the Crusader kingdoms, an event referred to by European historians as the "fall" of Acre in 1291—there was intense if mostly violent contact between western Europe and the countries bordering the eastern and southern shores of the Mediterranean. Crusade followed crusade, solidifying the competitive alliance between northern and southern Europe and, most importantly for our purposes, establishing regular trading channels that connected northern Europe, through the Italian intermediaries, to the preexisting circuits of commerce that joined the Middle East with India and China.

Thus, although the Crusades eventually failed, they had a significant consequence. They were the mechanism that reintegrated northwestern Europe into a world system from which she had become detached after the "fall of Rome." It is no wonder that the thirteenth century should have been such a time of efflorescence on the continent. Not only were her horizons expanded; so were her resources.

Much has been made of the new "tastes" that were whetted in Europe by her contacts with the East. Spices, silk cloth and brocades, damascene blades, porcelain, and a variety of luxury goods previously undreamed of made a rich prize for the Crusaders. The Crusades may have been initiated by a desire to capture souls, but they were sustained, in part, by the capture of booty. When conquest failed, however, purchases were necessary. At first, Europe had little to offer in this exchange, except for slaves, precious metals (primarily silver), and wood and furs (the former a scarce resource in a land area with extensive deserts, the latter unobtainable but scarcely "needed" in hot climes). But it appears that the need for items to sell in eastern markets stimulated European production, particularly of the fine woolen cloth made from the fleece of sheep that grazed on its plains and plateaus.

The renaissance of agriculture, mining, and finally manufacturing in northwestern Europe during the twelfth and thirteenth centuries must be attributed at least in part to the expansion of its horizons and to the heightened opportunities for trade generated by the Crusades. This was a time of rapid urbanization throughout the continent, both in Flanders and France—which had access to the western Mediterranean basin through Marseille, Aigues-Morte, Montpellier, and particularly, its chief seaport, Genoa—and in the central section served by the Rhine, which allowed a connection from the North Sea all the way to Venice, its chief outlet to the Mediterranean (Ganshof, 1943). Although originally such trade was conducted at "Fairs" held periodically at first and then continuously in towns designed to host merchants from a variety of directions, eventually the heightened industrialization, stimulated by a rapid population increase and the growing demands of the eastern trade, led to the growth of true trading emporia with outlets to the sea, of which Bruges was a chief example.

Connections with the East through Constantinople were main-

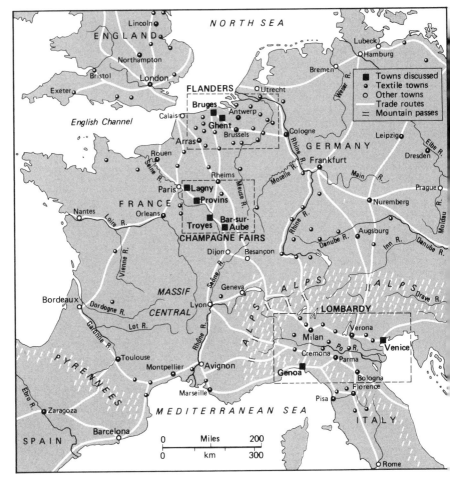

FIGURE 2. The European subsystem: locations of the four Champagne fair towns, the Flemish cities of Bruges and Ghent, and the Italian ports of Genoa and Venice.

tained throughout the Middle Ages, but this gave access only to the northern overland route to China, which was neither secure (it was traditionally a battleground for seminomadic tribes in a war of all against all) nor cheap, since travel by land was always more expensive than by sea. Not until the area was "unified" in the early days of the Mongols under the "world conqueror," Genghis Khan (d. August 18, 1227), did it become feasible for Europeans to traverse this long and treacherous route.

In this first part of the book we examine three key participants in the European subsystem of the thirteenth-century "world system:" the towns of the Fairs of Champagne (Troyes, Provins, Lagny, and Bar-sur-Aube) that handled Europe's new interactions with each other and with the East, particularly during the twelfth and early thirteenth centuries; the industrial/commercial towns of Flanders (Ghent and Bruges) that took over this crucial role in the later thirteenth and early fourteenth centuries; and the key seaports of Italy (Genoa and Venice) that linked northwestern Europe to the entrepôts of the Middle East (Figure 2).

Note

1. As can be seen from these remarks, we consider the form of feudalism that developed in northwestern Europe a specific social formation that one would never expect to find exactly replicated, since no other milieu inherited the precise Roman laws and Germanic customs that came together at that particular time and place. On the other hand, some features found in medieval European feudalism have appeared in other times and places; we see no harm in pointing to these similarities by employing the term "feudalism" to refer to these other formations, as long as it is understood that not all parts are glossed.

The Cities
of the
Champagne Fairs

Fairs as Economic Exchange

In societies in which the population is relatively sparse, the level of development not high, and the system of transport poor, one finds the phenomenon of the periodic market. In essence, in periodic markets merchants bring goods to customers at regular intervals (local markets are usually held once a week for consumer goods), following a circuit that in some cases even gives rise to the nomenclature of the marketing centers.

Thus, in North Africa in which a few periodic markets are still held, there are towns called Suq al-Khamis or the Thursday Market, Suq al-Arba or the Wednesday Market, and Suq al-Talata, or the Tuesday Market. The system, well studied by Mikesell (1961),[1] operated this way. Merchants, based largely in neighboring cities and dealing with manufactured and/or imported goods, worked a regular circuit in which they appeared with their goods at the town of, say, the Monday market; at the end of the day, after completing their transactions, they packed up their remaining stock and moved on to the location of the Tuesday market, and so on.

Each of the marketing towns had a large open space in which the traveling merchants set up their tents and stalls; important regional centers even had permanent stalls left from market day to market day. Agriculturalists from the region within walking or donkey radius would head downhill (usually) to the weekly market early in the morning, bringing produce or animals they wished to sell, as well as any money they had to make purchases.

Market day still has an air of excitement and festivity (recall Debussy's tone poem, *Fêtes*) engendered by the gathering together of large numbers of persons whose lives are usually quite isolated. Cooked foods and tea are available from special stalls. The barber sets up his chair and opens for business. The scribe settles on the ground to write letters or fill out documents for his illiterate clientele. Tinsmiths and other repairmen lay out their spare parts and tools, preparing for jobs. If there are any specialized craftspersons in the vicinity (such as women tent and rug weavers, potters, and other artisans) they too will take advantage of the collection of potential customers. Sellers, both local and itinerant, set up displays of their wares and prepare to bargain. The market has it own topography that is reconstituted each time, even in the absence of permanent installations. Animal sales, slaughtering, and butchers are off toward the periphery. Foodstalls and the goods of the "foreign" traders are closer to the center. The latter, mostly items of high value, have been brought from afar by the urban traders who display their cloth, their manufactured items, and their silver jewelry (and now watches and transistor radios) on more elegant carts, rather than on a sheet on the ground, as do most locals. By early afternoon, when the high sun makes it too hot to remain, after a glass of tea to fortify themselves, people begin to wend their way home, and the merchants pack up their inventories and prepare to move on.

Although market fairs originally used much barter and little money, once larger itinerant merchants began to frequent them, the need for currency became greater—and with it, the need for a money changer. This may have been how the role of banker and the institution of credit began. A wealthy farmer wants to purchase an item (possibly a major consumer durable for an upcoming marriage or a tool to clear more land) the urban merchant does not ordinarily stock. The farmer, therefore, orders the item, which the merchant promises to bring with him next time. The farmer either "gives" credit to the merchant by paying in advance, "gets" credit from the merchant by promising to pay once the item is delivered, or some compromise is worked out through a down payment. If the buyer does not have the sum required, he may "borrow" from the capital stored by the money changer or he may "borrow against" (mortgage) part of his expected harvest, either from the money changer or the merchant himself. As a result, a complex economic system is introduced, once the weekly market expands from barter between neighbors to the monetized system required by long-distance trading.

And should any market center attract urban traders from different and distant directions, the possibility arises that a "higher circuit" of trade will develop. Although traders may initially be drawn to the market to sell to local customers, it is very probable that, should they consistently meet at the same markets, they will arrange at their next scheduled encounter to bring special items for exchange—items not necessarily demanded by the local agriculturalists but for which markets exist in their home towns. The credit and exchange arrangements may become more complicated in this instance, particularly if the currencies in their towns of origin are different. The money changer becomes even more important, since he must stock several currencies. Furthermore, reserving credit for the next transaction may be preferable to handling specie, which means that records must be kept. Then, just as the local farmer may place an advance order, customers from the towns of origin of different traders may begin to place their orders, not for the onions sold in the local market but for the cloth woven in a distant town that his trader can order from his counterpart at a Monday market in which he otherwise has no interest. And in this way a central meeting point, which in itself produces little of interest, becomes the focus of long-distance trade.

Once that meeting point becomes institutionalized and attracts many merchants from a variety of points, however, there is always the chance that local production may be encouraged to tap the market created by the long-distance merchants. Thus, a local potter may gain wide renown for his craft and expand his production to sell to the long-distance merchants who come through, or a merchant may "commission" a number of pots of a particular kind that he knows he can sell elsewhere. He may even help the local artisan expand his production by advancing a sum to allow him to buy more material or hire a few helpers. Weaving is an even better example. Local wool, cotton, or flax production may be sufficient to supply the looms of local weavers for local uses, but an expansion of production may require the importation of raw materials. The traveling merchant may bring such supplies—and, in addition, contract to buy the finished products for export. It is only a short and treacherous step from independent production to a form of wage labor in which the merchant provides the material in a putting-out system and pays for the labor entailed in manufacturing the final product. This may, indeed, prove even more economical than having the weaving done in the merchant's home town where weavers are probably "organized" into protective guilds.

There seem to be a few basic prerequisites for the expansion of long-distance trade. One is certainly security. As the value of the goods being transported over long distances increases, the trader's need for protection becomes salient. As long as it is only farmers carrying onions and tomatoes for local exchange, theft is not a major problem. But when rich merchants carry valuable stock through poor regions, they constitute an attractive temptation. Robin Hood's men, who "stole from the rich to give to the poor," were in less glorified terms poor woodsmen who stole the goods of itinerant wealthy merchants on their way to market. Wherever unequal accumulation is present, safe conduct must be guaranteed; when that is not feasible, merchants travel in "caravans," together with their own guards, to ensure their safety and that of their goods. Such caravans were found not only in the exotic East but also in thirteenth-century Europe.

A second prerequisite is some agreement on a rate of exchange if currencies are not the same and, even more important, some way to enforce repayment of debts and fulfillment of contracts. Without these sine qua non's, trade would quickly stop. And as already noted, some mechanisms of credit need to be established for transactions beyond the immediate purchase and sale.

As to where such markets are likely to be established, several factors are crucial. At the very least, the trading site needs to connect two or more separate regions whose products are complementary rather than the same, for there must be a motive for exchange. Secondly, the trading site must be accessible to the traders, and transport costs must be minimized, given the current level of transport technology. This is why trading sites often change when means of transport undergo significant changes. Other things being equal, transport by water is considerably less expensive than transport by land, particularly for heavy bulky goods. Small high-value goods, of course, can incur high transport costs per unit and still yield an attractive profit, whereas low-value heavy goods are not worth carrying very far. That indeed was why, in the thirteenth century, as today, long-distance trade favored luxury items, capital goods, and weapons.

The Fairs of Champagne and Their Towns

In the example above—drawn from contemporary towns and an exotic locale—we explored some of the logic of the periodic market. We now move to northeastern France and back many centuries to examine how one of the crucial centers of trade in the thirteenth century world economy, the Fairs of Champagne, exemplified many of the same principles of operation. To do this, we must first reconstruct the situation of western Europe as it emerged from local to world markets.

After the break up of the empire, settlements that had been links in the Roman military and commercial network fell into disuse. Later, once the economy began to revive, they often served as the nuclei of fairs and then towns. Troyes, for example, had been the site of a Roman *castrum* (fortress) and there is evidence that it hosted periodic fairs as early as the fifth century and probably before. Under the reunification attempted by Charlemagne in the eighth century, both Troyes and Provins were selected as administrative centers. Troyes became the administrative capital for the county that became Champagne, whereas Charlemagne's administrative center for the county that became Brie was the less venerable town of Provins, whose chief asset was her defensible site on top of a sharp cliff overlooking the plain that any invader would have to cross (Mesqui, 1979: 7–8; Bourquelot, *Histoire de Provins*, original 1839–40, reprinted 1976, I: 407). Later, two more towns were added to the commercial circuit of the fairs: Bar-sur-Aube, situated at the intersection of Roman roads, in which the fairgrounds hugged the zone around the count's castle (Chapin, 1937: 111), and Lagny, in which the fair was set up on the grounds of a Benedictine Monastery (Chapin, 1937: 24). Each of the towns was situated at the intersection of Roman highways and, in addition, was near a river that offered a water supply, a source of water power that would figure in their later industrial development,[2] and some transport, although only Lagny was located on an easily navigable stream. In the tenth century, the economies of these towns began to prosper, and in the eleventh and particularly the twelfth and thirteenth centuries, they played a leading role in the economic renaissance of northern Europe, both as places of exchange and, in the case of Troyes and even more so Provins, as centers of textile production.

Although natural and administrative advantages account for the existence of cities at these points, certainly there were many other modest bourgs, scattered throughout France, whose characteristics were equally propitious for development. No unique qualities ensured that these towns would become the heartland of northern Europe's entry into the world economy in the twelfth and thirteenth centuries. Nor, once they had become established as the famous emporia in which Flemish merchants exchanged their high-quality textiles for the spices and silks of the Orient through the intermediation of Italian long-distance traders, was there much to predict that only one century later they would sink back to their former positions as sleepy towns, bypassed by the rising currents of world trade.

And yet, during their moment "on stage" they played a crucial role in extending the world system of production and trade to Europe, even though none of the four cities ever became large (Russell, 1972: 154). What accounted for their significance? And why did their site, and not another, attract the burgeoning trade? These are two separate albeit interrelated questions. Let us address the first.

Fernand Braudel (1984: 111) offers an overview. *Some* place midway between the commercially developing port cities of Italy, with their links to the Orient, and the industrially developing textile region of Flanders was likely to be selected as a common meeting ground:

> Thus it was that the two major economic zones [of the twelfth and thirteenth centuries]—the Low Countries and Italy—slowly and simultaneously came into being. And it was between these poles, these two potential "core zones," that the Champagne fairs had their day. Neither North nor South triumphed . . . in this early form of the European world-economy. Its economic centre lay for many years midway between the two . . . as if to satisfy both, in the six fairs held annually in [the four towns of] Champagne and Brie. . . . They were a rendezvous for the whole of Europe. . . . The trade caravans would converge on Champagne and Brie in assembled and guarded convoys, not unlike the other caravans with their camels which crossed the great deserts of Islam on their way to the Mediterranean.[3]

But why did these caravans converge on Champagne rather than on some even more centrally located point served by even more important Roman highways—a place such as Lyon, for example, strategically set at the confluence of two major navigable rivers, to which Italian merchants had flocked during classical times? It is necessary to seek a more complex and political explanation for why the region of Champagne became the "permanent year-round commodity market and money exchange for Western Europe" in the twelfth century (Gies and Gies, 1969: 12).

We return to our example of the periodic markets of Morocco and their prerequisites for success. First, safe conduct must be assured. Second, there must be mechanisms of exchange and credit, as well as an enforcement system to guarantee easy and secure transactions over time and space. And finally, since many localities are in competition with one another to become *the* site, there must be someone particularly motivated to make this site more attractive than others. Someone must gain enough to compensate for the concessions that have to be offered to traders. All three essential elements were present in Champagne and Brie in the twelfth and thirteenth centuries, of which the third was perhaps the most important. For, as we shall see, when the special motivation was removed in 1285 the Champagne fairs lost their edge.

In Champagne, then, the all important factor was the independence and motivation of the counts. They were periodically at odds both with the kings of France (although there were also alternating periods of intermarriage and alliance) and with the Pope who, from time to time, excommunicated one or another and once even the entire town of Troyes, exempting only the Cathedral! This tension between authorities, so typical of the period before the consolidation of the "nation-state," freed the counts from royal restrictions on trade and created an opportunity for them to offer better terms to traders. Their motivations were not only political, however; they were clearly financial, for the fairs brought great profits. The lords received tolls (*tonlieux*) on the goods in transit. They received high rents on the halls, stables, and houses they leased to the itinerant merchants. Furthermore, they charged license fees for all sorts of economic enterprises, and collected fees for their seals that ratified contracts, for registering defaults, and for imposing forfeits (Boutiot, 1870, I: 372).

In return, "the Counts of Champagne accorded to the merchants attending the fairs very active protection of their persons, their men and their goods. This protection began the day they set out for the fair" (Boutiot, 1870, I: 363), even if that were the Levant, and followed them through territories protected by others. As early as the end of the eleventh century, such guarantees were offered by the Count of Champagne (Laurent, 1935: 258). Thibaut II sealed a "remarkable treaty" with the kings of France in which the latter "pledged themselves to take under their protection all merchants passing through the royal territory on the roads to and from the Champagne Fairs" (Gies and Gies, 1969: 14). Later, when the regency fell to Blanche of Navarre, Philip Augustus (in 1209) placed under his protection all the Italian and other foreign merchants going to the fairs, promising to give three months warning if he wished to withdraw safe conduct, allowing them time to return home with their goods (Boutiot, 1870, I: 357; Baldwin, 1986: 348). Thus, merchants were guaranteed safety against pillage along the way. Agreements concluded with the nobles of the adjacent territories actually indemnified traveling merchants against any losses they might incur while passing through the territory under the jurisdiction of the given noble.

Furthermore, and this was of perhaps even greater importance, the counts of Champagne and Brie facilitated a local system of justice within the fairs themselves that enforced order among the traders of the various participating nationalities. The so-called "Guards of the Fair," who were officials appointed by the counts, policed the large number of people gathered on the fairgrounds, heard complaints, enforced contract promises, and collected fines to punish cheating. These officials, who numbered several hundred at times, were under two notables who constituted a tribunal of justice, hearing cases, adjudicating conflicts, and imposing penalties (Bourquelot, 1865, II: 211–256; Boutiot, 1870, I: 369).

By the middle of the thirteenth century these guards had become a force unto themselves. They had their own seal, different from the count's, recorded summaries of contracts in the Registers of the Fairs, and notarized agreements and enforced their performance (Bautier, 1942–43: 158–162). Their ultimate weapon, however, was to bar from future fairs any trader found guilty of not paying his debts or fulfilling his contracted promises (Bautier, 1953: 123). This was evidently so severe a penalty that few willingly risked this denial of opportunities for future profit. Short of that, however, the guards could seize the goods of a defaulting debtor and sell them for the benefit of his creditors (Bautier, 1942–43: 163).

These specialized institutions provided by the counts of Champagne and Brie created a nonnatural monopoly for the fairs, which assured that they would be preferred to those held elsewhere under less attractive conditions. To some extent, the loss of this monopoly was inevitable once these territories, hitherto under independent rule, came under the jurisdiction of the King of France in 1285. With the annexation, the fair towns lost their special status, and much fair activity shifted to other places, settling eventually on Lyon, whose more centralized location half-way between Italy and Flanders made it a natural meeting point. A second factor that led to a decline in the fairs of Champagne was a political controversy with Flanders, during which the Flemish merchants were actually prevented from attending the fairs. A final factor was the opening of an Atlantic sea route that allowed the Italians to reach Flanders without passing through France. But we shall reserve to later a discussion of the decline of the fairs, for we have not yet seen how they worked.

The Organization of the Fairs

Although we lack documentary evidence to reconstruct the original organization of the fairs, by the middle of the thirteenth century a very elaborate institution was fully operative, having evolved out of patterns established by the middle of the twelfth century. A variety of descriptions have been compiled, of which those of Félix Bourquelot (a native of Provins who produced a highly significant two-volume study of the fairs in 1865) and Th. Boutiot (the nineteenth-century archivist who put the archives of Troyes in order and then compiled the information in a four-volume chronicle plus one-volume bibliography: see Boutiot, 1870–1880) must serve as essential benchmarks.[4]

Although the Troyes fairs were known as early as Gallic Roman times (Bourquelot, 1865, I: 67), it is not certain to what extent they persisted after that, since the next authentic document we have dates only from 1114, when Count Hugues of Champagne, just before leaving for Palestine, granted to the local Abbey of Montier-la-Celle all the taxes on the sale of animals at the fair of Bar-sur-Aube (Boutiot, 1870, I: 190–191). From the context, and from other mentions of fairs in Troyes, Lagny, and Provins dating from the second third of the twelfth century, it is apparent that, by then, the fairs were of long standing.

Under the protection and auspices of the counts of Champagne and Brie, six fairs, each lasting approximately two months, were held annually on a regular and predictable circuit tied to religious (and movable) feast days. The trading year opened the day after New Year's[5] at Lagny, closest to Paris, and continued there until the Monday before Mi-Carême,[6] sometime in mid-February. Two days later, on a Wednesday, the fair opened at Bar-sur-Aube, at the easternmost extremity of the circuit, running until Monday in the week of Ascension. (Chapin indicates the Bar-sur-Aube fair opened between February 24 and March 30 and closed between

April 13 and May 17.) From there it moved, the very next day, to the larger town of Provins for the May fair which continued "until the Tuesday after the fortnight following the feast of St. Jean, but if the Fête falls on a Tuesday the closing takes place eight days later" (Boutiot, 1870, I: 354). (Chapin, again, gives more flexible dates and a shorter duration.) After the Provins fair closed, the circuit moved immediately to Troyes for the "Hot Fair" of St. Jean, which remained open until early September. On St. Croix day, traders returned to Provins for the St. Ayoul fair until Toussaint (All Saints' Day) around the beginning of November, at which point the "Cool Fair" of Troyes began, closing at the end of December or on New Year's day. Then the cycle repeated.[7]

One reason the sources do not agree exactly on the dates, and one thing that explains how merchants with heavy goods could have transported them over even those relatively short distances, given the slow transport of the times, is that each trade fair had its own cycle of assembling and dispersing, since it was a composite of local, regional, and long-distance trade whose products were neatly scheduled to permit those merchants requiring maximum mobility to arrive in time for their sale.

Each fair began slowly, with some eight to ten days allotted to the arrival of merchants and their installation in special lodgings and storage halls. (Again, I depend upon the description of Boutiot, 1870, I: 368.) The highlight of the fair, however, was when the town crier called "Hare," a signal that the cloth fair was about to open. Until that time, no sales of cloth were permitted and during the official ten days of the cloth fair no other transactions were allowed. This was clearly the economic heart of the fair, for it involved the long-distance merchants—the traders from Flanders who brought their manufactured goods for export to Italy and the Levant, and the Italian merchant-bankers who had come laboriously over the Alps for a chance to bid on them, bringing eastern products in exchange. Eleven days after the "Hare," the sale of leather goods and furs was permitted, and on the next day the trade in spices and bulkier local products—items sold by *avoir du poids*—commenced. Since cloth was the chief item exchanged by the foreign merchants, the presence of bankers and money changers was essential; their work continued for one month after the sale of cloth ended, since they still had to arrange to convert currencies, to credit bills of the fairs in the home communities of the foreign merchants, to repay debts or pass them on to third parties, and the like. Within a cycle of about 52 days, the fair wound down, which gave participants time either to proceed home or to make their way to the next one.

The Participants in the Fairs

Who were these merchants and how did they conduct their business? Granted, the fairs and those who attended them changed over time. It is neither feasible nor, for our purposes, necessary to document this precisely. What is of most interest are the goods they exchanged and the variety of places from which they came. For convenience only, the traders may be classified as (1) local merchants from the fair towns themselves, as well as locals who provided services to the foreign ones; (2) merchants from other French and Flemish towns, organized into a Hanse (confederation of urban merchants) that was called the "Hanse of Seventeen Cities," even though it eventually grew to include merchants from over sixty cities;[8] (3) merchants from various other French cities, both west and south of the Champagne region; (4) merchants from the northern Italian city-states, both from the ports of Genoa and, to a much lesser extent, Venice, and from the inland cities of Tuscany;[9] (5) relatively unorganized merchants from more peripheral European areas such as Spain, Portugal, Germany, England, Scotland; and even (6) some traders from the Orient (Greece, Crete, Cyprus, Syria), although the evidence for this is still ambiguous. Although many of the big businessmen were "bankers" as well as merchants, the higher circuit of long-distance trade was an almost exclusive monopoly of the Italians.

Each of these groups brought different commodities to the fairs, played different roles in the exchange process, and had a different degree of commitment to the particular fairs in which they participated. The local merchants, hostel keepers, and fair officials of the four towns were, of course, most committed to the Champagne fairs themselves, for their activities were fully dependent upon the prosperity induced by the fairs. Clearly, those local citizens who provided food and lodging to foreigners, who often held their goods and money in safekeeping, and who worked as notaries, local agents, scribes, fair guards, or even porters, had a fully vested interest in the continuation of the emporium (Chapin, 1937: 125–128).

But there were other locals whose prosperity depended at least in part on the demands generated by the fairs. Recall the example of the hypothetical periodic market, in which the presence of external long-distance traders helped to stimulate increased production for export. This certainly occurred in Troyes and even more so in Provins, in which a highly advanced textile industry, geared to export, developed. Not only did industry absorb the slack of peak labor, needed only when the fair was in session, but it attracted even more population to the cities that burgeoned around the walled towns and associated fairgrounds. As Chapin (1937: 53) describes it:

> At Provins, the geographic conditions were favorable for the development of the cloth industry. Wool was furnished by the sheep raised in . . . Champagne . . . [and] the plateau of Brie. In fact, the raising of sheep and the sale of wool constituted one of the principal sources of revenue of religious establishments.

The rivers in the Provins valley furnished water to make the cloth while the existence of the fairs facilitated its sale.

Although we have little information about the cloth industry during the twelfth century, by the thirteenth century there is evidence of a strong alliance between the counts and the local bourgeoisie for the purpose of protecting the textile industry. By then the cloth merchants constituted a powerful guild, having obtained from the count the exclusive right to make cloth in their towns.[10] As Chapin notes (1937: 54, italics added), "in 1223 Thibaut IV, *at the request of the bourgeois at Provins*, decreed that it was forbidden for all people coming to Provins to make cloth other than a man of the count [i.e., a serf under his tutelage] or an inhabitant [free bourgeois] of the city." Since there were many immigrants who sought refuge in cities from their feudal bonds, this provision was clearly an attempt to protect both feudal rights and the business monopoly of the bourgeoisie.

The expansion of the cloth industry in Provins gradually yielded what might even be termed an industrial class structure. As in other textile towns of the time, an urban patriciate,[11] made up of landlords and capitalists, ruled the workers who were increasingly shut out from view; they were concentrated in peripheral and unsavory industrial districts.

In Troyes the case was somewhat different for, although textiles played a major role in the economy, the town was known more for its commercial and financial functions than its industry. Furthermore, because it was the "seat" of the count's government, the line between feudal lords, industrialists, and financiers was less sharp. In spite of all the efforts to portray medieval European towns as "autocephalous," it must be stressed that in the thirteenth century, towns were deeply entangled with rural feudalism (Evergates, 1975).

The role of the counts in the cities was an active one. Even after Count Thibaut IV granted Troyes its charter in 1230, he continued to hold the monopoly over flour mills and other economic ventures in town, and he owned much property in the city (Gies and Gies, 1969: 19–20). And the famous charter (see Chapin, 1937: 147 for its text) that presumably "freed" the urban population from serfdom, imposed, in place of the infamous *taille* (head-tax), personal property and real estate taxes that were just as onerous. According to a later charter of 1242, Troyes should have been governing itself through a twelve person council, but we do not find any evidence that this council functioned until 1317 (Boutiot, 1870, I: 383). As late as 1270, Thibaut V was still referring to himself as the "king" of Champagne and Brie (Boutiot, 1870, I: 384) and presumably of its cities as well.

Nor were the roles of cloth merchant and banker, the two most lucrative activities, well separated. "Very commonly the two [were] combined by a single entrepreneur" (Gies and Gies, 1969: 98). On the other hand, the gap between merchant-bankers and laborers was growing wider. Although originally almost every artisan was also a merchant (Gies and Gies, 1969: 77), this system was undergoing a profound transformation in the thirteenth century.

> Troyes merchants invest their pennies . . . above all in wool. . . . [But a merchant buys in quantity at a lower price and] then in turn supplies weavers, specifying the kind of weave he wants. In theory he sells raw wool to individual weavers and buys finished wool back, but since he

usually buys from the same weavers, a wool merchant actually operates a factory [sic] scattered through town. (Gies and Gies, 1969: 100)

The workers were thus becoming proletarianized.

This class structure, increasingly pronounced, was reflected on the ground. The artisans were grouped chiefly near St. John's church; leather workers, furriers, and cloth makers were in their own quarters near the canals, with threadmakers nearby. The grain market next to St. Nicholas church was a second magnet, with bakeries and, on the street between it and St. John's, the stalls from which bread was sold. Farther out were quarters occupied by wool sellers and charcoal makers, as well as horse merchants. The abattoirs and tanneries were in the least desirable lower zone, which had formerly been a swamp (Chapin, 1937: 82–85). All these industrial activities owed at least part of their prosperity to the operation of the fairs and the extra demand they generated.

The textile industry of Troyes and even more of Provins was clearly geared to export. Although local merchants did not travel far afield,

they sent their cloth materials, by the intermediary of the fair merchants, through Europe and the Levant. From 1230, the textiles of Provins are mentioned in Italy.... In 1248, cloths of Provins were sent from Marseille to Messina and to Acre.... Among the belongings of two Florentine merchants, confiscated in Paris in April 1277, were found ... [cloth from Provins]. (Chapin, 1937: 74)

Provins cloth is mentioned in Marseille (1271), Paris (1296), and Barcelona (1309) documents and "the cloth of Provins still figured in the tariff bills of Florence and Pisa in the XVth century" (Chapin, 1937: 74).

The famous cloth had even reached the Levant. A remarkable fourteenth century source, *La Pratica della Mercatura* by Balducci Pegolotti, notes that Champagne linens were marketed in Constantinople and that Troy weights (still in use) and measures were used, or at least convertible, in Acre, Alexandria, Cyprus, and Tunis. This should not surprise us. Champagne had early and prolonged contact with the Middle East. Henri the Liberal, Count of Champagne, spent most of his time on Crusades, married the Queen of Jerusalem, and even became its king at the end of the twelfth century.

In contrast, the smaller bourgs of Lagny and Bar-sur-Aube were less stimulated by the fairs. Some cloth was produced in the former and some of its inhabitants had become money changers,[12] but the town remained chiefly a site for agricultural production and fairs. Throughout, Bar-sur-Aube retained her bucolic atmosphere, with fields and pastures providing more employment to the town's people than either industrial production or trade.

As we have suggested, cloth production in the fair towns was more a result of the fairs than an independent generator of them. Without the textile products and other items brought to the fairs from neighboring French and Flemish towns, the fairs could not have attracted the all-important Italian traders who intermediated the commerce with the Near and even Far East.

Among the French cities whose merchants sold cloth at the Champagne fairs were Rouen, Louviers, Bernay, Caën, Neuchatel, Montevilliers, Arras, Amiens, Beauvais, Roye, Peronne, Montcornet, Montreuil, Paris, St.-Denis, Chartres, Toulouse, Montpellier, Aurillac, and Limoges. Flemish and Brabantine merchants came from the towns of Malines, Ypres, St.-Omer, Diest, Ghent, Valenciennes, Huy, Lille, Bruges, Namur, Douai, Dixmude, Hesdin, Cambrai, Louvain, and Brussels (Bourquelot, 1865, I: 249). These towns appear on the various lists of the Hanse of XVII Cities (which by 1206 had some 60 members), but some also belonged to the Hanse of London.[13] French merchants also brought other items to the fairs. Chief among them were the still-famous wines of Burgundy, but many other regional agricultural items were traded, and merchants from as far away as Languedoc traveled north to the fairs to market their products.

Merchants from the various towns seem to have formed associations for several mutually reinforcing purposes. First, they joined together in convoys to travel to the fairs, thus ensuring their safety. Second, they acted as (multinational) cartels, obtaining from the count identical and favorable terms of trade. They enjoyed "most favored nation status," to apply an anachronistic term. Third, although merchants from the larger towns (Douai, Ypres, Arras) maintained their own independent hostels, storage caves, and merchandising halls, those from smaller ones often shared facilities, scribes, porters, and other personnel. This merchant cartel seems clearly distinguishable from the producers' cartel (the

London Hanse), which was rather an association to ensure favorable terms in the import of raw high-quality wool from England.

It was the products of these other cities that constituted an irresistible attraction for the key participants of the Champagne fairs, the Italian merchant-bankers whose presence *made* the fairs—and whose final disappearance from them in 1350 signaled their demise. The Italians were the largest customers; it was they who introduced the techniques of banking, credit, and bookkeeping without which so complex a set of transactions could not have been negotiated; and finally, they were the key intermediaries, expanding demand and supply to the regions beyond Europe. They made the fairs truly *international*.

The Role of the Italians

To understand the crucial role of the Italians and to explain their higher level of sophistication, it is necessary to recall that during the so-called Dark Ages of Europe the Italian ports never lost their continuity nor their connections with the East. Venice, in particular, was affiliated with Byzantium, which, after the fall of the Roman Empire, remained an admittedly truncated but nevertheless serious rival to Muslim developments in the eastern Mediterranean. As will be seen in Chapter 4, the Italian port towns of Genoa and Venice maintained an intense trade with Anatolia as well as with the Fertile Crescent, Egypt, and North Africa. In the process, they learned from their eastern counterparts, Christian and Muslim alike, many of the institutional arrangements that facilitated long-distance and cross-societal trade.

Few European historians, with notable exceptions such as Lopez and Ashtor, have paid adequate attention to these eastern precedents; historians and social scientists (including even Max Weber) have often credited the Italians with unique business creativity. They did not fully deserve this reputation, although they did make crafty use of the lessons they learned. But they were subsidiary to the Middle East. Venetian and Genoese merchants, up until the second half of the thirteenth century, employed the gold coins of Constantinople and Egypt rather than striking their own, a rough indicator of their semiperipheral status in world trade.

As early as the late twelfth century (which we know from notarial documents in Genoa), caravans of Italian merchants traveled together to each of the six fairs, although for the Genoese the fair at Lagny was most important. The people of Asti provided the mules and carts that trekked goods over the Alps in a regular transport service (Reynolds, as cited in Laurent, 1935: 265), a trip that took some five weeks (Chapin, 1937: 105). By the thirteenth century, according to a manuscript of the time (used in the following account by Bourquelot, 1865, I: 209–212), not only the port cities but increasingly those of Lombardy and Tuscany began to take part in the trade with northern Europe. The cities of Pisa and Milan were bringing high-quality cloth to the fairs and the Florentines were buying Flemish woolens to carry back to Florence for further processing into the luxurious "Kalimali" cloth for which they were world famous (Bourquelot, 1865, I: 211–213). A complete list of the Italian towns participating in the trade also included Rome, Cremona, Pistoia, Siena, Lucca, Parma, Piacenza, and Urbino (Bourquelot, 1865, I: 164).

The chief products brought by the Italians—those that made their presence indispensable—were the spices and silks they had imported from the Orient, either directly from North Africa and the Middle East or, via Muslim intermediaries, from the Far East. According to lists from contemporary documents (reproduced in Bourquelot, 1865, I: 206–208), North Africa provided, largely through its Genoese intermediaries, alum, wax, leather and fur, cumin, and dates, whereas Muslim Spain sent honey, olive oil, almonds, raisins, figs, and even silks. The Middle East exported pepper, brazilwood, feathers, damask cloth (named after Damascus), and elaborately embossed and inlaid metal objects. Gold and silk cloth came from Tartary (really China).[14] But the most precious cargo carried by the Italian merchants were the exotic spices[15] they obtained chiefly through Arab intermediaries, from India and beyond: saffron, cinnamon, nutmeg, mace, citron, licorice, cloves, ginger, cardamon, cumin, and of course all varieties of black and white peppers (Bourquelot, 1865, I: 285–294). They also brought items of extreme importance to the textile trade: alum (needed by the cloth fullers), as well as indigo, rose madder root, and other natural dyes. These, plus the occasional lapis lazuli and even more precious stones that came from India and Ceylon, constituted the quintessential items of long-distance trade—small, light, but having very high value.

As noted above, the Italians were welcomed not only for the rare and valuable products they brought but for their expertise in business and banking practices. Although some, such as the notorious Lombards, specialized in money changing and money lending, most of these early bankers were also merchants who, as part of their transactions, handled the all-important function of currency exchange, by which the credits accumulated in fair transactions could be used later or transferred "by paper" to the merchant's home-town office, since the carrying of specie was both cumbersome and risky. Although this topic will be discussed in greater detail in Chapter 3, which deals with Bruges, and in Chapter 4, which focuses directly on the Italian city-states of Venice and Genoa, at least a brief introduction is warranted here.

Braudel claims that the true originality of the Champagne fairs lay not in the goods they exchanged but "in the money market and the precocious workings of credit on display there" (Braudel, 1984: 112), things that were in the hands of the Italians. Their equipment was simple: a bench (or *banco*, from which our word bank is directly derived) or table, covered with a cloth, a pair of scales, and a few sacks of metal coins. "[A]ll the international and above all most of the modern aspects of the Champagne fairs were controlled, on the spot or at a distance, by Italian merchants whose firms were often huge concerns" (Braudel, 1984: 112). Bourquelot goes so far as to state that it was "through the Fairs of Champagne and Brie that the Italians passed on to France the commercial customs of their country and the science of banking of which they were without doubt the first [sic] to possess the secret" (Bourquelot, 1865, I: 164).

Although it still remains to be determined how original this knowledge was, there can be no doubt that the Italians did control foreign trade, leaving to the Lombards and Cahorsins the less international parts of money lending and to the Jews, pawnbroking. In Troyes, Jews had to purchase a "table," that is, obtain a special license from the count, to practice their trade. Furthermore, since they amassed local capital, they were often approached by local lords for loans (Gies and Gies, 1969: 105), some of which were actually confiscations, since there was no intent to pay back. But there is no doubt that pawnbroking, money changing, and banking were the financial base on whose existence the fairs and their towns depended.

The Decline of the Fairs

By mid-thirteenth century the Champagne fairs constituted the most important emporium for European trade, to which flocked not only the "big" traders from France, the Low Countries, and Italy, but those from lesser places as well (England, Scotland, Scandinavia, Germany, and the Iberian Peninsula). One century later, they had been supplanted completely.

Many scholars have sought to explain why this happened, each giving special emphasis to one cause or another. Among the factors often cited are (1) politically inspired interference with the passage of merchants; (2) the unification with France, which undercut Champagne's competitive edge; (3) a new and larger form of Italian ship that permitted navigation on the Atlantic, facilitating a direct sea link between the Italian ports of Genoa and Venice and the great textile towns of the north through Bruges; (4) the Black Death, which struck down the populations of Italy and southern France with greatest force and which ushered in a period of slower development in Europe; (5) the industrialization of Italy herself, which reduced her dependence upon Flanders; and (6) changes in the administration of business, which led Italian merchants to give up travel and stay at home, doing business by correspondence, resident "factors," and letters of payment. Clearly, no monocausal explanation is adequate, since the decline of the fairs was gradual. But although the negative effects were not sudden, they did prove cumulatively lethal.

Political difficulties were certainly capable of undermining the prosperity of the fairs for, as we have seen, safe passage and special concessions from the counts gave the fairs their competitive advantage. The death of Henri III (1274) placed the rule of the counties in the hands of a regent (Blanche d'Artois) who had other concerns and who was, in fact, allied to the King of France (not to mention the royal house of England through her second husband, the Duke of Lancaster) whose interests were actually antithetical to those of Champagne and Brie (Chapin, 1937: 215). The ensuing wars between the kings of France and Flanders led to a serious breach of the rules of safe conduct.

As early as 1262, Flemish merchants, who had been maltreated by the border toll collectors at Bapaume, temporarily boycotted the fairs (Bourquelot, 1865, I: 195). The significant turning point, however, came in 1285 with the final annexation of the counties of Champagne and Brie to the French crown. Philip the Bold, heir to the throne, had taken the kingdom of Navarre under his "protection" in 1274 and occupied the counties of Champagne and Brie on behalf of Henri III's minor successor, his daughter Jeanne. She eventually married Philip in 1284 and, when the latter became king of France one year later, Champagne's last remnants of independence vanished forever (Boutiot, 1870, I: 390–391). The difficulties that Flemish merchants had in reaching the fairs intensified. In 1302–1304 there was frequent harrassment of Flemish merchants and in 1315 they were even banned from attendance (Bautier, 1953: 140). When they were allowed to come again, they were subjected to progressive increases in their import taxes (Bourquelot, 1865, I: 190), a more lucrative solution. Furthermore, once the monarchy had absorbed Champagne and Brie, the French government placed restrictions on the access of Italian merchants to the fairs. This seems to have intensified the motivation of Italians to forge a new path to Bruges.

They had already succeeded in doing this by 1277 (Braudel, 1984: 114), although it was not until 1297 that regular maritime connections with Bruges were finally in place (Braudel, 1973: 313), thanks to the larger, more sea-worthy vessels Genoa was by then producing (Byrne, 1930: *passim*). Genoa's example was soon followed by Venice, which, as we have seen, had not been a major participant in the Champagne fairs. In addition, at about this time the Venetians developed a better Alpine route to Germany, which further served to reduce the importance of France (Braudel, 1984: 114). In any event, as soon as the Italians, "who had been the most important patrons, began using their ships to go directly to the North Sea coast and established permanent offices in Flanders, the Champagne fairs withered away" (Lopez, 1976: 90). Apparently, the last Italian merchants to visit the fairs came in 1350, and, when they ceased coming, so did almost everyone else.

The maritime route to Bruges was only one factor in the disappearance of the Italian merchants from the fairs. It is significant that the last time Italian merchants visited the fairs was the peak year for the Bubonic Plague, when half the population of Venice died and high casualties were also experienced in Genoa as well as in other Mediterranean ports. Perhaps there *were* no traders available to travel after that year. The Black Death certainly shook other routine institutions; it may also have caused a final break with the habits of the fairs.

De Roover certainly takes the latter position. After dismissing the usual explanations presented above, he concluded that "the determining factor [in the decline of the fairs] seems to have been the introduction of new methods in international trade, especially the growing tendency to do business by correspondence and the establishment of the Italians in Flanders near the centers of production.[16]

> ... instead of forming partnerships for the duration of a single venture, ... [there were new] terminal partnerships ... intended to last for several years, ... perhaps first developed in connection with ... the fairs of Champagne by the merchants of the inland cities of Sienna and Florence. ... A new instrument, the "letter of payment" or bill of exchange was created to meet the needs of the new type of sedentary merchants. The bill of exchange made it possible to transfer purchasing power from place to place without ... shipping ... coins. ... The development of maritime insurance made it possible to shift the sea risk to the underwriters. ... A more important development was the progress made in the keeping of accounts. ... The Italians were the first to master the new business techniques. ... [F]oreign trade in Western Europe became virtually an Italian monopoly ... until well into the sixteenth century, long after the trade of Italy itself had declined ... [due to] the shift in trade routes. (de Roover, 1948: 12–13)

One can only speculate about the possible connection between depopulation and the new business practices. Certainly, many of the advances de Roover itemizes occurred before 1350, when the Italians were still frequenting the fairs. The real change seems to have been after 1350 with the disappearance of itinerant merchants who, when hands were short, could no longer afford the time and trouble of the road and found it more efficient to work through agents placed permanently in the towns of their chief trading partners. We shall see this system in operation in Bruges.

A final set of explanations for the decline of the fairs is advanced by Bautier, who believes that the industrialization of Italy and a revolution in the market for precious metals were the root causes of the demise of Champagne (1953: 142–144). These factors, however, appear to be in addition to those already enumerated.

Far more significant for Champagne and its towns than the *causes* of the decline were the *consequences*. The towns apparently never recovered. Although drastic measures were taken in Troyes to prevent the spread of the Black Death (Boutiot, 1872, II: 88), the population was decimated; new methods of textile production had to be introduced to conserve the reduced and thus more expensive labor force (Boutiot, 1872, II: 90–91). Other towns were equally hard hit and in 1352 even the merchants of Provins abandoned their halls in Troyes, having little to trade (Boutiot, 1872, II: 92).

Troyes lost its role as trading center but, because it had another base of urbanism, it continued commercial and industrial functions into the second half of the fourteenth century, albeit on a smaller scale. Provins, too, did not disappear since she also had another means of support. But as Edith Chapin so perspicaciously points out in her book on the towns of the Champagne fairs, "fair sites did not necessarily grow into cities" (1937: xii), an allegation fully illustrated by the demise, once the fairs disappeared, of Bar-sur-Aube and Lagny.[17]

Lessons from the Champagne Fairs

One of the first lessons to be drawn from the Champagne fairs is that external geopolitical factors are absolutely crucial in determining whether or not a location will be "strategic" for world trade. It was not lack of local business acumen that killed the fairs. It was that, in time, the world system outgrew its need for a periodic market in east central France.

Second, the type of trading emporium required is heavily dependent upon the level of development in adjacent places. Just as the periodic markets of Morocco are disappearing in today's new era of economic sophistication, so the trading world of the thirteenth century passed beyond what the fairs, no matter how well run and administratively and financially advanced, could offer.

Third, to some extent, new levels of need both propel and respond to technological advances in transport and to shifts in the economic utility curves of relative costs. The Champagne fairs were left behind, in part, because of the growing importance of river transport in central western Europe and, even more so, because Genoese ships had gained the capacity to brave the open sea of the Atlantic, thus bypassing a route that had become less attractive, not only for economic reasons but for reasons of political instability and even hostility.

There was, in fact, little the Champagne fair towns could have done to avert either the natural or the geopolitical factors that now worked against them. Throughout history, the core zones of world economies have been displaced successively from one location to another.[18] Cores become peripheries and peripheries are thrust into the core, often through no fault or virtue of their own. And if blame cannot be attributed, so success need not be "deserved."

In Chapter 1 we criticized western historians for seeking in the unique virtues of western development a justification for Europe's success. And yet, in this first example we already see that virtue need not be rewarded. Champagne did not deserve to fail, and Bruges, the subject of the next chapter, did not necessarily deserve to succeed, albeit for only another brief moment before natural events overtook her, leaving her literally stranded in backwater when silt closed her opening to the sea. And if inadvertent failure occurred in two European cases, why should we wonder about the defeat of other even more promising regions, such as the Arab world or China? The Champagne fairs prepare us to look for more than internal virtue or defect in explaining what happened in other parts of the world system.

Other lessons might be drawn from the case of Troyes, although space has not permitted us to examine in detail the issues of urban and industrial modernization. Conventional treatments of medieval European cities stress their autocephaly or municipal self-governance and attribute their economic advances to this characteristic.[19] But closer inspection of the relationship between feudal and municipal institutions in Troyes shows a much more complicated and indeterminate picture. The fair towns were not independent of the authority wielded by either the religious institutions or the Counts of Champagne and Brie. Although Troyes was finally given a home-rule charter by the count in 1242, its terms never seem to have been implemented. The count "ruled" Troyes directly, although he seems to have had less freedom in Provins, somewhat out of his immediate range. His knights and retainers played a much more dominant role in the cities than the gloss of sociological knowledge would suggest. It is true that citizens (bourgeois) were, either through dispensation or purchase, freed from paying the seigneurial headtax (the *taille*) and could marry a similarly free person outside their area without the count's permission, but they continued to be taxed and subjected to special levies and license fees by the count who still monopolized many key functions. The landed nobility was deeply involved in collecting revenues from the fairs and participating in real estate investments and other nonnoble pursuits.[20]

Nor could this capitalism be described as laissez-faire. Just as will be shown in the cases of Flanders, to be treated in Chapter 3, and the Italian city-states, to be covered in Chapter 4, the "state" played an important role in regulating trade and commerce, in making laws that enhanced the position of its merchants vis-à-vis outsiders and workers, and in guaranteeing that the feudal authority would take its healthy share. Confiscations of merchant fortunes were not unknown, nor was commerce as secure as western scholars have sometimes claimed. The Middle Eastern merchants who handled the trade between the Italian trading ports and the Orient were no more at the mercy of their feudal lords (the Mamluks) than were the poor traders of Champagne.

As suggested in Chapter 1, similarities in our cases often outweigh differences. This is apparent in the case of Flanders where fairs, textiles, and urbanization also went hand in hand. We turn to this case in Chapter 3.

Notes

1. Although I use the past tense in the following description, it should be noted that periodic markets persist to this day in rural Morocco.

2. See Gies and Gies (1969: 12) for a description of Troyes' eleven water mills, established in the second half of the twelfth century; these provided power not only for milling grain but for oil pressing and an embryonic iron industry.

3. An almost identical point was made earlier by Postan (1952: 181) in his article, "The Trade of Medieval Europe: The North."

4. Where later scholarship, for example, that of Bautier and Benton, has corrected errors in these sources, I have amended their accounts.

5. Here I use Boutiot (1870, I: 354) unless otherwise noted but stress that he admits that the fairs did not *always* occur on the same dates.

6. Chapin (1937: 107) dates this as February 19.

7. These periodic markets differed drastically from the Moroccan ones described at the beginning of this chapter because they each lasted not a day but several months.

8. Bourquelot, in *Etude sur les foires* I (1865), seems to have confused this Hanse with the quite distinct Hanse of London that was organized in Flanders to secure English wool for their looms. As Bautier points out (1953: 126), Bourquelot's view was completely refuted in Henri Pirenne's *La Hanse flamande de Londres* (1899, reprinted Pirenne, 1939, Vol. II: 157–184), which shows the latter to be an entirely different confederation.

9. The Venetians were conspicuously absent from the Champagne fairs until the middle of the twelfth century (Desportes, 1979: 97), since their route north into the continent was more likely to pass through what are now Austria and Germany, terminating at Lubeck on the North Sea.

10. Chapin (1937: 54–55); but compare this to the similar monopolistic privileges enjoyed by urban cloth merchants in the textile towns of Flanders—Bruges, Ypres, and Ghent—as described by Nicholas (1971). See the next chapter.

11. Chapin (1937: 227–228), but also Lestocquoy (1952a) for a description of a similar alliance in the contemporaneous towns of Flanders and Italy. See the next chapter.

12. According to Chapin (1937: 102), as early as the twelfth century there was a corporation of money changers in the town.

13. These two associations have been hopelessly confused in the works of Bourquelot and, hence, Boutiot, an error to which Bautier has called attention. Fortunately, for our purposes we do not need to straighten these out.

14. Since ancient times silk had been known to the Chinese, Greeks, and Romans. This new industry expanded in the Arab realms, in Greece, and even in Moorish Spain at the time of Charlemagne but had not yet penetrated France. In the course of the thirteenth century, a small silk industry was begun in Italy, but it depended upon silken threads imported from India, Georgia, China, and Asia Minor (Bourquelot, 1865, I: 258–259). "Gold and silver cloth, . . . the taste for which spread through the Crusades, were, for the most part, made in the Levant, in Syria, Persia and Egypt, at Alexandria, at Damascus . . . " (Bourquelot, 1865, I: 269).

15. In the age before refrigeration, such items were essential to mask the taste of "high" meat.

16. See de Roover (1948: 12), who recommends Pirenne's *Economic and Social History* for more details.

17. The former is a pleasant but tiny town today whereas the latter has taken on a renewed life as it became absorbed into the metropolitan region of Paris.

18. See the incisive article by Ekholm (1980: 155–166). The examples in her article, however, are taken from ancient rather than medieval times.

19. Max Weber makes much of this in his essay on *The City* (excerpt from *Economy and Society*, translated by Martindale, 1958a) in which he all but says that no one had "real" cities but medieval Europe, and credits the institution of municipal freedom there with the birth of laissez-faire capitalism.

20. See the fascinating description not only of rural but urban feudalism in Champagne by Theodore Evergates (1975). His study refutes most of the generalizations school children are taught about medieval feudalism.

Bruges and Ghent: Commercial and Industrial Cities of Flanders

France was not the only economy that revived between the tenth and thirteenth centuries, nor was it the only site of fairs. In the low lands of Flanders (now western Belgium), after the Viking incursions had finally eased off, there was an efflorescence of urban growth, as populations that had earlier fled from the coast spread out and as more secure land and sea routes once again permitted traders to travel.

However, the dynamics of town formation were somewhat different and considerably more sophisticated in Flanders than they were in central France. In Champagne, location and political independence created special, albeit temporary, circumstances that favored the establishment of trading emporia; their existence then stimulated the development of industry that never became the major economic base and that did not long survive the demise of the fairs. In Flanders the situation was the reverse. After humble beginnings in the countryside industrialization expanded, leading to increased urbanization, which led quite directly to the growth of commercial functions in the city.

Two of the major towns in thirteenth-century Flanders provide outstanding examples of these processes. The larger was Ghent (in French, Gand),[1] which, along with Paris, ranked among the most populous cities of northern Europe.[2] From the beginning, Ghent's economy was based on the production of high-quality cloth, although she also transshipped grain and hosted a periodic fair. Furthermore, her development was sensitively linked to the expanding demand for textiles, which, at the time of peak production in the thirteenth and early fourteenth century, created employment for a third to a half of the labor force.[3]

The second city, eventually destined to play a central role in international commerce and finance far out of proportion to her smaller size (40,000 residents), was Bruges, a market for the world, as Haëpke termed it.[4] A port with access to the North Sea and thus to England and Germany, its first significant role was as a staging point for regional sea trade on the North Sea and the Baltic. As early as the tenth century Flemish merchants were venturing forth to buy raw materials (chiefly wool from England) and to sell iron, bronze, and, by the eleventh century, manufactured cloth (produced in Bruges but even more in the predominantly manufacturing cities of Ypres and Ghent) to purchasers as far away as Novgorod and western France (Doehaerd, 1946: 38–40). With the decline in the Champagne fairs the Italians no longer had a place to meet their Flemish counterparts and purchase Flemish cloth; as they developed their direct sea link to Bruges in the later thirteenth century, that city gradually expanded its commercial and financial functions until they became the driving forces in its development. Only as the successive harbors silted up did those functions decline, moving finally to Antwerp (Antwerpen in Flemish; Anvers in French).

The Origins of Ghent and Bruges

As a result of the "disappearance of the state" in the fifth century, there was considerable depopulation of earlier Roman-related towns in the region that was to become Belgium; during the sixth century, the only settlements surviving were those associated with religious institutions (Doehaerd, 1983a: 33).[5] Although it is likely that there had been Roman settlements near both Bruges and Ghent (Verhulst, 1977: 178), no traces seem to have been left, and the two "begin again" or at least come to be noticed in the ninth century when they are identified both as *porti*, that is, settlements reachable by boat whose residents had the right to conduct trade,[6] and as capitals of *pagi* (singular *pagus*), an administrative unit of Charlemagne's empire.[7]

By the end of the ninth century, the disintegration of Charlemagne's empire bequeathed substantial autonomy to the various counts who controlled subareas. Baldwin I, Count of Flanders, and his successor, Baldwin II, fortified their settlements against the Vikings and, once the invaders had been repelled, presided over the revival of Flemish cities whose expansion would continue even more vigorously during the subsequent centuries of Europe's rising fortunes. It was at this time that Ghent was refounded (van Werveke, 1946: 16–17) and that the *castrum* of Bruges, around which the town developed, was built (Doehaerd, 1983a: 40; Verhulst, 1960; van Houtte, 1967: 11). Coins struck in the later ninth century in the name of the *castrum* at Bruges (details in Duclos, 1910: 14) suggest that she was already of some administrative and commercial importance; this promise was more than fulfilled a century later when Bruges became the administrative capital of Flanders (Dusauchoit, 1978: 27).

In the eleventh and particularly the twelfth century there were enormous changes in these small towns that still huddled under the protection of the counts' castles. By about 1100, periodic fairs—much like those of Champagne, although lasting only one month and drawing buyers and sellers from a somewhat less diversified hinterland—were being held in a circuit that included Ypres, Thorhout, Lille, and Messines, to which the old Bruges fair (which had been held since 958) was officially added in 1200.[8] The fairs were already linked to the textile trade, since there is evidence that in the eleventh century Flemish merchants were buying wool in London and English wool was being sold in the fairs.[9] Furthermore, Flemish merchants were traveling even farther as agents whose chief item of sale was cloth. These activities were the result of the growth of the textile industry, without which the Flemish would have had little to sell and therefore to buy.

Textile towns in the north were gaining some element of autonomy. In 1002 Liège became the first textile town to be surrounded by a wall (Ganshof, 1943: 37), and by the end of the eleventh century, the major textile towns had all constructed walls and/or moats to enclose their enlarged circumferences.[10] They were to outgrow those fortifications many times, and by the thirteenth century, the proletarianized textile workers, who lived on the outskirts of the towns, were intentionally "walled out" of Ypres and possibly Ghent by an "upper class" (formed through a coalition between impoverished nobles and rich merchant/industrialists), to keep them from "causing trouble."

Thus, urban growth, the appearance of an incipient class structure, and the development of international trade and finance in Flanders were consistently related to the expanding textile industry.

The Origins of the Flemish Textile Industry

High-quality cloth was being made in the monasteries and rural areas of Flanders certainly by the ninth century and probably even earlier (Espinas, 1923, I, see Livre II). Many conditions were favorable to this development, although they were by no means unique to Flanders. Espinas argues (1923, I: 25–26), however, that a unique conjunction of forces facilitated the growth of this specialty in Flanders: a terrain and soil favorable to sheep raising, an ancient tradition of craftsmanship (Flemish cloth was known in Roman times), a propitious location at the edge between continent and sea, and most importantly, a high population density that "forced" residents to supplement agriculture with other production.[11] As early as the tenth century, Flemish merchants were frequenting London to buy wool and exporting their cloth to the English and Irish markets (Doehaerd, 1946: 38),[12] and by the middle of the eleventh century, textile production began in earnest as rural weavers, spinners, and fullers were drawn to cities specializing in textile production. Weaving underwent a technological "revolution" in the middle of the eleventh century that increased the productivity of workers from three to five times, as a result of the shift from the traditional horizontal to a new vertical loom (Cipolla, 1976: 164).

At that time, trade was still fairly local. Flanders' major trading partners were on the North Sea and Baltic, since these areas could be reached by their own ships. By the end of the eleventh century, for example, Ypres was regularly exporting cloth to Novgorod to the east, as well as to France, from which she received wine in exchange, and to German towns such as Cologne (Doehaerd, 1946: 39). Her production was evidently so large that by 1100, according to van Werveke (1955: 552), the city had already begun to take on an industrial character.

It is not clear whether textile production began in certain towns because they were the sites of fairs or whether places in which cloth was produced became attractive sites for markets. But whatever the case, there was at least potential synergism between the two functions. The fairs were quite sophisticated and, as with their parallels in France, quite capable of generating additional demand and of satisfying international as well as local customers. In addition, as van Houtte points out (1953: 206),

> The Belgian fairs were centers of financial traffic. The Flanders marts developed an important traffic in letters obligatory, the so-called bills of fairs, which declined [only] in the 14th century as a result of the first wave of Italianization of business life, and of the ascension of the bills of exchange which followed out of that.

But they were not really international enough, since a sea route from the Mediterranean to the North Sea was not yet feasible. To connect with southern Europe, an intermediary point was needed.

Thus, merchants/industrialists of Flanders began to frequent the Champagne fairs in the early twelfth century. By mid-century, merchants from a number of the textile-producing towns of Flanders began to maintain "halls" in the cities of Troyes and Provins, although at that time merchants from Arras and Douai, rather than Ghent or Ypres, played the leading role. Participation in the Crusades exposed the Flemish counts and knights to all the desirable goods for which their cloth could be exchanged, if only they exported it eastward, rather than to the less developed regions in the north. The Italian merchants at the Champagne fairs proved to be the means by which Flemish textiles began to reach a much wider market. Arriving in large quantities in Genoa by the middle of the twelfth century (Laurent, 1935: 54–56, 64), the cloth was transported to the Levant where its value helped to balance the payment deficit that Europe had previously settled by shipping silver and gold (Doehaerd, 1946: 43).

These arrangements continued, more or less, until the last few decades of the thirteenth century, when they were significantly disrupted by politics and "labor unrest" and substantially reshaped by new shipping capacities. The effects were complex. First, there was a growing gap between producer towns such as Ghent, and the commercial/financial capital, Bruges. Second, there were internal political struggles that challenged the power of the elite, formed by the alliance between the count and the *poorter* class, often replacing ordered oppression with the anarchy of multiple contending parties. External political conflicts exacerbated and were manipulated in a three-way contest between France, England, and local "patriots" seeking autonomy. Toward the end of the thirteenth century, conflict between the King of France, who had recently annexed the counties of Champagne and Brie, and the Count of Flanders prevented the sale of Flemish cloth to the Italians at the Champagne fairs. This intensified the motivation of Italian merchants to expand their direct sea route to Bruges, an ability they had only recently achieved by means of a new and larger galley.

Although Italian shipping catapulted Bruges to a first-rank international port, there were several ironic twists to this new-found importance. First, once the Italian merchant/bankers arrived and became permanently installed in resident colonies in Bruges, they gradually supplanted local merchants who, with respect to international trade at least, were reduced to serving as requisite "courtiers." (A parallel to the later concept of *comprador* easily suggests itself.) And second, just as the port became increasingly crucial to the economic success of the city, the deterioration of the harbor became irreversible. Silting of the harbor had earlier required the development of the nearby port of Damme, built in 1180 because Bruges was no longer accessible; by the end of the thirteenth century even that port no longer accepted deep draught ships. A new and much more distant seaport had to be opened at Sluis in 1290 (for details, see van Houtte, 1966: 251–252, 263–264). Ironically, now that large ships could sail from the Mediterranean to the North Sea and this became a major route, sand was sealing the entrance to the city. It would eventually result in a relocation of port functions to Antwerp (van Werveke, 1944), although assuredly there were other factors involved in this transfer. Let us now back up a little to examine these changes in greater detail.

The Height of Textiles (Ghent)
and the Shift to Commerce (Bruges)

Although trade with Italian cities, particularly Genoa, was well established by the last quarter of the twelfth century (Doehaerd, 1941: Chapter I) and had led to substantial internal changes in Flemish cities by the first quarter of the thirteenth century, it was not until 1250 to perhaps 1320 that Flanders reached the apogee of her significance to the premodern world system. Textile production was intensified as demand burgeoned throughout Europe and in the Mediterranean world beyond. By 1234, Flemish textiles were reaching Syria and "on the feverishly active eve of St. Louis' departure [from Marseille] for Syria April 1, 1248, hundreds of contracts were negotiated in which textiles from Douai, Arras, and Ypres are mentioned" (Laurent, 1935: 66). By then, not only Genoa but numerous other cities in Italy were engaged in transshipping the precious cargo eastward.[13] So great was the production of Flemish mills at that time that Laurent has forcefully argued that it constituted a virtual "industrial revolution only a little less advanced that that of the end of the XVIIIth and beginning of the XIXth century" (Laurent, 1935: xiii).

In some ways it *was* an industrial revolution (albeit still using primitive technologies of handwork that can still be seen today in the famous lace of Brussels) and a capitalist one at that, since the nascent class system that became increasingly evident was moving toward the kind we associate more with the modern era than with the multiplicitous ties of feudalism. At one extreme were members of the "patriciate";[14] at the other extreme were the textile workers—the weavers, fullers, and threadmakers who had only their labor to sell. (Interestingly, in the accounts of labor conflict at the time, the spinners, who were women, are never mentioned.)

As in Manchester in the nineteenth century, the two groups were for the most part physically segregated and juridically distinct. The *poorters* lived in the old bourgs (the original walled settlements) in palatial dwellings built like fortresses, whereas the workers were relegated to peripheral quarters where their "factories" were located. In Ghent, according to van Werveke (1955: 559), workers lived *outside* the outermost wall, although in Bruges, which had managed to buy so much land around its old bourg that it could be considered "overbounded," the walls were successively enlarged to enclose them. Only the *poorters* had the right to hold city land in freehold tenure and only citizens enjoyed the privilege of being tried in the urban magistrate; workers could neither own land nor receive "city justice," crucial issues in medieval times.

Furthermore, the city elite was able to pass laws and regulations in their own interests. "The rules that they imposed on the textile industry were generally to the advantage of the cloth merchant. The patricians opposed with all their energy the creation of autonomous trades" (van Werveke, 1955: 562). In Ghent, an oligarchy of 39 persons who rotated the 13 aldermanic posts among themselves every three years (Lestocquoy, 1952a, *passim*), constituted the "autocephaly" so admired by Max Weber. And in 1297, even when Guy de Dampierre broke with the French monarch and deposed the 39 incumbents of Ghent, he replaced them with another 39 members of the patriciate (van Werveke, 1946: 35). As in nineteenth century England, there was much intermarriage between the landless sons of the nobility and the rich daughters of the major bourgeois families (van Werveke, 1946: 57; Blockmans, 1983: 67), which further strengthened the alliance between feudalism and urban capitalism.

The poor, however, were not without their own resources. They were involved in labor uprisings in Valenciennes in 1225, Douai in 1245, and Ghent in 1252 and 1274 (Blockmans, 1983: 67–68), largely directed toward protecting their rights. In 1280 workers took to the streets in virtually every textile town in Flanders (including Ghent and Bruges) to protest their conditions,[15] even being drawn, in 1302, into the struggle for power being waged between the French and English, both with one another and for control over Flanders. By then, the Flemish nobility was so allied with both the French monarch and the local bourgeoisie through intermarriage that the only way the workers could try to overthrow them was by taking the side of the English invaders. Groups of worker militias joined the English forces that, with their help, defeated the French in the famous battle of Courtrai, which altered not only the internal governance of Flemish cities but the outcome of international politics.

But it was not until the time of Jacques van Artevelde (1338–1345) that the social transformation in Flemish cities was extensive enough to undermine the power of the aristocracy (van Werveke, 1943; but see Nicholas, 1988, for a different view). By then, however, it was too late. The textile industry was in decline as other producers, particularly the English, broke the Flemish monopoly. In the ensuing period of retrenchment, worker movements no longer struggled for freedom; rather, they were directed largely toward preventing competition from rural "nonguild" weavers and fullers for a share of the contracting market.[16]

The economic difficulties in the Flemish textile industry were caused in part by the necessity of acquiring, as the industry expanded, larger and larger quantities of imported high-quality English wool, without which the fine cloth for which Flanders was famous could not be made. This dependence, which had begun as early as the opening of the twelfth century, became progressively more pronounced in the thirteenth century. Indeed, this was the reason the merchants had such complete control over their workers, for it was they who assured the steady supply of the all-important wool. From earliest medieval times Flemish merchants had traveled to London and Scotland to buy fine quality English wool. By the thirteenth century these merchants were organized into the Hanse of London, a cartel of buyers who banded together to obtain special uniform privileges from the English ruler and to help set prices (Pirenne, 1899).

However, the political battles between France and England often had repercussions in the economy of Flanders; an English embargo on the export of wool to Flanders was a frequent weapon in the conflict. The alliance of Guy de Dampierre, then the textile workers, and finally Jacques van Artevelde with England was in part economically motivated. Each time a Flemish city sided with England, it obtained preferential treatment in the wool market. Even after England gained a monopoly on the sale of her wool by setting up "staples" (entrepôts that held the exclusive right to sell wool) on the continent, the support that Bruges had rendered ensured that at least from time to time she would host the "staple."

And yet nothing could prevent the eventual disappearance of English wool from Flemish spindles and looms. It was the development of a local textile industry in England, more than anything else, that eventually undermined the Flemish monopoly. As more and more wool was used at home, less was available for export. And when Flanders had little high-quality wool, the attractiveness of her product declined. Later, inferior quality wool was imported from Spain, but this yielded a rough and uneven cloth.

It is therefore understandable why, during this period of decline, the Flemish textile workers directed so much of their efforts to "protecting" themselves from rural competition. Urban wages were high; since the inferior cloth they produced no longer commanded premium prices, capitalists sought to cut their costs by moving operations into the countryside where lower wages could be paid. The artisan guilds responded by pressing for a "closed shop,"[17] but these efforts were in vain. Some skilled workers migrated to England in search of work and some even went to Italy (Doehaerd, 1946: 99–105), but most remained to await better times. These did appear briefly in the late fourteenth century, after their ranks had been thinned by the Black Death. The ensuing labor shortage resulted in an enhanced market position and therefore more favorable work conditions. But the golden era of Flemish supremacy in textiles had ended.

Before it did, however, the city of Bruges had her moment of glory as a world city. Bruges had never been as directly dependent upon the textile industry as had other Flemish cities such as Ypres and Ghent. From the beginning Bruges had supplemented her production functions by commerce and port activities, serving as the link between outside suppliers and markets and the nearby centers of production. This role was substantially enhanced in the late thirteenth century when, instead of working through the intermediaries of the Champagne fairs, merchants from the Italian city-states made direct contact with Bruges, which stood ready to handle cloth sales.

The Genoese had first sailed their newer heavy galleys out the Strait of Gibraltar up the coast of Portugal and France and into the North Sea in 1277, docking at Damme, linked by a short canal to Bruges and by a longer one to Ghent. But there was as yet no regularly scheduled service between the two ports. The more matters in Champagne deteriorated, however, the more attractive the alternative sea link became. By 1290, once the new port at Sluis was built, regular galley service between Genoa and Bruges was established, permitting the two parties to bypass the Champagne fairs, at least when necessary. Venice was slow to follow, but by 1314 even she had been forced to supplement her usual route (over the Alps and through Germany to the Low Countries) with boat service to Bruges. She could not afford to delay, for by then Bruges was the most important European market north of the Alps (van Houtte, 1966: 253; 1967: 51). By 1294, when the English set up their "wool staple" on the continent, Bruges also became the place where traders had to buy their wool.

Bruges and the Foreign Financiers

This propulsion of Bruges into a world market city changed the longstanding economic base of the city. Whereas her merchant sailors had previously gone forth to buy and sell, now, more and more, they stayed at home and waited for customers to come to them. In addition to the Germans, who had begun to come in force after the organization of their League,[18] and the Spaniards, specifically the Castilians, who, although they had arrived as early as the beginning of the thirteenth century, were still not numerous, there now came the Italians, who really transformed Bruges' economic role from import–export and production to true entrepôt— not only for goods but for money. And thus, even when textiles declined, Bruges persisted as the Bourse[19] of Europe.

Unlike the situation in the fair towns, the Italians came not just as periodic visitors but as permanent residents. And they soon took over not only the functions of international exchange but the more local one of arranging the sale of Flemish cloth. As de Roover points out, "the native upper-class in Bruges, during the fourteenth and fifteenth centuries, was not made up of merchants, save for a few exceptions, but of brokers, inn-keepers, *drapiers*, and commission agents" (1948: 13). These occupational roles existed to "service" not their own economy but the Italians (and one suspects to try to supervise them). Only the fact that foreigners were forbidden to deal in retail trade, were prohibited from buying up local goods for resale in the city (de Roover, 1948: 16), and, at least until the turn of the century, could not deal directly with local buyers or sellers (van Werveke, 1944: 32–33) prevented them from taking over all the commercial operations of the city.

The rights of the Italian merchants were particularly restricted with respect to commerce in cloth, still the major product traded. According to Espinas, all cloth produced in Flanders and then exported had to go through local brokers or commercial intermediaries called "courtiers." These were local agents with quasiofficial status who acted "on behalf" of the foreign merchants and oversaw a rough sort of justice. They bear a suspicious resemblance to the Guards of the Fairs. The "courtiers," in turn, hired their own scribes to keep official records of transactions and their own porters, measurers, and weighers, for they had responsibility for honest exchanges. All these intermediaries were "official" because they were appointed by the urban authority (Espinas, 1923, I: 305–321). But there were other locals who played a more informal role in trade.

The previously mentioned vander Beurse family of innkeepers, who gave their name to the Place de la Bourse, were only the best known of many. When a foreign merchant arrived in Bruges he had to find lodgings and a place to store his goods. Much like the caravanserais that dotted oases and cities alike in the Muslim world, there were facilities in Bruges in which a merchant could sleep and take his meals, warehouse his material, stable his horses (van Werveke, 1944: 33), and, it later developed, store his funds for safekeeping and even change them into a different currency (see de Roover, 1948). It was perhaps natural that the innkeeper and his employees would guide the stranger in town and help him make business contacts. The Germans, in particular, seem to have frequently used these facilities.

But the Italians, relative newcomers, were too numerous to be accommodated and, because they were more permanently installed, preferred to set up their own halls. In de Roover's words:

> As soon as the Italians established themselves permanently in Flanders, they began to organize "nations" or colonies which were composed of all the merchants from the same city. . . . Genoese, Venetian, Lucchese, Florentine . . . Milanese nations. . . . One of the first tasks of the newly formed nations was to secure official recognition of their incorporation and to obtain commercial privileges from the local authorities. (de Roover, 1948: 13)

These privileges protected them from arbitrary seizures of property, fixed the port dues and tariffs they would have to pay, and protected them from seigneurial law. From this it is obvious that isolated traders were the exception. Indeed, "the charters granted to the Italian merchants were . . . commercial treaties" that were negotiated between the city-states, taking on the appearance of actual "diplomatic documents" (de Roover, 1948: 16).

Nor were the "nations" or foreign colonies simply informal groupings of friendly compatriots; they were tightly organized, like guilds, with their own chiefs (called consuls) and their own rules and means for enforcing them (de Roover, 1948: 17; van Houtte, 1967: 55–56).[20] Similar to the situation so well described for medieval England by Lloyd (1982) and the one that prevailed in the Ottoman Empire much later under the Capitulations, the foreign colonies constituted a kind of extraterritorial authority, exempt from many of the customs of the host country and expected to maintain discipline over their own members (de Roover, 1948: 28). By the end of the Middle Ages there were some sixteen "nations" in the city of Bruges: the Germans (called "Easterners"), the Venetians, the Lucchese, the Genoese, the Florentines, the people of Milan-Como, the Placentines, the Pisans, the Catalans, the Aragonese, the Castilians (called the "Spanish"), the Biscayans, the Navarrese, the Portuguese, the English, and the Scots. In general, merchants from the various "nations" preferred to live on the same street or place, forming their own quarter in which they maintained their own national houses or consulates (Maréchal, n.d.: 153–155). The single men ate together, met socially, and often had their offices on the premises.

In these halls maintained by the various "nations" in Bruges, as opposed to those kept by the trading towns participating in the Champagne fairs, the installations and their members were permanent. Although many Italians kept themselves aloof from the local population, some remained and intermarried; a number of family names in Bruges today reveal their Italian origins. The language of business was heavily infused with Italian, and many of the financial aides and advisors to the local nobility were Italians. Indeed, nothing so sensitively captures the real difference between a periodic market and a city as these not so simple facts. How had this change occurred?

During the thirteenth century, the organization of business was undergoing a significant change in Italy. Rather than traveling, the head partners of Italian firms stayed home while "factors" ran their branch offices abroad. Factors were managers and assistants who were not partners in the firm, but rather received salaries (de Roover, 1948: 32).[21] This evolution in the way business was done was so drastic that de Roover claims it was a true commercial revolution whose "permanent result ... was to pave the way for the advent of mercantile capitalism which, in most European countries, was not displaced by industrial capitalism before the middle of the nineteenth century" (1948: 11).

Such firms were not large. At the beginning of the fourteenth century, the third largest Florentine company had "fifteen branches and employed forty-one factors, the home office not included" (de Roover, 1948: 39), but this size was large enough to require rational administration and careful bookkeeping. It was also large enough to amass large amounts of capital and, like a multinational company of today, to switch capital from unprofitable to profitable investments and from unpromising places to places offering higher returns. Mobility of capital, however, required a sophisticated money market.

Thus, the second thing that changed was that commerce in money and credit became as important as commerce in goods (van Werveke, 1944: 43). And it was with respect to this trade that Bruges assumed her true world-market significance. Here again, it was the Italians who were responsible for the transformation. Before their arrival, there had certainly been pawnbroking and money changing in the city, but international money and banking were undeveloped. To borrow large sums or to send or receive money from abroad, Flemish nobles and merchants had to travel to Champagne. By the end of the thirteenth century they no longer had to.

Jews, and later Lombards and Cahorsins,[22] were essentially pawnbrokers, lending money at extremely high rates (30 to 40 percent per annum) to nobles and bourgeois alike. Given the religious injunction against interest, they were sometimes persecuted, often tolerated because their services were needed, and almost always "controlled" through licenses, for which high fees were charged.

In contrast, money changers were "respectable" local citizens; in fact, they had to be burghers of the town, and in lists of money changers in Bruges in the fourteenth century, Flemish names predominate (de Roover, 1948: 171–172). Interestingly enough, women could become money changers.

> In the Middle Ages money-changing was apparently one of the few professions where there was no discrimination against women. In this respect the conditions found in Bruges are duplicated in Ghent, and elsewhere in Western Europe. No less than six women appear on a list of eleven money-changers ... doing business ... in 1368 at Frankfort-on-the-Main. (de Roover, 1948: 174)

The number of money changers was strictly limited; the licenses were hereditary, which may be why women, many of them widows, were allowed to practice the profession. In Bruges, only four money changers held fiefs from the Count of Flanders that allowed them to practice their monopoly trade. Even after 1300 when their numbers were increased because of expanding business, their activities were closely regulated and the city of Bruges owned all of their stalls (de Roover, 1948: 174–175). Although eventually the money changers served deposit banking functions, minted and traded in money and bullion, accepted deposits payable upon demand, arranged for transfers of funds between their depositors, and reinvested, either directly or through loans, the money left in their safekeeping (de Roover, 1948: 215), their activities did not extend to international trade (de Roover, 1948: 238).

That function was left to the Italian merchant-bankers who monopolized the international exchange of money and credit. De Roover argues strongly that contrary to the thesis of Bigwood (1921) that banking grew out of money lending in the Low Countries, the two had separate origins. True banking was imported to Bruges in an advanced form by the Italian merchant-bankers whose system was perhaps two centuries ahead of Flanders'. Because of this discrepancy, it was inevitable that the Italians would quickly dominate high finance there. Their chief contribution was the "bill of exchange," essentially a contract governing later payment somewhere else. The bill of exchange grew out of a more primitive form of contract, namely the exchange contract.

One of the oldest examples of an exchange contract mentioning Bruges dates from 1306; it is a notarized deed, acknowledging receipt of "imaginary" funds and agreeing to repay the equivalent at the forthcoming May Fair of Provins. It is not, however, a true bill of exchange because it involves two, not three, parties to the agreement (de Roover, 1948: 49, but based upon Doehaerd, 1941). At this time there were two kinds of exchange contracts, both of which required the contracting parties to appear before a notary: the *cambium* or ordinary contract, and the *cambium nauticum*, a sea contract in which payment was made contingent on the safe arrival of goods. But once the Italian merchants began to stay home, a more complex instrument was required. A third party somewhere else was involved, namely, the factor who was ordered to pay a certain amount to someone else. For this, the bill of exchange was necessary. During the early fourteenth century, this new method increasingly replaced the ordinary *cambium*, whereas later in the century marine insurance eliminated the need for the *cambium nauticum*.

A bill of exchange was essentially a document in which buyers and sellers agreed that payment would be made in a place different from the one in which goods were to be delivered and (usually) in the home currency of the seller. It was essentially a time bill in which a distant location and a conversion of currency were involved (de Roover, 1948: 53). The flexibility introduced by this instrument greatly facilitated foreign trade. (But we shall also see in Part II that this instrument existed even earlier in connection with trade through the Middle East.) Inspite of the fact that at that time the bill of exchange was "neither discountable nor negotiable" (de Roover, 1948: 53),[23] it did permit a mobility of capital that had hitherto not existed in European trade.

This mobility, however, proved a mixed blessing for Bruges, for it increasingly put her fate in the hands of foreign "nations" less committed to her solvency than to their own profits. The capital accumulated by the Italian merchant-bankers was lent out to local producers, either as time deposits or in return for shares of stock, for during the Middle Ages Italy was perhaps the only European country with "foreign investments" (de Roover, 1948: 42). Once the Flemish textile industry began to decline, however, the Italians moved their capital to other more profitable investments. And once the port facilities had become less convenient, because of the silting of the channel to Sluis,[24] they moved their destination—and thus the offices of their factors—eastward to Antwerp, a better port for deep draught ships and a more strategic location for capturing the land trade routes that now ran not through France but through Germany (Brulez and Craeybeckx, 1974).

The Black Death

To some extent, this latter shift had come about after the Black Death, which was an epidemic so severe that it shattered all customary ways of interacting. There had been other natural disasters that interrupted the increase in the Flemish population in the fourteenth century, notably the famine of 1316–1317, but none so catastrophic in effect as the "Pest" that arrived in Flanders from Asia Minor by way of Genoa in the middle of the fourteenth century.

It is impossible to overemphasize the significance of this epidemic for the course of world history.[25] Around 1330–1340, Europe's population had reached about 80 million. Of these, some 25 million died in the first two years of the plague (Cipolla, 1976: 146) and recurrences further decimated the population to a low point just after 1400, when Europe's total population was only 50–

60 percent of the preplague level (Russell, 1972: 23). Postan (1952: 204–215), after carefully examining all factors involved in the European depression of the late fourteenth century, concludes that the chief cause was the precipitous drop in population due to the plague.

Although areas still peripheral to the world system of trade (for example, England and Germany) seem to have been better protected from the disaster, heartland zones—Italy in particular but also France and Flanders—suffered more. The death rates were so high that two new cemeteries had to be created in Bruges in 1349, cadavers were piled in the streets of Ypres between 1350 and 1352, and the number of orphans in Ghent shot up astronomically (Blockmans, 1983: 74–75). Whereas in 1340 the population of Bruges had been about 35,000 to 40,000,[26] it declined precipitously at mid-century, and natural increases continued to be wiped out by additional recurrences of the plague in 1360–1362, 1368–1369, 1382–1384, 1400–1401, 1438–1439, and 1456–1459 (Blockmans, 1983: 75). By mid-fifteenth century its size was little more than it had been before the Black Death. The great period of population expansion for Bruges, Ghent, and the other cities of Flanders had come to an end. When recovery appeared, it showed elsewhere. Indeed, the boundaries of both Ghent and Bruges did not have to expand beyond those of the Middle Ages until the growth period of the modern age.

Lessons from the Case of Flanders

The primary factors underlying the decline of Bruges and Ghent were natural, epidemic, political, and economic, and it is hard to see how "policy" could have averted any of them. The coup de grâce to Bruges' preeminence in the thirteenth and early fourteenth century world system was delivered by natural events such as the final silting of her access to the sea and the reduction in her population caused by the Black Death. But if these had been the only problems, they would not have proven fatal. Today, a deep-draught canal links Bruges to a sea even more distant that it was in the fifteenth century when all sea-borne traffic came to a halt.

And in the pandemic of 1348–1349, other places, notably the Italian ports, suffered even higher mortalities than did Flanders, only to rise again and continue their active role in international trade for several centuries more. In themselves, these factors were not determining.

Political and economic variables seem to have been more decisive. These may be summed up under the anachronistic concept of dependency, which gradually eroded both the textile industry on which the prosperity of Flanders had rested and the commercial money-market functions that, over time, had taken its place. The textile industry depended upon outside sources of raw materials, notably wool, control over which rested with an independent political power. England could withhold the supplies at will and eventually developed to a point at which it could more fully utilize them at home, thus undercutting the competitor it had previously provisioned. In addition, the textile towns gradually lost control over the marketing of their products—at first partially when this system was centralized at Bruges, and then completely, after the Italians supplanted the merchant-bankers of Bruges in the export and marketing of Flemish textiles. (See Figure 3 which shows that Flemish cloth traveled much farther than Flemish merchants.)

Monetary capital accumulated by Italian firms was lent to local industries in advance purchases but, when textiles began to experience difficulties, such capital was free to move on. The merchants of Bruges became "passive" agents, trying unsuccessfully to monitor the actions of Italian "multinationals" who increasingly made the decisions and controlled the outcomes. Multinational firms are notoriously footloose, as we know from today's international division of labor, moving investment funds freely to places with lower labor and transport costs and higher returns.

Dependency thus "killed" the highly developed industrial capitalism that had grown so promisingly in thirteenth and early fourteenth-century Flanders. Even if the port had not dried up, the entrepreneurial abilities of the Brugeoises had. The *comprador* role extended the period of prosperity, but it could not stand alone; it depended on the real decision makers, the Italians, who not only mediated foreign trade but determined when and where investments were to be made.

We move on, then, to the Italian city-states that played so crucial

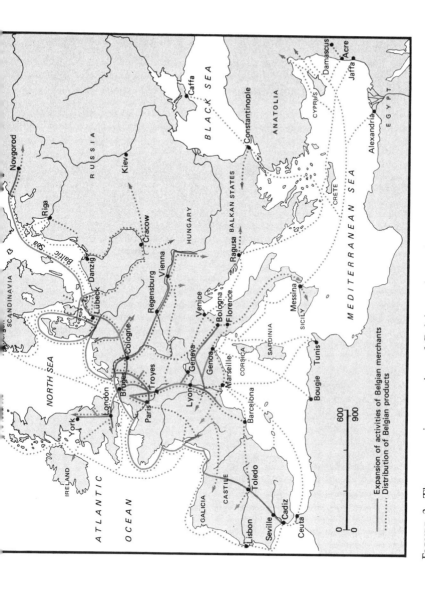

FIGURE 3. The economic expansion of Belgium: the paths of merchants and products (based on Doehaerd).

a part in making and breaking entrepôts in Europe and in connecting them to the world system of trade centered on the eastern Mediterranean and beyond. Chapter 4 examines two of them, Genoa on the west and Venice on the east coast of Italy.

Notes

1. Modern Belgium, created in the nineteenth century from an uneasy union of the French-speaking population of the south with the Flemish-speaking population of the east and north, remains extremely sensitive to linguistic symbols of nationalism and to internal economic and social rivalries. I have been uncomfortable in having to choose between the French and the Flemish names of the cities. In the end I have decided to be "even-handed," and to use the names that have maximum international recognition: hence the Flemish-based name, Ghent, instead of Gand, and the French Bruges, instead of Brugge.

2. By the mid-thirteenth century, both Ghent and Paris had populations of about 80,000, whereas Bruges probably had less than 40,000. However, it is significant to contrast these "true" cities with Troyes whose population at the same time was only about 15,000 (Russell, 1972). After the Black Death and the ensuing depression, Ghent with only 60,000 was considerably smaller than Paris and only 50 percent higher than Bruges (Nicholas, 1985: 1).

3. Fris (1913: 67) suggests one-third, which van Werveke has increased to half. It appears that these figures refer to a time after the industry had declined, however. Nicholas is somewhat more precise. He believes that circa 1356–1358, about two-fifths of the population was involved in textile production, a proportion that dropped to only about one-fourth toward the closing years of the fourteenth century (personal communication). See also Nicholas (1985: 1), however, when he estimates that one-half to two-thirds of Ghent's labor force worked in textile production in the fourteenth century.

It should not be assumed that the labor force in textiles consisted only of adult males. Production would not have been as high without the substantial contribution of women and children. The thirteenth century was a period during which the various *Beguinages* were established. These institutions housed single women who had not taken religious vows but lived collectively as lay persons. Many of the women supported themselves through textiles. The English term *spinster* comes directly from the textile function they performed. The French term *fileuse* (spinner) is related to both *fil* (thread) and possibly to *fille*, an unmarried woman. It is quite clear what function unmarried women performed in the medieval economy of Europe.

4. See Haëpke (1908). This has been an issue of contention among medieval historians, the debate centering on definitions. Proponents, mostly Belgians, stress, perhaps overenthusiastically, the prominent role of Bruges. Henri Pirenne claimed it was even more important than Venice in medieval international trade; I agree with Braudel (1984: 101) that this is going too far.

5. Neither Bruges nor Ghent seems to fit even this modest image, since apparently

Bruges did not survive as a religious place and the origin of Ghent can be traced back only to the seventh century when two monasteries were founded on its site. See Pirenne (n.d. xix).

6. See, inter alia, van Werveke (1955: 551). Although Ghent is definitely mentioned as a *portus* that early, Bruges may not have been one until later. According to Pirenne (Vol. I, 1929: 188–189), a *portus* was a place of disembarcation and an entrepôt on a gulf or river in which colonies of foreign merchants and artisans gathered, usually under the protective shadow of an episcopal settlement or a *castrum*. This image of the first "urbanites" as "foreigners" or strangers, established by Pirenne and accepted by many other historians (see in particular Ganshof, 1949: 69–70, who refers to adventurous caravan merchants), has recently been criticized for disindigenizing the process in an unnecessary way. The term *portus* gives rise to the Flemish term for the bourgeoisie (in its original sense as a free resident of a burg or town), *poorter*.

7. Again, Bruges seems to have been less important than Ghent. Although the first textual notice of Ghent as a commercial center (and *pagus*) is not until the third quarter of the ninth century, as early as 811 Charlemagne is reported to have visited Ghent to inspect the fleet that was being built there to defend the area from Normand (northmen or Viking) raiders (van Werveke, 1946: 15). It is very probable that the port of Bruges was founded (or refounded) then to serve a similar defensive purpose.

8. For details, see J. J. Carlier (1861–1872: 127–139). Van Houtte (1953: especially 183) gives the fair cycle in the thirteenth century (the earliest recoverable) as Ypres from February 28 to March 29; Bruges from April 23 to May 22; Thorhout from June 24 to July 24; Lille from August 15 to September 14; and Messine from October 1 to November 1.

9. A document cited by van Werveke (1946: 18) mentions wool being brought by riverboat to the fair at Ghent.

10. Although at an earlier time the chief function of walls had been to protect settlements from external threats, by the later Middle Ages the wall had taken on a different significance. It demarcated the boundary of a franchised (free) town from the rural land still under feudal ownership and authority.

11. I am a bit uncomfortable with his causal reasoning here since, if anything, the line runs in the opposite direction. During the revival of the eleventh century there were substantial improvements in agricultural technology, not the least of which in Flanders was the ability to canalize and drain land, which added substantially to the fertile area under cultivation. Windmills and waterwheels, probably introduced from the Middle East, intensified this process in the twelfth century (Braudel, 1973: 261–268; Cipolla, 1976: 162–168). This higher agricultural productivity supported a larger and denser population and even allowed surplus laborers to escape from seigneurial obligations. These escaped serfs migrated to the urban settlements, even though the latter were not yet autocephalous.

12. For a good insight into the situation of such merchants in England, albeit for a somewhat later time when they were more common, see T. H. Lloyd (1982). On English fairs, see Moore (1985).

13. The role of the Italian city-states in mediating Belgian contacts with the Orient should not be overstressed. Flanders had her own direct connections as well. Count Robert the Frisian had embarked from Genoa in 1190 on the Third

Crusade and Baldwin IXth of Flanders participated in the Fourth Crusade that, in 1204, was deflected to conquer Constantinople. For his troubles, the Count of Flanders was elected the first Latin Emperor of Constantinople; his heirs continued to append the phrase "of Constantinople" after their names, even though Baldwin IX lost his life on a campaign shortly thereafter.

14. The word "patriciate" was certainly not in use at that time. Rather, it is a term employed by modern historians to draw an analogy between the Roman antecedent and the rich bourgeoisie/entrepreneurs (van Werveke, 1946: 30–31) who ruled the cities of French Flanders inter alia and who controlled an increasingly proletarianized labor force. There were, of course, important differences with respect to both ancient Roman times and today. David Nicholas, in a careful critique of an earlier draft of this chapter, for which I remain indebted, has strongly objected to my imposing class categories on fourteenth century Ghent, a position he has also opposed in his 1985 book. Although he remains the leading authority in this field from whose accounts, indeed, I derived many of my own conclusions, I believe that the automatic resistance by many medievalists to class, as a sensitizing concept, prevents them from finding earlier precedents to modern capitalism. This is, in the last analysis, a subject that bears further study.

15. One of the unexpected consequences of the "disorders" was that the bell tower on the city hall of Bruges caught fire, destroying the 1241 Charter of the city and many of the documents archivists would need to reconstruct the city's history prior to that date.

16. By far the best book on this complex and fascinating subject is David Nicholas, *Town and Countryside: Social, Economic, and Political Tensions in Fourteenth-Century Flanders* (1971), to which the reader interested in the early history of labor movements is directed.

17. I am struck by some of the parallels with twentieth-century America, when the shoe and textile industries of New England moved south to lower their labor costs.

18. Misnamed the Hanseatic League, which literally translates as "Leaguely" League, this organization of merchant guilds from various German cities functioned informally much before the fourteenth century (Lopez, 1976: 114–115; Braudel, 1984: 102; Rorig, 1967: 37–39). It was like a combination of the League of XVII Cities (active at the Champagne fairs and headed by the merchant guild master of Ghent) in that it was a collective that protected its merchants and negotiated common terms of trade, and of the Hanse of London (headed by Bruges) whose goal was to import goods, chiefly wool, from abroad. See the classic work by Dollinger (1964, English trans. 1970).

19. See de Roover (1968). The term "bourse" may even have had its origin in Bruges. As we shall see, foreign merchants often stayed in special hotels that assumed increased functions as the intermediaries between Italian traders and Flemish hosts. Since the middle of the thirteenth century, there was such a hotel near the center of the city, run by the vander Beurse family, which gave its name to the open space outside it (eventually called in French Place de la Bourse). The Italian merchants were concentrated in this zone, and the halls of the Genoese, Florentine, and Venetian merchants were later located there (where they still stand). So intense were the financial dealings of these merchant–bankers that this area became known as "the exchange," hence, the "bourse." See inter alia, Frans

Beyers, "De familie 'vander Beurse' in de oorsprong van de handelsbeurzzen," an offprint of which I saw in Bruges but unfortunately not identified by source; also van Werveke (1944: 47). However, it is entirely possible that the etymology was in the reverse order, since the Old English *purs* may have been the origin of the family name itself. I am indebted to A. Stinchcombe for pointing this out to me.

20. It is interesting to contrast this with the organization formed by the Italian merchants visiting the fairs of Champagne. Perhaps patterning themselves after the Hanse of XVII Cities they encountered there (Laurent, 1935: 93), the Italian merchants formed a similar organization called the University of Lombards and Tuscans, whose title was expanded in 1288 to include other Italians (Laurent, 1935: 119). But the needs of temporary merchants differed from those more permanently settled.

21. One of the most famous of these factors was Francesco de Balducci Pegolotti, who worked for the Bardi firm of Florence and was stationed in Flanders and then in England during the early fourteenth century (de Roover, 1948: 33). We will return to him in a later chapter when we investigate Europe's trade with the Levant, for it is his merchant guide manual that constitutes a precious and unique document for the study of medieval trade.

22. According to de Roover (1948: 99–104), the Lombards and Cahorsins first appeared in Flanders toward the end of the thirteenth century along with the other Italians. The first charters granted to Lombards date from 1281; the license fees they had to pay to practice their profession were exorbitant.

23. The right to endorse such "checks" to someone else (that is, to be allowed to buy and sell them) did not evolve until the early seventeenth century in Antwerp (de Roover, 1948: 35).

24. By the end of the fourteenth century the harbor conditions at Sluis were so bad that the larger ships had to anchor at an offshore island and forward their cargoes to Sluis by barge (van Houtte, 1966: 40).

25. See Gottfried (1983) for a recent account and McNeill (1976) for a more global exploration of its causes and consequences.

26. This estimate, which appears in most sources on the city, was derived from a list of persons enrolled in the militia at that time, multiplied by the estimated ratio of militia to nonmilitia population. It is, therefore, very tentative. See de Smet (1933: 636).

CHAPTER

4

✠✠✠✠✠

The Merchant Mariners of Genoa and Venice

William McNeill (1974) gave his book on Venice the subtitle, "The Hinge of Europe"; the awkwardness of the term is compensated for by its precision. He may, however, be accused of pro-Venetian bias (a prejudice not uncommon in the literature on Italian cities) since Genoa could lay equal claim to that key position as link between Europe and the Orient.[1]

Both cities played pivotal roles in joining Europe to the ongoing world economy of the east. Both became great naval and merchant powers, struggling for supremacy over the Mediterranean, hitherto an "Arab Sea," and for exclusive and/or preferential trading concessions in the Black Sea areas, along the coast of Palestine, and in Egypt, which guarded the gateway to India and beyond. And from the eleventh to the end of the fourteenth century when Genoa finally capitulated, both were locked in a deadly battle to preserve their own sea lanes and destroy those of their rival.

Each was a vanguard. Geographically, each tried to reach as far as possible in Asia. Institutionally, each tried to devise better ways to do business, to accumulate larger amounts of less risky capital, to administer companies, and to monopolize the markets for commodities and money. Technologically, both developed impressive sophistication in navigation, shipbuilding, and armaments. Either could have accomplished the task of connecting the cultural islands of the thirteenth-century world system. Tragically, these two giants proved one too many, for they spent as much energy fighting one another as they did conquering the East. Both were fated to take to the sea, being insulated by politics, water, or high terrain from strong land-based hinterlands.

Origins of the Two Port Cities

Genoa, a superb harbor town huddled at the base of a mountainous escarpment that insulated her from the mainland behind, was from earliest times a port and, from time to time, a victim of invasions. Settled as early as the fifth century B.C., virtually destroyed by the Carthaginians in the Second Punic War, rebuilt by the Romans who encircled it with new walls in the fourth century A.D., it fell to the Ostrogoths and then the Lombards who occupied it until it was retaken by the Byzantines in 588 (Renouard, 1969, 1: 228). It remained under the nominal rule of Constantinople between the sixth and tenth centuries, but only as a modest fishing and agricultural town whose inhabitants lived at subsistence levels (Renouard, 1969, I: 228); trade was only beginning.

It could be said that the Crusades actually commenced in the tenth century, for by then Genoa was already "at war" with the Muslim states of the western Mediterranean. In 934–935 a Fatimid fleet stormed and sacked the city. Only much later did the Genoese, assisted by the Pisans, counterattack, sending expeditions in 1061 against the Muslims in Sardinia and Corsica, and later even against the former North African capital of the Fatimids, Mahdiya; they captured that town briefly in 1087, exacting tribute and the first, but not last, trade concession from its Muslim rulers—an exemption from the tolls.

By the end of the eleventh century, the Genoese had gained de facto independence from the Eastern Roman Empire and had established a self-ruled *compagna*, an association of citizens under the authority of six and later ten consuls elected for three-year terms (Renouard, 1969, I: 232–233). Appetites whetted and abilities tested by prior sea battles and seeking to expand their horizon from the western basin of the Mediterranean to the eastern, the Genoese enthusiastically answered the call of the Pope for the first foray of that bloody and eventually unsuccessful venture—the conquest of Palestine. Begun in 1095 and not abandoned until the last Crusader foothold in Acre fell to the Mamluks in 1291, the Crusades brought West and East into admittedly antagonistic but nevertheless permanent involvement with one another.

Venice was less eager than Genoa to enter that struggle, however, for she had a very different and earlier link to the east that she was reluctant to disturb. In spite of Edith Ennen's generally true contention that Italy, unlike the regions of northern Europe, had an unbroken continuity of urban settlement throughout the so-called "Dark Ages,"[2] Venice must be counted, unlike venerable Genoa, as a "new town," albeit one with urban roots. It was founded in about 568 (at a preexisting fishing village) when a stream of migrant mainlanders fled the invading Lombards to seek refuge at the lagoons off shore (Lane, 1973: 4). Venice remained firmly attached to Byzantium, even after the Lombards had conquered all of the Italian mainland, including Ravenna, which had been the Italian capital of the Byzantine Empire. And even after the Lombards were incorporated into Charlemagne's domains, the Venetians, with the help of a Byzantine fleet, were able to resist Charlemagne's attempt in 810 to include her as well. In the treaty of peace finally concluded between the Byzantine emperor and Charlemagne, Venice was explicitly protected (Lane, 1973: 5), which thus "laid the foundations for the absolute primacy of Venice over the other Italo-Byzantine seaports in western trade" (Lopez, 1952: 277).

Although Venice benefited from this allegiance, gaining certain trade privileges in Byzantine ports, she was not yet able to take full advantage of the commercial opportunities they made possible. Even though before 1000 A.D. "some Venetians were seamen expert enough to cross the Mediterranean, . . . Greeks, Syrians, and other Easterners carried most of the trade between Venice and the Levant" (Lane, 1973: 5), as indeed they did in other European ports.[3] At that time, Venice could only offer for trade local supplies of salt, fish, and timber, as well as slaves captured primarily from her not-yet-Christianized neighbors across the Adriatic (Lane, 1973: 7–8; Renouard, 1969, I: 131). As Braudel stresses, up to the time of the Crusades "Italy was still only a poor 'peripheral' region, intent on making her services acceptable to others as a purveyor of timber, grain, linen cloth, salt and slaves from the European interior" (1984: 107).

But Venice had already begun to play a more active role in commerce, even before the Crusades began. In 1080 she finally broke through the blockade of the Norman kingdom that controlled the lower waters of the Adriatic. Coming to the rescue of the Byzantine fleet, she assisted in freeing that crucial waterway, for which she was rewarded by the Byzantine Emperor Alexius I in 1082 with a special charter (the Golden Bull) granting her virtually full trading privileges and exemptions from tolls (Lane, 1973: 27–29; Braunstein and Delort, 1971: 44–47) throughout the empire and most importantly in Constantinople, Christendom's largest and most prosperous city and the gateway to Central Asia.[4] Having gained this concession and now able to expand her trade in the Levant, she was understandably reluctant to risk her ships and her reputation to follow the first Crusade.

At this point, Genoa and Venice still occupied relatively separate spheres. Genoa, on the west coast of Italy, commanded the western basin of the Mediterranean, gaining significant territorial or trading concessions from the Muslims of Spain, from the islands off her shore, and in littoral North Africa. The Venetians were similarly strengthening *their* lines of communication in the eastern basin of the Mediterranean, having gained access to ports of call throughout the Aegean and at least some of its islands, as well as Constantinople and the Black Sea. Her reluctance to tamper with this status was matched by Genoa's eagerness to "break into" the richer markets of the East.

The Impact of the Crusades on Venice and Genoa

It was thus Genoese and Pisan ships that came to the rescue of the French, Flemish, and other European knights[5] who had eagerly answered Pope Urban the Second's call in 1095 for a "reconquest"

of the Holy Land from the Muslims who, ever since the second
half of the seventh century—hardly a new threat—had converted
most of the resident population to Islam. It is difficult today to
comprehend the earnest zeal with which kings and counts gathered
their retainers and headed for a place more fabled than known.
Some cynics suggest that it was more eagerness for booty than for
divine redemption that motivated the counts of Champagne, Brie,
and Flanders and the kings of France and England, inter alia, to
set off on so perilous a journey. Yet the documents of the time
are both more naive and otherworldly than such an interpretation
would predict.

Nevertheless, the relative levels of civilization in Europe and
the Levant do suggest that the Crusaders were more akin to the
barbarians who periodically preyed on the settled wealth of high
cultures than to carriers of the *mission civilisatrice*. As Cipolla
(1976: 206) puts it, "there is no doubt that from the fall of the
Roman Empire to the beginning of the thirteenth century Europe
was an underdeveloped area in relation to the major centers of
civilization at the time . . . [—] clearly a land of barbarians." Archibald Lewis (1970: vii) uses this discrepancy to account for the
asymmetrical interest East and West showed in each other. Although Europeans eagerly sought out Muslim lands and their
wealth and "copied many facets of Muslim culture," their interest
was not reciprocated. Not only did "the average upper-class Moslem [feel] superior to most Western Europeans," but the wide
geographic lore of the Arabs never extended to western Europe,
an area they considered had little to offer (Cipolla, 1976: 206).
Even after the Crusades thrust a European threat into their heartland, Muslim attitudes remained condescending at best and aghast
at worst, whereas their invaders were filled with a strange mixture
of hatred and romantic (if reluctant) awe and admiration.

In the twelfth and thirteenth century the literature in both societies reflected this asymmetry. The best summary of European
views is by Sylvia Thrupp[6] who points out that

> *Chansons de geste* and romances that bring their heroes into contact
> with Muslims are our best clues to the views of the various Muslim
> peoples prevailing among French nobles and probably among the upper
> bourgeoisie in the twelfth and thirteenth centuries . . . The elements of
> the pattern are the cosmopolitanism of the world of Islam, its power

and wealth, the splendor of its cities, the cleverness of its people. . . .
The Muslims are openly envied because they know even better than
the French how to live. (Thrupp, 1977: 74, 82)

Such an exalted view of the enemy, however, was belied by the
Crusaders' behavior toward them, which evoked revulsion in their
Muslim victims. Muslims saw the "Franks"—as westerners were
consistently referred to in Arab literature—"as beasts superior in
courage and fighting ardour but in nothing else, just as animals
are superior in strength and aggression."[7]

This characterization was not totally unfounded. In 1098 Crusader destruction of the Syrian town of Maʿarra had been accompanied by acknowledged acts of Frankish cannibalism. Graphically
described in the chronicle of Radulph of Caen (he admits that "In
Maʿarra our troops boiled pagan adults in cooking pots; they im-
paled children on spits and devoured them grilled"), they were
later "justified" in a letter sent to the Pope by the Christian commander, who blamed the lapse on extreme hunger. Needless to
say, this excuse was dismissed by Arab historians who continued
to describe their bloodthirsty enemies as eaters not only of people
but, what was worse, even of dogs, considered the uncleanest of
species (Maalouf, 1984: 39–40).

The barbarians, however, met with some success in this first
military incursion. The Genoese and Pisans, who had so eagerly
supported the Crusaders in their attack on Palestine, reaped their
promised reward. They were given one-third of the city and suburbs of Acre as well as similar portions in the other cities they
helped to conquer. Once the Crusader state was set up, they also
received, retroactively, one-quarter of Jerusalem and of Jaffa
(Heyd, 1885, I: 138).

Venice held back until the operation looked as though it might
succeed. Not until "1099, after the Frank armies had battered their
way into Jerusalem, slaughtering every Muslim in the city and
burning all the Jews alive in the main synagogue . . . did a Venetian
fleet of 200 [leave] the Lido port" (Norwich, 1982: 76). It finally
arrived in the summer of 1100 just in time to assist in the recapture
of Jaffa and other towns. As a reward the Venetians were also
allotted one-third of the towns' land and environs and given special
trading concessions in the new Crusader kingdom (Heyd, 1885, I:
137). Later, Venice received her usual third when the ports of Tyre

and Ascalon were taken with her help (Heyd, 1885, I: 143–144). Venetians were allowed to form their own quarters and enjoyed a position privileged to exploit the commercial opportunities of expanding trade.

This direct entrée to the riches of the East changed the role of the Italian merchant mariner cities from passive to active. The revival of the Champagne fairs in the twelfth century can be explained convincingly by both the enhanced demand for eastern goods stimulated by the Crusades and, because of the strategic position of the Italians in coastal enclaves of the Levant, the increased supplies of such goods they could now deliver.

The Genoese and to a lesser extent the Venetians had begun the long process of tipping the fulcrum of the world system. By the thirteenth century "the center of gravity [of Europe at least] had definitely moved to the 'big four' of northern and central Italy (Venice, Milan, Genoa and Florence) whose powerful merchants had a firm grip on the routes towards the fertile and industrious European hinterland and endeavored to reach far beyond the declining Islamic facade into the depths of Asia and Africa" (Lopez, 1976: 99). But that process—aided not a little by the thrust into the Near Eastern heartland of "other barbarians" arriving from the east, the Mongols—would take all of the twelfth and most of the thirteenth century and would not be decisively achieved until the opening years of the sixteenth century, when the fruits would be gathered not by the Italians who planted them but by the Portuguese who succeeded (albeit with the help of Genoese capital and sailors) in outflanking them.

Colonial Expansion Abroad

During the twelfth century the Italians expanded and consolidated their imperial reach, building and arming larger ships,[8] plundering weaker vessels—Muslim and Christian alike—for their booty, vying with one another for more profitable terms of trade, and occupying any vulnerable port along the shores or on the islands of the Mediterranean. Their two eastern destinations were the Crusader enclaves of the Levant, which received goods from the Orient—either totally overland or, more commonly, via caravan routes that connected to the Persian Gulf—and, less commonly,

Constantinople where the Genoese had gained trading concessions as favorable as those enjoyed by the Venetians.

However, in the last third of the twelfth century, military events forced a renewed focus on the northern outlet. Crusader enclave after enclave succumbed to the Muslim forces of Seljuk Turks who entered the region from the northeast under the leadership first of Nur al-Din and then of his successor, Salah al-Din al-Ayyubi (the Saladin of European documents). By 1187 Saladin had routed the Crusader armies and Muslims reoccupied Tiberias, Jaffa, Ascalon, Gaza, and, finally, Jerusalem. The Ayyubid dynasty now held all of Egypt and most of the Fertile Crescent, as well as eastern Anatolia. Only a few western colonies remained in the Levant.

As matters deteriorated for the Christian side, Papal injunctions against trade with the "infidels" (a pious but futile prohibition) were increasingly enforced, which enhanced the relative position of Christian traders based in Constantinople and on the islands of Crete, Cyprus, and Rhodes. Competition between the Italians and the Byzantine "Greeks" came to an exasperating head in 1182 when in Constantinople there was a "wholesale massacre of the Latins" [that is, Italians] whose quarters were set afire (Runciman, 1952: 100). Although five years later the situation had been normalized and the traders were able to reestablish their colonies (Venetians within the city proper, Genoese across the Golden Horn in Pera), the underlying competition festered for several decades until Venice, in an underhanded but terribly brilliant ploy, succeeded in adding Constantinople to its growing empire, displacing by one dramatic act both its Greek and Genoese rivals for the northeastern trade.

The Fourth Crusade of 1204: The Latin Empire of Constantinople

The somewhat sordid details of this event have come down to us in a primary document, *The Conquest of Constantinople*, written by a knight from Champagne with estates not far from Troyes, Geoffrey de Villehardouin.[9] In the summer of 1202, he tells us, Crusader forces began assembling from all over Europe at the Lido of Venice where arrangements had been made to rent an impressive number of ships to take them to Egypt and then the Holy Land. They were to be joined by a second fleet from Flanders that carried the forces of Count Baldwin IX. But not all who promised to join appeared nor were those who did able to raise the steep fee demanded by the Venetians. A compromise was reached, whereby the Crusaders, in return for a reduction in the price, agreed first to travel to Zara to recapture that city from the Hungarians (Villehardouin, 1985: 40–46). By winter the combined forces reached and subdued Zara, whose spoils were divided equally between the Venetians and the Crusaders.

The Venetians, however, refused to set sail again until Easter, and when they did, they headed not south to Cairo as planned but eastward to Constantinople. Exclaimed Villehardouin (1985: 58–59) as the Venetian fleet put into that port, "[one] never imagined there could be so fine a place in all the world. . . . [with] high walls and lofty towers encircling it, and its rich palaces and tall churches . . . so many that no one would have believed it to be true." After such a paean of praise, it is hard to believe that the next action should have been an assault on the city. Between July 1203 and April 1204 the "Latins" who had set out to fight the infidels instead besieged their fellow Christians and, when the city was finally entered, set it on fire, plundered its riches,[10] and then piously celebrated Palm Sunday and Easter Day "with hearts full of joy for the benefits our Lord and Saviour had bestowed on them" (Villehardouin, 1985: 93).

The Count of Flanders and Hainaut, Baldwin IX, still in his twenties, was elected Emperor of the Latin kingdom of Constantinople, his coronation taking place a few weeks later in the great Church of Saint Sophia.[11] The Venetians wanted no high office; they wanted only to expand their merchant empire. They "appropriated the best part of the imperial territory" (Norwich, 1982: 141), claiming three-eights of the city and empire, including all of Crete, from which Venice would direct her spice trade into the fourteenth and fifteenth centuries. She excluded Genoa and Pisa, her arch rivals, from her hegemonic domain, which now stretched from the Caspian and Black Seas on the north to the Levant, through the eastern Mediterranean and its islands, up the Adriatic and, overland, beyond the Alps into Germany and the North Sea. This, when added to her continuing Egyptian connection, made

Venice the dominant force controlling European access to the spices and silks of Asia.

As a result the thirteenth century was a period of Venetian efflorescence at home—in culture, in politics, in industry (particularly shipbuilding and transport), and in business. But it was no less so for Genoa, which still had no serious rival in *her* hegemonic zone—North Africa and northwestern Europe, where the trade at Champagne far outshone that in Lubeck. Toward the end of the century, as seen in Chapter 3, she would further solidify her hold by moving westward out into the Atlantic and then on to Bruges.

New Technologies at Sea

The Crusades stimulated a remarkable increase in the naval power of the mariner states. The heightened demand for ships—to carry Crusaders, burgeoning loads of pilgrims heading for the Holy Land, and the goods facilitated by the new trading concessions gained by Pisa, Genoa, and Venice—all led to a virtual frenzy of shipbuilding. Although most ships were still built and owned by wealthy families, the initial construction in 1104 of the Venice Arsenal (a municipal facility for shipbuilding) signaled that an activity so central to the economic base of the marine cities needed more than individual entrepreneurs. It had to involve the state and, with it, virtually the entire populace, as we shall see later. Even in Genoa where shipbuilding was financed by privately pooled capital, the state played a regulatory and facilitating role.

In the twelfth and thirteenth centuries the Italians used three types of ships for long-distance transport: the sailing ship (called the *navis* or *bucius*) with two decks and, by the thirteenth century, even three, propelled by four to six lateen sails, divided equally fore and aft; the galley (called *galea*, *galeotis*, or *sagitta*), a warship propelled by large numbers of oarsmen but equipped with a few light sails for auxiliary use; and the *tarida*, a cross between the two, having both oars and a full set of sails on two masts, which was both heavier and slower than a galley but had a greater carrying capacity (Byrne, 1930: 5). The galleys were first used in connection with the Crusades but, when that demand wound down at the end of the thirteenth century, both sailing ships (sometimes called round ships or cogs) and large galleys were equally used for trade.

Over time, ships became larger and larger. Byrne (1930: 9) provides some estimates of their dimensions. In preparation for his 1248 Crusade, St. Louis not only leased hundreds of ships from Genoa and Venice but ordered the construction of new and larger ones. The biggest ship the Genoese provided was the Paradisius, some 83 feet long, which could transport a hundred Crusaders, their horses, armor, and attendants or, in later times, accommodate about 1000 passengers for trade or pilgrimage. Although this appears puny today, the 600 tons of cargo a large Genoese ship could carry in the thirteenth century was roughly equal to the shipping capacities of fourteenth- (Unger, 1980: 169) and even sixteenth-century vessels (Byrne, 1930: 10–11) and compared favorably with the ships Columbus used to "discover" the New World."[12] The galleys could respond sensitively to direction changes; the addition of special rudders on the cogs and hulks enhanced the maneuverability of this type.

Not only were ships becoming larger and more maneuverable but navigation techniques were undergoing significant improvements at the same time. Although a "floating magnetic needle" had long been used as a compass on Chinese ships[13] and Arab sailors used this guide to navigation to supplement the sidereal-dependent astrolabe (unfortunately of little use on stormy nights when stars were obscured), its adoption (in the form of the *bussola*) by the Italians in the latter part of the twelfth century meant a real improvement. Particularly in combination with "the [later] creation of nautical charts of unprecedented accuracy and the compilation of the navigating tables called *tavole de marteloio*, referred to in a rare manuscript of 1290 as already well established, the compass made year-round sailing possible" (Lane, "The Economic Meaning of the Invention of the Compass," reprinted in 1966: 332). Hitherto, there had been only summer sailings; now there could be convoys in the winter as well, although Lane claims that it was only in the fourteenth century that the double *muda* became common (Lane, 1966: 334).

Improvements were not confined to the physical technologies of sailing, however. Parallel developments in social and economic techniques were equally essential to harness the enhanced transport capacities. Of greatest importance were the ways devised to pool ships to reduce hazard and, perhaps as significant, the ways invented to pool capital and distribute risk. The first involved the convoy and the fighting merchant marines; the latter required new forms of capitalism.

Given the endemic war on the high seas, no merchant shipping was very safe without the organization of convoys protected by warships, backed by the full power of the "state." Safe passage had been essential for the development of periodic fairs; for the Champagne fairs, protection was provided by the feudal warlords. But over water, safe passage could not be arranged in such a way. Just as Britannia's hegemony was later to be assured by her naval gunboats, the success of the Italian merchant fleets depended in the last analysis upon how well they fared in the marine war of all against all—sometimes called piracy, but only when the acts of enemies were being described. This protection could not be bought from someone else; the Italians had to provide it for themselves.[14]

This need for a citizen "militia" may have been one of the reasons the governments of the Italian port states were both "more democratic" and more directly involved in economic ventures than was the case in either France or Flanders.[15] As Lane put it, "the crews of the merchant marine and the navy were the same people" (Lane, 1973: 48). All sailors were also fighters, and the convoys that circled the Mediterranean twice a year stayed together in caravans, the ten to twenty rather small ships (*naves*) accompanied by "one or two really big round ships [cogs] or a few galleys for protection" (Lane, 1973: 69). The crews were expected, when necessary, to seize their swords, daggers, javelins, and lances for the hand-to-hand combat that was de rigueur, for there were as yet neither canons nor, of course, guns on board (Lane, 1973: 48–49). Strength in numbers, therefore, was a crucial strategy, and this was undoubtedly the underlying reason why the Commune set the date for a convoy sailing, the *muda*, a term that was applied at first to the convoy itself and later to the time set for its sailing (Lane, 1957, reprinted 1966: 128–141).

The Alliance between the State and Private Capitalism

We have already alluded to the special relationship between private entrepreneurial or venture capitalism and the city-state government that existed to defend and assist it. But in this instance, Genoa and Venice developed quite different patterns for its expression. In Venice, the arrangements were closer to state capitalism with a strong subcomponent of individual enterprise. In Genoa the mix was reversed; individual citizens were more involved than the state in direct investment.

The variation may have derived from the different origins of the two cities. Venice, as a "new city" that did not import its elite from the hinterlands but developed it indigenously, was less fractured by the kinds of interfamily feuds and competitive struggles that plagued most Italian city-states, including Genoa (Heers, English trans. 1977: *passim*) The latter, because the nobility derived, in part at least, from a landowning class that came from the hinterlands, tended to perpetuate old battles in the new arena—moving from rural military conflict to modern urban cut-throat competition in business and government.

Both Genoa and Venice used the institution of the public debt, in lieu of taxation, to fund investment in infrastructure and defense at home and on the high seas. Even before 1200, the Italian city-states had developed the institution of the "public debt," by which citizens voluntarily lent money to the commune. In return they were granted "shares of stock" that paid a regular if variable interest and could be redeemed any time funds were plentiful. During the course of the thirteenth century, however, a system of forced loans came to prevail in Venice and Florence, particularly to finance large merchant-military campaigns. In contrast, in Genoa, "where the system developed further and lasted longer than anywhere else" and in line with her more individualistic approach, the loans to the commune were actually purchases of shares in a given revenue-producing state function (Luzzatto, English trans. 1961: 123–124). This system later resulted in the kind of "tax farming" associated more with Muslim feudalism than with the communes of Europe.

The institution of the public debt, whether subscribed to voluntarily or levied according to a percentage of family wealth,[16] shaped a peculiar relationship between city government and merchant wealth. With the state seen as yet another outlet for profitable capital investment, it was natural that merchants would be eager to participate in (that is, control) state decision making. Indeed, in describing the relationship between political power and merchant wealth in Venice and Genoa, Le Goff points out that in fourteenth- and fifteenth-century Genoa and Venice, speculations on the true "value" of shares in the public debt "constituted . . . a larger and larger part of the affairs of the big merchants" (1956: 24). That government was run as a corporation fits well with merchant capitalism.

Merchant Capitalism

In the "Great Debate" on the origins of capitalism, attention focuses closely on the Italian city-states of the thirteenth century. The *bête noire* of the Italian medievalists is Werner Sombart, who claimed that the level of economic sophistication and affluence in thirteenth-century cities (even in Italy, by far the most advanced) was too ludicrously low to qualify as "capitalism." On the other side of the debate are most scholars of medieval Italy, who make an ardent plea for "complimenting" the latter by calling it capitalism.[17] Although their evidence is drawn largely from studies of economic institutions, some even claim that Max Weber's nebulous "spirit" of modern capitalism also existed in Italian towns of the thirteenth and fourteenth centuries.[18] This seems to be a sterile debate. I think we can assume that the forms of any given "ideal type" shift gradually from point of origin to full development and that, particularly at the early stages, the innovative form exists within a social formation with which it is in conflict. Much depends upon the definition of "capitalism" used.

Lane (1964, reprinted 1966: 57), adopting what he called the "sensible" definition of Oliver Cox (1959), argues that "Venice was the first [European city] to become capitalistic in the sense that its ruling class made their livelihood by employing wealth in the form of commercial capital—cash, ships, and commodities— and used their control of government to increase their profits." But this seems to be too particularistic and superficial.

I prefer the position taken by Le Goff (1956: 39–40) who says it is better to think of Italian medieval merchants as "precapitalist" in the Marxian sense, because "feudalism" was still the dominant form of social organization. In the midst of this, however, was a cadre of new types struggling to overturn that order—industrialists (in Flanders) and merchants (in Italy), who were *preparing for capitalism*. He distinguishes sharply between urban merchant-artisans, not yet capitalistic, and larger scale merchant-bankers, who clearly were the vanguard for the system then being born.[19] We now turn to this group to examine how far along that path the merchant mariner states of Italy had advanced.

As contrasted with an imperial economy, "free-enterprise" capitalism is characterized by its capacity to mobilize for concerted investment, through "extrastate" means, more capital than any one individual, no matter how wealthy, can provide. The usual distinction between the collectively pooled capital in a state socialist system and in entrepreneurial capitalism is that, in the latter, the contributors invest *voluntarily* for the purpose of making a profit. This return may then be reinvested, at least in part, for the purpose of gaining even more profit. Investors not only try to maximize their chances of profit but diversify their "portfolios" to minimize the risk of losing all. If we use this definition, there can be little doubt that the city-states of Genoa and Venice (not to mention Florence and other commercial hill cities of Italy) were *almost* capitalist by the thirteenth century, albeit in slightly different ways.[20]

The method of capital pooling used first, which continued to be favored in Venice even after Genoa moved beyond it, was the family firm called the *fraterna*, whose capital came from the undivided shares of family heirs (brothers). The usual arrangement was for the partner brothers to divide labor, one remaining at home to supervise family interests (arranging for the purchase of goods for export and the sale of imports in the local market) and the other traveling with the exported goods to foreign ports to sell them and to make purchases for the return trip. Such organizations were hardly innovative. Their advantage, however, was that the partners presumably could trust one another and were prepared to work together for a lifetime. Thus, as Heers (1977: 221–222) has so forcefully argued, the family, even after the fourteenth century, was still the basic unit of economic organization.

However, not all merchants who inherited money were equipped with brothers and not all adventurous entrepreneurs were born with the capital they needed. Therefore, even before the thirteenth century began, a variant had been developed, called the *commenda* or, in Venice, the *colleganza*. In this type of partnership, initially formed for only one overseas venture at a time, the first partner put up two-thirds of the required capital and the second partner contributed the remaining one-third plus his labor to accompany the goods abroad. Reflecting their differential input, once the venture was successfully concluded they divided the profits equally, after deducting the traveling partner's expenses.[21]

Gradually, to take into account young "active partners" who had not yet amassed any capital, an alternate form was devised in which a "sleeping" partner (the so-called *stans*) provided all the capital and an "active" partner, after covering his expenses, obtained only a quarter of the profit. However, this did not work well for small merchants whose exports did not warrant the labor of a full-time partner. The traveling agents, therefore, also accepted supplementary consignments from a variety of sleeping partners, taking a commission for their services. Such agents often remained abroad for several seasons, receiving shipments, selling the goods, and often exercizing considerable discretion about what the return load would contain.

Eventually, larger firms employed factors who worked not for commissions but for salaries, remaining in the major branch office abroad to handle ongoing transactions. This, however, was more common across Europe, since the fast post there could deliver detailed orders to the factors. On the islands of the Mediterranean, in Syria, and in the port towns on the Black Sea, more autonomy had to be granted to the permanently installed commission agents. Many of these began as agents but eventually became independent traders as they amassed capital, running a very complicated itinerary through various local ports, rather than a simple one to and from Genoa or Venice. In the Orient, agents even began to take on "investment banking" functions.

> Debts owed by men in Syria to residents of Genoa were collected by reputable factors going to Syria, under contracts made with the creditor in Genoa. The creditor authorized a factor to collect the debt for him, and directed the factor to take the amount collected in accomendatio to use it in trade as he saw fit. (Byrne, 1916: 166)

As forms of trade and types of partnerships became increasingly complex and more removed from the family, better records were needed—both for accountings, which had to be rendered to investors, and for complex agreements, whose terms could not be trusted to memory or faith. Although double-entry bookkeeping as we know it was not formally in place until the late fourteenth century, even before that, records were kept so carefully that a contemporary scholar can, with a bit of effort, transform them into present-day accounting forms. And although the earliest Venetian sources refer to agreements under the name of *rogadia* (by prayer),[22] soon such contracts were being written down and made official by a notary. In Genoa this notarizing of documents became a virtual obsession, with thousands of contracts recorded annually at home and in various colonies abroad.

Historians have conscientiously mined both account books and notarial documents to understand how business was conducted in medieval Europe. But as Sapori (1952, translated 1970) has sardonically pointed out, businessmen as crafty as the Italians were as likely to use official documents to deceive as to reveal. Thus, two sets of books seem to have been kept, one for the "investors" and possibly the tax assessors and one that showed the real accounts. Furthermore, the profusion of notarial documents often resulted from the subdivision of a given transaction into multiple (and separately recorded) parts designed to conceal the existence of interest, forbidden by the Church's injunction against usury. Nevertheless, the sheer volume of recorded transactions suggests that in the Italian port cities business investment was not restricted to a small group of upper class entrepreneurs but permeated the entire economy.

In Marco Polo's Venice virtually every "dandy" in the city had money invested in ships at sea (Power, 1963: 43), which meant that capital was being accumulated by more than the top elite. In Genoa participation was even broader. An ingenious system had been developed to tap not only the large capital of ship owners and merchants but the petty capital of sailors, artisans, and even members of the "lower classes." Not only did sailors carry goods on commission and artisans and housewives send small quantities of their production for marketing in other ports, but ownership of ships and their cargoes became so infinitely divided that even a poor worker could invest a pittance—as in a lottery—hoping that his ship would come in.[23]

This Genoese institution was so similar to a joint stock company (not invented until much later) that it deserves to be described. Byrne (1930: 12) tells us that before the thirteenth century, when ships were relatively small, they were owned by individuals or in simple partnerships and were operated by one of the owners. However, as commerce expanded and larger ships were built in the thirteenth century, the ownership of vessels was subdivided into shares called *loca*. This system was particularly prevalent in the sea trade with the Levant. On any ship "the number of *loca* . . . was the same as the number of mariners required to man the vessel" (Byrne, 1930: 15), so the owner of a *locum* evidently assumed responsibility for the expenses associated with a mariner; indeed, a *specific* mariner was intended, for *loca* owners could even transfer "their" mariner to a different ship (Byrne, 1930: 16). The owner was entitled to merchant quarters during the journey and was given a unit of storage space. Although at first large merchants bought or rented whole shares for their own use, these spaces gradually were divided and subdivided again until individuals could hold one-twenty-fourth of a *locum* or an even smaller share. In the process, the *locum* became a "commodity" that could be bought and sold on the market, "pledged for loans . . . to pay mariners' wages, to buy goods for export" (Byrne, 1930: 17–18), or given in *accomendatio* or as security in a mortgage. In short, the "stock share" was treated as any other piece of merchandise or personal property. According to Byrne (1930: 14):

> Men and women from all ranks in society owned shares; members of a family pooled their resources . . . to purchase shares, individuals sometimes owning a mere fraction of a *locum*. *Loca* were regarded as particularly good security for one of the favorite forms of investment across the sea, the sea loan . . . which was repaid only if the ship arrived safely.

It would be hard to find a more advanced form of the institutions we associate with modern capitalism than this example in full flower in Genoa by the first half of the thirteenth century.

However, this seems to have been only a temporary expedient. Although "[o]wnership by *loca* characterized the entire field of Genoese shipping until about the middle of the thirteenth century . . . [eventually] the accumulation of vast fortunes by families and individuals and the increasing security of overseas trade made it no longer imperative" as a way of distributing risk and pooling capital (Byrne, 1930: 12). By the end of the thirteenth century both the small ships owned by their captains and the small holders of *loca* had been displaced by a commercial aristocracy that had accumulated vast wealth and experience in foreign trade (Byrne, 1930: 65).[24] Through their control over the admittedly laissez-faire communal government, they achieved almost as much as their counterparts did in the more socialized system of shipping investment that prevailed in Venice.

Changes in the System of Trade, 1260 to 1350

The relative positions of Genoa and Venice, the two contenders for naval/commercial hegemony, shifted toward the end of the thirteenth century within the context of a changing political and geographic environment. Genoa's recovery signaled a renewed struggle between the two "superpowers" that ended only in 1380 when the Genoese, poised on the Venetian island of Chioggia ready for the kill, were finally defeated. The Peace of Turin (1381) bequeathed the Mediterranean and in particular the oriental trade to a Venetian monopoly. Why did this occur?

During the second half of the thirteenth century, Italy's eastern connections underwent a series of realignments that removed the "center" and split the rest beween the southern and northern routes. This divergence in the paths of European expansion into the Middle East heartland began in 1258 when the Mongols destroyed Baghdad and established their rival capital at Tabriz, farther north and east. This reduced the attractiveness of the old caravan route that passed overland from the Crusader kingdom to Baghdad, before following the Tigris River to Basra, and then setting out by sea through the Arab-Persian Gulf and the Indian Ocean beyond. Toward the end of the thirteenth century, the loss of the Crusader footholds in Palestine further undermined this old pathway. After that, some traffic shifted either north through Central Asia or south through Egypt to the Red Sea and then to Aden, before entering the Indian Ocean.

The beginning of this new period was signaled on the north by the fall in 1261 of the Latin kingdom of Constantinople, which effectively destroyed the Venetian monopoly over the Black Sea land trade. It is no surprise that Genoa assisted the Byzantine contender in recapturing the city and, in return, was restored as the hegemonic European force in that zone. Genoa's prime rank was still contested by her old ally, Pisa, but that competition virtually ended by her decisive defeat of the Pisan fleet in 1284. With a free hand, the Genoese settlements at Pera, on the Golden Horn, and at Caffa, between the Black and Caspian Seas, exploited the growing overland trade to the east, which was facilitated by the temporary *pax mongolica* (see Chapter 5). It is of some significance, perhaps, that when Marco Polo's father and uncle made their first trip in 1261 from Venice to the land of the Khans, they went via Constantinople. However, their return trip in 1268 was via Acre, still in Crusader hands. And when they set out again in 1273, this time accompanied by seventeen-year-old Marco, they avoided Constantinople entirely, passing instead through Persia to the Arab Gulf.[25]

Displaced from their northern domain, the Venetians refocused their attention southward, where major changes were taking place. In Egypt, the Mamluk sultanate, after an interregnum of ten years (1250–1260), finally replaced the dynasty of Saladin's successors, the Ayyubids. Venice's countermove vis-à-vis her Genoese rivals was to strengthen her relationship with this new military caste of slave and former-slave soldiers, a strategy that assumed heightened significance in 1291 when the Mamluks completed Saladin's work by recapturing Acre, the "capital" of the Crusader kingdom and the last remaining European foothold in their empire.

This end to the "great venture" required an even more drastic realignment of trading routes and partners. Mamluk Egypt became the key transit point for the sea-borne eastern trade. Thus began the strangely ambivalent relationship between the Venetian traders who tried to gain monopolistic control over the spice trade and the equally monopolistic Mamluk state, trying to gain advantageous terms through tolls and tariffs.

Genoa did not cede the sea trade with the East to Venice without a struggle. Her countermove was to set out westward through the Atlantic. It was not without significance that Genoa's first real attempt to reach the Indies by circumnavigating Africa came in

1291. (If the ships of the Vivaldi brothers had made it the Genoese might have played the role in the world system achieved by the Portuguese two centuries later.) It was also in the late thirteenth century that Genoa established her first commercial sea connection with countries on the North Sea—both England and Flanders. Although up to then the Muslims had more or less controlled passage through the Strait of Gibraltar, a limited number of Genoese ships had always made their way through. However, once the Muslim sea forces had been decisively defeated in 1293 by a joint Castilian–Genoese fleet, direct trade with Bruges was established on a regular basis.

As can be seen from this account, during the latter part of the thirteenth century and, even more, in the early part of the fourteenth century, the port cities of Genoa and Venice expanded their reach to incorporate virtually every part of the developing European world-economy. And even though each was hegemonic in a somewhat different part of the system (Genoa at Bruges, Venice at Antwerp and Lubeck; Genoa in the Black Sea, Venice in Egypt), neither succeeded in fully excluding the other. Both participated in the entire system. Not only did they trade in all parts of western Europe but they had made significant inroads into the Central Asian and Middle East-North African world economies that continued to mediate the Far Eastern trade. (See Figure 4.)

In the developing world system, however, the Italians were still only one of the participants on whom trade depended. They in turn were dependent on their counterparts from other regions if the interchange was to persist. What did they offer that made them so welcome in Middle Eastern ports? Perhaps the best way to answer this, as well as to illustrate the complexity of the trade patterns established by the early years of the fourteenth century, is to quote Le Goff (1956: 16). He invites us to follow a group of merchants embarking at Genoa for the east.

The cargo is mostly cloth, arms, metal. The first port . . . reached . . . is Tunis, the second Tripoli. At Alexandria, merchandise of all sorts—products of local industry and above all oriental imports—joined the cargo. If one stopped in Syrian ports— . . . Acre, Tyre, Antioch—it was to load travelers, pilgrims, or [those] coming from the East by caravans. But it is Famagusta, on the island of Cyprus, which is the great entrepôt of spices. . . . At Lataqiyah, at the point of the arrival

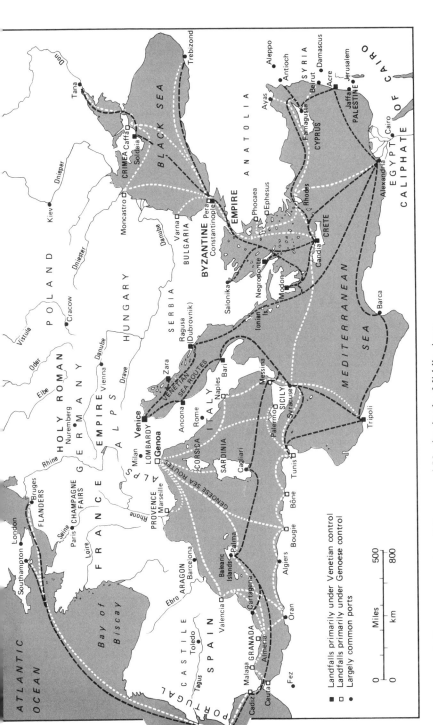

FIGURE 4. Mediterranean routes of Genoa and Venice in the Middle Ages.

of routes from Persia and Armenia one found also, according to Marco Polo, "all the spices and silk and gold cloth of the world." At Phocea, it is the precious alum that one took on board whereas Chios is the port for wines and gums. . . . Byzantium is the next obligatory stop at the great crossroads of the routes of the Levant. Then, traversing the Black Sea, one received at Caffa in the Crimea the products of Russia and Asia coming the length of the Mongol route: wheat, furs, wax, salted fish, silk, and above all perhaps, slaves. Many of these products, which they did not bring back from the Orient, they stopped to sell at Senope or at Trebizonde. The most audacious left from there, escorted up to Sivas by the tartar police, for Tabriz and India . . . , for China . . . by the land route to cross Central Asia or by sea from Basra to Ceylon.

Had we followed Venetian rather than Genoese traders we would have been led on a similarly circuitous route, dropping off cargo in one place and picking it up for sale elsewhere, although the stop in Egypt would have probably been preceded by a northern pick-up of slaves from the Caucasus, since it was the Italians' ability to replenish the ranks of the Mamluks that essentially gave them their bargaining power vis-à-vis the Egyptian rulers. To command such supplies, the latter had to ensure a steady and expanding volume of spices, as well as locally manufactured cotton and linen cloth and, as their position deteriorated, raw cotton as well (Ashtor, several articles reprinted in 1976, discussed in Chapter 7).

By the early decades of the fourteenth century there was clear evidence of increased integration of the various world economies that were forming into what might, with little difficulty, be called a world system—a large portion of which was capitalist. Linked by the Italian merchant mariner states to a vital eastern trade that connected Asia Minor to China on the north and Egypt to India, Malaysia, and China by the southern sea route, western Europe had finally entered that trading system and, although she was not yet hegemonic, at least she was becoming a more equal partner.

The extent to which the world was "unifying" is reflected in the fact that prosperity was pandemic. Genoa was at her highest point, as were Bruges and Cairo (as we shall see in Part II), although the Champagne fair towns had passed their prime, as had Baghdad and Constantinople. Chinese expansion had entered a new phase. An aggressive trade policy was being pursued by the Mongol rulers of the Yuan dynasty whose merchants were actively reaching out toward the west. It seemed only a matter of time, with the continuation of the trends already in motion, before the subsystems would intermingle even more, converting the "cultural islands," or to use Chaunu's term, *les univers cloisonnés* (1969, second ed. 1983: 54–58), into a truly interdependent world system.

The basic problematic of this book is to understand why that did not happen. As we shall see, it would be erroneous to assume that everything came to a halt in the middle of the fourteenth century. The linkage between Venice and the eastern trading system continued into the latter part of the fourteenth and throughout the fifteenth centuries. But instead of becoming more and more reticulated, the system simplified to a few narrow paths over which a smaller number of "players" had increasing control. Thus, it is only an apparent contradiction to note that many parts of the European–Middle Eastern subsystems atrophied at the same time that Venice and Cairo continued and even expanded their commercial connections. They increased their "market share" over what was temporarily a smaller whole.

The Mid-Century Depression

Using the cities of Venice and Genoa as examples, there are several ways to track the effects of the heightened trade that characterized the first half of the fourteenth century and the economic collapse that followed the Bubonic Plague of mid-century. One of these is clearly population. In 1200, before her imperial expansion, Venice's population stood at about 80,000. By 1300, the population had doubled, with 120,000 within the city and another 40,000 in the rest of the lagoon area. A house-to-house count of male adults in the city, made in 1338, suggests that this represented an apogee that was sustained until the plague years (Lane, 1973: 18). Genoa's population peaked somewhat earlier, around the turn of the century, at about 100,000 (Kedar, 1976: 5), but even she continued to add suburbs to her environs throughout the first decades of the fourteenth century (Hyde, 1973: 181).

Ironically, it was Venice and Genoa's imperial outreach that

proved their undoing. The Bubonic Plague came to Italy from
Caffa, the trading post in the Crimea used by both cities; there,
the Mongol troops besieging the city had fallen prey to a virulent
epidemic. The disease was then transmitted to Europe by rats
aboard a Venetian galley that reached home port in the fall of
1347. The results were catastrophic.

> Something like three-fifths of the inhabitants of Venice died within the
> next 18 months. . . . Three plague-ridden centuries followed 1348. . . .
> In 1500 the population [of Venice] was about the same size as it had
> been two hundred years earlier. (Lane, 1973: 19)

Genoa suffered a similar fate. By 1350 her population was only
about 60 percent of what it had been in 1341 (Kedar, 1976: 5) and
never did recover fully.

Kedar (1976: 16) developed a number of ingenious indicators
to trace the differential fates of Venice and Genoa through the
cycles of good and hard times and the postplague recovery. One
indicator was physical changes in the port facilities. In Venice,
work on the waterfront was finally completed in 1324, after which
no further improvements were made until 1414. In addition, the
state Arsenal, begun in 1103, was tripled in size in 1303 and expanded again in 1325, after which no expansions took place until
1473. The pattern for Genoa was similar, although the sixteenth-
century revival noted in Venice's port installations is *not* paralleled
in Genoa, which had, by then, given up her pretensions to maritime
dominance. Genoa's harbor, the "Mole," was substantially length-
ened in 1300 and again in 1328, but after that no changes were
made until 1461. "Thus, in both Venice and Genoa, the extension
of the main port facilities came to a stop about 1325, and was
resumed only in the following century. This virtual standstill in
the development of the harbors of the two cities suggests a stagnation in maritime trade" (Kedar, 1976: 16).

The second indicator Kedar (1976: 17) used was the declining
size of the convoys of merchant galleys leaving the Venetian port.
"In the 1330's, eight to ten galleys sailed to Romania and the Black
Sea every year; between 1373 and 1430, there were convoys of
only two or three galleys. . . . [T]he reduction in the size of the . . .
convoys must be regarded as a rudimentary indication of a contraction of maritime trade." Although the drop was dramatic—

and even sharper for Genoa than for Venice—it is interesting to note that it had already begun *before* the arrival of the plague, which proves that the epidemiological explanation accounted for only a portion of the decline.

Hyde argues forcefully that the Black Death "was preceded in Europe by a series of lesser misfortunes of various kinds which suggests that something was seriously wrong with the economy" (Hyde, 1973: 179). In Italy, economic decline began in the countryside with poor crops,[26] and this placed particularly heavy burdens on municipal finances. Communal expenditures and the taxes that supported them peaked in the 1330s and 1340s; the public debt of Italian city-states grew very high and lost its ease of redemption. This may in part have been the factor underlying the bankruptcy of several of the most important Italian banking houses—Peruzzi in 1342 and Bardi (Balducci's employer) in 1346— all *before* the arrival of the plague (Hyde, 1973: 181–187). But it should be noted that these were all Florentine firms; in Venice and Genoa such credit failures had not yet appeared.

Another factor to which decline has been attributed is the political factionalism that, by the 1340s, led a number of Italian city-states to more or less abandon the old communal rule by a merchant oligarchy in favor of more dictatorial rule by a single, and in the case of Genoa external, leader—the *podesta* in Genoa (initially, the leader of the *popolo* or people) and the *signoria* (or "lord") in other towns.[27] Indeed, Waley deplores this trend in his chapter entitled "The Failure of the Republics" (1973: 221–239). But Waley's fascinating book is almost exclusively focused on the hill towns; Genoa and Venice are conspicuous by their absence. Other scholars—particularly those emotionally attached to Venice—make an invidious distinction between Genoa and Venice, attributing the eventual success of Venice to its "fine government" and blaming Genoa's eventual collapse on the rampant individualism of her warring "big" families.[28] These political differences, however, had always existed. It is therefore difficult to attribute Genoa's later collapse to a condition that had also been present earlier when she was even more successful than Venice in her overseas trade and, as late as 1340, had been the more prosperous of the two.

Kedar (1976), although accepting the general stereotypes, poses a more complex question. His book begins with the assumption that patterns of behavior that serve well during times of expanding prosperity may be less functional when a contraction occurs. He therefore examines the responses of Genoese and Venetian merchants during the "Great Depression" of the second half of the fourteenth century to see why Venice survived the challenge, going on to monopolize what was left of the eastern trade, whereas Genoa did not. His analysis focuses on the different entrepreneurial styles of the merchants of each city and on the degree to which merchants could or could not count on the state to support their ventures and cover their risks. He suggests that individualistic Genoa was poorly positioned to mobilize communal wealth to create a safety net for its merchants, whereas the state in Venice had always provided subsidies and insurance to its merchants through the provision of collective goods—whether ports, vessels, or defensive arms. Thus, state "socialism" or the "welfare state" tided Venice over the shoals of depopulation and economic contraction on which Genoa foundered.

But these explanations seem to leave out the kinds of international factors we have tried to trace here. Genoa's natural zone of dominance had always been the western Mediterranean and later the Atlantic. Her "captured" zone of dominance was the northern area of Asia Minor—Constantinople, the Black Sea, and the overland route through Central Asia. Neither of these advantageous outlets was as useful to her during the second half of the fourteenth century. The Portuguese and Castilian Spanish were better situated on the Atlantic itself and therefore did not have to contend directly with the last remnants of Muslim power in southern Spain. They began to challenge Genoa's hegemony on the North Sea. And, as we shall explain in Part II, the northern route across Asia was increasingly disrupted as the Mongol empire, which had been so remarkably unified in the thirteenth century and therefore so receptive to transit trade, underwent fission and fragmentation. Tamerlane was not Genghis Khan.

Genoa's failure to recover from the Black Death and her eventual naval defeat at the hand of Venice, first in 1378–1384 and then finally after 1400, must have been the result of her own weakness as much as Venice's strength. She was losing her commercial empire either to other European competitors or to Central Asian events far beyond her control. In contrast, Venice's "bet" on the southern sea route proved a fortunate one. As we shall see, her eastern trade continued via Egypt and the Red Sea up to the opening decades of the sixteenth century, sustaining the old thirteenth-century world system on a narrow thread until the tapestry would be rewoven in a different pattern in the sixteenth century.

Lessons from Genoa and Venice

There are several routes to importance in an international system. The role of trade fair site is one, well illustrated by Troyes and Provins. A specially protected entrepôt, in which traders from a variety of points can come together under auspicious conditions to exchange goods, free of restraints or arbitrary intrusions and at low cost, is always of potential significance, particularly when such freedom of trade is facilitated by a lack of monetary restrictions. Singapore and Hong Kong today, no less than the Champagne fairs of the thirteenth century, occupy such niches. The survival of an entrepôt, however, requires, at the minimum, the continued availability of a surplus generated elsewhere, the continued comparative advantage obtained through low transport costs and low protection rent, and the existence of motivated middlemen, either local or foreign, who gain more from its use than they could by going elsewhere.

A second route to international importance is to become a powerful industrial producer whose goods are so desired that merchants will come from a variety of foreign places to make advantageous purchases, bringing with them whatever can be exchanged for the goods produced locally. The textile towns of Flanders, and particularly the port through which their goods were exported, Bruges, illustrate this second functional niche. The requisites for continued prosperity include the ability to produce a unique good, which of course requires assured supplies of raw materials and talented labor, and sufficient outlets for distribution. The availability of surplus capital for reinvestment and technological improvements in production are essential, although secondary, to the existence of customers with money to spend.

A third route is that of the commercial shipper, whose chief role is as middleman or jobber, transferring goods from where they are produced and plentiful to where markets for them exist. Particularly when combined with business expertise and the capacity to accumulate, invest, and exchange money and credit, this role offers a secure niche—as long as the producers continue to produce and the buyers continue to buy. And as long as the routes of transportation are traversible and the safety of goods can be ensured without unduly high protection costs, those who capture the shipper–jobber role tend to persist in it. Genoa and Venice, whose economic base remained that of the trading state, illustrate this third route. Changes in all these factors eventually altered the market situation of both and undermined that of Genoa.

Although the immediate and direct effect of the Black Death was to wipe out large proportions of the population of both Genoa and Venice, the long-term and indirect effects were probably more significant. In the core cities, once the first effects—wandering bands searching the countryside for safety and sustenance—had worn off, the lost population was soon replaced, albeit not entirely, by immigration from the countryside. Depopulation in more peripheral areas, however, could not as easily be made up. A return to agricultural activities by the smaller population and an accompanying contraction in industrial production reduced the surplus available for exchange; at the same time, in spite of an improvement in wage levels, the smaller population meant a drop in total demand. Thus, the volume of trade decreased and cities that played the role of middleman obviously were affected most.

Their first response was to intensify competition for a larger share of the smaller market. The death struggle between Genoa and Venice escalated, and with it, what might be called the costs of "protective rent" (McNeill, 1974). More and more of the carrying capacities of ships had to be given over to arms and fighters, which raised the costs of transportation. Similarly, ships and cargoes ran greater risks of capture or destruction, which also inflated the ultimate cost of getting goods to port. It was not until Venice established a virtual monopoly over the Mediterranean routes that trade once again became more secure. That monopoly was all the more important because alternative routes to the Orient were experiencing blockages.

Although those changes will be examined in detail in Part II, it is important to note here that it was the inability of the Italian mariner states to determine what would happen in regions far beyond their control that ultimately aborted their bid for hegemony over a world system that had formed but then dissolved. The strength of the Mamluk state blocked direct Italian expansion into the Indian Ocean via the Red Sea, and Venice was therefore never able to displace Middle Eastern merchant intermediaries to develop a direct commercial link to the Orient. The only way she could have done this was to deepen the access paths across the Central Asian land mass. But this was not only more expensive (transport by land being some twenty times more costly than by sea) but proved, in the last analysis, impossible. The break up of the *pax mongolica*, more than anything else, prevented the full reticulation of a world system that died soon after it was born. We move now to that part of the story.

Notes

1. It surprised me to find that these two cities—both of central significance to the story of the thirteenth century and so equivalent in power during that time—were treated unequally in the literature. There are literally scores of studies of the city of Venice, many of them cited in the bibliography; in marked contrast, Genoa has been of primary interest to only a handful of non-Italian scholars and the subject of far fewer urban biographies. Even those works that set out to compare the two (for example, Kedar, 1976) show a marked distaste for Genoa and an affection for Venice that exceeds rational judgment. It is as if the present-day beauty of the latter relegates the often destroyed Genoa to the status of the "ugly step-sister," in spite of her greater economic importance. My private explanation is that scholars find significance for places they want to be in and therefore study; only this can explain, for example, why Toulouse, a perfectly wonderful town but not of greatest historical significance, has been better studied than almost any other French city except Paris!

2. See Ennen "Les différents types de formation des villes européennes," in *Le Moyen Age* (1956) and her *The Medieval Town* (1979: *passim*).

3. In a fascinating article, Henri Pirenne (1933–4: 677–687) details the role of Syrians in the spice and other trade that persisted from antiquity. Not only during

antiquity but after the ninth century recovery of sea trade, Syrians were regularly provisioning the town of Cambrai (for which a rare document exists) "with papyrus, pepper, cinammon, cloves, ginger, gums . . . and other oriental goods" (Pirenne, 1933–4: 679–680). Throughout the ninth century they continue to frequent France but, after that, they disappear (Pirenne, 1933–4: 686–687).

4. See in particular the article by Steven Runciman in *The Cambridge Economic History of Europe*, II (1952) for a detailed description of this capital and its relations with both the Crusades and the Italian merchant mariner cities, particularly Genoa and Venice.

5. In this first Crusade, the sea route was secondary; most Crusaders passed overland via Constantinople, a route they were not to follow again.

6. See Thrupp's "Comparisons of Culture in the Middle Ages: Western Standards as Applied to Muslim Civilization in the Twelfth and Thirteenth Century" (reprinted 1977: 67–88).

7. These are the words of a contemporary chronicler, Usamah Ibn Munqidh, as quoted in Maalouf (1984: 39).

8. See Byrne (1930) and Unger (1980) for information on technological improvements in both the cargo-carrying cog or round ship and the later developing oar-assisted armed cargo ship, the galley.

9. In the account that follows I depend heavily on this document, available in English translation in *Joinville & Villehardouin: Chronicles of the Crusades* (1963, reprinted 1985). In this account, the contempt that Villehardouin feels toward the Venetians, whom he describes as venal, cruel, and cowardly, is ill-concealed. The document blames the Italians for all disasters and double dealings. However, it is questionable as to how much credence should be given to his account, which completely exonerates the Crusaders from any responsibility for what happened. That a fully armed force, without its consent and compliance, could have been maneuvered by the Venetians into doing what it thought was wrong is difficult to accept, particularly given the enthusiasm for the task later shown by Villehardouin himself, as evidenced by the quotation we present in the text.

10. Perhaps Norwich (1982: 141) goes too far in his final judgment:

The Fourth Crusade—if indeed it can be so described at all—surpassed even its predecessors in faithlessness and duplicity, brutality and greed. Constantinople, in the twelfth century, had been not just the greatest and wealthiest metropolis of the world, but also the most cultivated. . . . By its sack, Western civilization suffered a loss greater even than the sack of Rome by the barbarians in the fifth century . . . [It was] perhaps the most catastrophic single loss in all of history.

11. As seen in Chapter 3, he soon paid for his newly won glory with his life. After less than a year, his body was buried in the church in which he had been crowned.

12. It is hard to find better proof of the Eurocentric character of historical writing than this usual way of putting matters. Black writer Jan Carew shocks us when he begins his article, "The Origins of Racism in the Americas" [in Ibrahim Abu-Lughod, ed., *African Themes* (Evanston: Program of African Studies, 1975), pp. 3–23], with the sentence: "It is extraordinary that in the 482 years since the Ara-

wakian Lucayos of San Salvador discovered Columbus and his sailors on their beaches, so little research has been done on the origins of racism in the New World." We reread the sentence with new insight. And yet even Carew refers to the "New World" as if it had just been created, rather than newly brought within the purview of Europeans.

13. Although some scholars apparently doubt this, the leading authority on Chinese science, Joseph Needham, shows no hesitation at all in his 1960 lecture on "The Chinese Contribution to the Development of the Mariner's Compass" (reprinted 1970: 239–249). He references a clear mention of the magnetic needle in a Chinese sea manual of about 900 A.D. (p. 243) and notes that by the eleventh and twelfth centuries magnetic compasses were definitely being used to navigate Chinese ships. On the *busolla*, see Commune di Genova Servizio beni Culturali, *Navigazione e Carte Nautiche nei secolo XIII–XVI*, the catalogue for the Naval Museum in Pegli (Genoa: Sagep Editrice, 1983), p. 6 and, for an illustration, p. 25.

14. McNeill (1974: 22) perhaps goes too far when he attributes the Venetians' success on the sea to their "extreme readiness to resort to violence." However, it is clear that much "primitive accumulation" was going on.

15. Clearly, another factor was that Genoa, and even more so Venice, lacked a true land-based hinterland in which competing clan power could grow through appropriation of agrarian wealth; the fate of all, "nobles" and populace alike, depended upon the success of the sea trade and the military prowess needed to sustain it.

16. There is a fascinating connection between this "tax" on wealth and the efflorescence of investments in works of art by the great Italian families during the Renaissance. The forced contribution to the public debt was assessed on the basis of wealth, excluding items of household furnishing and domestic consumption. Wealth was therefore sheltered in the form of paintings, wall hangings, and objects of silver and gold. For how this worked in Florence in the fifteenth century, see the fascinating article by David Herlihy, "Family and Property in Renaissance Florence," in Miskimin, Herlihy, and Udovitch (1977: 3–24, particularly 4–5).

17. The writer who most readily comes to mind is Armando Sapori (1952). See in particular the diatribe against Sombart throughout his *The Italian Merchant in the Middle Ages* (English trans., 1970).

18. For example, the venerable A. Fanfani, in his *Le Origini dello Spirito Capitalistico in Italia* (1933).

19. As a subpoint, Le Goff stresses that in the Middle Ages a worker proletariat was forming in large-scale capitalist industry only in the textile industry of Flanders and the naval industry of Italian ports (1956: 49).

20. In the section that follows I depend inter alia on the following sources: Lane (1966, 1973), McNeill (1974), Lopez (1976), Lopez and Raymond (1967), Postan (1952), Byrne (1916, 1930), Heers (1977), and Sapori (1952, trans. 1970).

21. The parallel between this system and the type of partnership agreement commonly employed much earlier by Arab traders, described in A. Udovitch's *Partnership and Profit in Medieval Islam* (1970a), is so close that it is virtually impossible to resist the conclusion that it was borrowed directly. Even though Lopez (1976: 76) cautions that we "cannot rule out the independent emergence of similar contracts" in the Byzantine-Islamic and European culture areas, this seems

suspiciously unlikely, since Byrne (1916: 135) traces the origin of the Genoese *societas* back to the period just after trade began with Syria. We return to this point in Part II, which deals with the Middle East system.

22. This type of agreement was and still is common among Muslim merchants, and in the Middle Ages it was also popular among North African Jewish traders, although it early fell out of favor in Venice (Lopez, 1976: 73–74).

23. A similar system seems also to have been used in Venice but, because of the direct involvement of the government in shipbuilding, it never reached the same development as in Genoa. See, for example, McNeill (1974: 16–17).

24. Following the usual pattern of other capitalist institutions, as scale increased, banks eventually became the chief owners of *loca* whose management was entrusted to agents (Byrne, 1930: 19).

25. Significantly, they returned by way of Constantinople only in 1295, *after* the Crusader kingdom had fallen.

26. I find these types of ex post facto explanations extremely suspicious. Crop failures, fiscal tightness, etc. tend to be very short-term cyclical events to which historians pay little attention when the long upswing of a secular trend is occurring. However, when a major decline sets in, these recurring events are scrutinized more closely.

27. Such factionalism was imprinted on the landscape of the Italian medieval town in the form of the bristling fortified private towers that each big family maintained for use in what often deteriorated into a war of each against all. Indeed, Genoa may have been less wracked by internal fissures than many other commercial towns and seems to have been able to transcend or transmute the hottest parts of factionalism because it was so "bad for business."

28. It is almost impossible to find a scholar (with the possible exception of Queller, 1986) of the economic history of medieval Italy who does not subscribe to this view, although perhaps Renouard (1969: I) puts it most emphatically. But as seen at the beginning of this chapter, there is enormous partisanship in Venice's favor, which casts a shadow over some of the judgments scholars have rendered. It seems not accidental that the harshest critique of Venice's government should come from a Florentine booster. Thus, J. Lucas-Dubreton, in his *Daily Life in Florence* (English trans., 1961), calls the Venetian aristocracy "a clique of conspirators, standing aloof from the populace who trembled in face of a 'mysterious and invisible' police state," in contrast to Florence, "the home of a higher culture."

PART
II

The Mideast Heartland

The Three Routes to the East

As a result of the military/colonizing venture of the Crusades and the heightened trade that followed, Europe, in the twelfth and early thirteenth centuries, finally attached itself more firmly to the ongoing world system. But we have not yet examined this preexistent and complex system of trade that, at least from the ninth century, passed through the geographic heartland of the system, the land bridge of the eastern Mediterranean that guarded three routes of access to the Orient (Figure 5): the northern route from Constantinople across the land mass of Central Asia, the central route connecting the Mediterranean with the Indian Ocean via Baghdad, Basra, and the Persian Gulf, and the southerly route that linked the Alexandria–Cairo–Red Sea complex with the Arabian Sea and then the Indian Ocean. During the twelfth and thirteenth centuries, these routes grew more reticulated as, in ironic partnership, both war and peace brought distant trading partners in contact with one another. By the second half of the thirteenth century, all three routes were functioning—for the first time since Rome had controlled the gateways to the east.[1]

This beginning seemed promising. It appeared that the separate world economies were coalescing, evolving into an interdependent world system. And yet, by the second half of the fourteenth century vast sections lay in ruins, tragic evidence that the fates of each had become inextricably linked to the fates of the rest. Indeed, the degree to which a world system has been integrated is most sensitively indicated by the extent to which disruptive events in any part have serious repercussions in the rest.

In Part II we explore the processes by which these linkages were forged and, perhaps of even greater significance, the events that

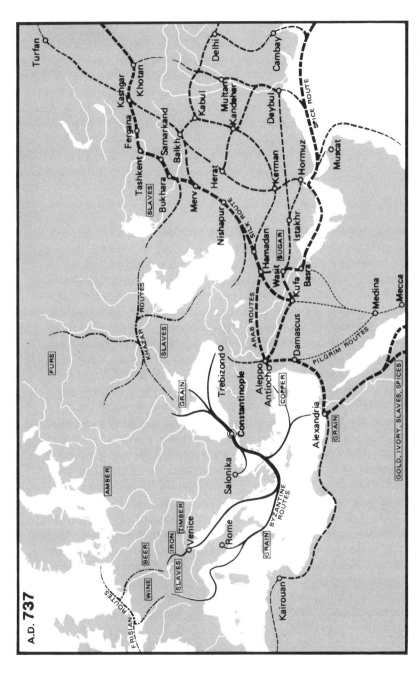

FIGURE 5. The gradual reticulation of routes from the Mediterranean across Central Asia and toward the Indian Ocean (based on McEvedy).

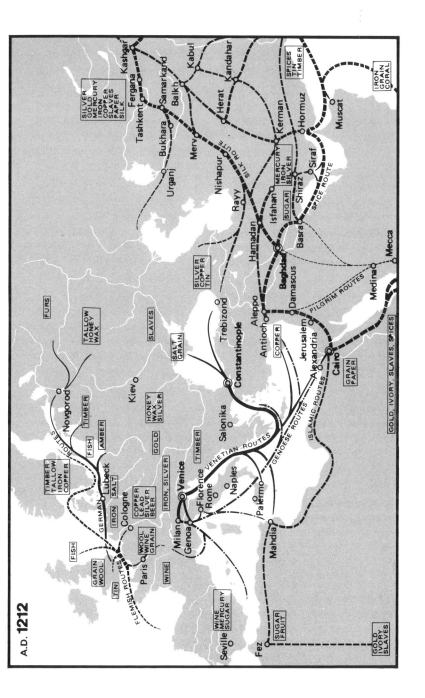

A.D. **1212**

Kashgar
Fergana
Tashkent
SILVER GOLD MERCURY IRON COPPER SLAVES PAPER SILK
Samarkand
Balkh
Kabul
Kandahar
SPICES TIN TIMBER
Bukhara
Merv
Herat
Urganj
Kerman
Hormuz
Muscat
IRON GRAIN CORAL
Nishapur
MERCURY IRON SILVER
Siraf
SILK ROUTE
Rayy
Isfahan
SUGAR
Shiraz
SPICE ROUTE
Hamadan
Basra
FURS
Baghdad
SILVER COPPER TIN
Damascus
Mecca
TALLOW HONEY WAX
Trebizond
Aleppo
Medina
PILGRIM ROUTES
SLAVES
Antioch
COPPER
Jerusalem
SALT GRAIN
Constantinople
Alexandria
Cairo
GRAIN PAPER
ROUTES
Novgorod
Kiev
HONEY WAX SILVER
Salonika
ISLAMIC ROUTES
GOLD, IVORY, SLAVES, SPICES
TIMBER
GOLD
TIMBER
VENETIAN ROUTES
FISH
AMBER
Lübeck
GERMAN
IRON, SILVER
GENOESE ROUTES
TIMBER
TALLOW IRON COPPER
IRON
SALT
COPPER LEAD SILVER BEER
Florence
Venice
Rome
FISH
Cologne
Milan
Naples
GRAIN WOOL
Paris
WOOL TIN GRAIN
Genoa
Palermo
TIN
WINE
Mahdia
FLEMISH ROUTES
WINE MERCURY SUGAR
SUGAR FRUIT
Seville
Fez
GOLD IVORY SLAVES

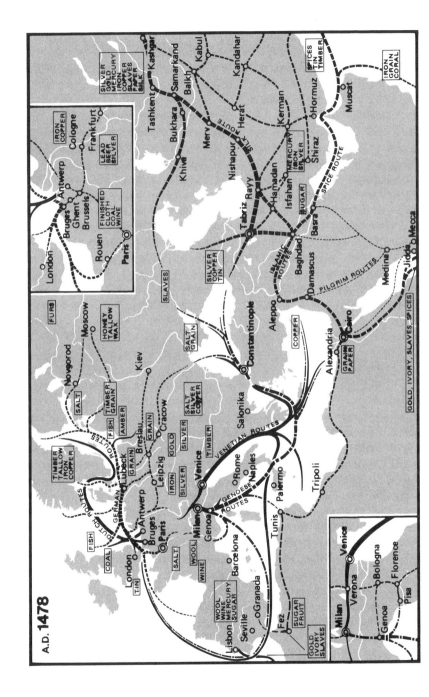

A.D. **1478**

caused their eventual rupture. Although this drama was played out primarily in the region we have termed the "heartland," its plotline was scarcely independent of events taking place as far away as China, the pivotal element of the entire system, as we shall later see.

The Northern Route

During the thirteenth century, the heartland region not only absorbed Crusader incursions from the West but a new thrust of nomadic invasions from the East. Whereas the westerners came by sea, facilitated by the growing naval strength of the Italian city-states, however, the easterners came, as they traditionally had, on horseback across the Central Asian steppes, pressing their fast mounts in a strategy that some scholars describe as the earliest precursor to modern mobile warfare.

The thirteenth-century Mongols, under the leadership of a self-styled "world conqueror," Genghis Khan, were scarcely the first nomadic tribe to head westward.[2] The Huns under Attila had sped overland as far as Germany at the collapse of the Roman empire (Grousset, 1939, reprinted 1948). Later, another Turkic tribe, the Seljuks, had pressed westward and by the twelfth century controlled virtually all of Iraq, the Fertile Crescent, and Egypt, whereas still another, the Khwarizm Turks, held Transoxiana. And now a new coalition of nomadic tribes was following a similar route with what promised even greater success. By 1225, having already defeated the Khwarizm, the vanguard of Mongol forces arrived at Hungary, poised for an invasion of Europe. (See Figure 6.)

Europe, however, was not the only or even the primary object of their ambitions. The richer prize of China was more attractive. Thus, Genghis Khan suddenly turned his back on Europe to focus attention eastward. Two years later in 1227, however, the World Conqueror was dead, struck down by an illness contracted during his Chinese campaign.[3] A temporary halt to the campaigns was called until succession could be ratified. The nascent empire he had amassed but not yet fully subdued was divided among his sons, each of whom was charged with pacifying a different region. To his son Jochi (whose prior death left this task to *his* son, Batu) he assigned the Russian and eastern European zone; Chaghatai was

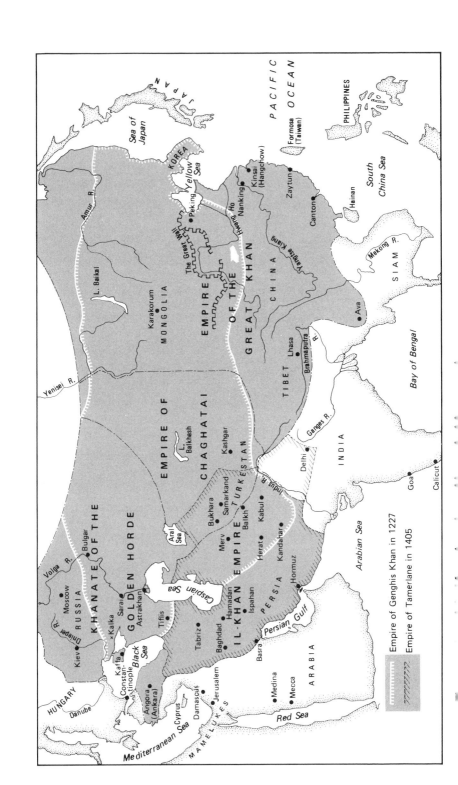

Empire of Genghis Khan in 1227
Empire of Tamerlane in 1405

charged with the conquest of Persia and Iraq, and indeed the whole Muslim world. Following Mongol custom, he left to his youngest son, Tolui, the least challenging task of governing the Mongolian homeland, while Ogodei became his true successor as Khan, the *primus inter pares*.

The campaigns resumed once succession was ratified. By 1241 the troops of Batu (the so-called Golden Horde)[4] had completed their conquests of southern Russia, Poland, and Hungary—leaving destruction and burned cities in their wake. Various accounts were circulating in Europe about the frightening power of the Mongols who were now ready for further conquests. Batu's expeditionary force had already entered Austria to prepare for a full-scale attack and, by 1242, was poised only a few miles from Vienna (de Rachewiltz, 1971: 77–81). Farther south, Chaghatai, the leader of the White Horde, was making similar inroads into Muslim territory. It appeared that, at least in the western regions, the successors to Genghis Khan would finally achieve his ambitions.

Once again, however, the Muslim and Christian worlds were both "miraculously saved." When news of Ogodei's death (some say from a surfeit of fermented mare's milk, the Mongols' intoxicating drink) reached the generals in the field, they left only a portion of their troops behind when they returned in haste to the Mongol capital of Karakorum to participate in the selection of the next khan. That election, however, proved less than determinate. Hence, it was not until the election in 1251 of Mongke as fourth supreme Khan that the task set by the founder of the dynasty was finally resumed.

Although western Europe was never again under imminent threat, within a decade all of Central Asia and parts of the Middle East were under Mongol control. Hulegu, Mongke's brother, subdued Baghdad in 1258 and established his Il-Khan empire in Persia and Iraq; it was only with great difficulty that the Mamluks managed to repel him from Damascus a year later. And Mongke's brother and future successor, Kubilai Khan, had established *his* hegemony over northern China. Twenty years later (1280) even the southern Sung had capitulated to Mongol rule, to be known as the Yuan dynasty.

It was during the second half of the thirteenth century that western Europe gained its first direct introduction to the world of the Far East. It made contact through Mongol intermediaries who had unified under a single system a region that had previously been fragmented, penetrable only with difficulty and hazard. (The ancient silk route that had brought the fabulous Asian cloth to Rome had long since dried to a narrow trickle of uncertain caravans presided over by Muslim and Jewish merchants.) At first, European hopes were unrealistically raised by the prospect of forming an alliance with the still-mysterious Mongols. All that Europeans knew at that early time was that the Mongols were *not* Muslims; given the setbacks the Crusaders were increasingly facing in holding on to shrinking enclaves in the Holy Land (Saladin's reconquest of much of Syria/Palestine in 1169 was followed by St. Louis' disastrous campaign against Egypt in 1250), it seemed logical to them—albeit somewhat incredible to us in hindsight—to attempt an alliance of east and west against the Muslim empires between them.

Thus, the second half of the thirteenth century witnessed a series of Papal missions to the Mongols and, perhaps of greater long-term significance, trade missions undertaken by merchants from Venice (Marco Polo the most famous) and Genoa (leaving less of a record but having more substance) who managed to reach Cathay, the eastern "edge" of the then-known world. By the beginning of the fourteenth century there was even a Catholic mission in Khanbalik (Peking), although it was soon destined to disappear when hopes dissipated and the connections frayed.

The administrative partition of Genghis Khan's world empire shortly after his death had not fragmented his empire. And even when the realms were reapportioned after the demise of Ogodei and then Mongke, unity was sufficient so that safe passage granted by one regional ruler was honored by the next. Berke, third Khan of the Golden Horde, controlled southern Russia and eastern Anatolia; the Il-Khans, under Hulegu, controlled Persia, Iraq, and portions of northern India/Pakistan and Afghanistan; and Kubilai, the fifth supreme Khan since 1260, was fast becoming the master of China. All of this facilitated the conduct of both trade and diplomacy.

However, although originally unified in basic culture and allegiance, these subgroups, as they became assimilated in their conquered territories, grew increasingly diverse and, perhaps not unexpectedly, progressively at odds with one another. In some regions (for example, those under the Golden Horde and then later even under the Il-Khans), the Mongol rulers converted to Islam, dashing Europe's hopes for allies in the Crusades; in others, the Mongols were assimilated to Chinese culture and the Buddhist faith. And as successor followed successor, the once-unified empire fragmented into factions more likely than not to be at war with one another. The promise of the great trans-Central Asian route as an alternative to the Indian Ocean collapsed under the burden of their conflicts.

By the second third of the fourteenth century, plagues and in-surrections weakened the once powerful Mongols. These factors compounded the problems of fragmentation and eventually de-stroyed this land bypass of the Arab heartland. Evidence for the changed circumstances is clear. Toward the end of the fourteenth century, Tamerlane sought to replicate the lightning successes of his forebears by reunifying all of Central Asia, but his rapid con-quests were indicative more of the internal weaknesses of the Cen-tral Asian states than they were proof of his own strength. If 1250 marked the opening of the Central Asian route, Tamerlane's cam-paigns, which carried destruction through the gates of Damascus, ironically signaled its end. Thus, from a promising beginning as facilitators of the expansion of the world system in the thirteenth century, the Mongols eventually became the agents who sundered the northern route.

The Middle Route

The middle route was similarly affected by the pincer action of western Crusaders and Mongol armies. Beginning at the Mediter-ranean coast of Syria/Palestine, this route crossed the small desert and then the Mesopotamian plain to Baghdad, before diverging to follow either the land or sea alternatives. The land route con-tinued across Persia to Tabriz and from there either southeastward to northern India (which by the mid-thirteenth century was ruled by the Muslim Sultanate of Delhi) or due eastward to Samarkand and then across the desert to China.

The sea route, however, had always been the most important. Following the Tigris River down to the Persian Gulf, goods transited the key Arab-founded port of Basra and from there passed the trading princedoms of (alternately) Oman, Siraf, Hormuz, or Qais, guardians of the link between the Gulf and the Indian Ocean beyond. Even during the pre-Islamic era this had been a prime route, but it became increasingly hegemonic during the early centuries of Islamic expansion when Baghdad was the prime Muslim center of trade, culture, and religion.

Founded in A.D. 750 as the capital of the 'Abbasid empire, home of the Caliph (the regent of the Prophet on earth) who commanded the loyalty of most of the Muslim world, and commercial and intellectual center par excellence of the lands east and west of it, Baghdad was, in the eighth to tenth centuries, a true world city. The sea route between it and the Far East was carefully detailed by Muslim sailors, geographers, and savants. Arab and Persian knowledge of the East was set down in classic works to which we must still refer for our understanding of the world-economy linkages that underlay its prosperity and that of its Gulf guarders. Even after the Crusaders established their footholds on the Mediterranean shore, such trade continued, the Europeans merely benefiting by holding the westernmost ports.

Yet the route through Baghdad was also to be crushed between Crusaders and Mongols. By 1258, the troops of Hulegu, Mongke's younger brother, had surrounded, besieged, and plundered Baghdad, destroying the last vestiges of the city's centrality and putting to death its most important Islamic symbolic head, the 'Abbasid Caliph. The capital was severely damaged and, thereafter, the region of Iraq was ruled from Persia. Just as in the fifth century, when Persia under the Sassanids temporarily isolated itself from the world system, thereby breaking the connection between the Gulf and the Indian Ocean, so the creation of the Mongol Il-Khanid dynasty initially inhibited, although did not destroy, trade through the middle route.

The final eclipse of this route came with the recapture of the Syrian coast from the Crusaders. When the Mamluk military state of Egypt finally evicted the last Crusaders in 1291, they razed virtually every port town on the Syrian coast, which effectively sealed the western terminus of the route.[5] European merchants repaired northward to Little Armenia or to islands in the Mediterranean to continue their trade, but in this new arrange-

ment Palestine played a distinctly subordinate role. Thenceforth, Palestine and Syria were ruled from Egypt, which was
not likely to yield its competitive advantage to a dependent
province. Although Syrian/Palestinian agriculture recovered,
and its products, primarily cotton, continued to be marketed in
Europe, the industrial and commercial base that had yielded so
high a level of return in earlier times never regained its former
preeminence.

With the decline in the middle passage eastward, the endemic
rivalry between the Persian Gulf route and its Red Sea alternative
was decisively resolved. The latter was to dominate for many centuries to come. This shift to the south reshaped the world system
that persisted into the fourteenth and fifteenth centuries and that,
once the Portuguese made their end run around Africa, ultimately
was transformed into a Eurocentered one.

The Southern Route

The Mamluk state, established in Egypt between 1250 and 1260,
was also the direct result of the double-edged threat to the Middle
East heartland posed by Crusaders and Mongols. Even though the
Pope's naive invitations to an alliance were haughtily rejected by
the Mongol ruler, who sent back imperious requests for the Pope's
submission instead, the de facto situation on the ground often had
the Arabs–Turks fighting on both fronts. Threatened simultaneously by Mongols and Crusaders, the industrial and mercantile
society of Egypt, which had adventurously expanded eastward to
bridge the "Greek" (the Mediterranean) and "Green" (or China)
Seas in the early centuries of Islam, was gradually forced into
increasing militarization. Although this transformation into a garrison state allowed Egypt and Syria to regain and then preserve
their territorial independence, it did so at great cost to economic
development and commercial vitality.

An incipient system of militaristic feudal organization had been
introduced in the twelfth century by the Kurdish forces that, under
Saladin, had succeeded in repelling the Crusaders from Egypt and
driving them out of several of their enclaves in Palestine. Their
new dynasty, the Ayyubids, supplanted the Fatimids, once famous
for their naval power as well as their highly developed industry

and their commercial trade with the East. The Fatimid mercantile state, however, had proved powerless to defend its capital, Cairo-Fustat, from the Christian invaders. Indeed, Cairo had to be rescued by the Kurdish forces who then set up the Ayyubid dynasty (after Salah al-Din al-Ayyub) that ruled Egypt and Syria until the middle of the thirteenth century. Between 1250 and 1260, the slave-soldiers on whom the defense of the country had grown increasingly dependent finally succeeded in placing one of their numbers at the head of state, ushering in the so-called Mamluk or slave sultanate.[6] Its hand was strengthened by the same forces that had brought it to power.

The reduced state of Baghdad left Cairo the most important capital of the Muslim world, a fact symbolized by the reestablishment of the Caliphate in that city. Baybars became the first "legitimate" Mamluk Sultan of Egypt. He had attained his unrivaled position by defeating the Mongol forces at Ain Jalut in Palestine in 1260 and later consolidated it by similar victories against the Crusaders. In at least the first instance, luck was with him. Just as Europe had been "saved" in 1241 by the death of Ogodei, so Mongke's death in 1259 rescued the Muslims. When the news of Mongke's death, with its possible ramifications for a succession struggle, reached Hulegu, who had been successfully subduing inland Syria, he returned to Persia, leaving behind a reduced force that was easily overcome at Ain Jalut. As de Rachewiltz (1971: 148) simplified it:

> The immediate outcome of the battle [of Ain Jalut in 1260] was the recapture of Aleppo and Damascus by the Turks and the momentous rise of Baibars (1260–77), . . . the real founder of the Mamluke empire. . . . Once in control of Egypt, Baibars's chief concern was to extend his rule over both Syria and Palestine while keeping the Mongols at bay. . . . [I]n less than ten years he dislodged the Franks from . . . Caesarea, Antioch and the Krak de Chevaliers. . . .

The animosity between Mamluks and Mongols was not absolute, however. Baybars, in order to reconquer Syria, actually formed an alliance with Berke, the third ruler of the Golden Horde and the first Mongol ruler to convert to Islam.[7]

The expulsion of the Crusader states from the coast of Syria/Palestine had forced European traders out onto islands in the

Mediterranean, in particular, to Crete and Cyprus. In practical terms, this meant essentially that they had access to only two functional routes to Asia. One went overland from the Black Sea; the other went through Egypt to the Indian Ocean, and was the longer but historically preferred passage. Whoever controlled the sea route to Asia could set the terms of trade for a Europe now in temporary retreat. For the rest of the thirteenth, and indeed up to the beginning of the sixteenth century, that power was Egypt.

The southern route through the Red Sea became the single thread connecting the two bodies of water that constituted the central axis of the then-known world. As a result, Cairo, the "mother [city] of the world" as she was described in Arab writings, flourished in the thirteenth, fourteenth, and even early fifteenth centuries, recovering from the ravages of recurring plagues and surviving in spite of the depredations of an extractive military caste.

That the Italian mariner states played a crucial role in linking Egypt to European markets is very well known. What is less often recognized is that the Italians rendered another indispensable service to the Mamluk state, which guaranteed them access to Egyptian ports even when Christian–Muslim animosity was at its peak. It was the Italian mariner nations who ensured a steady supply of new military recruits to the slave elite that governed Egypt. To that unique institution, in which neither feudal nor political position could be inherited but had to be continually recreated, the Italians provided the manpower needed to perpetuate its strength. That was the price for continued trading rights in Egypt. Ironically, then, the Italian trading nations assisted the very state that blocked their direct contact with the East and that exacted so high a price for goods in transit.

Part II explores these changes so central to the rise and fall of the thirteenth-century world system. Chapter 5 details the unification and then dissolution of the Mongol world and the implications it had for the northern route, Chapter 6 examines the decline of the previously crucial Baghdad–Persian Gulf subsystem, and Chapter 7 traces the increasing centrality of the Italian–Egyptian–Red Sea linkage. In Part III we examine the Indian Ocean system to which it was the gateway.

Notes

1. For an account of the earlier system, see Loewe (1971: 166–179), Charlesworth (1924), and Warmington (1928). Both Lombard (1975) and Hodgson (1974: particularly 330–335) make strong cases in support of the position that the Middle East constituted the center of a "world system" in the thirteenth century, although neither uses that term.

2. Nor to head east, the more usual direction. Barfield (1989) traces three cycles of the relationship between China and the peoples of the inner Asian steppes between 209 B.C. and the twentieth century. He hypothesizes a positive correlation between a strong China and strong empires on the steppes. Interestingly enough, the sole exception to this pattern occurred in the thirteenth century, the only time in history when Central Asian nomads ever ruled China. This exceptionalism helps to explain the rise of the world system in that period, whereas its reversion in the post-Yuan period contributes part of the explanation for why the system broke up in the late fourteenth century.

3. We are fortunate that, in spite of the fact that the Mongols had no written language until their spoken dialect was transcribed into the Uighur script, several primary documents have come down to us from the thirteenth century. There is, first of all, the collection of "historical texts" referred to as *The Secret History of the Mongols* that, although it may have started to be assembled as early as 1241, appears actually to date from 1251–1252 (Boyle, 1962, reprinted in Boyle, 1977: 136–137). The original Uighur text has never been found. A German edition of an early Chinese translation of this work, however, is available (Haenisch, 1941). The English translation of Spuler's *History of the Mongols* (1972) contains many excerpts from this document. Most recently, the first part of the text has been translated into English by F. W. Cleaves (1982). *The Secret History of the Mongols* concerns the life of Genghis Khan and his immediate successors, but more in the form of an Icelandic Saga than what we would call "history." The opening lines on the genealogy of Genghis Khan give hint of the flavor of the text: "There was a bluish wolf which was born having [his] destiny from Heaven above. His spouse was a fallow doe." This text was apparently used by Ala-ad-din ʿAta Malik Juvaini to compile his *The History of the World Conqueror* (trans. Boyle, 1958). Then, we have the universal history of the Persian physician, Rashid al-Din, composed in the late thirteenth century and translated by Boyle under the title, *The Successors of Genghis Khan* (1971). For an evaluation of these works, see Barthold (1928: 37–58). These voluminous texts, however, constitute a frustrating source for someone interested in economic history. Although genealogies are presented, campaigns detailed, personal anecdotes recounted, and intradynastic disputes noted, the internal administration of the Mongol Empire is virtually ignored, except by Rashid al-Din.

4. The term "horde" was not originally pejorative. The Mongolian word "ordu" referred to the household "tent" and, by extension then, to the tribe(s) owing allegiance to the master of the tent. Thus, the term "horde" referred to any Mongol tribe or tribal confederation.

5. Unlike the sea-going Fatimids who had hailed from the Tunisian port of Mahdiya, the land-locked Mamluks were frightened by oceans. Of Turkish stock

(Baybars himself was a Kipchik) drawn from Central Asia, they preferred cavalry battles; ports were viewed chiefly as potential beachheads for their European enemies and were thus destroyed. Once the Palestinian coast was no longer in Christian hands, Europeans intensified their use of the northern route from the Black Sea across Mongol territory.

6. Mamluk in Arabic means "one who is held or owned." Although even before Ayyubid times the state was becoming dependent on a military caste of "owned" soldiers for its protection, this corps remained a praetorian guard subordinate to the ruler. As military demands increased, however, larger numbers of soldiers had to be recruited, and by a novel means. The new recruits were young boys captured as children (or, increasingly, bought as slaves through Italian traders at the Black Sea), converted to Islam, raised to absolute fealty in the households of advanced and already manumitted Mamluks, and trained in the skills of battle and administration. This feudal military caste was supported through the agricultural surplus it wrested from assigned districts and provinces; in return for such milk farms, the chief Mamluk lords were responsible for providing a given number of troops. Until this military caste usurped the Sultanate, however, it is not possible to speak of a Mamluk state.

7. Berke's opposition to Hulegu's campaigns against the Muslims led to a war between the two Mongol domains. This was indeed the precipitating factor that forced Marco Polo's father and uncle eastward to the lands of Kubilai Khan, since their return to Constantinople from Berke's headquarters was blocked by the fighting (Latham, 1958: 23). Furthermore, the alliance between Baybars and Berke resulted in one of the anomalies of history. Berke, after the death of Baybars, was for three years (1277–1280) the titular "Sultan" of the Bahri Mamluk state of Egypt!

The Mongols
and the
Northeast Passage

Some economic units in the thirteenth century owed their importance to their entrepôt functions—to their competitive edge as neutral ground at a crossroads. These were places at which traders from distant places could meet to transact business, their persons secure in passage and their goods protected from confiscation or default. The towns of the Champagne fairs and, as we shall see later, the port entrepôt of Aden, the towns along the Strait of Malacca, and, to some extent, those of the Malabar Coast offered such a haven.

Other units, such as Bruges and Ghent, enjoyed a comparative advantage in the production of unique goods in high demand. It was their industrial output that drew them into the world market. And although from time to time they supplemented this role by shipping and finance, even when others preempted those activities their economic viability was sustained by production.

Commerce, finance, and transport constituted the economic underpinnings of the mariner city states of Italy. These functions would have been of little value, however, had they not also had sufficient naval military prowess to protect their own passage. Whereas feudal lords and bourgeois governing classes, respectively, offered these guarantees in Champagne and Flanders, the Italian fighting sailors, supported by a mercantilist state, were responsible for the defense of their ships and of the goods they carried. Without this sine qua non, trade would have been impossible.

The thirteenth-century Mongols offered neither strategic crossroads location, unique industrial productive capacity, nor transport functions to the world economy. Rather, their contribution was to create an environment that facilitated land transit with less risk and lower protective rent. By reducing these costs they opened a route for trade over their territories that, at least for a brief time, broke the monopoly of the more southerly routes. Although their social and political organization could not transform the inhospitable physical terrain of Central Asia into an open and pleasing pathway, it did transform its social climate.

The Physical and Social Environment
of the Central Asian Steppes

Barren, empty, sparsely populated by scattered tribes of nomadic herders, weeks of travel with no local resources to draw on, vast desert expanses—such are the medieval descriptions of this forbidding terrain. Thus, Marco Polo's journey eastward from Kerman takes him through desolate stretches until he reaches the city of Kuh-banan, then through another desert that takes eight days to cross, and later across another vast barren desert, inhabited by only infrequently encountered nomads (Latham, 1958).

Balducci Pegolotti, in his manual for merchants, is even more explicit in describing the hardships of the journey that, by the time of his writing (ca. 1340), had been considerably ameliorated as a result of safe transit and comfortable stations established along the way. He advises a merchant to let his beard grow, to obtain a good dragoman and several servants (as well as a woman since "she will make the trip more comfortable"), and to lay in sufficient provisions at Tana before starting out (Yule, II, 1924: 291). This is understandable because, according to his itinerary, it will take 25 days by ox-wagon to go from Tana to Astrakan, another 20 days by camel-wagon to reach Organci, another 35–40 days by camel to reach Otrar, 45 days by pack-ass to Armalec, another 70 days with asses to reach Camexu on the Chinese frontier, 45 more days to the river that leads to Cassai (Kinsai or Hangchow), and then finally 30 days overland to Peking (Khanbalik) (Yule, 1924: II: 287–290). Since by the time he wrote, the route had reached its point of greatest ease and safety,[1] imagine what it must have been like before such "ease" and "security" had been established!

The inhospitable terrain was the place of origin for a long succession of groups that left it to plunder richer lands. From earliest times, nomadic groups poured out of this marginally productive zone, seeking better grazing land, more space, or a chance to appropriate through "primitive" accumulation the surplus generated in the more fertile oases and trading towns.[2]

The Mongols, in the beginning, differed little from their predecessors. As is usual in the case of nomads who prey on settled agriculturalists, their economy developed less *out of* nomadic pastoralism than out of extraction from a new type of herd—human. The sedentary populations conquered by the nomads were forced to use their own productive surplus to pay the "tribute" that supported their new masters. As de Rachewiltz (1971: 65) explains, once conquest was achieved

> The court was empowered to distribute the revenue collected by Mongol governors from the subject populations amongst the imperial relatives and the Mongol nobility. Thus Chingis Khan's conquests had the effect of transforming a nomadic and semi-nomadic tribal society into a kind of feudal society in which the military leaders . . . enjoyed the fruits of their conquests without having to relinquish their traditional mode of life.

This was not an economic system designed to create a surplus, nor could it be perpetuated indefinitely. As de Rachewiltz (1971: 66–67) points out, the continuous military campaigns took the common tribesman away from his cattle-breeding and domestic occupations and led, furthermore, to high death rates which decimated Mongol ranks. Thus, their leaders were forced to rely increasingly on slave labour at home and on foreign troops in their campaigns abroad. Massive deportations of civilians, especially craftsmen, were carried out in Chingis' time. These unfortunate people, forcibly removed from their towns and villages in Persia and north China, were resettled in Siberia and Mongolia where they had to weave, mine and make tools and weapons for their oppressive master. . . . [G]radually [the Mongols] changed their policy, concentrating more on the exploitation of the settled population of the conquered territories. . . . When Ogodei was elected in 1229, one of his first tasks was to work out a more efficient system of levying taxes and corvée from his subjects. . . . At . . . Karakorum . . . were Chinese serving as scribes and astronomers, Christian Kereit and Uighur advisers versed in the languages and cultures of Central Asia, as well as a large group of Central and Western Asian Moslems engaged in trade operations for the Mongols. With the help of these people, Ogodei set up in 1231 a State Secretariat to deal with the administration of his vast empire. A more regular system of taxation was introduced . . . and a more complex network of post-relay stations was established. . . .

One of the difficulties of using tribute to support the state, however, is that revenues can be increased only by raising taxes on existing subjects or by expanding the domains from which surplus can be extracted. Ogodei, following the advice of some Muslim merchants at court, tried to meet the court's increasing need for goods and wealth by raising taxes (de Rachewiltz, 1971: 81), but he had also opted for the second strategy, resuming his offensive against China in 1230. By 1234 the kingdoms of Hsi-Hsia and Chin in northern China had been occupied, which brought the Mongols directly up against the Sung empire that ruled the southern half of the country. In 1235 Ogodei declared war on the Sung (de Rachewiltz, 1971: 68).

A second limitation of tribute is that exploitation, if too rapid and ruthless, can actually "kill the cow" itself. This evidently happened in Russia. There (de Rachewiltz, 1971: 83)

the "Tartar yoke" lasted two and a half centuries. During the first hundred years of Mongol domination, the Russian subjects had to pay a heavy tribute to the Golden Horde. . . . This harsh economic exploitation . . . had the effect of plunging Russia into a culturally dark age.

But the Mongols were not dependent solely upon foreign conquests. They also derived profits from trade across their domains. Although the zone remained *terra incognita* for Europeans until the first exploratory missions at mid-thirteenth century, this was not true for the Middle Easterners whose trade had never fully disappeared. Even before the unification of the Central Asian trade route under the Mongols, that forbidding region had been regularly traversed by Muslim and Jewish merchant caravans (Lombard, 1975: 204–211). Thus, Ibn Khordadbeh, writing in the latter part of the ninth century, recounts how the activities of the Jewish Radhanites already linked zones that were to become more integrated in the thirteenth century. Goitein (1964b: 106) quotes a relevant passage from this early source:

These [Radhanite] merchants speak Arabic, Persian, Roman [i.e., Greek . . .], the languages of the Franks . . . , of the Andalusians . . . , and the Slavs. They journey from west to east and from east to west, partly on land, partly by sea. They take ship in the land of the Franks, on the Western Sea [the Mediterranean], and steer for Farama [. . . near the present Suez Canal]. There they embark into the Eastern Sea [Indian Ocean] and go to India and China. . . .

It is evident from Ibn Khordadbeh's other descriptions that they also followed the land route across Central Asia itself, passing through the land of the Jewish converts, the Khazars, and going all the way to China. Goitein (1964b: 107) believes that such merchant travelers had been going over similar routes even before the Islamic era.

With the Islamic conquests of Transoxiana in the eighth and ninth centuries, the western end of Central Asia became more hospitable to merchants from various parts of the Muslim world. When there was peace a vigorous and profitable transit trade plied the overland caravan route. Samarkand was, of course, the great meeting place for the land routes—those coming north from India, eastward from the Black Sea through the Caucasus, and westward from China (see below).

And yet, passage could be interrupted for many reasons. With control of the region fragmented among dozens or sometimes hundreds of rival tribal groups, each competing to wrest lucrative surplus from the limited number of prosperous oases, eruptions of warfare over territory were inevitable and frequent. Each time, the safe transit on which the caravan trade depended was threatened and often lost. Furthermore, with so many groups guarding limited stretches along the way, demands for protection money at times reached prohibitive levels.

In spite of these perils and costs, however, Muslim merchants moved precious cargo from west to east and back. Their importance is clearly illustrated by an incident that occurred early in Genghis Khan's first excursions westward. Transoxiana was then ruled by the Muslim Khwarizm-shah, vis- à-vis whom Genghis was cautious, a sentiment that, with even more justification, was reciprocated. Each ruler, seeking to placate or at least "test" the other, dispatched great caravans headed by merchants who accompanied impressive quantities of "gifts." It is significant that each of these caravans was said to be "manned" by Muslim merchants (Barthold, 1928: 395–398, based upon the primary source, Juvaini). The exchange was, however, only a respite before Genghis Khan invaded and then defeated the Khwarizm as his forces sped west.

The unification of the vast region under Mongol control reduced the number of competing tribute gatherers along the way and assured greater safety in travel, not only for the usual caravans of Jewish and Muslim merchants well accustomed to traversing Central Asia, but for the intrepid Italian merchants who now joined them, vying to share in the profits to be gained from the generous and acquisitive Mongol rulers.[3]

In contrast to the sophisticated knowledge that Muslims had of these regions, however, Europeans were at first abysmally ignorant. Newcomers to the ongoing world system and disdainfully overlooking the merchants already there, Europeans viewed themselves as great adventurers "discovering" new regions and peoples. The first European clerics who ventured into the territories controlled by the Mongols wrote incredulous (and frequently incredible) accounts that were read avidly by their sedentary compatriots. Friars were soon followed by merchants hoping to break into the game. It must be remembered, however, that when they first traversed the great Central Asian route to Cathay during the last third of the thirteenth century, bringing back wondrous tales of rich lands and prosperous trade, Europeans were describing a preexistent system of international exchange from which Latin merchants had previously been excluded except in their entrepôts on the Black Sea. It is to this entry of Europe we now turn.

Reducing Europe's Ignorance of the Mongols

Although Ogodei's death in 1241 spared western Europe forever from the threat of a direct Mongol invasion, this miraculous salvation did little to enlarge Europe's knowledge of either the "new barbarians" or the land from which they came. Indeed, the Mongols were initially consigned to the same mythological region reserved for other strange creatures populating the unknown world of Asia. Based on a misinterpretation of the term Tatar (the name for only one of the tribal groups later joining the Mongol confederation), the Mongols were identified as Tartars, that is, coming from the Biblical region of Tartarus or Hell.[4] It is difficult to see how, at the same time, they could have been viewed longingly as potential allies in Christendom's holy war against the Muslims. Yet, perhaps even those creatures from the lands of Gog and Magóg (another feeble attempt to identify their provenance) might be mobilized in their struggle.

European ignorance of the east was vast, a simple indicator of how isolated she still was from the system she sought to join. This was hardly surprising. If the classical Romans who maintained trade contacts and received imports from the far eastern world in the early Christian era remained basically ignorant of their ultimate trading partners, how could medieval Europe, cut off for hundreds of years, have been expected to know more.

It is instructive—and amusing—to look back to classical times to see how precipitous was the atrophy in Roman knowledge as one moved eastward. Although Chinese silk was being regularly imported to Rome through Middle Eastern intermediaries, the myth remained that the "Chinese combed silk out of the floss growing on the leaves of their trees" (Virgil as cited by de Ra-chewiltz, 1971: 21; and by Yule, 1913: I: xliv). Nor, in all fairness, were the Chinese more knowledgeable about the textile goods they imported from the Middle East. According to the Han Chinese, cotton "was made of hair combed from certain 'water sheep' " (de Rachewiltz, 1971: 23). To Roman citizens at the time of Trajan, India was not only the source of "pearls, precious stones, aromatic woods and spices, but also the home of men with a dog's head . . . or a single foot . . . or with heels in front. . . . It was the country of headless people with faces between their shoulders, of wild men without mouths . . . " (de Rachewiltz, 1971: 22). The Han Chinese, on the contrary, were certain that these fabulous creatures pop-ulated the Mediterranean world.[5] The very same stories—of islands in the Indian Ocean inhabited by naked dog-faced or headless people—punctuated the generally more credible geographies and travel accounts produced by Muslim geographers in the ninth cen-tury and even later. It seems legitimate to use these fanciful images as indicators of the lacunae that were to be systematically filled in the course of the thirteenth century, as distant peoples made direct contact with one another.

Certainly, now that reports about approaching Mongols were reaching Europe, more exact information was needed and for very practical purposes. Such information was as yet scanty. The Rabbi Benjamin of Tudela claimed, upon his return to Spain in 1173, to have traveled as far as India and China, although most scholars doubt that he ever reached the Far East, and in any case, his journey to visit eastern Jewish communities had not been primarily overland.[6] Of far greater interest to contemporary Christians were fabulous rumors of what eventually turned out to be a nonexistent Christian colony in India, under the presumed kingship of one Prester John. The crusading nations were so eager to find natural allies in the east that the very first western envoy sent out by the Pope as early as 1177 was ordered to search for Prester John. However, not only did the envoy not find the Christian king of India but he himself disappeared (de Rachewiltz, 1971: 19). But if either Indian Christians or Asian Mongols were to be enlisted in the war against the Ayyubids, further exploratory missions were called for.

Papal Envoys

In 1245 Pope Innocent IVth sent the first serious emissaries to the Mongols: a Dominican friar, Simon of Saint Quentin (see Guzman, 1968), and a Franciscan, John of Pian di Carpine (see de Rachewiltz, 1971: 84–89). Their reports constitute the first European accounts of travel to Central Asia. John of Pian di Carpine, who had instructions to proceed all the way to the Mongol court to deliver the Pope's letters, left from Lyon on Easter Sunday 1245, returning from Mongolia two and a half years later. Portions of his detailed report to the Pope (known by its later title, *History of the Mongols*) were incorporated into Vincent of Beauvais' 1253 *Speculum historiale* (de Rachewiltz, 1971: 88–89). Simon of Saint Quentin authored an account when he returned in 1248, which was similarly extracted in Beauvais' history (Guzman, 1968: 1–4, 70–76). Although these reports were filled with both inaccuracies and prejudices (little wonder, since in the Mongol camp the envoys had been treated more as prisoners than as emissaries), they constituted the data on which Europeans made their first judgments of the Mongols—enemies or allies, they knew not which.

Somewhat more accurate, yet still hardly "true," was the account rendered by William of Rubruck, a Franciscan friar who went to Mongolia in 1253–1255. [See Rockhill's translation in Hakluyt Series II (1900), now superseded by Dawson, 1955, reprinted 1980: 89–220.] Born in French Flanders sometime between 1215 and 1220, Friar William accompanied St. Louis in 1248 on his Crusade to Egypt and stayed with him in Palestine until 1252. From there, apparently on his own initiative, he journeyed to Cathay, taking copious notes on the "manners and customs of the natives," particularly their religious practices. After returning from Mongolia, he went to Paris in which he met Roger Bacon who was intensely interested in his experiences. Bacon refers to him at length in his *Opus Majus*, which indeed "is the only contemporary record of him that we possess" (Dawson, 1955, reprinted 1980: 88–89).

We know that Friar William set out overland from the Black Sea in the spring of 1253 and soon encountered his first Mongol camp. In spite of maltreatment he persisted eastward. He reports the very first European impression of the people of the east (Dawson, 1955, reprinted 1980: 143–144).

> They [the Mongols] are little men and dark like Spaniards; they wear tunics like a deacon's tunicle with sleeves a little narrower, and on their heads they have mitres like bishops. . . . Next is Grand Cathay . . . [whose] inhabitants used to be called Seres. From them come the best silken materials. . . . The inhabitants of Cathay are little men, and when they speak they breath heavily through their noses . . . they have a small opening for the eyes. They are very fine craftsmen in every art, and their physicians know a great deal about the power of herbs and diagnose very cleverly from the pulse. . . . There were many of them in Caracorum. . . . There are Nestorians and Saracens living among them like foreigners as far as Cathay. . . .

The magnitude of Europe's ignorance of the east is easily illustrated by the gullibility of William of Rubruck who gives the following account of the source of the red dye for which Chinese silks were famous. Here is the translation that appears in Dawson (1955, reprinted 1980: 171):

> On one occasion there sat by me a priest from Cathay, wearing a red material of a very fine hue, and when I asked him where he got such a colour from, he told me that in the eastern district of Cathay there are lofty crags in which dwell creatures having in every respect a human form except that they do not bend their knees but walk hopping . . . ; they are but a cubit high and the whole of their small bodies is covered with hairs. . . . When men go hunting them they carry with them . . . very intoxicating [mead], and they set traps among the rocks in the shape of cups which they fill with this mead. . . . [Then] these animals come out of their caves and taste the drink and they cry out "Chinchin;" from this shout they got their name, for they are called Chinchins. Then they assemble in vast numbers and drink the mead and, becoming drunk, they fall asleep . . . the hunters . . . bind them hand and foot as they sleep. Next they open a vein in their necks and . . . extract three or four drops of blood . . . and that blood, so I was told, is most valuable for dyeing purple.

And so—Europe's first rediscovery of Cathay or of the sense of humor of its inhabitants!

Within the next few decades, this ignorance would begin to dissipate as a result of Venetian traders who followed in the footsteps of the Papal missionaries and Genoese traders who, although less loquacious than the famed Marco Polo, seem to have been more successful in business. Poised in their trading posts on the Black Sea, which were simply outer extensions of Constantinople, the Italian merchants were the first to come to terms with the Mongol invaders, undoubtedly using their merchandise to entice their would-be-conquerors into relations. But their deeper forays into the Mongol domain evidently had to await the accession of Kubilai Khan as head of the empire.

The Polo Adventure

Certainly, the first European merchant adventurers of whom we have record who traversed Mongol territory, taking the overland route to Cathay, were the brothers Niccolo and Maffeo Polo. They left Constantinople in 1260 and did not return to Venice until 1269. Being astute businessmen, they did not freely share their discovery of the great new possibilities for trade. They set out on a second, longer journey in 1271, this time taking Niccolo's young son Marco with them, not returning to Venice until 1295 (Petech, 1962: 553). Much of what is known, not only of their travels but of the world of the Mongols, is learned from the memoirs set down a few years later by a fellow cellmate in a Genoese prison, after Marco's capture in one of the recurrent sea battles between Genoa and Venice. The ballyhoo that introduces the memoirs does nothing to allay suspicions that at least some of the contents have been sensationalized to attract an audience. Recognizing the low literacy of his times, the scribe invites

> Emperors and Kings, Dukes and Marquises, Counts, knights and townsfolk, and all people who wish to know the various races of men and the peculiarities of the various regions of the world, take this book and have it read to you. (Latham, 1958: 21)

The book begins as the elder Polo brothers sail eastward on the Black Sea to the Venetian colony at Suduk, from which they depart by land, coming at last to the court of the Khan of the Golden Horde. Berke, the third khan, received them with honor and accepted the jewels the brothers offered him, giving in return "goods of fully twice the value [which] . . . he allowed them to sell . . . very profitably" (Latham, 1958: 22). Their stay in Berke's domain was rudely interrupted after a year by a war between Berke and Hulegu, in which the latter's forces were victorious. Since their route back to Constantinople was blocked by strife, they set out eastward and, after traversing a desert for seventeen days, came to Bukhara. Three years later an envoy from Hulegu, stopping at Bukhara on his way to Kubilai Khan, was surprised to find the two brothers there "because no Latin had ever been seen in that country." On learning that they were merchants, he invited them to accompany him to meet the Khan who "has never seen any Latin and is exceedingly desirous to meet one" (Latham, 1958: 23). Protected by his safe conduct, the Polo brothers arrived at the court of Kubilai Khan who evinced great interest in learning more about the West and Christianity.[7] He proposed to send them as his emissaries to the Pope, with a request that the latter send him 100 priests and some oil from the lamp in the sepulcre of Jerusalem (Latham, 1958: 24). (One wonders at these strange requests.)

Equipped with a gold tablet bearing the Khan's seal, which ensured their safe conduct throughout the Mongol empire, they set out again overland, taking three years to reach Acre. Since the Pope had died and a successor had not yet been elected, they returned to Venice to visit their families. By this time Niccolo's wife was dead, leaving a son of fifteen, Marco, who would accompany the brothers when they returned to Acre several years later. After the new Pope had been selected, the Polos began their return journey to the Khan's capital, entrusted with messages and gifts but only two priests, far short of the 100 requested. Although the two fearful priests soon eluded them, the Polos did manage to complete their trip in some three years, being welcomed back with great enthusiasm. They remained for the next seventeen years, during which Marco served the Khan and traveled widely on his behalf.

There is thus reason to believe that his geographical measurements *cum* observations on the eastern regions are well grounded; they are certainly much more sophisticated than any preceding accounts. Whereas William of Rubruck seemed primarily interested in chronicling the religious practices of the strange people he met, Marco Polo was much more his father's son, observing what people made, what they traded, and what had commercial value. His account presents an image of the Mongol domains as containing prosperous agriculturalists, skilled industrial producers, and many foreign traders (whom Polo dismisses with a brief aside, since they were "only Mohammedans").

His account follows the route from west to east. In Turkey he exclaimed over the "choicest and most beautiful carpets in the world" (Latham, 1958: 33); beyond was the land of the Georgians, in which "silk is produced . . . in abundance, and the . . . cloth of gold woven here . . . [is] the finest ever seen. . . . There are ample supplies of everything, and commerce and industry flourish" (Latham, 1958: 35). Mosul and Baghdad in Iraq are both described as flourishing cities (Latham, 1958: 36–40), even after the devastations of Hulegu, which he recounts from hearsay. But it is Tabriz that captures his full admiration. Not only are silk and cloth of gold produced in great quantity by its artisans, but it is a great city for trade. "The city is so favorably situated that it is a market for merchandise from India and Baghdad, from Mosul and Hormuz . . . ; and many Latin merchants come here to buy the merchandise imported from foreign lands. It is also a market for precious stones . . . [and] a city where good profits are made by travelling merchants" (Latham, 1958: 43). Persia he describes as a prosperous land in which trade and industry abound. "They make cloth of gold and silk of every sort. Cotton grows there in abundance. They have no lack of wheat, barley, millet, panic-grass, and every type of corn, besides wine and all kinds of fruit" (Latham, 1958: 47). In Kerman, turquoise is mined, along with "steel" [sic] and ondanique. "The inhabitants . . . manufacture . . . all the equipment of a mounted warrior— bridles, saddles, spurs, swords, bows, quivers, and every sort of armaments" (Latham, 1958: 47) and the women embroider silk with "beasts and birds and many other figures" (Latham, 1958: 48). Crossing a great plain one then reaches the Persian Gulf at an excellent harbor called Hormuz. "Merchants come here by ship from India, bringing all sorts of spices and precious stones and pearls and cloths of silk and of gold and elephants' tusks and many other wares. . . . It is a great centre of commerce" (Latham, 1958: 51).

Rather than describing the sea route to India here, his account turns north from Kerman into a desolate stretch that takes days to cross before reaching the city of Kuh-banan in which "they make steel mirrors of large size and excellent quality" (Latham, 1958: 54). After Kuh-banan, another desert appears that takes eight days to cross. The inhabitants all along the route are Muslims, living in scattered oases throughout the desert. Although he enumerates many of these towns and villages, he describes none of their products and dismisses their inhabitants as only half-civilized. After passing through another desert, he reaches Kan-Chou, and then the "countries of Cathay" (Latham, 1958: 84).

The most interesting part of his account is the description of Cathay itself, including a sycophantic description of his patron, Kubilai Khan, "the wisest man and the ablest in all respects, the best ruler of subjects and of empire and the man of the highest character of all that have ever been in the whole history of the Tartars" (Latham, 1958: 102). On the site of the old city of Khanbalik, Kubilai had built a new city as his capital, which he called Taidu. Since this is contemporary Peking, we quote at length from his description because there are remarkable parallels to the city and Great Palace of today.

> Taidu is built in the form of a square with all its sides of equal length and a total circumference of twenty-four miles. It is enclosed by earthern ramparts . . . all battlemented and white-washed. They have twelve gates, each surmounted by a fine, large palace. . . . [T]he streets are so broad and straight that from the top above one gate you can see along the whole length of the road to the gate opposite. All the way down the sides of every main street there are booths and shops of every sort. . . . the whole interior of the city [being] laid out in squares like a checker-board. . . . (Latham, 1958: 106)

The most significant statement contained in Marco Polo's description of Peking, however, is one whose implications elude him. He notes that the suburbs contain as many inhabitants as the walled city itself and that in each suburban quarter there are "many fine hostels which provide lodging for merchants coming from different parts; a particular hostel is assigned to every nation. . . . [for] merchants and others come here on business in great numbers, both because it is the Khan's residence and because it affords a profitable market" (Latham, 1958: 106–107).

But who are these merchants from "every nation" who live in the suburban hostels assigned to them? Certainly *not* the

Italian traders, for Polo continually insists that his family is unique! It is obvious from other evidence that these foreign merchants are Muslims from all parts of the heartland of the thirteenth-century world system. For them the Khan's domains are no new discovery; they are a natural and integral part of their world. And indeed, Polo goes on to tell a story of Ahmed, a Muslim governor in the city to whom the emperor gave power for some 22 years!

These extracts are sufficient to illustrate an important point. European merchants first traversed the great Central Asian route to Cathay during the last third of the thirteenth century, bringing back wondrous tales of rich lands, of prosperous trade, and of an ongoing system of international exchange from which Latin merchants were still essentially excluded. In the decades that followed, many traveled in the footsteps of the Polos but, in spite of the later widespread activities of Italian merchants, few written records were left and none that rival the rich detail of Marco's account. Only the merchant handbook of Francesco de Balducci Pegolotti, produced in the fourth decade of the fourteenth century when this pathway was about to close, stands as conclusive evidence that Italian merchants once traded extensively over this northern route.

Italian Merchants in the Mongol Empire

Luciano Petech[8] provides some rare details about the Italian merchants who were too busy making money to write their memoirs. According to Petech (1962: 549–552), the Pax Mongolica and safe travel accounted only partially for the flourishing of Mediterranean-Mongol trade. The intensification of trade was also the result of the commercial revolution that sent Italian traders on wide missions, including those to the Mongol empire (although, at this time, most European traders still favored the sea route through the Persian Gulf). The primary item in that trade was the silk of Cathay that, as early as 1257, was being sold by Genoese merchants at the fairs of Champagne. Interestingly enough, this silk was in particular demand in Europe because, even then, it was lower in price (albeit also in quality) than the silk that came from Persia and Turkestan. A clear indicator of the preeminence of the Genoese in commerce with China is the fact that Balducci Pegolotti's manual used the Genoese terms for weights and measures in describing the land route to Cathay.

Commercial, religious, and "political" missions were frequently intermixed. Thus, a merchant named Peter of Lucalongo accompanied Friar John of Monte Corvino to Cathay. The Italian friar left Tabriz (Persia) in 1291, spending some thirteen months in India before meeting the merchant who would escort him to China (Lopez, 1943: 165; Dawson, 1955, reprinted 1980: 224). Two of the priest's letters have been preserved. In the second, sent from Khanbalik on January 8, 1305, he proudly reports that he has set up a Catholic mission (although his accomplishments appear a bit dubious).

> I have built a church in the city of Cambaliech [Khanbalik or Peking] where the chief residence of the king is. . . . I am constantly baptizing. Also I have purchased by degrees forty boys of the sons of the pagans, between seven and eleven years old, who as yet knew no religion. Here I baptized them and taught them Latin and our rite. . . .

He also reports what Balducci Pegolotti was later to confirm. Inviting other churchmen to join him, he assures them of their security.

> As to the road [across Central Asia]: I report that the way by the land of Cothay [sic] . . . is safer and more secure, so that, travelling with envoys, they [the priests] might be able to arrive within five or six months. But the other route is the most long and perilous since it involves two sea voyages, the first of which is about the distance of Acre from . . . Provence, but the second is like the distance between Acre and England and . . . is scarcely completed in two years. But the first was not safe for a long time on account of the wars. (quoted in Dawson, 1955, reprinted 1980: 225–226)

At the time he wrote this letter, John of Monte Corvino was 58 years old. He had learned the Tatar language and script and had translated the whole New Testament and Psalter into that language.

John of Monte Corvino was not the only Italian in China. We also have a record of a physician from Lombard who arrived in Khanbalik in 1303 (Petech, 1962: 553) and a 1326 letter from Andrew of Perugia, a bishop in the famous port of Zaytun, who mentions many Genoese living there (details and text in Dawson, 1955, reprinted 1980: 235–237). Genoese merchants served diplomatic functions as well. "The most eminent personage in the Genoese colony of China...was Andalo de Savignon" whose name is first encountered in 1336 when he was sent by the Yuan emperor, Toghon Temur, as an ambassador to the Pope (Petech, 1962: 554). But direct contact was about to end. The last date for which there is any evidence of Genoese merchants using the land route to Cathay is in 1344, when a court case was recorded involving the inheritance of a merchant who died along the way (Petech, 1962: 555). Diplomatic missions also were coming to a close.

In 1339 the Pope sent his last emissary via Central Asia when the Franciscan, Giovanni de' Marignolli, left Naples for Caffa to make the land crossing to Peking (Petech, 1962: 555). But by then the Mongol empire was tottering, the victim of insurrection and epidemics. Now it was the Mongols who pleaded for an alliance. The Mongol emperor, Temur, entrusted his conciliatory answer to Marignolli who, accompanied by a military escort of 200 guards, left for home in 1345. By then, however, the land route was no longer usable, having been cut by civil war in the Chaghataid dominion. Signaling that the weakened structures of the Mongol empire were collapsing everywhere, the convoy went through China to the port of Zaytun, from which Marignolli embarked by sea for India and the Persian Gulf. His account is virtually the last we have of any European traversing the route between China and Europe—until the circumnavigation of Africa reopened direct contact in the sixteenth century.

Marignolli's return itinerary took him through the impressive cities of Hangchow and then Zaytun, from which he sailed in December 1345, arriving at the port of Quilon on the Malabar coast of India in April 1346. From there he sailed up the coast to Hormuz and then traveled circuitously overland to the Mediterranean via Baghdad, Mosul, Aleppo, Damascus, and Jerusalem, before setting sail for Cyprus. He finally reached Avignon in 1353 to deliver the Khan's letter which, inter alia, contained a request for more Christian preachers (de Rachewiltz, 1971: 197–201).

The request could not be granted and, in fact, that was the end of the Christian missions in China for some time. Why? Not only had the land route across Central Asia been closed but there were simply no preachers to spare. By then, the Black Death had virtually "emptied the Minorite convents in Europe (two-thirds of the friars had perished within a year)" (de Rachewiltz, 1971: 202). Nor, by then, were preachers of high priority to the Mongols. The vast regions unified under Genghis Khan and his successors were wracked by internal dissension and depopulated by the plague, for whose spread they were largely responsible (McNeill, 1976).

The Unintended Consequences of Mongol Success

The unification under the Mongols of much of the central Eurasian land mass put the termini of Europe and China in direct contact with one another for the first time in a thousand years. Although this facilitated the expansion of trade by opening up the northern route between China and the Black Sea outlet to the Mediterranean, its very success led ironically to its eventual demise (see Figure 7). The unintended consequence of unification was the eruption of a pandemic that set back the development of a world system for some 150 years. When the system revived in the sixteenth century, it had taken on a quite different shape.

William McNeill has developed elaborate hypotheses concerning the causes and consequences of disease in human history that are particularly relevant to our inquiry. He suggests that by the start of the Christian era "four divergent civilized disease pools had come into existence" (1976: 97)—China, India, the Middle East, and the Mediterranean (including Europe)—each of which contained a population of some 50–60 million people (McNeill, 1976: 93) and had reached relative equilibrium with its environment, including endemic diseases. Their relative encapsulation from one another prevented the transfer from one system to the next of "strange" diseases (those for which local populations had not yet built up natural immunities or cultural patterns of avoidance and treatment).

During the first two centuries A.D., however, contacts among them intensified, both over the land route the Romans called the Silk Road and through the Indian Ocean, once sailors had mastered the art of riding the monsoon winds.[9] Now that previously isolated groups came into direct contact with one another, the chances for the transmission of diseases to unprotected populations increased, particularly in China and Europe, "the two least disease-experienced civilizations of the Old World" (McNeill, 1976: 102). Certainly, the limited information at hand suggests that serious outbreaks of measles, smallpox, and then bubonic plague made their appearance in both Europe and China between A.D. 200 and A.D. 800, often acting "like new infections breaking in upon a virgin population" (McNeill, 1976: 103–120; quotation: 119).[10] Gradually, however, adaptations to disease seem to have followed parallel paths in Europe and China and, from about A.D. 1000 on, population began to expand in both peripheral regions (McNeill, 1976: 121). This balance was to undergo a new challenge in the thirteenth century when contacts again intensified.

It is McNeill's contention that the Mongol successes once again bridged these relatively encapsulated zones, thus facilitating the spread of life-threatening infections that culminated in the Black Death pandemic of the second half of the fourteenth century.

At the height of their power (1279–1350), the Mongol empires . . . of China . . . Russia . . . central Asia, Iran and Iraq. . . . [were knitted together by a] communication network comprising messengers capable of traveling one hundred miles a day for weeks on end. . . . [In] addition to . . . [the old silk route over the desert,] caravans, soldiers and postal riders [now] rode across the open grasslands. They *created a territorially vast human web* that linked the Mongol headquarters at Karakorum with Kazan and Astrakan on the Volga, with Caffa in the Crimea, with Khanbaliq [Peking] in China and with other caravanserais in between. From an epidemiological point of view, this northern extension of the caravan trade net had one very significant consequence. *Wild rodents of the steppelands came into touch with carriers of new diseases, among them, in all probability, bubonic plague.* (McNeill, 1976: 134, italics added)

He reconstructs the following scenario, combining information from scattered textual references drawn from the period with evidence from more recent medical investigations of plague transmission.

There probably existed, among communities of burrowing ro-

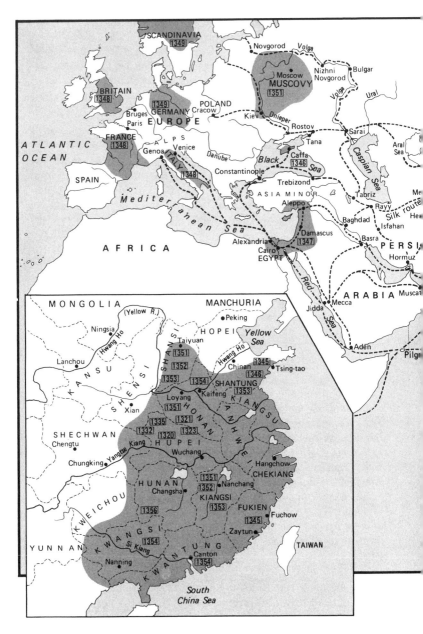

FIGURE 7. The congruence between trade routes and the spread of the Black Death circa 1350.

SIBERIA

MONGOLIA

L. Baikal

Irtysh

Amur

Karakorum

MANCHURIA

L. Balkhash

TRANS-
OXIANA
kent

Almalik

Beshbalik

Shangtu

Sea
of Japan

Balasagun

Anhsi

Peking

Silk route

Samarkand
ukhara

Kashgar

Ningsia

Khotan

Cherchen

Lanchou

Hwang Ho

SHANTUNG
1345

Balkh

Leh

Kabul

HIMALAYAS

TIBET

Lhasa

Xian

Kaifeng

1320

Chengtu

HUPEI

East
China
Sea

Indus

Delhi

Ganges

Patna

Wuchang

Yangtse

Hangchow

Hwang Ho

CHINA

FUKIEN

INDIA

Cambay

Yunnan

Zaytun

Canton

TAIWAN

PACIFIC
OCEAN

Puri

Pagan

rabian
Sea

Calicut

Bay of

Pegu

Angor

South
China
Sea

te to Mecca
n the East

Quilon

Bengal

CEYLON

NDIAN   OCEAN

SUMATRA

Malacca

BORNEO

Palembang

JAVA

Mekong

Irrawaddy

| 1345 | Areas of outbreak of plague with first known dates (sample) |
| ------- | Trade routes |

dents in the Himalayan mountain region between China, India, and Burma, an endemic focus of the plague bacillus to which the local population was somewhat inured by prior exposure and protected by cultural patterns of avoidance. This focus zone remained somewhat insulated from other regions by unpopulated zones, rivers, and other natural barriers (McNeill, 1976:140) until the penetration of Yunnan and Burma by the Mongols after 1252 created a means for the export of the plague bacillus. Not only did the Mongols have little resistance to the disease, but their mounts offered a safe harbor for the rapid transport of infected fleas to the burrows of underground rodent colonies in their northern grasslands (McNeill, 1976: 142). There, the bacillus could survive even the ravages of winter.

McNeill (1976: 143) does not believe that the Black Death was transmitted directly to Mongolia, but rather that it began in 1331 in inland China and spread from there to the overland route and then to the sea. In his cautious words:

> What seems most likely . . . is that . . . [the plague] invaded China in 1331 . . . [and] must then have traveled the caravan routes of Asia during the next fifteen years before reaching the Crimea in 1346; whereupon the bacillus took ship and proceeded to penetrate almost all of Europe and the Near East along routes radiating inland from seaports. . . . What probably happened between 1331 and 1346 . . . was that as plague spread from caravanserai to caravanserai across Asia and eastern Europe . . . a parallel movement into underground rodent "cities" of the grasslands occurred . . . where the bacillus found a permanent home. . . . All these circumstances converged at the middle of the fourteenth century . . . [T]he Black Death . . . broke out in 1346 among the armies of a Mongol prince who laid siege to the trading town of Caffa in the Crimea. This compelled his withdrawal, but not before the infection entered Caffa itself, whence it spread by ship throughout the Mediterranean. . . . (McNeill, 1976: 145–147)

Although no sufficient data exist to confirm (or disprove) McNeill's speculations, his account is convincing and corroborated by at least some if not all evidence.[11]

In Part I we noted the anomalous facts that Flemish textile production was in trouble by the late 1320s and that an economic contraction (including major bankruptcies) had already begun to occur in Italian banking circles by the late 1330s and early 1340s, even though the plague had not yet made its appearance. We noted above, in the section concerning European traders and missionaries in the Mongol empire, that references to them begin to decline by the late 1330s and have all but disappeared by mid-century. It is not illogical to connect these disturbances to the decline in overland trade between the two places. It will be recalled that although the overland route had been the preferred one around the turn of the century, Marignolli, the last Italian in China of whom we have record, was forced by unstable inland conditions to follow the longer sea route when he set out for home in 1345.

Nor does it seem far-fetched to assume some connection between the epidemic deaths recorded in China from 1331 onward and the weakening of Mongol rulers that left them the targets of increasing rebellion. If indeed the Pax Mongolica had been one of the important factors in permitting an increased linkage between European merchants and China, any disturbance in that environment that made it less secure—whether for military or health reasons—could be expected to reduce trade and thus prosperity among trading partners. One way to explore this hypothesis might be to look at the actual caravan cities along the way. Of these, Samarkand was probably the most important.

Samarkand and Other Caravan Centers

Overland trade is a complex matter. From all accounts, such trade was maintained through the activities of a large variety of agents. Some were simple peddlers, perpetually on the move, investing relatively small sums with an immediate flexibility, depending upon what they could buy cheaply at one point and sell dearly at the next. Some were large-scale merchant bankers who remained at home, lending money to itinerants, entering *commenda* contracts with them, or supervising large numbers of quasi-independent "factors" who were little different from the petty peddlers. Finally, there were those who ranged between these two extremes, perhaps beginning small but developing virtual "empires" in long-distance trade.

Prerequisites for overland trade can be classified as physical, political, and institutional. The physical prerequisites are easiest to list but usually have relatively little impact on the volume of trade. Routes must be passable and means for transport must exist. In the northern overland route that stretched some 5000 miles from end to end, however, neither could be taken for granted. The quality of the roads that threaded the inhospitable terrain, the existence of stopping places at regular points in the sparsely inhabited regions, the ability to obtain water and provisions for a journey that at best took months and might, if one stopped to trade along the way, take years—were all physical variables that were sensitive to other events. Let us look at some of the limiting factors.

In arid terrain, water is the major one. The domesticated beast of burden for transport in such zones is the camel, for it can live off the sparse vegetation of desert areas and go for three to four days without water. The camel can carry loads of some 500 pounds for long distances, but it travels at a steady pace of only three miles per hour. (See Wellard, 1977: 11–37, for a graphic description.) Thus, given roughly 30 miles per day and 3–4 days between water intake, the maximum distance between settlements or at least wells should ideally be no more than about 100 miles. This requirement severely restricted the choice of paths across Central Asia. It did not predetermine any given route, however, for there were usually alternatives.

In the mountains also scattered across the zone, a different set of imperatives is even more compelling. Travel over mountains requires pack-asses, and their paths must be carefully selected to take advantage of the lowest grades and the location of passes. Selection is not quite the word; routes through mountainous terrain are, by trial and error, established along the paths of least resistance and are fully determined by the major passes. Even more frequent water resources are essential, but they are usually present in mountain streams.

Finally, across the plains, the volume of travel determines the smoothness of the roadbed, for unpaved roads harden and become more passable with every additional traveler. Settlements are encouraged to grow wherever major routes cross and they, in turn, help to set the routes in firmer locations. Thus, the great trans-Asian routes were shaped through physical factors.

They were, however, particularly sensitive to political factors as well. The unification of Central Asia under the Mongols was certainly significant for both the physical and social channeling of trade. Although they could scarcely be called highways, the major lateral routes underwent substantial improvement as a result of the steady horse movements of the Mongols—both troops and post communications. By the end, there was a real road network, provided with way stations and points around which caravanserais flourished. Even more important was the safety of travel that a unified and regularized administration eventually produced.

It is difficult for us today to appreciate the extent to which trade depended on risk reduction, or the proportion of all costs that might have to be allocated to transit duties, tribute, or simple extortion. Unfortunately, there are no figures from the thirteenth century with which to estimate the proportion of transportation costs that went for protection. However, on the basis of evidence from the seventeenth century, over at least the westernmost part of the land route, Niels Steensgaard (1973: 37–40) has concluded that protection costs (including duties) far exceeded transport expenses themselves, which, according to his calculations, were a great bargain. The spread between purchase/transport costs and gross sale prices might be considered enormous—until one calculates not only what was added in transit dues but the risks involved in shipments that were confiscated or lost, as well as in buying goods whose eventual market price could not really be estimated.

The relative order introduced by the Mongols must have reduced many of these costs, while their generosity and receptivity to merchants encouraged additional trade through their territories. However, such trade would obviously seek alternative routes once these favorable conditions disappeared, as they did during the second half of the fourteenth century.

The third variable has to do with institutional arrangements for business. Although this is discussed in more detail in Chapter 7, it is important to note here that the operations of the myriad small traders along the caravan routes would not have been possible or at least not as efficient if means for getting credit, transferring debts, and exchanging funds between one trader and another and between one trading point and the next had not existed. The check (or rather a demand note to be paid at a distant point and in a different currency at a preestablished exchange rate) was first institutionalized in Persia and seems to have been linked to the caravan trade. As was later usual in Egypt, however, only large merchants availed themselves of this formal means. Most traders dealt more informally, using the network of fellow nationals (or what we would call "ethnics") to settle accounts that were not always translated into monetary terms but might be phrased in terms of commodity exchanges. Again, it is uncanny to read seventeenth-century accounts of an Armenian itinerant merchant or excerpts from merchants' letters to one another (as reported in Steensgaard, 1973) and compare them with the correspondence among Jewish merchants in Fustat in the eleventh and twelfth centuries (as recounted by Goitein, 1967). Little seemed to have changed in the nature of trade.

Although most points along the caravan route were modest burgs—oases or agricultural settlements for which the periodic arrival of a string of camels was an exciting festival but not their staff of life—a few of the cities located at the crossroads of heavily traveled routes grew to large size, particularly if they occupied fertile sites and also served political or religious functions. Then, permanent trade and industry were likely to appear, stimulated by local demand and supplemented heavily by long-distance trade. Tabriz, along the southerly route, was one such place, as were Balkh, Merv, and other towns along the northerly one. But when one thinks about a trade oasis city par excellence, Samarkand (and to a lesser extent, Bukhara) comes to mind.

Set near the point at which the east–west lateral route intersected the north–south "highway" between India and Russia, embedded in a fertile garden fed by an elaborate irrigation system from a river that flowed into it, eventually the political capital of Tamerlane but routinely at least a regional capital for earlier dynasties, Samarkand was perhaps the quintessential caravan city. Barthold (1928: 83) says of it:

> In extent and population Samarqand was always the first city of Transoxania, even in the age when . . . Bukhara was the capital of the kingdom. This importance is explained chiefly by its geographical position at the junction of the main trade routes from India (via Balkh), from

Persia (via Merv), and from the Turkish dominions. The extraordinary fertility of the neighbourhood of the town also made it possible for an enormous number of people to be collected in one place.[12]

Samarkand was one of the oldest cities of Central Asia. Its persistent commercial importance derived from its location at the juncture of trade routes, which made it an attractive prize. Alexander the Great captured it in 329 B.C., and later it was ruled successively by Turks, Arabs, and Persians. With the expansion of Turkic and Mongol tribes westward, it was inevitable that they would seek its wealth. In the eleventh century it was conquered by the Karakhanids and later by the Seljuks; in the twelfth century it was ruled by the Kara Khitais, and at the beginning of the thirteenth century it came under the domination of the Khwarizm-shahs, from whom Genghis Khan wrested it in 1220.

Given its strategic location, it was no accident that fortifications defined the city. Ibn al-Faqih gives us the earliest description of Muslim Samarkand. He tells us that, like Balkh and Buhkara, Samarkand and its suburbs were "encircled by a wall (twelve farsakhs[13] long) with twelve wooden gates; this enclosed a second wall around the city itself, which in turn contained an inner third walled area, called the shahristan, which included the cathedral mosque and the walled citadel containing the ruler's palace" (Barthold, 1928: 84). The Arab geographers of the tenth century confirm that the shahristan had already been walled in pre-Islamic times (Barthold, 1928: 85). The physical expanse of the city was tremendous because, like any oasis, dwellings and vegetation needed to be contained within a common space. According to the geographer, Istakhri, "a considerable part of the area was occupied by gardens, almost each house possessing one; in viewing the town from the summit of the citadel no buildings were to be seen because of the trees in the gardens" (as cited in Barthold, 1928: 88).

In spite of the horrendous tales of Genghis Khan's conquest of the city—accounts of mass murders and massive deportations of artisans—it managed to survive. An eyewitness description of Samarkand in 1221 belies the scorched-earth image, suggesting instead that life continued, albeit on a much more modest scale. The account was written by a disciple who accompanied the Taoist hermit Ch'ang-Ch'un, who had been summoned by Genghis Khan in 1219 to give him religious instruction. Between 1221 and 1224 master and escort traveled throughout the Muslim territories. The *Si Yu Ki*, dated 1228, has been translated by Bretschneider (1875, I: 35–108). Toward the end of 1221 they entered Samarkand, which is described as being laid out on the borders of canals. "As it never rains in summer and autumn, the people have conducted two rivers to the city, and distributed the water through all the streets, so that every house can make use of it" (Bretschneider, 1875, I: 77–78).

Barthold uses this account to demonstrate that "life there [in Samarkand], not withstanding the devastation caused by the Mongols, went on its way. At the call of the mu'adhdhins both men and women hastened to the mosques . . . and those who failed to carry out this duty were severely punished. During Ramadan nights feasts were held as usual. *In the bazaars there was much merchandise*" (Barthold, 1928: 451, my italics). But the *Si Yu Ki* takes a dimmer view. It notes that only one-fourth of the former population was left after the conquest, that Muslim inhabitants were prevented from selling their lands but had to manage them under the supervision of Kara Khitais and the Chinese, and that "Chinese workmen are living everywhere" (Bretschneider, 1875, I: 78). In the spring of 1222, Ch'ang-Ch'un and his disciple returned by way of Samarkand but offer only additional ethnographic information (some of it bizarre).

There is very little information about the city during the ensuing 145 years when it was a provincial capital of the Mongols. However, assuredly, when trade flourished, so did Samarkand, and so did its sister city, Bukhara, connected by a "royal road" that allowed travelers to bridge the distance between them in 6–7 days (Barthold, 1928: 96). Like Samarkand, Bukhara was an ancient caravan city whose Magian merchants had been supplanted at the time of the Arab conquest (Barthold, 1928: 108). In Samanid times it, too, was divided into citadel, shahristan, and rabad, each separately walled (Barthold, 1928: 100), and like Samarkand, the city was irrigated by a diversion of the river and by canals. Al-Muqaddasi described the water system during Arab times: "The river enters the town on the Kallabadh side; here sluices are constructed, forming wide locks and built of timber. In the summer flood season, one after another of the beams is removed according to the height of the water . . . " (as cited in Barthold, 1928: 103). The prosperity of both cities depended on the state, not only for its water but, even more importantly, for the political and economic prosperity of the wider region. Since they were essentially critical stopping places, like other smaller caravanserais their vitality ultimately depended on the traffic. Soon there would be few to stop.

When trade declined, however, Samarkand survived by other means. Indeed, for a brief time it attained even greater importance. During the middle third of the fourteenth century the Mongol forces were in growing disarray, not only from internal dissension but from a thinning of their ranks from disease. Throughout the various parts of the empire, the ruled revolted. In China the rebellion resulted in the overthrow of the Yuan dynasty and its replacement in 1368 by the Ming. In Samarkand, the outcome was different. The beneficiary of the unrest was a Mongol, Timur i Leng (the lame Timur, known to us as Tamerlane), born near Samarkand and a putative, albeit distant, descendent of Chaghatai himself. He rose to prominence first in the 1357 disturbances in Transoxiana. These uprisings were followed by much confusion but the outcome was eventually clear, at least with respect to Samarkand. In 1370, Tamerlane proclaimed himself the new sovereign (and would-be restorer) of the Mongol empire; he did this in Samarkand, which became his privileged capital.

Thus, during that period of sharpest retrenchment in Central Asia, the late fourteenth and early fifteenth centuries, the condition of Samarkand improved relative to her rivals. During Tamerlane's rule Samarkand became the most important economic and cultural center of Central Asia. From a wide region Tamerlane asembled artisans and craftsmen who not only produced goods for a luxurious court life but embellished some of the still-standing architectural masterpieces. From Samarkand Tamerlane's troops set out in all directions to regather the fragmented pieces of the empire over which the former Pax Mongolica had been established. However, whereas the unity achieved under Genghis Khan and his immediate successors brought relative peace to his realms and encouraged travel and trade, the unity so brutally wrested by Tamerlane had the opposite effect. It severed the trans-Asian land routes, forcing commerce into increasingly narrow channels that had to pass through only a few land bottlenecks before spreading out into the Indian Ocean.

Chapters 6 and 7 examine these alternate passages eastward, but before moving on to a discussion of the Persian Gulf and Red Sea axes to the Indian Ocean, we might pause to consider a few of the lessons to be gleaned from the Mongols.

Lessons from the Mongol Case

The most striking lesson is that the economic role of facilitator, depending as it does on an ability to enforce its control over a wide zone, is basically an unstable one, subject to chance political and demographic fluctuations. In itself, unification does not necessarily reduce the overall costs of transit, but it has the potential to do so, depending upon policy choices. The chief contribution made by an administration based on "law and order" is a reduction in unpredictable protection rent. By eliminating competing tribute gatherers and by regularizing tolls, unification makes transport costs calculable. Furthermore, although it can scarcely eliminate natural disasters, such as droughts that dry up watering holes, it can reduce overall risk by virtually eliminating human predators. As long as these advantages can be assured, trade will flourish, but when roads become insecure, merchants seek other routes.

A second instability arises from the parasitic nature of tribute as a basis for the state. Since the Mongols neither traded nor produced, they were inordinately dependent upon the skills and the labor power of the peoples they conquered to ensure their livelihoods; their subjects therefore provided the means used to perpetuate their own continued oppression. An economy so ordered could not be generative. Enlightened self-interest might dictate the encouragement of commerce and industry and a certain restraint in appropriating surplus, but the demands of defense had their own imperative. If they went up, new sources of surplus had to be found.

Thus, the third instability comes from the need for continual geographic expansion. Like the Red Queen, the Mongols could not stand still. Expansion of surplus required the conquest of more and more productive units. And when new peoples could no longer be conquered, the system did not stabilize, it contracted. This contraction initiated an exponential cycle of decline. If expenses for control were cut back, restive captives might rebel; if oppressive measures were escalated, production might suffer, for surplus extraction was already at its maximum. Given this inherent instability, any new shock might topple the precarious system.

The shock appeared in the second third of the fourteenth century with the outbreak of the Black Death, which apparently spread fastest among the most mobile elements of the society, the army. Demographically weakened, the Mongols were less able to exert their control over their domains, which, one by one, began to revolt. Such revolts disturbed the smooth processes of production and appropriation on which the rulers depended, which in turn led to a reduced capacity to suppress the revolts. Once the process began, there was little to prevent its further devolution.

As the plague spread to the rest of the world system, the impulse to conduct long-distance trade was similarly inhibited, although it did not entirely disappear. But when trade revived, the myriad number of small traders sought more secure paths. These were, however, no longer in the forbidding wastes of Central Asia. The lower risks, and therefore lower protective rents along that route, were forever gone.

Notes

1. Balducci Pegolotti, of course, never claimed to have made this journey himself. But he had no hesitation in reassuring his readers that "The road you travel from Tana to Cathay is perfectly safe, whether by day or by night, according to what the merchants say who have used it" (Yule, 1924, II: 292).

2. Barfield (1990) offers a different interpretation. He suggests that the Central Asian tribes before Genghis Khan preferred "pay-offs" to direct conquest and therefore made deals with the Chinese state *not* to invade. However, this preference can only be conjectured. They *might* have wanted to conquer but been too weak to do so.

3. It is fascinating to read Rashid al-Din's vignettes on *The Successors of Genghis Khan* (Boyle, 1971: *passim*). The values of the society and its image of the "good ruler" projected through anecdotes and *biligs* (wise sayings) refute western and

and Muslim stereotypes of the Mongols as barbarians. Justice, wisdom, and generosity are the traits most admired. The latter, in particular, is routinely illustrated by the Khans' dealings with foreign merchants who are paid far more than the goods they offer are "worth." The elder Polo brothers slyly rejoice in the "gullibility" of Berke (Latham, 1958: 22), but the Khans, in turn, seem to have considered their largesse the ultimate demonstration of noblesse oblige.

4. The English historian, Matthew Paris (1200–1259), writing in 1240, certainly collapses these two identifications (see the lengthy extract quoted in Boyle, 1970, reprinted 1977: 6–7).

5. Compare, for example, the illustrations in de Rachewiltz (1971) with those in Lach (1965).

6. See J. Voporsanger, "The Travels of Benjamin of Tudela in the Twelfth Century," *Bulletin of the Geographical Society of California* II (May 1894): 77–96.

7. This account of graciousness, hospitality, and openness to trade is clearly at odds with the idea of "men from Hell," but is consistently maintained throughout Marco's memoirs.

8. "Les marchands italiens dans l'empire mongol" (Petech, 1962: 549–574).

9. The first Roman merchants arrived in China in A.D. 166, according to McNeill (1976: 101).

10. McNeill (1976) goes so far as to suggest that the rise of Islam in the seventh century was facilitated because Persian and Roman forces were weakened by the plague, but caution is required in using epidemiological conditions as a deus ex machina to account for change. Furthermore, it should be noted that McNeill's epidemiological explanation for the rise and fall of societies is particularly weak when applied to the two central regions—India and the Middle East—where contact had never been broken.

11. A Chinese historian has mapped for me the data, presented in McNeill's appendix, on dates and places of disease outbreaks. For the period in question, McNeill's hypotheses are not supported, since after the first inland outbreak, the disease appears to move immediately to the coast. See insert, Figure 7.

12. Barthold (1928: 88) claims that there were about 100,000 families in the town prior to Genghis Khan's invasion. "If we bear in mind that several years before this the town was devastated by the Khwarazm-shah, and that the Qara-Khanid epoch was on the whole one of decay in culture and consequently in civil life also, then we may, without exaggeration, conjecture that the Samarqand of the Samanids had more than 500,000 inhabitants." I am certain, however, that this *is* an exaggeration, given the economic base of the city. As we shall see, at its height the multifunctional capital of Cairo attained this size only briefly.

13. A farsakh is the distance a mule can travel in an hour, which makes it difficult to translate it into a linear measure. However, it is often estimated at three miles on flat terrain.

CHAPTER

6

Sindbad's Way:
Baghdad and the Persian Gulf

Of the three routes between Europe and the Far East, Sindbad's "middle way" through the Persian Gulf was the easiest, cheapest, and, not unexpectedly then, the most ancient and enduring. When it functioned well, this middle route through the Levant and Baghdad took precedence over all alternatives. When it experienced blockages, however, the routes north of it, overland from Constantinople, or to the south, by land through Egypt and then water via the Red Sea, became more essential.

Blockages occurred in the second half of the thirteenth century. One cause was the Mongol conquest of Mesopotamia and the subsequent demotion of Baghdad from Islamic capital and world trade emporium to provincial center of Mongol military rule and fiscal exploitation. In itself, this did not close European access to the Persian Gulf, for at first the traders simply shifted to the Il-Khan's preferred route, bypassing Baghdad and Basra and heading instead for Tabriz and its port outlet, Hormuz.

But two events made this alternative less attractive. When the

Il-Khans converted to Islam in 1295, they came under the same Papal injunction against trade with the "infidels" as the rest of the region. Furthermore, when the Crusaders lost their last port outlet on the Levant coast with the "fall" of Acre in 1291, many European traders repositioned themselves farther north (in Little Armenia), which made the northern overland route more attractive. Both of these events encouraged Europeans to follow the northeast passage through Central Asia, a process already described in Chapter 5. Other European traders relocated to Mediterranean islands from which the sea journey to Alexandria could easily be made; the transfer of their attention to Mamluk Egypt will be explored in Chapter 7. In the process, the middle route declined.

Muslim/Christian Trade

Neither the violence of the Crusades nor the repeated Papal injunction enjoining Europeans from trading with Muslims could interfere with the prosperous trade that in the twelfth and thirteenth centuries traversed the middle route. A deeply symbiotic relationship had developed over the years between the Christian merchants of the Crusader kingdoms and the Muslim merchants who brought them goods from the orient beyond. (See Figure 8.)

The prosperity of Acre, the chief port for the Crusader colonies from 1191 to 1291, depended on that trade. By mid-thirteenth century, Acre was firmly controlled by the Venetian colony that had gradually managed to exclude its rivals, the Genoese and the Pisans (Jacoby, 1977: 225–228). Busy buying and selling land, constructing buildings, concluding contracts, and conducting their affairs through a locally empowered court (see, for example, Prawer, 1951: 77–87 and Richard, reprinted 1976: 325–340), the Venetians seemed oblivious of the fact that their privileges were about to end.

Even after the establishment of Mamluk rule over Egypt and Syria in 1260, the Italians in Acre continued to receive both bulk goods from the immediate hinterland (taxed heavily) and the more precious goods of long-distance trade (more lightly taxed), which

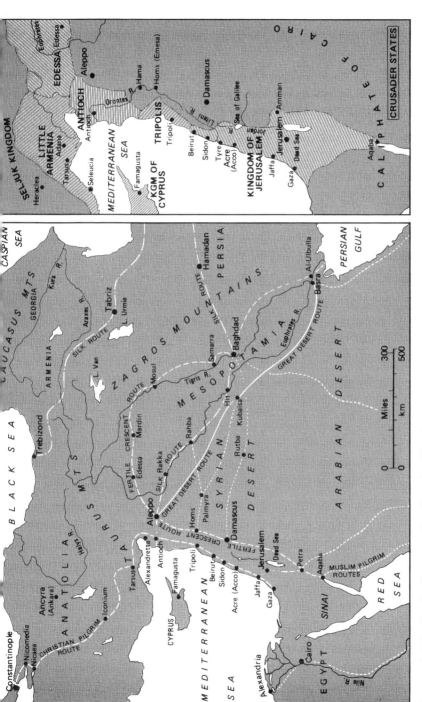

FIGURE 8. The Fertile Crescent, the Crusader Kingdoms and the way to India.

they reexported to Europe. Their trading partners were Muslims. According to Hilal (1983),[1] the Muslim merchants from the interior

did a profitable business with the Latin ports. . . . Syrian cities of the interior, such as Aleppo, Hama, and Hims, depended in part for their prosperity on the trade that they carried on through the Latin ports. . . . [T]reaties [between] . . . the Mamluk Sultan and the Latin powers guaranteed the safety of each other's traders, their ships, money and merchandise and their freedom in movements through their territories.

During the first half of his reign (ca. 1280–1285), the Mamluk sultan, al-Mansur Qalawun, maintained ostensibly peaceful political relations with the Latin states of Syria (Hilal, 1983: 119). As late as 1290, Qalawun, needing replacements for his troops, which Genoa provided by ship from the Black Sea area,[2] concluded yet another treaty with the Genoese that guaranteed the mutual safety of each's merchants (Hilal, 1983: 157). By then, however, the general level of trade across the inland route had already declined precipitously. It was to diminish even more, once the marriage of convenience between Crusaders and Mamluks broke down.

The truce between the two ended in 1291 when Qalawun's son and successor, al-Ashraf al-Khalil, finally drove the Crusaders from their last port stronghold at Acre. Although a Papal injunction against European trade with the "infidels" had been in force throughout the Crusades, it had hitherto been honored mostly in the breach. Now, however, "[i]n the face of the final collapse of the Christian holdings, and in view of the impossibility of gathering sufficient forces for an immediate reconquest, the effective enforcement of an embargo seemed to be the only reprisal possible."[3]

What were the Venetians and Genoese to do? If, indeed, Muslim intermediaries could no longer be used to gain access to the silks and spices of the Far East, new routes had to be found to bypass the heartland. One alternative, of course, was the northern overland route, which was increasingly used, as already seen. Another was to work through the Il-Khans of Persia who were not then adverse to European merchants crossing their territory. The conversion of Ghazan to Islam in 1295, however, soon put an end to this. The most daring alternative was to circumnavigate Africa via the Atlantic and thus gain sea access to the Indian Ocean. Interestingly enough, this was first attempted seriously in 1291.[4] Although the exact details of this event are shrouded in mystery, it appears that two brothers from Genoa, Ugolino and Vadino Vivaldi, set out by sea down the west coast of Africa, presumably in an effort to reach the Indies. They were never heard from again. Lopez speculates that "if the voyage of the Vivaldi brothers had been successful it would have supplied the Genoese with an alternative sea route to the Indies" (1943: 170). But the successful completion of their attempt had to wait another two centuries.

In the meantime, for trade to continue, the Europeans, whichever way they turned, had to deal with Muslims, the Papal injunction notwithstanding. Both land routes to the Indian Ocean passed through Muslim territory. The Egyptians were adamant that no European trader would be permitted to transit their country, either to carry European goods to India and China or to bring back far eastern goods. In Egypt, therefore, the Italians had no alternative but to deal with the powerful Karimi Muslim merchants (see Chapter 7) who monopolized the spice trade. The state was actively involved in these contacts. Not only were relations with European merchants regulated by the Egyptian state but, increasingly, the Mamluk sultans monopolized trade with the foreigners. The only "free" passage to the eastern seas theoretically open to European traders, then, was through Il-Khan territories to Hormuz on the Persian Gulf. From there they could set sail for India.

It is necessary to glance backward to the "Golden Age" of Islam (eighth and ninth centuries) to understand how important the route through the Persian Gulf had formerly been. Baghdad stood at the key crosspoint where the most heavily traveled land and sea routes to the Far East intersected; even after her decline, these routes persisted, albeit at lower levels.

Baghdad

A tenth century geography of the world (*Hudud al-'Alam*, Minorsky trans., 1937: 137)[5] described Iraq as "situated near to the centre of the world," and as the "most prosperous country in Islam," a "haunt of merchants, and a place of great riches. . . . "

Baghdad is called "the most prosperous town in the world" (*Hudud al-'Alam*, Minorsky trans., 1937: 138). However, in spite of this glowing description, the city had already declined since the days of Harun al-Rashid. By the late tenth century, when the Buyids were in control, the city was no longer of first rank, as al-Muqaddasi's detailed geography clearly reveals.

Al-Muqaddasi wrote his description of the Middle East in about 985–986,[6] based, in part at least, on his own direct singular experiences. He had traveled widely, combining scholarship with trade, not an atypical arrangement that he describes in his introduction (Ranking and Azoo trans.: 3, 14):

> I was wont . . . to buy and sell in every town, and associate with people of all classes, giving everywhere close attention to . . . this science [of geography]. I have measured the extent of the provinces . . . ; have travelled round the frontiers and defined their limits; visited the country towns. . . . I have also inquired into the revenues and estimated their amount. . . . I, myself, have travelled a course of about two thousand leagues over it and have made the circuit of the whole Peninsula from al-Qulzum [Red Sea] to 'Abbadan [Persian Gulf]. . . . I have plied [sailors] with questions . . . I have also seen in their possession charts and sailing directories which they constantly study and follow with implicit confidence.

He is quite explicit in explaining why, *ceteris paribus*, the Persian Gulf rather than the Red Sea was always the preferred sea access to the Orient. In contrast to the easily navigated Gulf, the Red Sea was treacherous for sailing because "the ground is overspread with huge rocks. . . . On this account, the passage is only made by day . . . " (Al-Muqaddasi, Ranking and Azoo trans.: 16). Furthermore, transit from the Red Sea to India required crossing the open sea, whereas ships traveling from the Gulf could hug the shore all the way.

We shall return to al-Muqaddasi's book when we trace the sea route to the east, since his work gives convincing evidence that Arab and Persian sailors and merchants were well acquainted with all parts of the Indian Ocean long before his time. At this point, however, let us look at his description of Baghdad toward the end of the tenth century, even though there is some ambiguity as to whether he is describing the metropolitan area of Baghdad, largely on the east bank of the Tigris, or is focusing more exclusively on Madinat al-Salam, the former royal city on the west bank, known to have been abandoned. He says (Ranking and Azoo trans.: 51)

> Know further that Baghdad was once a magnificent city, but is now falling to ruin and decay, and has lost all its splendour. . . . The Fustat of Misr [old Cairo] in the present day is like the Baghdad of old; I know no city in Islam superior to it [Fustat].

Or later (Ranking and Azoo trans.: 187–189):

> Baghdad is the great metropolis of Islam. . . . [Formerly, the Madinat al-Salam] was the best of all the possessions of the Muslims, and a most splendid city . . . but after that the power of the Caliphs declined, it fell from its former state, and its population dwindled. The City of Peace itself [the round city, Madinat al-Salam] is now in ruins . . . the town is daily going from bad to worse, and I fear it will one day become [abandoned] like Samarra.

According to Wiet (1971: 106), the Caliph had first been reduced to a figurehead under the Buyids, and the capital was further demoted by the Seljuks who did not even live in it. Nonetheless, something clearly remained, as seen in Khatib Baghdadi's (d. 1071) hyperbolic description of Baghdad under the Seljuks circa 1060 (as quoted in Wiet, 1971: 118):

> There is no city in the world equal to Baghdad in the abundance of its riches, the importance of its business, the number of its scholars and important people, the extent of its districts, the width of its boundaries, the great number of its palaces, inhabitants, streets, avenues, alleys, mosques, baths, docks and caravansaries. . . .

But even Baghdadi acknowledges a decline from the previous era (as quoted in Wiet, 1971: 118–119):

> The buildings and inhabitants were most numerous during the time of Harun al-Rashid. . . . Then the riots began, an uninterrupted series of misfortunes befell the inhabitants, its flourishing condition came to ruin to such an extent that, before our time, and the century preceding ours, it found itself, because of the perturbation and the decadence it

was experiencing, in complete opposition to all capitals and in contradiction to all inhabited countries.

Wiet's history of Baghdad chronicles an endless series of catastrophes in the late eleventh and twelfth centuries that cumulatively had major consequences: a famine in 1057, a fire in the same year followed by another two years later (Wiet, 1971: 107), damaging floods between 1069 and 1075, and numerous religious conflicts from 1075 on. Five months of disorder in 1077 were followed by pitched battles in the streets in 1088. Fires also recurred. In 1092 a major fire "destroyed the money-changers' markets and the *suqs* of the goldsmiths" and other fires broke out again in 1102, 1108, 1114, 1117, 1134, 1146, and 1154. Natural disasters compounded the problems. There was a bad flood in 1106, an earthquake in 1117, and other floods in 1174 and 1179. "Disorder in the streets went on as usual" in 1100, 1104, 1110, and 1118. And in 1123, "the lord of Hillah's Bedouins [even] attacked Baghdad. [Only] The Seljuk's help saved the caliph . . . " (Wiet, 1971: 122–127). Thus, Wiet (1971: 135) concludes that even before the Seljuk break up, "Baghdad had been nothing more than a regional capital. . . . After the departure of these Turkish masters, the caliph fancied himself the uncontested sovereign of the provincial city. . . . [but] Baghdad was merely the center of a phantom caliphate."

Even the Spanish pilgrim Ibn Jubayr, who stayed in Baghdad five days in 1184 (just at the end of Seljuk rule), lamented that although Baghdad was an ancient city that still served as the capital of the Abbasid Caliphate, "most of its traces have gone, leaving only a famous name. In comparison with its former state, before misfortune struck it and the eyes of adversity turned towards it, it is like an effaced ruin, a remain washed out, or the statue of a ghost" (as quoted in Wiet, 1971: 137–138). In all fairness, however, Ibn Jubayr seems to be referring only to the royal Round City, for in the rest of his description he speaks glowingly of the eastern bank city (as quoted in Wiet, 1971: 141–142).

The eastern part of the city has magnificent markets, is arranged on the grand scale and enfolds a population that none could count save God. It has three congregational mosques. . . . The full number of congregational mosques in Baghdad, where Friday prayers are said, is eleven. . . . The baths in the city cannot be counted.

Clearly, the sources are inconclusive. When they compare Baghdad with the past, they see decline, but when they compare her to most other places, they see an undeniably active economy, in part bolstered by the heightened demands of the export trade.

Industry continued to thrive throughout. During the Buyid period cloth-making remained important. "Eager to have luxurious materials manufactured in their capital, the caliphs brought teams of weavers from Tuster, in Susiana." City workshops produced "a growing output of superb silk and brocaded materials." In medieval Italy there was a special cloth brocaded with gold, known by the word for Baghdad, and also a cloth called *attabi*, made of silk and cotton, named for one of the city quarters (Wiet, 1971: 101). Furthermore, even during Seljuk times "Baghdad produced cotton cloth, silk materials, matting, shaped crystal, glass, ointments, potions and electuaries . . . [which] were the principal exports" (Wiet, 1971: 117).

These activities, however, declined drastically in the second half of the thirteenth century with Hulegu's conquest of Iraq. Not only did the Mongols bleed the economy but they established their capital at rival Tabriz, which deflected European traders away from Baghdad and her port, Basra, to the Mongol's Gulf outlet at Hormuz.

The Fall of Baghdad

In marked contrast to European ignorance about the Mongols, the Baghdadis were keenly aware of the potential threat they posed. Indeed, early in the thirteenth century a panic-stricken Caliph Nasir had called upon the Ayyubids for protection against Genghis Khan. Fortunately, it was only a false alarm, since the Ayyubids were then too busy battling the Crusaders to come to his aid (Wiet, 1971: 151). Several times subsequently—in 1236, 1238, 1243, and again in 1252—the Mongols made forays in the direction of Baghdad; each time the population mobilized, only to be saved when the Mongol forces veered off or withdrew after inflicting damage

(Wiet, 1971: 151–163). Perhaps these false alarms lulled the city into complacency. For even when there was a persistent rumor in 1257 that the Mongol army under Hulegu was approaching the city, the Caliph remained transfixed, unable to organize an adequate defense. By January 11, 1258, the Mongols had completely surrounded the city and by February 5, their banners flew in triumph above the city walls. Five days later, the Caliph was executed (Wiet, 1971: 164–165).

We have a number of graphic descriptions of the fall of Baghdad in 1258, some based on hearsay (Ibn Athir and the Chinese sources)[7] and some based upon eyewitness accounts at the time or soon after the event. Most have the tone of tragic poetry, for the Muslim world viewed this as one of the great catastrophes of history. My favorite is the account (in Persian) by Wassaf, reproduced here in the English translation of Spuler (1972: 120–121):

> In the morning, when the orange of Zulaikha' [the sun] was placed at the rim of the dish of the horizon and the light by sleight of hand had conjured away from the mercury blanket of the sky the imprint seals of the stars, the Ilkhan [Hulegu] ordered the army to carry the torch of plunder and robbery into Baghdad. . . . First of all they razed to the ground the walls . . . and filled the moat which was as deep as the contemplation of rational men. Then, they swept through the city like hungry falcons attacking sheep, with loose rein and shameless faces, murdering and spreading fear. . . . The massacre was so great that the blood of the slain flowed in a river like the Nile, red as the wood used in dyeing, and the verse of the Koran: "Both seed and stem perished" was recited about the goods and riches of Baghdad. With the broom of looting, they swept out the treasures from the harems of Baghdad, and with the hammer of fury, they threw down the battlements head first as if disgraced. . . . And a lament reached the ears . . . from roofs and gates. . . . Beds and cushions made of gold and encrusted with jewels were cut to pieces with knives and torn to shreds; those hidden behind the veils of the great harem . . . were dragged like the hair of idols through the streets and alleys; each of them became a plaything in the hands of a Tatar monster. . . .

No European description of the People from Hell rivaled this tale of horror. And yet, was Baghdad fully destroyed or did it, like Samarkand, rise again?

Scholars have yet to provide a definitive answer to this question, although to date, Ashtor's chapter on "Irak Under Mongol and

Turcoman Feudal Lords" (1976: 249–279) gives the fullest account of the general context. Keith Weissman (University of Chicago: lecture January 23, 1986) is examining the chronicles to evaluate the condition of Baghdad under the Mongols. He suggests that the lacuna of information about Baghdad between 1258 and the Ottoman conquest some 600 years later is, in itself, an important indicator of the reduced importance of the city. The fact that Islamic scholars no longer discuss the city and travelers seldom mention it suggests that the major trade routes no longer went through Baghdad.[8] Weissman argues that Baghdad's decline was political, economic, demographic, and social. Ashtor provides the larger context within which this was happening. For both, the primary account of Rashid al-Din (vizir to a later Muslim "reformist" Il-Khan) constitutes a central source. (See the relevant selections from this document that are reproduced in Spuler, English trans., 1972: 115–164 variously.)

Political demotion certainly occurred. After 1258 the city was reduced to a provincial capital, ruled from Tabriz; the Mongol presence was in the form of a military garrison headed by an amir and, during the thirteenth century, the Il-Khan visited it only a few times (Weissman, 1986). That did not, however, indicate a lack of interest in Baghdad's potential as a source of revenue. The feudal regime established by the Il-Khans imposed oppressive taxes, particularly on the townspeople who incurred great losses through forced purchases, commercial taxes, and the billeting of tax collectors (called messengers!). "The taxation of the townspeople was ... a merciless exploitation. The contemporary Arabic chronicler Ibn al-Fuwati relates how quite often heavy contributions were extorted from the inhabitants of Baghdad" (Ashtor, 1976: 250). These heightened taxes were imposed in spite of the general decline in the region's prosperity and productivity.

Economic decline also was evident, since long-distance trade routes bypassed Baghdad, although it remained a center for regional commerce. Ashtor (1976: 263) tells us that for fifty years after its conquest by the Mongols, Baghdad's regular trade with Syria and Egypt was cut off, resuming only at the beginning of the fourteenth century. What was even more serious, the trade with India was disrupted (Ashtor, 1976: 264).

> Until its conquest by the Mongols a great part of the spices and other Indian articles had been shipped to Basra and thence carried via Baghdad and Antioch to the shores of the Mediterranean. After the establishment of Mongol rule, Tabriz became not only the capital of the Il-Khans but also a great emporium of international trade. . . . Ten years after the conquest of Baghdad the sultan of Cairo captured Antioch, which had been the great commercial town at the other end of the overland route along which the Indian articles were transported from the Persian Gulf to the Mediterranean. The enmity between the rulers of Tabriz and Cairo, or rather the almost permanent state of war between them, was another reason for the shift of this great trade route. From that time a considerable part of the Indian articles which arrived on the shores of the Persian Gulf were sent to Tabriz and then on routes north . . . to Little Armenia.

These bypassed not only Baghdad but also the older Mediterranean outlets of Aleppo and Antioch[9] whose Christian merchants had moved to Famagusta on Cyprus or to Little Armenia to keep the letter, if not the intent, of the Pope's injunction against trade with Muslims.

Agricultural productivity also declined under the Mongols, and Baghdad suffered from periodic famines. Rashid al-Din (as cited in Ashtor, 1976: 260) complained that only one-tenth of Iraq's land was being cultivated and Weissman claims that the revenues of the province fell 90 percent between 1258 and 1335. Because of the shortages, there was constant inflation and currency devaluation. The disastrous combination of falling wealth and an exploitative revenue-extraction system placed a heavier tax burden on the smaller population that remained.

"The decrease of population which had begun shortly after the dismemberment of the caliphate became rapid after the Mongol conquest" (Ashtor, 1976: 253). In Baghdad, this was reflected in a gradual abandonment of parts of the city. By the latter thirteenth century, Baghdad contained many deserted neighborhoods, particularly on the western bank, and new construction was minimal. Furthermore, between 1290 and the 1330s, there was even some emigration from Baghdad to Cairo, as evidenced by the Iranian–Iraqi influence on Cairo constructions during the time of al-Nasir Muhammad (Weissman, 1986).

The decline of Baghdad was paralleled by difficulties in the port outlet of Basra, which had always mediated its Indian trade. Basra was one of the two planned towns (the other was Kufa) established by the Arabs when they first conquered Mesopotamia in the seventh century. Al-Muqaddasi, writing toward the end of the tenth century, considered Basra superior even to Baghdad, "on account of its ample resources and the great number of godly people in it" (Al-Muqaddasi, Ranking and Azoo trans.: 184).[10] It produced fine quality silk and linen cloth, was a source of pearls and precious stones, and a place in which antimony and verdigris were processed, but above all it was an indispensable seaport and emporium through which passed the goods of the Indies and from which dates, henna, floss silk, violets, and rosewater were exported to all countries (Al-Muqaddasi, Ranking and Azoo trans.: 205–206).

However, Basra's fortune was distinctly tied to that of Baghdad whose port it was. With Baghdad's decline, its prosperity could not be sustained, particularly after Tabriz, the Il-Khanid capital, became the major emporium. An alternative route to the Gulf— one that went directly to Hormuz on the Persian side near the mouth of the Gulf—began to draw commerce away from Basra.

Thus, during the second half of the thirteenth century, the middle route was undergoing a decisive reorganization. Baghdad, its gateway city Basra, and indeed the entire Gulf zone were declining. On the Mediterranean coast, the Crusader ports that had hosted the Italian merchants who transshipped eastern goods to Europe were tottering, one after the other, the last gone by 1291. It was inevitable that commerce in the Gulf should have been negatively affected. This was more than a minor loss. For this route to the Indies had been the most important link between the western Muslim world and "Hind" (India) and "Sin" (China) during the great period of Arab commercial hegemony. This had been Sindbad's Way.

The Gulf Route to the East

The rise of Islam in the early seventh century and its expansion to a vast empire by the end of the eighth century had created a unity that even the later Mongol conquests would never rival.[11]

This empire facilitated the flowering of the overland caravan trade in a fashion similar to that described in Chapter 5. It was in the expansion of sea routes, however, that the unification of the two great ancient river valley civilizations— Mesopotamia nurtured by the Tigris and the Euphrates, and Egypt nurtured by the Nile— was most evident.

Just before the unification, at the apex of Sassanid power in the fifth and sixth centuries, whatever sea trade still existed with the east was dominated by the Persians and passed through "their" Gulf; activity through the less navigable Red Sea had declined with the eclipse of Roman power (Toussaint, 1966: 45). However, this was to change during the early period of Islamic hegemony.

The Arabian Peninsula, from which Islam was carried in both directions, is bound on the west by the Red Sea and on the east by the Persian Gulf. As long as the center of the empire remained on the peninsula, both waterways were equally functional. With the Arabs, Egyptians, and Persians newly unified under the common rule and ideology of Islam, the Persian Gulf and Red Sea ceased to be rival routes (Hourani, 1951: 52) but became two arms of the same sea (the Erythrean), as they had been in the age of Alexander (Toussaint, 1966: 48).[12]

Dynastic rule did not stay in the peninsula, however. It moved first to Damascus, the capital of the Umayyads, and then to Baghdad, with the victory of the Abbasids. These shifts exerted a gravitational force on the trade routes, which became increasingly concentrated on the Gulf as the Red Sea became an ancillary arm of the mainstream.

Before the unification of Persia with the Arab world, Persian sailors had dominated the Gulf's long-distance trade with the east, even China (Hourani, 1951: 47). Now Arabs became equally active participants. Hourani's study (1951: 61) shows how

the Arabs inherited this traffic, prospering in it despite interruptions. This sea route, from the Persian Gulf to Canton, was the longest in regular use by mankind before the European expansion in the sixteenth century. . . . The . . . sea trade between the Persian Gulf and China at this period in history [seventh through ninth centuries] was made possible by the simultaneous existence of large empires at both ends of the route. The whole Moslem world from Spain to al-Sind was united under the Umayyad caliphs (A.D. 660–749), and for over a century

(750–870) under the 'Abbasids. . . . In China, the T'ang dynasty (618–907) ruled a united empire until its closing years. . . .

Under such felicitous conditions it was natural that trade should have flourished, even though the Persians continued to dominate it at first. References to their ships appear in Chinese documents as early as 671 and reappear in accounts of 717, 720, 727, and 748, when Persians are identified, along with Indians and Malaysians, as owners of ships at Canton (Hourani, 1951: 62).

The first time Chinese sources mention the Arabs specifically is in 758 in connection with a joint raid the Ta-shih (Arabs) and the Po-sse (Persians) made against Canton. This suggests that a noticeable Arab colony had been newly established in the far east (Hourani, 1951: 63; Toussaint, 1966: 51), a fact not unrelated to the founding of Baghdad as the Abbasid capital in 750, which clearly stimulated more adventurous sea travel to the East. After the attack, the Chinese closed the port to "foreign trade" (Toussaint, 1966: 51), but that proved only a temporary interruption to what continued to be expanding, if sometimes conflictual, relations between the Arabs and the Chinese. Canton was reopened in 792 and was visited steadily thereafter by Muslim ships and merchants.

One hundred years after the establishment of Baghdad as the capital of the Islamic empire, a remarkable document was written that detailed the extent to which Arab and Persian sailors, exiting the Gulf, had become "at home" in the Arabian Sea, the Indian Ocean, and even the South China Sea. The descriptions of the voyage and the ports of call leave no doubt that by 851, when Sulayman the merchant[13] wrote his account (to which Abu-Zayd al-Sirafi put his finishing touches a century later), the trade path between the Persian Gulf and China—via the Malabar coast of India, Ceylon, the Nicobar Islands, Kalah on the Malay Peninsula, the Strait of Malacca, past Cambodia and Vietnam to Canton—was already well established and of great interest to Arabic readers. Indeed, Mas'udi, who perhaps conferred with Abu-Zayd when he met him in Basra on his way to India (Shboul, 1979: 53–55), relates many of the same facts. These texts will be examined in more detail in Part III. Here we simply note that their existence indicates that considerable trade between China and the Arab world was already occurring before the mid-ninth century.

Although Toussaint (1966: 51) claims that the "frightful massacre" of Arabs in Canton in 878 "put an end to the Moslem settlement" in Chinese ports, and that afterward "the Arab merchants merely met the Chinese at the port of Kalah Bar in Malaya," this is not strictly true. The massacre had been but a symptom of the general unrest in China from 875 onward,[14] and once order had been restored, the trade voyages began again.

Direct sea voyages between the Gulf and the Chinese coast resumed sometime after the Sung came to power, since two primary documents from China give clear evidence of regular visits to Chinese ports by ships from Western Asia during those times. We have an early thirteenth-century document written by Chau Ju-Kua, the Chinese official whose job was to greet and then control foreign ships, including those of the Ta-Shih (Arabs from Mesopotamia), entering a Chinese "treaty port," and a second, based on the biography of a late thirteenth-century Chinese agent of Arab descent, P'u Shou-keng, who was in charge of foreign traders in Fukien during the transition from Sung to Yuan times.[15] (See Chapter 10 for more details.)

Ships sailing to China from Mesopotamia and Persia exited the Persian Gulf and then skirted the western coast of Sind (today's Pakistan) and Hind (today's India), making frequent port calls and seldom out of sight of land. The monsoon winds allowed them to cross the open sea from Muscat-Oman to India, but boats were small (see Bowen, 1949 and 1951, for information on twentieth-century dhows and their earlier prototypes) and navigational methods were still primitive. In the tenth century, the Arabs had only the sidereal rose, a method of plotting locations via the polar star that the Persians had used before them. By the thirteenth century if not before, however, Arab navigators were supplementing star navigation with the floating compass the Chinese had employed a century or so earlier (Teixeira da Mota, 1964: 51–60).

At the Malabar coast near the southwestern tip of the Indian subcontinent, often at the port of Quilon, they might meet other Arab sailors coming via the less important Red Sea route. Leaving Qulzum in Egypt or Jeddah on the Arabian Peninsula, such ships, after stops at Aden and Hadramaut, took off across the open sea to reach Malabar. There, the two routes joined, rounding the tip to skirt or stop at Ceylon, and then possibly continuing up the eastern coast of India to what is now Madras. From the Coromandel coast of India, the ships set out toward the Strait of Malacca, either meeting Chinese merchants there (whenever China closed its ports to foreigners) or proceeding all the way to such Chinese "treaty" ports as Canton and Zaytun (Ch'uan-chou) or sometimes continuing even farther north to the port that served Hangchow. In all cases, however, trade using the Persian Gulf had to exit that narrow waterway into the Arabian Sea by passing through the Strait of Hormuz. [See Figure 9.]

Guarding the Strait

A number of tiny city-states and principalities near the entrance to the Gulf took advantage of their strategic location to capture either parts of the transit trade itself or a direct "tribute" toll from merchant ships wishing to pass. Some, such as Suhar in Oman on the western shore and Siraf on the eastern littoral, became trade entrepôts in their own right. They were places at which merchants coming from Baghdad–Basra, from China and India, and from the Red Sea via Aden might exchange their wares with others arriving from diverse directions. These entrepôt ports were similar to the more important caravanserais located where land routes crossed. Others, such as Hormuz, were the port cities for imperial domains; they owed their competitive position not only to the advantages of their natural harbors but to the political preferences and the fluctuating strength of the empires to which they gave access. Finally, some, like the isle of Qais (Kish), might at times—to put it harshly—become mere pirates' lairs, from which predator vessels sailed to plunder the richly ladened merchant ships.

Although in the ultimate sense these small units could not increase the total amount of trade that passed through the portal they guarded—since *that* depended mostly on supplies and demands at core areas far away—they could from time to time and to a greater or lesser degree block the long-distance trade that normally used the route they guarded, either reducing overall trade by raising protection costs or deflecting it to alternative routes. As in the Central Asian overland route examined in Chapter 5, risk and the costs of protection went down when a single unifying power kept small entrepreneurial tribute gatherers and independent pre-

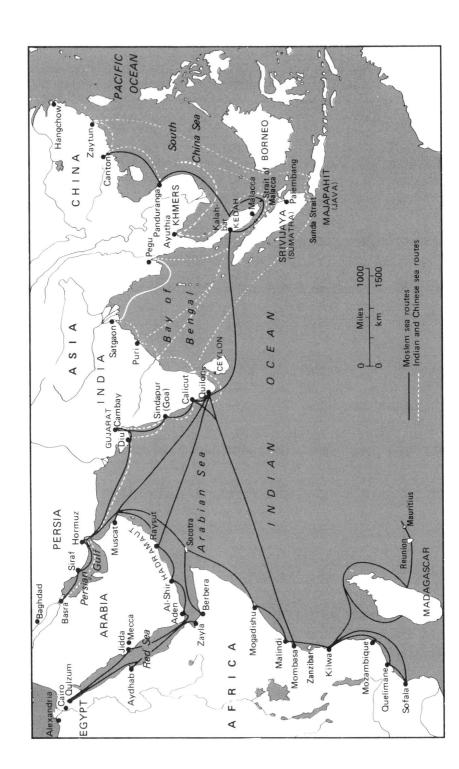

dators from interfering with goods transiting by sea; when imperial power broke down, both costs increased.

During the ninth and tenth centuries, when Abbasid power was strong, there seems to have been synergism between the growth of Baghdad's trade and the prosperity not only of Basra at the head of the Gulf, but of the entrepôts closer to the Strait. Oman, and particularly its port of Suhar on the Arabian Peninsula side, was a major beneficiary. Al-Muqaddasi (Ranking and Azoo trans.: 49–50), writing in the late tenth century, lists Oman as one of the three places in the Muslim world most conducive to gaining commercial riches (the other two were Aden and Fustat), and calls Suhar together with Aden "the vestibule of as-Sin" (China). With his usual exuberance, al-Muqaddasi notes (Ranking and Azoo trans.: 142) that

> Suhar is the capital of ʿUman. There is not on the Sea of China at the present time a more important town than this. It is a flourishing and populous city . . . of wealth and many merchants. . . . [It] is the gateway to China and the emporium of the East and al-ʿIraq. . . . The Persians are masters of it.

That it was a great entrepôt for exchange is clear from al-Muqaddasi's list (Ranking and Azoo trans.: 148) of its exports—drugs, perfumes (even musk), saffron, teakwood, ivory, pearls, onyx, rubies, ebony, sugar, aloes, iron, lead, canes, earthenware, sandalwood, glass, and pepper—since, with the possible exception of pearls, virtually every item listed originated somewhere else along the path of long-distance trade.

Although al-Muqaddasi has less to say about the entrepôt of Siraf on the Persian side of the Gulf, it too appears to have been a prosperous port. It will be recalled that the navigational and descriptive document begun by the merchant Sulayman in 851, was completed a century later by a man named Sirafi (coming from Siraf). Ibn Hawqal, a tenth century geographer, described Siraf as a great port of the Persian Gulf, although by then some of its merchants had relocated to Suhar. As we shall see, there is evidence that even after its presumed decline, it continued to be the home of extremely wealthy merchants trading with China well into the twelfth century (Aubin, 1959: 287–99; Heyd, 1885: 165).

It is therefore perplexing that so great a historian of the Middle

East as Jean Sauvaget (1940: 11–20) should have argued, on the basis of the *absence* of Arabic navigational instruction manuscripts between the eleventh and fourteenth centuries, that maritime traffic between the Persian Gulf and the seas of India was no longer of more than marginal and intermittent significance during those centuries (Aubin, 1964: 166). Just as likely an explanation for the lack of new manuscripts would be that the route had become so well known, and the earlier nautical instructions so perfected, that new ones were no longer needed.[16] Certainly, a similar absence of nautical manuals for the Red Sea area does not indicate an interruption of trade, as Aubin (1964: 165–171) points out in his critique of Sauvaget's theory. Aubin argues that there are multiple proofs that intense trade continued to ply the Persian Gulf throughout the period between the eleventh and fourteenth centuries, even though Arab sailors may no longer have dominated it.

In spite of Baghdad's decreasing dominance from the eleventh century on, which suggests that there may have been some shift in overall traffic away from the Persian Gulf and toward the Red Sea, commerce between the Gulf and China continued to yield large fortunes to merchants. To illustrate this, an anonymous twelfth-century annotator of Ibn Hawqal's geography gave the following description of some of Siraf's richest merchants (Stern, 1967: 10):

> I was told that one of them, feeling ill, made his testament; the third part of his fortune, which he had in cash, amounted to a million [gold] *dinars*, not counting the capital which he laid out to people who undertook to trade with it on *commenda* basis. Then there is Ramisht. . . . [His son] told me that the silver plate used by him was . . . 1,200 *manns*. . . . Ramisht has four servants, each of whom is said to be richer than his son. . . . I have met . . . Ramisht's clerk, and he told me that when he came back from China twenty years before, his merchandise was worth half a million *dinars*; if that is the wealth of his clerk, what will he himself be worth!

Even discounting exaggerations and the hearsay character of this evidence, it would be hard to argue that the China trade had dried up or that the entrepôts along the Persian Gulf lay in ruins! The weakened power of Baghdad does, however, seem to have allowed independent entrepreneurial enclaves to compete with one another for the trade or spoils that passed through the Gulf.

One such competitor was the island of Qais (Kish), whose sailors exploited its key location to block passage or to raid merchant ships. By the end of the eleventh century the so-called pirates of Qais were already operating freely, which reduced Siraf's viability as a port (Idrisi as cited in Heyd, 1885: 164, 378; Aubin, 1959; 1964: 164), and in the early part of the twelfth century these predators were notorious.[17] By then they seem to have bested all their competitors to become the "chief port of the India and China trade" (Stern, 1967: 14). In spite of the dominance of Qais, however, the ports on the Arabian side continued to receive trading ships up to the thirteenth century (Heyd, 1885: 164–165).

The Mongol conquest of Persia and Iraq in the second half of the thirteenth century served to speed up local changes that were already underway. Baghdad, already in decline, was deprived of its status as titular capital, and even Basra, with the demotion of her chief destination, lost her importance as the primary gateway to Baghdad and then the Mediterranean. The two intermediaries that gained most from the new arrangement of power were Hormuz and Qais. By 1291, when Marco Polo traversed the middle route, the main path used by Europeans went overland to the Il-Khanid capital of Tabriz and then down the Persian coast to the off-shore port of the empire, Hormuz.[18] The other intermediary entrepôt, of even greater importance for Muslim merchants, was the island of Qais, which, during Mongol times, operated a large fleet and had become a prime entrepôt for the Asian trade (Aubin, 1964: 14; Heyd, 1885: 165).

Hormuz continued to be the *primus inter pares*, however, for an Asian trade that continued throughout the next few centuries, even after the Il-Khans had been Islamized. Perhaps not without significance, it was the destination port for the very last ships from China to sail into the Gulf—the fleet of Admiral Cheng Ho that came in the early fifteenth century, just before the Ming Dynasty's sudden introversion (see Chapter 10).

The Decline (for Whom?) of the Middle Route

Thus, although the Mongol conquest of Iraq and Persia altered many of the local patterns of port distribution in the Gulf—patterns that had persisted throughout the period of increasing anarchy during late Abbasid times—the Mongols cannot be blamed for destroying the middle trade route to the Far East. Not only did trade with India–China persist after Hulegu's appearance but it took on a new life, as a result of the presence—albeit short-lived— of Italian merchants in the Il-Khanid realm. Even after al-Ghazan's conversion to Islam, Italians still attempted to continue its use, although it could no longer be defended as a viable alternative for the European traders seeking to avoid direct dealings with Muslims.

Ghazan's conversion did have one important effect, however. In the early fourteenth century it led to a temporary halt in the endemic war between the "Mongol" Il-Khans and the "Egyptian" Mamluks[19] (the latter, by then, ruling Syria, including its coastal plain at the Mediterranean). Trade between the two key regions of the heartland recommenced. When it did, the Italian traders lost out; they were no longer as needed and therefore as tolerated in the Il-Khan kingdom as they had been before. The Persians no longer offered them a less restricted and cheaper route to Asia than the one that passed through the Gulf's real competitor, Egypt and the Red Sea. And competitors they certainly were, in spite of the fact that both states were now ruled by Muslims. Whereas the early Islamic empire had unified the two major subregions, making both routes to the Far East part of the same trade system, the temporary truce between the Il-Khans and the Mamluks had no such effect. In the fourteenth century, the Gulf and the Red Sea were rival seas.

Nor was the middle route as attractive to the Italian traders, once the Christian footholds on the Syrian coast were gone. To understand why the middle route declined in importance in the thirteenth and fourteenth centuries, it is necessary to look not only eastward to the Gulf but also, and perhaps more significantly, westward to the Mediterranean. As seen, there were temporary interruptions and periods of slowdown in the Persian Gulf, but traffic to India and beyond never stopped. If the Europeans no longer depended so heavily on this route, it was not because the route had ceased to operate but because the European enclaves at the Mediterranean coast were no longer as conveniently located with respect to it. We have already discussed the end of the Crusader kingdom in 1291 and the retreat of the Italian merchants either to islands such as Cyprus and Crete or to Little Armenia farther north. This shift had two important effects.

On the one hand, for those traders who shifted to Little Armenia or the Black Sea ports, the attractiveness of the northern overland route was enhanced. Given the relative calm and safety throughout this region during the reign of Kubilai Khan and his immediate successor, this shorter direct route to Cathay became competitive, since (as John of Monte Corvino pointed out in his letter, quoted in Chapter 5) it was considerably shorter, taking less than a year to traverse in contrast to the two years required to go by sea via Tabriz and the Gulf. It was the route of the Genoese, par excellence.

On the other hand, for those merchants who transferred their operations to islands in the Mediterranean, other alternatives were preferable. The Venetians in particular, blocked from depending heavily on the northern route by the Genoese, who controlled the Black Sea gateway, and now deprived as well of their enclaves on the Syrian shore, concentrated their attention on the Mamluks who held the key to the sea route to the Indies. Although the Venetians might have preferred their old route—through Syria to Baghdad or Tabriz to the Gulf and then to the Indian Ocean— they were no longer in a position to exercise their preferences. They were at the mercy of the Mamluk state of Egypt, which now controlled coastal Syria and Palestine as dependent provinces, and of Mamluk–Ghazanid relations, which determined whether and how much transit between Syria and the Gulf would be allowed. We examine the relationship of the Venetians to the Mamluk state in Chapter 7, in which we also detail the way commerce and industry were conducted in Islamic realms. But before proceeding, we must consider what can be learned from the current case.

Lessons from the Baghdad–Persian Gulf Case

It is evident that the decline of Baghdad and of the centrality of the Gulf route is explainable only in part by purely local and exclusively economic factors. It can be fully understood only within the context of changes in the geopolitical system of the larger region and, indeed, of the world system.

The Gulf's strategic location on what Hourani termed the oldest water route of mankind was a geographic given of long-term historic significance. It was a navigable waterway linking the Indian subcontinent with the Middle East heartland and then the Mediterranean Sea via several good land routes—either paralleling the Euphrates River extension to Aleppo and then to Antioch on the coast or crossing a relatively narrow desert land stretch to Damascus and the Mediterranean beyond. As early as the third and second millennia before Christ, this route had connected (and indeed facilitated the rise of) ancient civilizations along it—Ebla near Aleppo, Sumer in lower Iraq, Dilmun on the island of Bahrain in the Persian Gulf, and the civilization of Harappa and Mohenjo-daro in the Indus Valley (now Pakistan). If ever a route had proven comparative advantage, this was it.

If location alone were the only or overriding factor, it could naturally be anticipated that trade routes would always be concentrated there. The general route would be a constant. The only variations would be in the quantity of goods flowing from one place to another and the range over which trade took place—sometimes contracting to the core connection between Mesopotamia and its nearest neighbors and sometimes spreading to more distant extremities, depending upon transportation, demand, and the state of peace.

However, as seen, the fluctuations were wider than geographic factors alone would have predicted. The centrality of location meant that even in the worst of times the Gulf would be used, albeit at a lower rate.[20] But location alone could not guarantee that the route would carry significant transit trade or would retain its prime position over its potential rivals. Three factors of larger significance determined these.

First, of lesser importance because it could simply interfere with but not generate trade, was the state of "order" in the Gulf itself. Fragmentation of control, then as now, increased protection costs and risks and might therefore encourage some merchant traders whose ultimate port of call was not on the Gulf itself to choose an alternative route. As will be seen in Chapter 7, then as now, the route through Egypt constituted the only real alternative until the circumnavigation of Africa and, for the heartland region itself, constituted the only *reasonable* alternative. Even though Arab sailors had rounded the Cape of Good Hope long before the Europeans, this did not constitute a valuable route for them, since they had access to shorter and more convenient ways.

Second, unification of Persia and Iraq usually encouraged trade through the Gulf by creating a secure transit environment and a prosperous hinterland that, by increasing local production and markets and stimulating the demand for imports, facilitated trade. When these two regions were joined and under common rule, as they were in the early Islamic period, not only was there an agricultural revolution of enormous importance (see Watson, 1981: 29–58) but all elements of civilization—from intellectual development to industrial productivity, as well as thriving commerce and trade—flourished. Conversely, the break up of that unity always inhibited trade and culture.

Unification, however, was not the only variable, as the period of the Mongol conquest proves. Iraq and Persia were unified under the Il-Khanids, but that was not sufficient. A final factor proved even more important. This was the relative health of economic conditions at both ends of the Indian Ocean trade path. In an ultimate sense, these determined just how much trade there would be—whether through the Gulf or via some other route. When the Arab World and China were both prosperous—as they were in the ninth and tenth centuries—the efflorescence of trade that occurred was to be expected. And when Europe was added to this mix by the twelfth century, the system received an added impetus. On the other hand, when conditions collapsed at both ends, as they did in the second third of the fourteenth century, the link between them inevitably declined as well. In the competition for a declining quantity of trade in the fourteenth and fifteenth centuries, the Gulf (under the Ghazanids) and the Red Sea (under the Mamluks) once again became rival routes rather than two arms of the same sea. And in that competition, the clear winner was Egypt.

Notes

1. See the very interesting unpublished thesis by Adil Ismail Muhammad Hilal, "Sultan al-Mansur Qalawun's Policy with the Latin States of Syria 1279–90, and the Fall of Acre" (American University in Cairo, 1983: quotation 114–115).

2. The Il-Khans had closed the overland route by which new Mamluk recruits had usually been sent, temporarily giving the Genoese a special monopoly of which they took full advantage.

3. See in particular Robert Lopez (1943: 164–174; quoted from p. 170).

4. There had been several earlier attempts to sail down the western coast of Africa. "About the year 1270 . . . a Genoese fleet commanded by Lancelot Malocello entered the Atlantic, and . . . reached the Canaries" (Toussaint, 1966: 95).

5. This universal geography is a remarkable demonstration of the sophisticated level of Muslim knowledge about the world. Not only are all areas from the Atlantic to the China Sea included, but the book begins matter of factly with a simple declarative statement—one whose validity would not be accepted in Europe until 500 years later! "The earth is round as a sphere and the firmament enfolds its turning on two poles, . . . the North Pole and . . . the South Pole" (*Hudud al-'Alam*, Minorsky trans., 1937: 50).

6. See Muhammad ibn Ahmad al-Muqaddasi, *Ahsanu t-Taqasim fi Marifati-l-Aqalim*, translated by G. S. A. Ranking and R. F. Azoo. Calcutta: 1897–1910.

7. See D. S. Richards, "Ibn Athir and the Later Parts of the *Kamil*: A Study in Aims and Methods" (1982: 76–108), for an evaluation of his biased account based on hearsay evidence. Contrast this with the rather bland nonevaluative renderings of the same event in the Chinese sources reproduced in Bretschneider (1875: I: 118–139), the *Si Shi Ki*, and the biography of Kuo K'an. Clearly, the "interests" of the writer determine the way an event is recounted.

8. Only a dozen years after its presumed destruction, however, Marco Polo describes Baghdad as a large and prosperous city. As seen, Arab/Persian sources often distinguish between the royal city (Madinat al-Salam) on the west bank of the Tigris, which was evidently completely destroyed, and the commercial city on the east bank, which continued as a center of production and trade. This distinction may account for the discrepancies among descriptions.

9. In 1260, the Mongol troops under Hulegu essentially destroyed Aleppo. "Ruined and half-deserted, Aleppo would not recover from the carnage for another century" (Humphreys, 1977: 349).

10. Al-Muqaddasi (Ranking and Azoo trans.: 180) calls Basra "a noble capital founded by the Muslims in the days of 'Umar, who wrote to his lieutenant saying, 'Build thou a town for Muslims between Persia and the country of the Arabs, at the extreme border of al-'Iraq, on the China Sea.'. . . . [It] derives its name from the black stones which were used as ballast by the ships of al-Yaman, and which were thrown here" (Ranking and Azoo trans.: 184).

11. It also led to what Watson (in Udovitch, 1981: 29–58) termed a "Medieval Green Revolution," as new crops or new strains of old crops diffused to the Middle East from Southeast Asia, Malaysia, and beyond (Watson, 1981: 30), brought by the "sailors and merchants of Oman and Siraf who plied between India and the headlands of the Persian Gulf" (Watson, 1981: 32). From there the new crops diffused westward to the Arab world and eventually to Europe (Watson, 1981: 35).

12. Evidence of Greek navigation throughout this area (but not beyond India) is found in the anonymous document, the *Periplus of the Erythrean Sea*. See, inter alia, Toussaint (1966: 39–40). For the original source in English translation, see W. B. Schaff, ed., *The Periplus of the Erythrean Sea* (London: 1912).

13. See Joseph Toussaint Reinaud (and with a lengthy introduction by the editor), *Relation des voyages faits par les Arabes et les Persans dans l'Inde et à la Chine dans le IXe siècle* (1845). A better translation of this document is available by Jean Sauvaget, *Akhbar as-Sin wa l-Hind, Relation de la Chine et de l'Inde* (1948).

14. The peasant revolts of the late ninth century left the country in ruins; in their rage, peasants had even destroyed their mulberry trees and the export of silk to the Arabs was interrupted for a long time (Heyd, 1885: 31).

15. Both of these crucial documents will be taken up in greater detail in Part III, but we might give the citations at this point. See *Chau Ju-Kua: Chu-fan-chi [His Work on the Chinese and Arab Trade in the Twelfth and Thirteenth Centuries]*, translated into English from the Chinese by Friedrich Hirth and W. W. Rockhill; and also Jitsuzo Kuwabara, "On P'u Shou-keng: A Man of the Western Regions who was the Superintendent of the Trading Ships' Office in Ch'uan-chou towards the End of the Sung Dynasty, together with a General Sketch of Trade of the Arabs in China during the T'ang and Sung Eras," in *Memoirs of the Research Department of the Toyo Bunko* (1928: 1–79; 1935: 1–104).

16. Furthermore, Sauvaget based his claim that there were no manuals between the eleventh and fourteenth centuries on only one albeit definitive document, the *Kitab al-Fawa'id fi usal al-bahr wa'l-qawa'id* by the fifteenth-century master navigator, Ahmad ibn Majid al-Najdi, which incorporated the major sailing instructions compiled before him. See the excellent translation of this source, with lengthy introduction, by G. R. Tibbetts, *Arab Navigation in the Indian Ocean before the Coming of the Portuguese*. London: The Royal Asiatic Society of Great Britain and Ireland, 1981.

17. See, for example, S. D. N. Goitein, "Two Eyewitness Reports on the Expedition of the King of Kish (Qais) against Aden," in *Bulletin of the School of Oriental and African Languages* XVI (1954): 247 ff.

18. Serjeant (1963: 11) described Hormuz as a "barren place, but . . . immensely rich, and though it had no food, fresh water, nor any green thing, and supplies had to be imported from the Persian mainland some twelve miles distant, it had grown nearly as large as Aden—due to its immunity from raiding and its splendid harbour. It was the centre of sea-borne traffic from India. . . . The Portuguese did not penetrate . . . [it] until the year 1529."

19. Both, of course, were scarcely "pure." The war would begin again with Tamerlane toward the end of the fourteenth century.

20. Contemporary events illustrate this clearly. In spite of a recent prolonged war between Iran and Iraq over the head of the Gulf, the escalation of risks to shipping generated by these political events, and the impoverishment of both countries as a result of the war, Gulf shipping continued, albeit carrying not the old objects of long-distance trade—dates, silks, spices, lapis lazuli, and obsidian—but the new one, petroleum.

Cairo's Monopoly under the Slave Sultanate

The great coalescence of the Mesopotamian and Nile valley civilizations that had created the golden age of Islam was broken by the Mongol preemption of Iraq and Persia. Even after the Mongol Il-Khans converted to Islam, the enmity between the Mongols and the Mamluks, who ruled Syria and Egypt, abated only briefly during the first half of the fourteenth century. This hiatus may have been partially responsible for the fact that Cairo reached her apex during the reign of Sultan al-Nasir Muhammad (1294–1340, with two brief interruptions), when her population reached half a million (Abu-Lughod, 1971: 32–36). By then it was one of the largest cities in the world, exceeded by only the cities of China, Hangchow and possibly Zaytun.

Egypt's strong position was the result of several factors. First, she controlled a large region including Egypt and Syria, having expelled the Crusaders and brought the Syrian provinces under her control. The last Crusader threat to Egypt was removed when St. Louis' invasion of 1249–1250 failed[1]—the victim of Mamluk defensive tactics aided not a little by the dysentery suffered by the European forces—whereas the fall of Acre in 1291 removed the Crusaders from Syria. Second, with the decline of the Persian Gulf, Egypt gained virtually exclusive control over the sea gateway to India and China, a monopoly she would consolidate during the second half of the fourteenth century after the northern overland route collapsed. Third, she had a strong, albeit militaristic, government that reinforced, at least until it supplanted, her merchants in long-distance trade.

However, the Mamluks needed manpower to sustain their system. They therefore had no choice but to deal with the Europeans who, gradually deprived of other alternatives, now came eagerly to Egypt's door. The Mamluk system had an insatiable need for military manpower to defend itself from the Europeans on one side and the Mongols on the other. However, its unique system of military feudalism meant that it could not recruit locally from indigenous Syrian and Egyptian Muslims. Only non-Muslims, particularly pagans, could be enslaved for military and governmental service. Once converted to Islam and moving up the ranks of service to his owner, a Mamluk could be manumitted—but still had to keep aloof from the indigenous population. The offspring of Mamluks and Circassian women might join the ranks of Mamluk service (particularly if they were the sons of the incumbent sultan) but the *awlad al-nas* (literally, the children of the people) born of Mamluk fathers and native women were theoretically excluded from the Mamluk governing elite, although practice seems to have diverged (Haarmon, 1984). It was this "peculiar" system that elevated the slave trade to such strategic importance for the governors of Egypt and created a strange symbiosis with Genoa.

As Ehrenkreutz pointed out, there was an "opportune convergence of economic interests of . . . [Genoa] with the sociopolitical interests of the Mamluks" (Ehrenkreutz, 1981: 335) in the second half of the thirteenth century. In the early thirteenth century the Ayyubid sultanate had obtained new troops from "the steady flow of slaves from central Asia and from the Caucasus, arriving . . . by way of the traditional routes running across Mesopotamia and Asia Minor" (Ehrenkreutz, 1981: 336). However, after 1243, the Mongols controlled the land routes between the Caucasus and Syria and, with the Il-khanid's "supremacy over Persia, Iraq, the Caucasus, and eastern Anatolia, the Mongols were capable of interdicting major land traffic between the Mamluk territories and the northeastern slave markets." They did this at the time of Hulegu, when "following the rupture between the Mongols and the Mamluks, slave caravans disappeared from Oriental trade routes converging on Syria and Egypt" (Ehrenkreutz, 1981: 337). When that happened, the Mamluks had to find some way to circumvent the Ilkhanid embargo.

Genoa eventually provided that way, but not until 1261, when the fall of the Venetian-dominated Latin Kingdom of Constantinople restored her trading rights in that city and the Black Sea area beyond (Ehrenkreuntz, 1981: 340–341, as well as Chapter 4 above). Once in control, Genoa, with the assistance of Hulegu's foe, the Golden Horde under Berke, was able to establish a sea route connection from the Crimea (the source of the slaves) to Egypt via the Bosphorus and the Mediterranean. The primary "good" transported over that route was male slaves.[2]

Genoa was more than happy to cooperate in this trade, since "the shipment of slaves to Egypt . . . constituted a decisive leverage by which her merchants could . . . [promote] European commercial hegemony in the Levant. . . . Genoa . . . [became] the most important supplier of Circassian slaves for the Mamluk army" (Ehrenkreutz, 1981: 341). It was only in the fourteenth century that their bargaining power was reduced, and that resulted from political developments over which they had no control.

[T]he defeat of the Crusaders eliminated one sector of costly military commitments. . . . More importantly, following the conversion of the Ilkhanids to Islam and the rapid decline of the Mongol regime in Persia, the Mamluk sultanate was relieved of the specter of extinction. . . . Furthermore, the reopening of the traditional overland caravan trails between Mesopotamia and Syria resulted in the resumption of an intensive and lucrative slave trade by local Middle Eastern merchants. (Ehrenkreutz, 1981: 342)

Thus, by the end of the thirteenth century, the Genoese were no longer indispensable to the Mamluks.

The Venetians, unable to offer slaves to the Egyptians, and

having, as noted at the end of Chapter 4, wagered on the southern sea route, were able to use European demand for eastern spices and silk and for Egyptian–Syrian cotton and linen textiles, inter alia, as bait. Whereas in Fatimid and Ayyubid times the Venetians shared the Egyptian market with nationals from other Italian trading cities (Genoa, Pisa, Amalfi), during Mamluk times they increasingly strengthened their position, gradually supplanting their competitors in the eastern trade. When Egypt came under the direct rule of the Mamluks, who became more active in regulating relations with the foreign merchants, the Venetians were quick to exploit the opportunity for preferential treatment made possible by state control.

In the thirteenth and fourteenth centuries both the Venetians and the Mamluk state made efforts to establish monopolies in trade. These monopolies had important consequences for both parties. The Venetians were able to exclude, or at least subordinate, merchants from rival Italian cities. In Mamluk Egypt, the state was able to subordinate the free-wheeling Karimi (wholesale) merchants by placing restrictions on their trade with foreigners and eventually by monopolizing the markets for particularly profitable products.

The repercussions caused by the Black Death in the middle of the fourteenth century provided the final denouement, at least for the next 150 years. Out of that chaos-generating event Venice and Egypt emerged, if not victorious, at least as among the most fortunate survivors. As seen in Chapter 4, Venice recovered from her incredible loss of population whereas Genoa, which suffered a somewhat lower mortality, did not. The explanation, sought by Italian historians in the internal politics of the two cities or in their "entrepreneurial spirits," can now be reformulated in terms of a world system.

Venice survived because Egypt survived, sustained by the persistence of the southern route to Asia. By 1346 Venice was running regular galley service to Alexandria (Ashtor, 1974, reprinted 1978: 17) and, in spite of the interruption caused by the Plague and its periodic recurrence, that line of communication between the two centers proved indestructible. In the fifteenth century the connection between Venice and Egypt was all that remained of the world system created in the thirteenth century (although, admittedly, the regional subsystem was to be reshaped by the Ottomans in the late fifteenth and early sixteenth centuries). Venetian relations to Mamluk Egypt and Syria will be discussed in greater detail, but first it is necessary to consider what the Muslim business world had to offer the Italians.

Islam and Business

Too often, European writings view the medieval Italian maritime states as "active" agents operating on a "passive" Islamic society. The Italians are credited with introducing enormous and innovative mechanisms for transport and trade into a presumedly less competent region. That argument, however, illustrates some of the fallacies mentioned in Chapter 1, namely, reasoning backward from outcomes and failing to discount perspective in evaluating narratives. Although it is true that the "West" eventually "won," it should not be assumed that it did so because it was more advanced in either capitalistic theory or practice. Islamic society needed no teachers in these matters.

It has been suggested that Islam, because it forbade usury, was inimical to capitalism. Nothing could be less accurate. Unlike Christianity, which not only forbade usury but tended to be "unworldly," from the beginning Islam assumed the existence of commerce and addressed itself to matters of business (Rodinson, 1974; Goitein, 1964a, 1964b, 1966a, 1967 inter alia; and Udovitch, 1970a). It might be considered strange that a religious document purportedly dictated directly by God should concern itself with the writing of business agreements (as the Qur'an does, inter alia, in Chapter 2, Verses 282–283), but it must be remembered that Mecca was an important caravan center and that Muhammad, before his religious experience, was a business agent.

Such commerce had long predated Islam in the region and it continued to sustain the prosperity of the expanding Muslim empire. Many of the business techniques used in that empire had been firmly established before the Qur'an codified them and counseled ethical business practices. Sumaria invented many of them and the Sassanids were using "banks," "checks," and "bills of exchange" before Islam was introduced (Toussaint, 1966: 46–47). The *commenda* contract was traditional practice in the caravan trade, if not before Islam, certainly by its time (Lopez, 1970: 345).

Islam took over these mechanisms and added to them a high moral evaluation of merchants and their contribution to society. Goitein (1964b: 104) argues that Islam's attitude toward commerce was particularly favorable.

> The income of the honest merchant is regarded in Muslim religious literature as a typical example of *halal*, as earnings free of religious objections. In addition, the merchant was particularly able to fulfill all the duties encumbent on a Muslim [prayer, study of religious books]. While traveling, a businessman ... [could more easily become] a pilgrim to Mecca [visit saints, give alms, keep fasts more easily] than his co-religionists with lower incomes who did physical labor.

After the Abbasids came to power in 750, capitalism flowered, as wealthy businessmen (who had financed the "bourgeois revolution" that overthrew the Umayyads) began to "use" the state in their own interests (Goitein, 1964b: 101–103). It is Goitein's thesis that "just as the rise of modern capitalism in Europe was accompanied by a new religious attitude toward making money, so the 'bourgeois revolution' of the Muslim Empire of the eighth and ninth centuries had a strong religious foundation" (1964b:105). Data to support this thesis remain elusive, however.

For Europe a large corpus of notarized contracts has been preserved that clearly indicates how business was conducted (with the cautionary condition of Sapori, see Chapter 4). Nothing comparable exists for the Middle East. Morgan (1982: introduction) laments the almost complete absence of archival data dealing with the quantity of goods traded and their prices and Udovitch (1970a) notes a similar lack of written contracts that would permit reconstruction of the actual practices relevant to *Partnership and Profit in Medieval Islam*.[3]

Because of the paucity of documentary sources, it is not possible to investigate quantitative aspects of trade (Udovitch, 1970a: 3) and, given the similar absence of contracts,[4] one can only study the legal texts that describe mechanisms (*shurut* or legal formulae) or set forth principles (*hiyal*) for their execution. This Udovitch does in his book, which addresses the institutions of partnership and *commenda* in the early Islamic period in an effort to determine whether Islamic constraints on business were responsible for the loss of Islamic commercial hegemony in the Middle Ages (Udovitch, 1970a: 4).

Law books, however, are an imperfect source. Just as the Italians bypassed the Church's injunction against usury, so in Islam there were discrepancies between law and practice. Nevertheless, law books constitute a place to start the investigation. Udovitch (1970a: 8) suggests that even though partnerships were found in Babylonian times, the *commenda* was "original with the Arabs." Both partnerships and *commenda* agreements were in common use in the medieval Muslim world, since both had been fully codified by the eighth and ninth centuries (Udovitch, 1970a: 14) in documents largely from Iraq.

Partnerships

The law recognizes two types of partnerships: *sharikat al-milk* (proprietary partnerships) and *sharikat al-ʿaqd* (contractual or commercial partnerships).[5] The former is simple joint ownership, not necessarily for commercial purposes. In contrast, the latter emphasizes "joint exploitation of capital and the joint participation in profits and losses" and is the dominant form of business organization, the subject of extensive discussion in legal treatises (Udovitch, 1970a: 19). While Shafiʿi law frowned on the *mufawada* (unlimited investment partnership), Hanafi law permitted it but preferred the *ʿinan* (limited investment partnership), in which only a specified portion of a partner's capital became part of the common fund (Udovitch, 1970a: 40–43).

A unique characteristic of partnership, at least in Hanafi law, was that in addition to money (Udovitch, 1970a: 55) and possibly goods (questionable, Udovitch, 1970a: 61), partners could "invest" labor. "Unlike the *commenda*, in which one party provides the capital and the other the labor, the capital in a work partnership consists primarily of the labor of both partners. The type of labor envisaged is usually a skill in some kind of manufacture such as tailoring, dyeing, weaving, . . . designated . . . [as] 'a partnership of work with their hands' . . . 'a partnership in work' . . . 'of bodies' . . . 'of crafts' " (Udovitch, 1970a: 65).[6]

Labor partnerships offered an alternative to the "putting out system" that had led to proletarianization in Europe. Since the "division of labor in medieval industry was usually such that the person who did the manufacturing did not necessarily own the raw material upon which he worked or have anything to do with the sale of the finished product" (Udovitch, 1970a: 66), partnerships could potentially put capitalists, workers, and wholesalers on a more equal footing. Furthermore, a partnership could be formed between the owner of a stall and the skilled craftsman who produced its goods, a share in profits substituting for rent (Udovitch, 1970a: 71–74).

It was also possible to form partnerships for "credit;" at least by the eighth century, these were important ways to finance trade and industry in the Muslim world. Udovitch confirms (1970a: 78, 80) that "the legal instruments necessary for extensive use of mercantile credit were already available in the earliest Islamic period" and that "buying and selling on credit were accepted and apparently widespread commercial practices." Indeed, long-distance trade would have been impossible without it. Not only could selling on credit yield higher profits but Islam's injunction against usury could be circumvented by skilled use of credit. Such credits could be transferred over and over again and there were even partnerships for buying and selling credit (Udovitch, 1970a: 81). Udovitch is clear in his conclusion: "Any assertion that medieval credit was used for consumption only, and not for production, is quite untenable with reference to the medieval Near East" (Udovitch, 1970a: 86).

Contracts

Although written documents were not required and the oral testimony of witnesses was preferred, many business contracts were actually recorded. Indeed, there were officials equivalent to notaries (Tyan, 1960) and a body of literature, *shurut* (Udovitch, 1970a: 88 seq.), that presented exemplar contracts (much as we buy rental forms rather than make them up ourselves). Copies of written contracts were given to each partner, but the true partnership began not with signing the contract but with the actual contribution of funds to start the business transaction (Udovitch, 1970a: 96).

The Commenda

In addition to partnerships, Islamic law governed the *commenda*, which, as seen in Chapter 4, became an important mechanism for Italian long-distance trade. In the usual *commenda* agreement, one partner put up the capital and the other accompanied the goods abroad. Although similar to a partnership between money and labor (Udovitch, 1970a: 67, 170), it was treated separately in Islamic law, since although the traveling partner shared in the profit and negotiated with third parties on behalf of his stationary partner, he was not liable for normal risks. Something similar to the *commenda* was already in use in the pre-Islamic Arabian caravan trade, since Muhammad seems to have been a *commenda* agent for Khadija (Udovitch, 1970a: 171). The institution continued in use and spread to other parts of the Islamic world in the first century Hegira, eventually reaching Europe.[7]

The *commenda* was a capitalist instrument par excellence. Through it, capital could be invested either in commerce or, unlike Europe, in industrial production (Udovitch, 1970a: quoted 185–186).

A person could entrust his capital to an agent on the condition that the latter buy raw materials and turn them into finished consumer products and sell them on the basis of shared profit.... An arrangement of this kind ... one might term an industrial or labor *commenda*, in which elements of manufacture and production are tied to the more usual commercial functions of the *commenda*.

Examples of industrial *commenda*s and partnerships can be found as early as the eighth century, and the Geniza papers (primarily eleventh and twelfth century in Fustat[8]) mention industrial agreements between capitalists and laborers in the sifting of gold dust at the mint, weaving, lead processing, tailoring and embroidering, baking, glass blowing, wine making, medicines, dyeing and manufacturing purple cloth, silk working, silver smithing, sugar refining, tanning, and the processing of cheese and dairy products (Goitein, 1967: 362–367). The primary difference between a labor contract (i.e., the employment of a factor) and a partnership or *commenda* arrangement was that in the latter two cases there was an agreed-upon distribution of the potential profits. As in the case of later Italian agreements, the distribution ratio of profits could vary, but it had to be specified in advance (Udovitch, 1970a: 190–196).

The *commenda* was also a flexible device for extending and transferring credit. Even capital deposited with a third party or credit from a debt owed to a businessman could be invested in a *commenda* agreement, at least in Hanafi law (Udovitch, 1970a: 187), with agents authorized to make such transfers. Such flexibility certainly assisted the conduct of long-distance trade. It facilitated the delegation to the active partner of either unlimited decision making powers (typical when really long distances were involved) or more strictly specified ones, but "even in a limited mandate *commenda* contract, the agent's freedom of action extend[ed] almost unto the commercial horizons in which he functioned," the only limit for the legitimacy of the agent's actions being "the customary practice of the merchants" (Udovitch, 1970a: 206). Agents had to keep detailed accounts, but they were not held liable for losses (Udovitch, 1970a: 237–240).

The Wakil (agent)

In contrast to the frequency of partnership and *commenda* arrangements for the conduct of commerce, commission agents (*wakils*) were seldom employed, although trusted slaves or young apprentices (called "boys") might "work for" the benefit of their masters (Goitein, 1967: 131–133). Extremely important in foreign places, however, was the role of the *wakil al-tujjar*, who acted as the professional representative for merchants from his area. According to Goitein (1967: 186–192), this respected official had three functions. He served as the legal representative for his fellow countrymen; he maintained a warehouse (the *dar al-wakil*) in which he stored the goods of absentee merchants that he might be asked to market; and finally, and perhaps most importantly, he served as the trusted

depository for the merchants and a neutral arbiter between them. . . . Since the warehouse of a wakil was a neutral meeting ground for merchants, it served them also as a bourse. . . . [T]here was a notary in the wakil's warehouse so that commercial contracts, such as the conclusion of partnerships and commendas, could immediately receive their proper legal form.... [The dar al-wakil had a] semi-official character.

In port cities the *wakil al-tujjar* might also serve as superintendent of the port, as tax farmer of the customs and other dues, and even as a postal address.

There are definite parallels between this role in Arab trade and the houses of foreign merchants at the Champagne fairs or the Consul houses of Italian merchants at Bruges and Antwerp. Neither a religious explanation nor the concept of "diffusion" is needed to account for these parallels. Common needs apparently gave rise to common solutions. The same was true with respect to money and banking, although here there were some important differences between the two culture areas.

Merchants, Credit, Money, and Banking

By meticulously analyzing a small fraction of the 10,000 items (of which 7,000 can be considered "documents") found in the Geniza repository, Goitein (1967: 13) has imaginatively reconstructed a picture of how money and credit may have worked in eleventh and twelfth century Fustat and, by extension, elsewhere and at later times.[9] He suggests that business, even retail, was traditionally conducted on credit, since payment could routinely be postponed for two months after delivery. "Occasionally, a longer delay could be gained by paying a price higher than had been agreed upon, which concealed interest" (Goitein, 1967: 197–199).

Eventually, however, payment had to be made. Currency was on the gold and silver standard by weight and a variety of minted coins circulated—some old and worn and lighter than marked, fewer newly minted and therefore accurate. To avoid the "tedious and time-consuming" task of continually reassaying the gold coins, "money was handled largely in sealed purses of coin the exact values of which were indicated on the outside." Since these "cases" were sealed and passed unopened from hand to hand, the identity and trustworthiness of the sealer were crucial. Some purses "bore the seal of certified money assayers, of a government office, or of a semi-official exchange, and others...the names of individual merchants.... As a rule, bankers' accounts indicated solely the real value of the dinars, namely their weight" (Goitein, 1967: 231). The less valuable silver coins were not sealed in purses.

Where there is money, there must be money changers. The bankers (who, as in Europe, were often merchants as well)[10] not only assayed and certified money but changed local and foreign currencies (Goitein, 1967: 234–237). Goitein notes that money changers were ubiquitous. There were special changers' bazaars in Alexandria and Fustat.

Bankers also accepted money on deposit for safekeeping although, unlike their European counterparts, they were not supposed to invest it (Udovitch, 1979). However, interestingly enough, they also accepted "promissory notes," which is another way of saying that they advanced funds. Naturally, as Goitein notes (1967: 245–247), "a banker would issue promissory notes only to a person for whom he had received payments, or ... deposits. ... It was customary to keep part of one's money with a banker." But bankers also entered *commenda*s of credit, advancing capital in return for a prespecified share of the profits. Although bankers did not charge for keeping deposits, they did charge fees for changing money, for lending money (often concealed as a partnership or *commenda* of credit to avoid the usury injunction), and for issuing bills of exchange (*suftaja*'s).

It was in the transfer of funds from one party to another or from one place to another that the banker played his most important facilitating role. Here a distinction must be made between a simple "order to pay" (the *hawala*) and the "demand note" at a distant location (the *suftaja*). Goitein gives us a description of the "order to pay" that reveals how similar to a modern check this instrument was.[11] At the upper left corner was the amount to be paid (in numbers), and in the lower left corner was the date and then the name of the payer. "Legally, orders of payments were in the form of a transfer of debt or assignment ... made before a court or notary. ... [T]he normal procedure ... was to have them paid through a banker" (Goitein, 1967: 241–242).

Furthermore, although European bankers did not develop the full bill of exchange until the fourteenth century, its precursor, the *suftaja*, of Persian origin, was in full use in Middle Eastern trade.

As a rule ... [suftajas] were issued by and drawn upon well-known bankers or representatives of merchants, a fee was charged for their issue, and after presentation a daily penalty had to be paid for any delay in payment. . . . Since the presentation of a bill of exchange required immediate payment, even great bankers refrained from issuing suftajas on large sums. . . . [T]he use of suftajas was fairly well developed, especially inside Egypt itself . . . and between international centers such as Cairo and Baghdad. (Goitein, 1967: 243–245)

Accounts

A few of the Geniza documents demonstrate that bankers kept careful accounts, as might be suspected. We have one document, identified as a Banker's Account and dated around A.D. 1075 (Goitein, 1967: 295), that shows entries for bills of exchange (*suftaja*s) deposited with him, a balance sheet of credits and debits, and then entries for payments in cash—all for a single customer. Another document is a twelfth–century account between a large merchant and the banker who was his "partner." It is in two columns, although not in modern double-entry form, and after adding up the debits and credits of each, there is a balance given (Goitein, 1967: 299). This seems to indicate a system of banking and accounting as sophisticated as was found in Europe several centuries later.

Thus, all the legal and institutional prerequisites for financing and administering "capitalist" production and exchange were in place in the Islamic world long before the Europeans would benefit from them (Udovitch, 1970a: 261). It is therefore not surprising to learn that the Muslim world hosted a highly developed economy; indeed, it was not only the spices and dyes and aromatics Egypt transshipped from the Far East that were sought after by the Italian merchant mariners but the fruits of her own agricultural production and urban industries. We must therefore go back a few centuries to trace how that economy developed and how it ran, since its prosperity made Cairo and, to a lesser extent, Alexandria, thriving centers of production as well as trade.

Fustat–Cairo[12] and the Processes of Production and Trade

Fustat, the newly planned town founded in A.D. 640 by the Peninsular Arabs who brought Islam to Egypt, began, like Basra and

Kufa in Iraq, as a military settlement. However, its strategic location on the Nile, just below the point at which the north-flowing river branches to form the Delta, made it a natural site for a political and economic capital for the same reasons that Memphis, just opposite, had dominated Pharaonic Egypt. By the ninth century, Fustat had become the chief inland port of Egypt as well as a vital center of industrial production and trade. Together with its successively added suburbs, it was fast becoming one of the largest cities in the Islamic world, an ambitious challenger to Baghdad. The decline of Abbasid power (centered in Baghdad) in the tenth century was reflected in the increased autonomy (and also chaos) of the Egyptian province, a process finally brought to an end in 969 by the invasion from Tunisia of a new Shi'ite dynasty, the Fatimids.

Jawhar, the conquering general, planned a new royal city for the Fatimid caliph, a walled enclave called Al-Qahirah (later Europeanized to Cairo) some distance away. In the tenth and eleventh centuries this settlement did not draw economic activity away from Fustat[13] but rather stimulated Fustat's growth by heightening the demand for its products and its imports. Al-Muqaddasi (see Chapter 6), writing soon after the Fatimid conquest, considered the dual city (Ranking and Azoo trans.: 322–324, italics added)

> a metropolis in every sense of the word; for in addition to having within it all the departments of the State, it is the residence of the [Fatimid] Commander of the Faithful [the caliph] himself.... [V]erily it is the capital of Egypt, *it has effaced Baghdad* and is the glory of Islam and the centre of the world's commerce.... Among the capitals none is more populous than this city.... The inhabitants are peaceable and prosperous, and very kind and charitable.... The houses in Misr [al-Fustat] are each of four stories, or five, like watchtowers.... I have heard ... that as many as two hundred persons live in a single house.

Al-Muqaddasi listed it, along with Aden and Suhar, as the best place to make one's fortune in commerce, since the

> fruits of Syria and al-Maghrib [North Africa] reach it in all seasons, and travellers are ever coming to it from al-'Iraq and from the eastern countries, and the ships of the peninsula and of the countries of Rum [Byzantium/Europe] are ever ploughing their way to it. Its commerce is marvellous, and its trades are profitable and its wealth abundant. (Ranking and Azoo trans.: 327)

Although both trade and industry flourished under the Fatimid administration, defense did not. In 1168, Saladin helped rescue the city from a Crusader invasion, eventually replacing the Fatimids by his own dynasty, the Ayyubids. Since Fustat had been intentionally burned to stop the advance of the Crusaders, the royal enclave of Cairo, formerly off limits, was opened to the masses. Thenceforth, Cairo and a rebuilt Fustat grew toward one another and shared the role as economic and political capital of the country.

The Fatimids had begun as a great sea power[14] and, when they moved from Tunisia to Egypt, they brought their naval forces into the eastern Mediterranean (Goitein, 1967: 34). A port and shipbuilding arsenal were constructed next to al-Qahirah (Cairo) and Fatimid ships moved aggressively throughout the Mediterranean and into the Red Sea and Indian Ocean. It was at this time that the "centre of Islam in the Indian Ocean shifted from the Persian Gulf to the Red Sea" (Toussaint, 1966: 51) and Aden rose to prominence. Although gradually the Italians broke the strength of the Fatimid fleet in the Mediterranean, they never managed to penetrate the Red Sea route whose link to the Mediterranean, via the ancient canal of Necho, was periodically filled in to prevent such incursions.[15] The Fatimids jealously guarded their "rear," and the trade with India expanded during the centuries of their rule.

The Fatimid administration gave free reign to the capitalist tendencies of its subjects, Muslims and Jews alike,[16] although, like the Italian mariner city-states, the lines between government and civil society were inevitably blurred. The state was the ultimate owner of most of the land and, as the monopolizer of force, it was needed to defend the ships used in trade. Although at that time the state did not direct commerce, as it later would, "the presence of government was very much felt" (Goitein, 1967: 267). Not only was the government the largest customer but agricultural products, particularly flax, "were largely bought from or through government agencies."

The connection between commerce and the government was particularly evident with respect to the Mediterranean, increasingly threatened by European vessels. Goitein collected details on about 150 Arab boats plying the Mediterranean during the eleventh century. He found that they were owned almost exclusively by single individuals (1967: 309); however, because of the constant need for military protection, the owners were disproportionately connected in some way with the government (1967: 310). Nevertheless, the "largest single group of shipowners were the merchants" (Goitein, 1967: 311). On the India route, protection needs were less pressing and merchants overwhelmingly ran the show. During that period a profusion of petty boat owners and merchants competed in the search for markets and sources of supply. Gradually, however, this process yielded greater inequality, with the so-called Karimi merchants eventually rising to the top.

The Karimi Merchants

Who were the Karimi, in what did they trade, and what was their relationship both to the state and to the producers? The answers to these questions changed over time, so we might look at the Fatimid period as a benchmark from which to measure later developments.

Orientalists have devoted considerable attention to the Karimis, attempting to construct a somewhat exotic image commensurate with their strange name; and yet, I believe the concept and the name refer to a more mundane phenomenon. *Karim* means "great" and, in this instance, was used as a descriptor to distinguish large-scale wholesale merchants from the host of petty entrepreneurs who dealt in smaller quantities closer to the point of ultimate sale, much in the same way that French distinguishes between a *marchand en gros* and a *commerçant* or tradesman.

Clearly, then, their appearance and their rising importance would be expected to follow an increase in the scale of operations. Ashtor notes (in his article on "The Karimi Merchants," 1956, reprinted 1978: 45–56) that the earliest reference he could find was at the time of the Fatimids, when Qalqashandi refers to "Karimi ships." Labib (1965: 60) expands on this. According to Qalqashandi, the Fatimids maintained a fleet of five ships in the Red Sea to defend merchants from piracy. The ruler of Qais [Kish] and an amir representing Fustat jointly supervised this fleet.

Protection continued under the Ayyubids, as ships previously used to transport soldiers to the Hijaz and Yemen were converted and deployed in the Red Sea where they proved more effective than the Fatimid fleet had been. Saladin increasingly supported the Karimis because he profited greatly from taxing them. (Maqrizi recounts that they paid four years of taxes in advance!) Saladin was also anxious to exclude Europeans from Cairo and the Red Sea. In 1182 the Karimi faced their gravest crisis under the Ayyubids, an attempt by the Crusaders to penetrate the Red Sea. The victory of Saladin in the Red Sea decided the issue in favor of the Karimi and in 1183 a nephew of Saladin and his viceroy in Egypt built the famous *funduk* (warehouse) of the Karimi at Fustat. Later the merchants built additional funduks in Alexandria, Qus and the Red Sea area (Labib, 1965: 61). Thus, although Labib (1970: 209) claims that their name first appears in the eleventh century, systematic allusions to them are not found until the twelfth century, when European demand for spices via the Egyptian route escalated.

Regardless of the disagreement about their origins, there is general agreement that they had become very important by the Bahri Mamluk period, particularly during the reign of Sultan al-Nasir Muhammad in the last decade of the thirteenth and first few decades of the fourteenth century (see Fischel, 1958; Ashtor, 1956; Goitein, 1958; Labib, 1970; Wiet, 1955), by which time the spice trade in the Indian Ocean had assumed central importance to the economy of Egypt. As Ashtor (1956, reprinted 1978: 52–53) stated:

> Under the rule of the Bahri Mamluks, the Karimis apparently monopolized the spice trade between Yemen and Egypt. . . . There was a great difference between the Indian spice trade of the Fatimid and the Mamluk periods. The small capitalists previously engaged in it were gradually supplanted by the Karimi merchants who accumulated great wealth. This was the result of the economic policy of the Mamluk government, which oppressed the small traders by its system of taxes and monopolies.

Labib (1970: 21), although agreeing in general with Ashtor, attributes the healthy growth of Karimi wealth in the early Bahri Mamluk period to the entrepreneurial skills of the merchants themselves, aided by the free-enterprise system the early Mamluks retained from Ayyubid times. What Ashtor calls the oppressive policy of the Mamluks, Labib calls valuable "protectionism by the

Egyptian government which profited the Arab merchants" (Labib, 1970: 209).

Regardless of the interpretation, however, all concur that Karimi importance peaked in the early fourteenth century when, according to Ibn Hajar, there were some 200 Karimi merchants in Egypt (as cited in Labib, 1970: 212). Gaston Wiet (1955) culled the histories and chronicles, compiling a list of over 46 merchants working in Egypt between 1149 and the fifteenth century who are identified in the original sources as "Karimi merchants." The biographical information available for names on this list indicates who they were and in what activities they engaged.

All seem to have been Muslims, although Ashtor claims that some Jews were also considered Karimis (1956, reprinted 1978: 55).[17] Many, as might be expected, were sons or relatives of other Karimis. Some occupied high positions in the religious hierarchy (a few were *qadi*s and one was the vice rector of al-Azhar, Cairo's mosque university) or in the civilian hierarchy, and at least two held the all-important position of provost of the Cairo markets. A few are referred to as "Chief of the Karimis of Cairo and Damascus," suggesting that the merchants may have been organized into a loose "guild."[18]

The data available give some insight into the activities of Karimis. Spices were indeed their primary, albeit not exclusive, stock in trade and their geographic range was wide. Some, but not many, are reported to have traveled as far as Cathay. Many are noted as having operations in India, particularly on the Malabar coast; the names of Indian ports such as Cambay and Calicut recur with regularity. Almost all seem at one time or another to have worked out of Aden/Yemen, particularly after the rebirth of that port's prosperity in 1229 under the Rassoulids (Wiet, 1955: 88). They not only were engaged in the sea trade with the Far East but in the overland caravan routes as well. Many had branch offices in the Levant, particularly in Damascus, and once the land route to Iraq opened at the end of the thirteenth century, they also dealt with Baghdad. Nor were their activities confined to the spice trade. On Wiet's list are cloth merchants, an owner of an emerald mine in Upper Egypt, dealers in silk, lead, porcelain, slaves, and diamonds, as well as bankers and shipowners. The diversity of their enterprises is striking. As Goitein notes (1967: 153–155), wholesale merchants dealt with an enormous variety of goods in diverse ports and places. The big merchant "had to diversify his activities and to accept orders from many different categories of customers in order to spread the risk and to meet fluctuations of the market."

The Karimi merchants seem to have persisted as important participants in the long-distance trade of Egypt even after the Mamluk state began to play a more active role in commerce and tried to monopolize the spice trade. Although some scholars claim that the Karimis began to lose their hegemony during the second half of the fourteenth century and blame the downfall of this merchant class on the increasing strength of the Italian traders in early fifteenth-century Egypt (inter alia, Ashtor, "The Venetian Supremacy in Levantine Trade," 1974, reprinted 1978: 26), alternative explanations are possible. As shall be seen when we examine in greater detail the relation of European merchants to the Egyptian state, the Karimi merchants remained important as providers of eastern goods, even after the state monopolized (set prices in) the spice trade with Italian merchants coming across the Mediterranean. Furthermore, the decline (or shift) coincides with the depression that followed the Black Death, which suggests that the state may have stepped in to fill the void created by the death of many of the merchants.[19]

Industries and Agricultural Production: A "Military–Industrial Complex"?

The collaboration of merchants with the government was also evident in the cultivation of agricultural products such as cotton, flax, and sugar cane, their processing into textiles or refined confections, and their marketing, either at home or abroad. Certainly since the time of the Ayyubids, when military feudalism began to characterize Egypt and Syria, the involvement of an alien elite in the Egyptian countryside became more intense. Under the Mamluk system, which assigned whole agricultural districts to amirs who were expected to use the surplus they could extract—either directly or, more commonly, indirectly through tax farming—to equip and finance their troops, a symbiotic relationship between the state and "civil society" was inevitable.

An impressive array of "manufactured" goods was produced in

Egypt, not in large factories but in small workshops (Goitein, 1967: 80) in which workers owned their own tools and often combined the activities of manufacture and sales (Goitein, 1967: 85–86). Among the industries of Cairo listed by Goitein (1967: 108–115) were workshops for metallurgy and metal objects, including military equipment and accoutrements, glass and pottery, leather tanning and the fabrication of leather objects, parchment, paper, bookbinding, construction, stone cutting, furniture manufacture, and food preparation and processing. The largest plants were the *matbakh*s (literally kitchens) in which sugar was refined or paper was made. These plants, many of them belonging to the sultan or high amirs, employed large numbers of workers.

But the most important industry in medieval Egypt was the one that dominated European economies as well, namely, textiles. The reasons for this are best presented by Goitein (1967: 101):

> Comparable to the place of steel and other metals in a modern economy, textiles represented the major industry of medieval times in the Mediterranean area. As far as the statistical data available allow us to gauge, a very large proportion, perhaps the majority, of the working population and certainly of the distributing classes was engaged in this branch of economy. Textiles in those days were more durable and more expensive than they are nowadays. . . . Fantastic prices were paid for single selected pieces. . . . Clothing formed part—sometimes a considerable part—of a family's investment, being transmitted from parents to children, to be converted into cash in case of an emergency. The furniture of a house consisted mostly of various types of carpets, couches, cushions, canopies, and draperies. . . .

One can illustrate the way agricultural production and urban industry interacted by looking at two of Egypt's major industries: textiles, which depended upon locally grown cotton and flax, and sugar refining and confections, which depended upon locally grown cane. In both industries, the state played major roles. It controlled the lands on which the raw materials were grown, owned many of the factories in which the goods were processed, and ultimately bought large quantities of the finished product, either to consume or to resell to the Italian merchants. By Fatimid times the sultan had already become the biggest "capitalist." State involvement in production became even more widespread during Ayyubid and early Mamluk times, although complete state monopolies were not achieved until the fifteenth century.

SUGAR AND ITS REFINING

Although sugar was grown throughout Egypt and Syria, Upper Egypt was the foremost producer in the region (Ashtor, 1981: 93). Most sugar-refining factories were located on the plantations themselves, but there were *matbakh*s (literally, kitchens) in small towns in Upper Egypt and even in Old Cairo (Fustat). In the early fourteenth century 66 sugar refineries are listed in Old Cairo alone, of which the largest number seem to have been founded in the second half of the thirteenth century when there was a "real boom in the Egyptian sugar industry . . . [as] the Mamluk amirs began to invest money in this profitable sector of Egypt's economy" (Ashtor, 1981: 94–95). Although prodigious quantities of sweets were consumed locally, in the thirteenth and early fourteenth centuries much was also exported to other Arab countries as well as to Italy, southern France, Catalonia, and even Flanders, England, and Germany (Ashtor, 1981: 97–98). Ashtor (1981: 99) categorically describes the Egyptian sugar factories as

> capitalistic enterprises, in the sense that big trusts systematically pushed aside the smaller enterprises. The sugar center of Mallawi, for instance, was in the first half of the fourteenth century dominated by the family Banu-Fudayl, which planted 1,500 feddans of sugar cane a year. The greatest sugar industrialists, however, were the Mamluk amirs and the directors of the sultan's financial administration. . . . [Amirs got fiefs to refine sugar.] The sultans themselves were very much involved in the sugar industry [through royal sugar plantations, presses, and factories].

Mamluk officials enjoyed significant advantages over the civilian bourgeoisie because their taxes were lower and they could mobilize peasant labor through the *corvée* (forced labor on the irrigation system); thus, they were in unfair competition with bourgeois industrialists (Ashtor, 1981: 99–100). It appears that in the fourteenth but particularly by the fifteenth century, the Mamluks took over direct sugar production since, when unfair competition did not work, they could also force people to buy the sultan's sugar; corruption was rampant (Ashtor, 1981: 99–103).

According to Ashtor, this inhibited technological development. Whereas in the thirteenth and fourteenth centuries, sugar technology in Egypt was considered advanced,[20] the state monopolies and poor management eventually stifled technological development. By the fifteenth century, European sugar refining techniques were improving whereas the "Egyptian and Syrian sugar industries were meanwhile adhering to their old methods" powered by oxen or water wheels (Ashtor, 1981: 106).

Apparently, the decline had already started early in the fourteenth century; Maqrizi dates the ruin of Fustat's sugar factories from then (Ashtor, 1981: 104), even before the onset of the economic crisis in the Mamluk kingdom at the beginning of the fifteenth century. No doubt the Black Death intensified this decline, as did Tamerlane's incursions fifty years later. In any case, as Ashtor (1981: 112–113) concludes, by the fifteenth century "Levantine industries could no longer compete on the international market with European sugar."

Although Ashtor tries hard to blame government monopolies and taxes, corruption, and technological stagnation for the collapse of Egyptian industries and the "triumph of Europe" in the second half of the fifteenth century, his arguments are not fully convincing. After discounting alternative explanations, even he concludes that of all the factors depressing industry, the decline in population was most important (Ashtor, 1981: 120)! We return to this later.

TEXTILES

Textiles constituted the second industry that linked rural production to the "industrial" economy. According to Labib (1965: 307), weaving was an extremely well-developed and important industry in Egypt. As early as Fatimid times (Goitein, 1967: 115), state looms produced silk, cotton, linen, and woolen fabrics, although the quality of Egyptian silk was low[21] and woolen cloth was of poor quality because Egyptian sheep and goats had thin coats as a result of the hot climate. Cotton and particularly linen were the specialties of the area.

Coastal towns such as Tennis and Damietta were the traditional centers for linen production before Crusader incursions interrupted their activities. Labib (1965: 308) offers a description of the industry in these cities that may also apply to inland Mehalla, whose textile industry absorbed workers fleeing Crusader attacks on the coast (El-Messiri, 1980: 52–54). The weavers occupied rented rooms, workshops, and factories, in which master craftsmen and their journeymen produced white (in Damietta) and colored (in Tennis) fabrics of high quality. In Alexandria there was even a municipal weaving center, the Dar al-Tiraz, that was closely guarded by the government. In addition, there were private textile factories that were important to the economic life of the city (Labib, 1965: 309). Since linen, rather than cotton cloth, constituted the primary output of these factories, production was tied to flax.

Flax was "the main industrial crop of Egypt" and "formed the main object of international trade" (Goitein, 1967: 104–105). A complex labor-intensive process was required to separate the fiber from the wood core and then remove seeds from the fiber. Interestingly enough, women, although they did not weave, were involved in this part of the production process. Cotton and flax traders employed women who, sitting on the open street in front of the shops, cleaned the cotton and flax of straw (Labib, 1965: 312).

Cotton weaving was more common in the provinces of Syria and Palestine in which the raw material was grown in large quantities. Cotton planting had increased in the Levant in the tenth century, primarily in Aleppo, northern Palestine, and Jerusalem. (See Ashtor, "The Venetian Cotton Trade in Syria in the Later Middle Ages," 1976, reprinted 1978: 675–715.) At that time the major outlet for the expanding textile industry was Egypt. The Crusader presence stimulated even greater demand for cotton and cloth, which was signaled by rising prices in the second half of the twelfth century, nor did this demand abate even after the fall of Acre and the subsequent injunction against trade with Muslims.

During the second half of the fourteenth century, however, the textile industries of both Egypt and the Levant seem to have undergone significant changes. In Egypt, production itself apparently declined as a result of increased competition from European goods, and in Syria the cotton crop was increasingly bought in its raw state by Italian (primarily Venetian) merchants. This is a precursor of what was to happen in more dramatic fashion five centuries later, when European textiles flooded "third world" markets and transformed industrial producers into "dependent" exporters of primary products.

Labib (1965: 311) documents the penetration of the Egyptian market by fabrics imported from Europe. Citing the fourteenth-century Egyptian historian, Maqrizi, Labib says that the Franks (i.e., Europeans) "flooded" the local markets with great quantities of their textiles. A special bazaar for European fabrics was set up in Cairo, and Turkish carpets and Indian fabrics, particularly silk and cotton, were traded in great quantities. Fabrics also came from Africa. The increased textile production and trade led to a proliferation of bazaars and qaisariyahs for textile traders and, for a time, even to the increased export of Egyptian textiles. However, the integration of Egypt with the world economy also encouraged her to export larger quantities of flax and raw cotton. Although Christian countries such as Sicily, Malta, Cyprus, Greece, and Italy also exported raw cotton, it was of lower quality. Given the prices offered, it was therefore hard for Egypt to resist selling her crop.

A similar process took place in Syria, although at a somewhat later time. At first, the integration of Syria with the European market stimulated her cotton cloth production, with Baalbek and other weaving towns experiencing a real boom. However, industrial developments underwent difficulties in the mid-fourteenth century and collapsed by the end of that century. The drop in population, caused first by the Black Death and then by the invasion by Tamerlane, who deported many of the skilled craftsmen of Syria to Central Asia at the turn of the century, had disastrous consequences for the Syrian cotton textile industry. By the early fifteenth century, she had become a region that exported raw cotton; the Venetians assisted this transformation by "dumping" cotton goods in the Syrian market (Ashtor, 1974 reprinted 1978: 5–53).

Although Ashtor consistently "blames the victim" by attributing Syria and Egypt's industrial decline in the later Middle Ages to internal factors—the increased role of the state, corruption, technological backwardness, and the like—the causes seem far more complicated to me. Two external factors were central in bringing about the transformation of Egypt (and to some extent Syria) from a hegemonic and enormously diversified economy, in which trade, agriculture, and industry worked synergistically, to a "dependent" economy whose limited strength came from only two sources, the production of raw materials and strategic control over access to the Indian Ocean. The first external factor was certainly the aggressive trade policies of Venice, but the second was the double impact of the Black Death and Tamerlane. By the fifteenth century only her strategic role was left, a slender thread that would be cut by the Portuguese.

The Impact of the Black Death on Egypt and Syria

During the second half of the fourteenth century several negative trends converged in Egypt–Syria, alerting us to look for a common cause. First, there was the decline in industrial production, as the raw materials of the Mamluk state—notably flax, cotton, sugar cane—were no longer fully processed into linen and cotton textiles and confections for local consumption and export but were increasingly bought up by Italian traders for processing in European factories.

Second, the import of goods from India and beyond (not only pepper and other spices but also porcelain, silk, and other manufactured goods) and their reshipping to Europe no longer ensured the prosperity of the Karimi merchants who, during the same period, lost to government monopolies their prominence as freewheeling entrepreneurs.[22] The Mamluk sultans sought to squeeze every possible drop of revenue from the transit trade, a strategy naturally deplored as confiscatory by the Italians.

And finally, the Mamluk state seems to have reached new heights of oppression during the era of the Circassian or Burji Mamluks (who supplanted the weakened Bahri Mamluks in 1382). It is clear that during this late period the ruling elite intensified the rate at which it extracted surplus from the Egyptian and Syrian countryside, forcing both sales of crops at depressed prices and purchases of government-monopoly products at inflated ones. Furthermore, there were other signs of economic distress: forced loans extracted from the remaining merchants, periodic government devaluations of the exchange rate, debasement of the metallic content of currency, and a general decline in productivity.

It is not unlikely that the common precipitating cause of this convergence of symptoms of economic decline was the Black Death of 1347–1350. Although it did not "kill" Egypt immediately, it so undermined its basic strength that even the continued infusion of wealth made possible by Egypt's monopoly over the sea route to India and China was barely enough to support her. The ultimate proof of this was how quickly the Mamluk enterprise collapsed, once the Portuguese pulled the plug in the beginning of the sixteenth century. By 1506 no spices were coming through the Cairo markets. Within ten years, the Mamluks were defeated by the Ottoman Turks and Egypt and Syria became provinces of the Ottoman Empire. Therefore, this epidemic must be examined closely, even though we lack the data available for the same period in Europe. In the absence of precise data we must try to deduce the logical connections between demographic losses and the symptoms of economic decline.

Michael Dols, using imaginative methods, has made the only detailed study of the Black Death in the Middle East. His 1977 book is summarized in his article in Udovitch (1981: 397–428). The account that follows draws heavily on his findings. The Plague arrived in Alexandria in the autumn of 1347, which means that it must have been carried there directly from the Italian outposts on the Black Sea. By spring it had spread southward through the Egyptian Delta. Its virulence peaked in Cairo between October 1348 and January 1349, after which it continued its destructive path to Upper Egypt. Maqrizi's description of the symptoms suggests that it was the highly fatal pneumonic plague, an accurate diagnosis. Although Maqrizi's mortality figures are clearly exaggerated, Dols (1981: 413) believes that it is not unreasonable to assume that daily mortality in the city of Cairo alone reached 10,000, based on extant records and on the death rate in a slightly later plague for which better accounts exist. In all, Dols concludes that some 200,000 persons died in Cairo alone in the course of the plague. My own estimates yield a total population for the city just before the plague of approximately half a million (Abu-Lughod, 1971: 131), which means that within a few years some 40 percent of Cairo's population was wiped out. This is not inconsistent with Maqrizi's view that from one-third to two-fifths of the combined population of Egypt and Syria died in the course of the plague.[23]

In 1345, just before the outbreak, Cairo probably contained some six percent of the total population of Egypt, which may have been about eight million. A one-third loss would have left the total population of the country at about five million, which was gradually reduced during the next fifty years as the plague periodically, albeit less virulently, reappeared. Further population decline is acknowledged to have occurred during the centuries of Ottoman rule. The population of Egypt was a scant three million when the French made their estimates at the time of Napoleon's invasion of Egypt in 1798. What are the implications of such a population loss?

In Europe the plague led to great shifts in the distribution of population, dislodging peasants and serfs from their land and causing an exodus of urbanites fleeing the worst conditions in their areas. In Egypt, the population was less free to move. Hemmed in by deserts and tied to the land as part of the Mamluk amirs' fiefs ('iqta'), the "serfs" had no forests to which they could flee and urbanites had no untilled land to clear and cultivate. Therefore, the unforeseen positive consequences experienced in Europe after the plague were not paralleled in Egypt.

On the other hand, the disintegration of industry that appeared in Europe as skilled craftsmen were decimated by the plague was fully paralleled in Egypt. Some of the decline in Egyptian productivity must be attributed to this dramatic loss of skilled manpower. A similar decline evidently occurred in the countryside as the loss of skilled farmers and sheer labor power destroyed the elaborate system of canals on which that hydraulic society depended. Losses in the commercial class must have been even more dramatic. The Karimi merchants, engaged primarily in long-distance sea trade, were particularly vulnerable to any disease that moved from port to port. That the state became more directly involved in international trade after the Black Death may have been related to a decline in the number of private traders. Thus, the three trends previously noted—declining industry, displacement of the autonomous Karimi by the state, and the heightened ruthlessness of the ruling elite—may all have been linked to the effects of the plague.

The Mamluk system was essentially a mechanism for mobilizing the natural resources and labor of the country to support an elaborate military machine and the luxurious style of life of its alien elite.[24] Given the labor-intensive methods of production of the time, that surplus depended, more than in contemporary societies, on the labor force that produced it. With labor supplies severely reduced by the Black Death, the system could no longer produce the same surplus. The increasingly exploitative strategies employed by Mamluk sultans in the late fourteenth and fifteenth centuries can be interpreted as desperate attempts to maintain revenues in the face of a severely eroded economic base.

After the Black Death, Egypt's economic foundation grew more dependent on long-distance trade. As Europe recovered from the depression of the second half of the fourteenth century, her demand for the goods of the East sharply increased. To obtain their supplies Europe had to maintain good relations with Egypt; to supply the goods Egypt, with its last remaining reserves of strength, had to guard its exclusive access to the Far East.

Relations between the Mamluk Regime and the Italian Traders

From the onset of the Crusades the Franks had been trying to reach the Red Sea; each time, the Egyptians managed to block them.[25] Saladin had devoted considerable effort to preventing European penetration from the Mediterranean. The last serious attempt by the Franks ended in disaster with the defeat of St. Louis in 1250, whereas the final enfeebled effort, known to few, was the unsuccessful Crusade led by Peter von Lusignan in 1365 (see inter alia, Labib, 1965: 337). The Mamluks took their responsibility as seriously as their predecessors. European merchants were absolutely prevented from passing through Egypt, and their arrivals and departures at the Mediterranean port of Alexandria were rigidly supervised and controlled.

The phenomenon of the *muda*, so remarked by historians of Venice (see inter alia, Lane, "Fleets and Fairs" and his "The Merchant Marine of the Venetian Republic," both reprinted in

Lane, 1966; also McNeill, 1974), is clarified by examining Egyptian policies. Lane notes in "Fleets and Fairs" (reprinted 1966: 128) that the Italian term *muda* had two meanings: it referred to a convoy of ships, but also to the period of time during which ships were loaded. The latter meaning seems to date from the early fourteenth century (McNeill, 1974: 60), by which time Venetian ships were owned by the Commune of Venice and rented to the highest bidders (Lane, "The Merchant Marine . . . " as reprinted in 1966: 143). Security of sailing explains only part of the *muda*'s function; arrival in the port of Alexandria may explain an additional amount.

Italian ships were required to assemble in the harbor of Alexandria and none could unload until all had arrived for the season. (As noted later, a similar policy was followed in Chinese treaty ports.) In part, this prevented unpredictable price fluctuations that irregular arrivals might engender, but it also served to facilitate control over trade. The "policing" of the land and sea borders of Egypt was not new, nor was it confined to Europeans. Earlier accounts (reported in Labib, 1965: 160–162) noted toll and "passport" stations on the land borders and a system to supervise the disembarkation of persons in Alexandria. This may well have been extended more strictly to Europeans.

When ships entered the harbor, everyone remained on board until the Divan al-Hims (the head of Customs) and the city governor met them offshore. Then, the merchants either registered themselves and their goods on board ship or were lighteraged to the port at which they gave information about themselves and filed a sworn declaration. Customs officials stayed on board until everything was unloaded (Labib, 1965: 243–244). Christian foreigners had to have a special permit (visa) from their consul, who assumed responsibility for their good conduct, and had to pay an import tax that was considerably higher than for Muslims.[26] Once they had "cleared customs" European merchants repaired to specified funduks, comparable to the houses maintained by "foreign" traders at the fairs of Champagne, at which they stored goods, conducted trade, notarized contracts, and came under the jurisdiction of their own law. They were not permitted beyond the confines of Alexandria—not even as far as the nearby port of Rosetta.

Given such restrictions on their movement, European traders

were completely dependent upon the Karimi merchants and, later, the governmental monopoly officials for their supplies of return cargo. Although much of the return cargo was in the form of bulk agricultural products or locally manufactured goods, the most prized purchases—and the real reason the Italians continued to come, even when wars heated up or piracy inflated the costs of protection—were the spices and dyes from Malaysia and Indonesia, the pepper and silk and cotton cloth from India, and the porcelains and silks of Cathay so demanded in Europe. All these came through the closely guarded Red Sea ports, either obtained in Aden from Indian merchants or brought from farther away on Arab ships.

The Red Sea and Aden: Gateway to the East

Al-Muqaddasi described Aden as a "centre to which travellers flock from every quarter" (Ranking and Azoo trans.: 109), "a large, flourishing and populous town, strongly fortified and pleasant" (Ranking and Azoo trans.: 135).

> It is the gateway of as-Sin [China] and the sea-port of al-Yaman, the granary of al-Maghrib and the depot of all kinds of merchant goods. There are many palatial buildings in it. . . . The town is in the shape of a sheep-pen encircled by a mountain which surrounds it down to the sea while an arm of the sea passes behind this mountain, so that the town is only approached by fording this arm of the sea and thus gaining access to the mountain.

In spite of its forbidding location, or perhaps because of it, Aden had traditionally been the entrepôt for any traffic heading out of the Red Sea, whether destined for African ports such as Kilwa (Chittick, 1974; Mollat, 1971: 304) and Zanzibar or for Gujarat and the Malabar coast of India, and even points beyond. Maqrizi reports that in his time (early fifteenth century) ships coming from India never entered the Red Sea but stopped at Aden (Heyd, 1885: 379).

The route to India via Aden was considerably more treacherous than the one that exited the Persian Gulf. It required a skilled use of monsoon winds and careful navigational techniques to cross the open sea out of sight of land. It is interesting that the term "monsoon" was derived from the Arabic *mawsim*, which originally referred to the time of departure of land caravans (Goitein, 1967: 276); if anything, the winds imposed a more stringent schedule for sailing the Indian Ocean than any caravan head, no matter how powerful, could. Ships sailed in convoys in the spring and fall. In between, merchants settled in ports to conduct business. It is this, more than any other factor, that accounts for the stable port enclaves occupied by Muslim Arabs and Persians along the west coast of India.

Although this subject will be discussed in greater detail in Chapter 8, we might pause here to consider its implications. Whereas European merchants trading in the Middle East seem to have had very little influence on the culture of the unreceptive Muslim societies in whose ports they were essentially quarantined, the Muslim traders established colonies throughout the Asian world, carrying not only their goods of trade but their culture and religion. Through them, Islam was transmitted to India, Ceylon, Malaysia, and Indonesia. There, it coexisted with the Hindu and Buddhist cultures that were being diffused from India and China along the same routes. This intermingling and coexistence gave a continuity and coherence to the Indian Ocean arena that, ever since the rise of Islam, the Mediterranean had lacked. This may account for the fact that the vicissitudes in contact and trade traced in the Mediterranean Sea—so often a divider rather than a connector—were not paralleled in the Indian Ocean, where a quite different periodicity of historical epochs prevailed.

The Asian system will be explored in Part III. But before we turn to that very different arena, we might quickly examine the lessons from the Egyptian case.

Lessons from Egypt

By the thirteenth century, as even Chaunu (1979 trans.: 58) has acknowledged, Egypt was a vanguard for the world system. By then,

> The link between the Red Sea, India, Malaya and the East Indies had been secured . . . [albeit] dependent upon the seasonal shift of the mon-

soons for navigation. . . . Both before and after the domination of the Mamluks, Egypt had a direct link to India and the East Indies and pushed its communication system as far as Mohammedan Spain and the western [sic] Maghreb. Thus, Egypt was the forerunner of Portugal. . . . At this time in Cairo . . . a group of wealthy people had a horizon which included nearly a third of the whole world.

Egypt's strategic position between the middle (Mediterranean) and green (South China) seas, coupled with her ability to defend that link from European ambitions, assured her continued importance even after her productive economy fell victim to depopulation, an oppressively extractive feudal system dominated by an alien militaristic elite, and ultimately the loss of her Levantine empire occasioned by Tamerlane's incursions.

Thus, in the long run, the undermining of her indigenous economy proved less important than her incapacity to control this key route of international trade. Although she and her primary trading partner, Venice, managed to hold their joint monopoly throughout the fifteenth century, neither survived the decline in that route. The circumnavigation of Africa by Vasco da Gama proved to be the undoing of both.

In July 1497 da Gama set sail from Portugal, eventually rounding the Cape and attacking Arab settlements at Malindi, Kilwa, Zanzibar, and Mombasa on the east African coast. He then struck out across the open seas to Calicut. "Following upon da Gama's second expedition of 1502, the Portuguese made the important policy decision that they would block the Red Sea to Muslim shipping" (Serjeant, 1963: 15). Soon afterward, the Portuguese attacked the seaports on the Persian Gulf. The Muslim sultan of Gujarat, the ruler of Yemen, and the Hindu head of Calicut all appealed to the Mamluks to defend them against the Portuguese, but the Egyptian fleet was soundly defeated in the Arabian Sea. Egypt's economy received a serious blow when, with this act, the India trade upon which she had become singularly dependent was thus cut off. Her conquest by the Ottoman Turks in 1516 sealed her defeat.

In this chapter we explored the many forces that conspired to weaken Egypt over the course of several centuries. The two-pronged military threat from European Crusaders and Central Asian Mongols set the process in motion. This led to a defensive militarization of the region that eventually undermined civil society and its vital economic institutions. The weakened economy was severely debilitated by the effects of the Black Death, which left only the India trade as the prime surviving source of wealth. When the Portuguese took over that trade, Egypt was undone. It was less her lack of business acumen than her lack of fire power (Ayalon, 1956), that caused her demotion from kingpin of the collapsing world system.

Notes

1. Louis IX was himself taken prisoner and ransomed only by paying a princely sum.

2. Ehrenkreutz (1981: 342–343) is particularly harsh in his evaluation of the role of the Genoese in facilitating the defeat of Europe in the region. He notes that

> the slave trade between Genoa and the Mamluk Sultanate [in the second half of the thirteenth century] performed a crucial function in the shaping of western Mediterranean history. Genoa exploited it to gain commercial hegemony. The Mamluks depended upon it to maintain and expand their hold in Egypt, Syria, and Cicilia. Crusader establishments and various Armenian principalities disappeared under the deadly blows inflicted on them by the hosts of military slaves supplied by the trade. . . . One can argue that Genoa's pro-Mamluk policy was instrumental in bringing about the extinction of Christian domination at the hands of Muslim warriors.

But it might easily be argued that Venice's collusion in long-distance trade was probably as important as Genoa's provision of slaves in contributing to the strength of the Egyptian state.

3. My own interpretation of the deficiency is that although the Muslims were no less astute in business than the Italians, or the Champagne merchants for that matter, two factors conspired to suppress the data. First, in Islam, verbal witnesses were required to attest to the validity of a contract; therefore, although agreements might be written down, in themselves they were unenforceable without the testimony of witnesses. That meant that some agreements probably were not written. Second, although Muslim businessmen used notaries to witness their transactions, copies of the actual paper agreement were given only to the contracting parties. Unlike their European counterparts, the notaries seem not to have kept the same "authoritative" records that were preserved in large notebooks (in the case of Genoa) or in bailiffs' books (as in the case of Champagne). What has been preserved, then, is a sample of contracts evidently thrown away when transactions were finished; these are some of the documents found in the Geniza "kitchen midden."

4. As we shall see, there are some documents found in the Geniza papers studied by Goitein (1967), but they are from a limited period and the sampling error is probably extreme.

5. Joint ownership specifies that nothing can be done with the share of a joint owner without his consent and that profits are to be divided according to ownership shares (Udovitch, 1970a: 25–26). Shafi'i law frowned on the indiscriminate merging of capital into joint ownership, whereas other schools tolerated it. The limited investment partnership was the only type permitted by the rigorous Shafi'i school.

> In this arrangement, each partner contributes a certain sum of money for the common fund; this capital must then be intermingled in order for the contract to become effective. The investors may contribute to the partnership equally or in any other proportion they see fit. Each partner's share in the profits or losses is in direct proportion to his share of the total investment. Any stipulation assigning to one of the partners a share in the profits larger than that of his share of the total investment is invalid. No allowance could be made for a partner's special business skills or contacts. (Udovitch, 1970a: 34)

6. See also Goitein (1967: 87, and, for examples, 362–367). These sources are not independent, however, since Udovitch depends upon Goitein's "The Main Industries of the Mediterranean as Reflected in the Records of the Cairo Geniza" (1961).

7. Udovitch (1970a: 172) notes that although "commercial arrangements resembling the *commenda* were known in the Near Eastern and Mediterranean world from the earliest times, it is the Islamic form of the contract (*qirad, muqarada, mudaraba*) which is the earliest example of a commercial arrangement identical with that economic and legal institution which became known in Europe as the *commenda*."

8. Although the Geniza documents were found in a repository next to a synagogue in Fustat (Old Cairo) that was used by Jews coming primarily from the Maghrib (now Tunisia and Morocco), the documents do not cover only Jews. Furthermore, as Goitein points out elsewhere (1964b), there was little real difference between Jewish and Muslim business practices.

9. A somewhat different view for Mamluk times is drawn by Labib (1965) on the basis of equally systematic analysis of historical chronicles, sources scarcely designed to answer economic questions.

10. Udovitch claims, in his contribution to *The Dawn of Modern Banking* (1979: 255–273), that "banks" were unknown in the Middle East until they were introduced by Europeans in the nineteenth century. However, this does not seem a fair comparison. Banks as we know them today were equally absent from thirteenth-century Europe, and many of the banking practices described by Goitein are already familiar from our study of fourteenth-century Bruges (see Chapter 3).

11. Goitein (1967: 241) points out that the French *aval*, the endorsement on a bill of exchange, is derived from the Arabic term *hawala*.

12. Much of what follows has been condensed from *Cairo: One Thousand and One Years of the City Victorious* (Abu-Lughod, 1971).

13. Cairo was reserved for the alien elite and commoners were actually barred from entering it.

14. As noted earlier, the naval clashes between the Genoese men-of-war and the Fatimids of North Africa in the tenth and early eleventh centuries were actually the opening phases of the Crusades.

15. In an explanatory note to their translation of al-Muqaddasi, who noted that the canal was closed, Ranking and Azoo (note on p. 28) give the following background: "This . . . refers to the canal of Trajan which connected . . . [one] branch of the Nile with Arsinoe . . . in the Red Sea. The original canal, known as the river of Ptolemy . . . was commenced by Pharaoh Necho II (B.C. 480) . . . completed by Ptolemy (B.C. 274) . . . restored by Trajan (A.D. 106) . . . [and was] still open to traffic . . . up to the tenth century." Heyd (1885: 40), on the other hand, dates its filling to the late eighth century, an unlikely timing.

16. Goitein (1964b) calls the tenth, eleventh, and twelfth centuries the apogee of Arab–Jewish symbiosis.

17. Labib (1965: 62) states unequivocally that in Ayyubid and Mamluk times the merchants had to be Muslims. "It is a fact that those merchants who wanted to join the Karimi group had first to accept Islam or already to be Muslims. In this way the group profited from the experience of Christians and Jews [who converted] and of those Muslim merchants who had settled in Egypt after the disturbances and insecurities in Iraq." Karimis could, however, be recent converts. Wiet (1955) lists, for example, a very important merchant who had converted from Judaism.

18. Fischel (1958: 70) certainly argues this, although Ashtor (1956, reprinted 1978: 51–52) and others demur.

19. Wiet's list of Karimi merchants includes many whose deaths are recorded in the necrologies of the Black Death years, but it also includes some merchants active in the second half of the fifteenth century, long after Ashtor claims they had disappeared.

20. Syrian specialists were imported to Cyprus to advise on sugar production and, according to Ashtor (1981: 105), Marco Polo mentioned Egyptian technical consultants teaching their methods of sugar refining to the Chinese in the second half of the thirteenth century, although I have been unable to find this in my translation.

21. Labib contrasts the low quality of Egyptian silk with the much better threads and fabrics produced in Iraq and Persia. Syrian silk, on the other hand, was highly regarded. Egyptian weavers mixed it with their own to get a higher price. Indeed, 500 Syrians lived in the Fayyum where they were commissioned by the government to cultivate mulberry trees and silkworms (Labib, 1965: 307).

22. The end came decisively in 1429–1434. In the earlier year, Sultan Barsbay established a government monopoly over the pepper trade; in 1430, he prevented the Venetian merchants from getting off their ships in the Alexandria harbor and, in defiance, the Karimi merchants boarded to trade with the Italians. This led to an outright struggle between the merchants and the state. In 1434 Barsbay forbade contacts between the Karimi merchants and the Venetians and completely cornered the pepper market, later expanding his monopoly to other items (Labib, 1965: 337–357 *passim*).

23. Egypt experienced a higher mortality rate than Syria, ironic testimony to her greater centrality in world trade routes. Ibn Habib estimated that only a quarter of Damascus' smaller population died in the plague (Dols, 1981: 415).

24. See Rabie (1972: *passim*) for a detailed explication of the institutions of

Mamluk "feudalism," a term he refuses to apply. Humphries (1977: 7) contrasts the Mamluk system with its predecessor in Syria in this way: "If one compares the armies of twelfth century Syria . . . with the Mamluk forces of the later thirteenth century, it is obvious that the latter were a distinctly heavier burden on society and that they formed a more tightly knit and self-conscious body, one better able to act in its own interests, yet more alien to the society which it dominated."

25. It would not be until the nineteenth century, with the digging of the Suez Canal by the French with the collusion of the British, that European designs on the shortest sea route to India would be achieved.

26. According to Labib (1965: 240–243), Christians from Europe and Byzantium had to pay various taxes. Every traveler paid an entry tax upon arrival (the *maks al-samah*, which amounted to about two gold pieces in the fifteenth century). They also had to pay a 2 percent tax on their cash. Merchandise from Dar al-Harb (literally, the Land of War, i.e., Franks) was subject to a custom tax of 20 percent in all Islamic countries. This tax was levied in Alexandria and Damietta but not in Rosetta, since merchants from Dar al-Harb were not allowed there. In contrast, Muslim merchants paid only the *zaqat* (theoretically 2.5 percent). There were similar taxes on Egyptian merchandise exported by the Europeans.

PART
III
ᘑᘑᘑᘑᘑ

Asia

The Indian Ocean System:
Divided Into
Three Parts

In the thirteenth century and considerably before as well, the Asian sea trade that traversed the Arabian Sea, the Indian Ocean, and the South China Sea was subdivided into three interlocking circuits, each within the shared "control" of a set of political and economic actors who were largely, although certainly not exclusively, in charge of exchanges with adjacent zones. (See Figure 10.) The primary basis for these divisions was geographic, although these geographically determined zones were gradually converted into cultural domains as well.

The westernmost circuit was largely inhabited by Muslims, with ship owners, major merchants, and their resident factors being drawn from the ports of the Arabian Peninsula or the more interior capitals of Baghdad and Cairo, earlier described in Chapters 6 and 7. As already seen, Muslim merchant ships exiting the Gulf made stops along the northwestern coast of India (usually at Gujarat) before proceeding to the Malabar Coast farther south, whereas those exiting the Red Sea, after a stop at Aden or Hadramaut, sailed directly to Malabar. Both at the port of Cambay in Gujarat and the Malabar port entrepôts of Quilon and Calicut they conducted their business through sizable resident "colonies" of Muslim merchants. Some of these merchants originally came from the Middle East but had settled, married, and generally assimilated to their new home; others, however, were indigenous to the region but, through the prolonged contacts of trade, had converted and adopted Muslim culture and language.

The middle circuit connected the south Indian coast—both Mal-

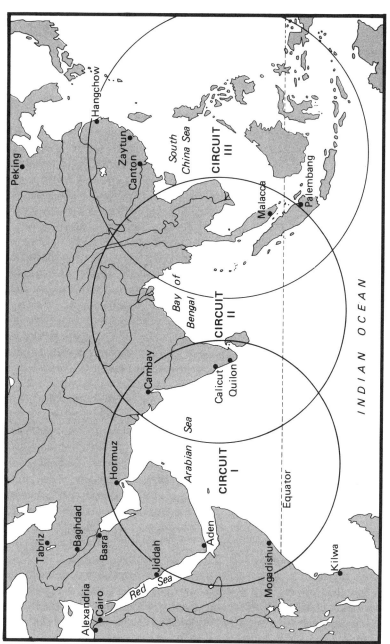

FIGURE 10. The three circuits of the Indian Ocean trade (based on Chaudhuri)

abar on the west and Coromandel on the east—with the region of Sumatra and Malaya that flanked the Strait of Malacca and with Java and the other islands of Indonesia just beyond. This zone was primarily "Hinduized" in culture, at least within its ruling circles, although there were also Buddhist connections and Chinese influences. Although Islam made major inroads from the fourteenth century onward, during the thirteenth century Muslim influences were still decidedly secondary.

The easternmost circuit was Chinese "space," the sea that joined the east coast of Indochina and the northern shore of Java with the great ports of south China being under the hegemony of the Sung and then Yuan navies. This was the realm of Buddhism and particularly Confucianism and was the domain par excellence of what scholars have called the tribute trade.

Although it is thus possible to delineate three "great cultural traditions" in the Indian Ocean's continuous expanse, it was not culture per se that set the boundaries between the three regions. Rather, cultural influences spread most freely *within* each of the three zones whose limits were, in the most fundamental sense, set by the wind patterns of the separate monsoon zones. Where countercyclical wind patterns met, as shown in Figure 11, they broke up the larger area into fairly discrete subsystems.

Although on occasion shippers of any subsystem might venture to trade in the adjacent circuit or even range freely over all three, the "natural" condition of the Indian Ocean was for several locally hegemonic powers to coexist; no single power ever exercised dominance over the entire system. (For a fuller exposition of this, see, inter alia, Chaudhuri, 1985.)

In the port emporia that were the meeting places for merchants and emissaries, representatives from the three culture zones were likely to mingle and to trade ideas as well as goods. Whenever there were major infusions from one cultural zone to another, such as the movement of Islam into Malaya and Indonesia, these were achieved through beachheads that had been established in the emporia. (See the discussion of Malacca in Chapter 9.) This was in sharp contrast to the situation in the hinterlands around the ports; regions off the "main track" of trade remained remarkably insulated from these international currents.

Because the boundaries between the major subsystems were set

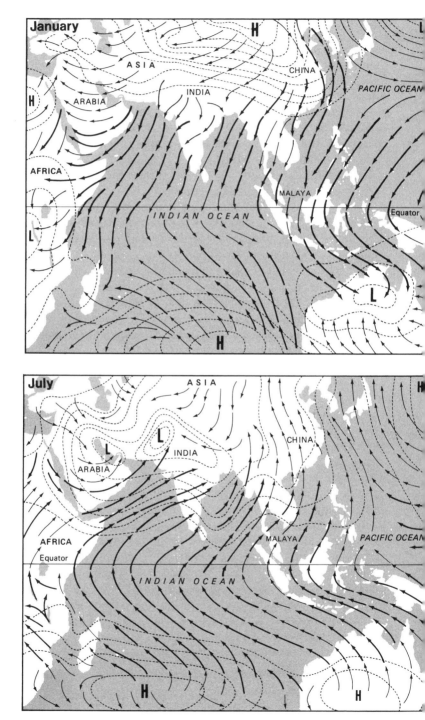

FIGURE 11. Monsoon wind patterns in the Indian Ocean.

by "natural" forces rather than imperial reach, the starting point
for Part III must be the monsoon imperatives that routinely subdivided the long Indian Ocean journey into the three circuits shown
in Figure 10: (1) the westernmost circuit, from the Red Sea–
Arabian Peninsula–Persian Gulf to the southwest tip of India; (2)
the middle circuit, from the southeastern coast of India to the
Strait of Malacca and Java; and (3) the easternmost circuit, from
the Straits of Malacca and Sunda and the Indian archipelago (Java
and beyond) to the great ports of southeast China.

There is no better guide to the monsoon seasons than the navigators' manual of Ibn Majid, written toward the end of the fifteenth century, just before the Portuguese arrived in the Indian
Ocean. This manual was not innovative; it was not a description
of new routes but simply a codification and detailed expansion of
earlier Arab sea manuals. In the Eleventh Fa'ida of this work (see
Tibbetts, 1981: 225–242), Ibn Majid gives detailed advice about
the "monsoons (sailing seasons) in which one is *compelled* to travel,
the intervals of the monsoons, their beginnings and ends, *showing
what is not good in each*" (Tibbetts, 1981: 225, italics added). He
makes explicit the break between the circuits and, as we shall see,
his omissions are as significant as his inclusions (Table 1).

He first looks at the Arabia to India circuit. He discusses the
timing of departures from the Arabian coasts (Yemen, Jiddah) and
notes that to reach Malabar in India such journeys *must* be undertaken by the end of March or the beginning of April, but in no case
later than early May. (It is possible to delay the time of departure
a little if the destination is only Gujarat, and by as much as one month
if the destination is merely Hormuz or the Persian Gulf.) The important thing was "to reach India before the Indian Ocean . . . closed"
(Tibbetts, 1981: 226) since, apparently, there were ninety days
during the year when it was suicidal to cross the open seas of the
western circuit of the Indian Ocean. The consequences of missing
the specific season for sailing were hardly trivial, since the cros-
swinds could immobilize an eastbound ship for up to a year.

Know that a man bound for India when he is forced to moor because
of the Ayzab [monsoon] in Al-Shihr or Fartak and desires to go to
India . . . must stay there for four months only, but he who is forced
to moor in Yemen must stay there for a whole year when bound for
India, but for seven months if bound for Hormuz.

Table 1. Monsoon Sailing Dates[a]

Itinerary	Dates Given	Source
Two Seasons from West to East (Arabian Peninsula to Malacca)		
Long Monsoon Season (Kaws) between February and May		
Arabian Peninsula to west coast of India		
Muscat to Malabar	2/20–4/11	Ibn Majid
Muscat to Gujarat	Leave until 5/1	Ibn Majid
Muscat to Sind	Leave until 5/11	Ibn Majid
Muscat to Malacca	Leave by 3/17–18	Celebi and Sulayman
Aden to Gujarat	3/17–5/6	Celebi
Aden to Gujarat	3/18–5/7	Sulayman
West Coast of India to Malacca		
Gujarat to Malacca	4/11–9/28	Ibn Majid
Gujarat to Malacca	Leave by 3/17–4/26	Celebi
Gujarat to Malacca	Leave by 3/18–4/27	Sulayman
Malabar to Malacca	Leave by 4/21	Ibn Majid
Malabar to Malacca	Leave by 4/16	Celebi
Malabar to Malacca	Leave by 4/17	Sulayman
Short Monsoon Season (Damani) Mid-August to End of September		
Arabian Peninsula to west coast of India and beyond		
Aden to India	8/29–9/18	Ibn Majid
Aden to India	Leave 8/24–28	Celebi
Aden to India	Leave 8/25	Sulayman
Aden to Malacca	Leave 8/14–15	Celebi
Aden to Malacca	Leave 8/15	Sulayman
Hormuz to Malacca	Leave 8/19	Ibn Majid
West coast of India to Malacca		
Gujarat to Malacca	Leave 9/3	Celebi
Gujarat to Malacca	Leave 9/14	Sulayman
Gujarat to Malacca	Leave 9/24	Ibn Majid
Malabar to Malacca	Leave 9/23	Celebi
Malabar to Malacca	Leave 9/24	Sulayman
Malabar to Malacca	Leave 9/28	Ibn Majid

Table 1. (*continued*)

Itinerary	Dates Given	Source
One Long Season from East to West (China to Arabian Peninsula)		
Ayzab Monsoon (mid-October to mid-April)		
China and Malacca to India and beyond		
China to Malacca	11/23–3/2	Ibn Majid
Malacca to Aden	1/1–2/20	Ibn Majid
Malacca to Aden	12/27–2/15	Celebi
Malacca to Aden	12/28–2/16	Sulayman
Sumatra to Aden	12/7–2/5	Celebi
Sumatra to Aden	12/8–2/6	Sulayman
Sumatra to Bengal	2/20–4/11	Ibn Majid
Sumatra to Bengal	2/15–4/6	Celebi
Sumatra to Bengal	2/16–4/7	Sulayman
India to the Arabian Peninsula		
Bengal to Aden/Hormuz	1/2–1/31	Ibn Majid
Bengal to Aden/Hormuz	12/27–1/26	Celebi
Bengal to Aden/Hormuz	12/28–1/27	Sulayman
Calicut to Gujarat	October–April	Ibn Majid
Gujarat to Oman	10/13–4/16	Celebi
Gujarat to Oman	10/14–4/17	Sulayman
Gujarat to Arabia	10/18–4/11	Ibn Majid
Gujarat to Arabia	10/13–3/27	Celebi
Gujarat to Arabia	10/14–3/28	Sulayman

[a]Adapted from information given in Tibbetts (1981).

In contrast to the tight schedule for open-sea sailing, however, it was always possible to hug the coastline and travel between the Persian Gulf and Gujarat (Tibbetts, 1981: 227) since this route was open virtually year-round.

The return trip from India to the Arabian Peninsula had to be made between late fall and early spring with a break in mid-winter;

Ibn Majid says that it is possible to set sail from Gujarat beginning around October 18, but that the return voyage should be delayed somewhat if setting out from Malabar, because otherwise the rains still falling there would soak the cargo. On the other hand, travel should be avoided after February 10, although it is possible, albeit slow, to hug the coastline to Gujarat. But Ibn Majid (Tibbetts, 1981: 231) adds the following ominous note:

> He who leaves India on the 100th day (2nd March) is a sound man, he who leaves on the 110th will be all right. However, he who leaves on the 120th is stretching the bounds of possibility and he who leaves on the 130th is inexperienced and an ignorant gambler.

The second part of Ibn Majid's exposition concerns travel in the Bay of Bengal (i.e., the second or central circuit between India and the Strait). According to him, only in January is the weather propitious for rounding the tip of the Indian subcontinent. However, having attained the southeastern coast, there is a long sailing season (from about February 20th to the end of April) in which to journey across the Bay of Bengal to the Strait of Malacca. It is almost impossible to make a round trip within a single sailing season, however. Ships coming eastward from India arrive in the straits area either at the same time as or slightly after those heading westward from the straits to India, which means that a layover in the straits could possibly last a year!

By the time Ibn Majid was writing, Arab ships no longer went beyond the straits area. (The third and final part of his chapter refers to travel to the East African coast.) Although his voluminous manual details an incredibly varied set of itineraries—including sailing directions for going down the east coast of Africa, rounding the Cape of Good Hope, sailing up the west coast of Africa, and entering the Mediterranean through the Strait of Gibraltar, that is, the reverse of the route Vasco da Gama was later to take—Ibn Majid ignores the easternmost circuit of the Indian Ocean–South China Sea, namely, from Java to the south China ports. Although we know that Persian and Arab boats had traversed that circuit as early as the eighth and ninth centuries, the itinerary is omitted in this otherwise comprehensive fifteenth-century document.

The explanation, as will be seen in the coming chapters, is simple. Arab sailors no longer needed directions because, by the fifteenth century, their ships no longer sailed to Chinese ports. Chinese seaports were closed to foreign traders in the latter part of the fourteenth century, a fact of supreme importance in accounting for the collapse of the premodern world system. This topic will preoccupy us in Part III because it seems to hold the key to both the decline of the old system and the opportunity this afforded for a new Eurocentered world system. When, after 1435, the Ming dynasty withdrew a powerful Chinese fleet from the ocean via which, hitherto, her ships had regularly visited southwest India and occasionally reached the Persian Gulf, an enormous vacuum of power was created that, some 70 years later, the Portuguese intruders filled with their own brute fire power.

The Indian Ocean, then, must be conceived of as a trading zone divided into three circuits or subsystems shared by numerous groups: the Persians and Arabs who acted in their own right but also as intermediaries for Mediterranean Europe; the Indians on the west coast of the subcontinent whose Islamic beliefs gave them a special affinity to Middle Easterners; the Indians of the east coast whose Hindu and Buddhist culture bridged the Bay of Bengal; the diverse population of Malays, Sumatrans, Javans, and long-term "foreign" residents who made the Strait of Malacca area a cultural melting pot, at least in the numerous trading entrepôts that dotted the coasts; and the Chinese and later Chinese/Mongols who dominated the easternmost circuit between Java and China. The wind patterns that divided the expanse into three circuits yielded two interchange points that remained relatively constant: the south Indian coast and Ceylon, at which circuits one and two met, and the Strait of Malacca, at which circuits two and three intersected.

Part III is organized accordingly. Chapter 8 examines the two coasts of south India: Gujarat/Malabar, which looked westward to the Arab world, and the Coromandel Coast, which faced the opposite way toward the Strait of Malacca and the so-called Indian archipelago, Indonesia. Chapter 9 examines the Strait area itself (which the sixteenth-century Portuguese writer, Tomé Pires, referred to, with good reason, as the "gullet" of world sea trade) and demonstrates the limits of its power to affect the overall world system. Chapter 10 takes up the most puzzling case of all, China, which, under the indigenous Sung and then the Mongol-ruled Yuan dynasties, seemed fated in the thirteenth century to become the hegemonic power if not of the world at least a goodly portion of it—via both the great land route across Central Asia and the great sea route across the Indian Ocean and its extensions. Chapter 5 analyzed the role the Black Death played in the collapse of the northern overland route. Chapter 10 chronicles the not unrelated collapse of the sea route.

This leads to the final question of the book, which will be explored in Chapter 11. Did the West rise or did the East fall? In Part III we intend to demonstrate that the East had already substantially "fallen" before the Portuguese men-of-war appeared in the Indian Ocean. That weakened world was a plum ripe for the taking. No special "virtue" inhered in the conquerors; they took control of the remnants of a preexisting world system, one they then ruthlessly honed to serve their own ends.

The Indian Subcontinent:
On the Way to Everywhere

During medieval times the Indian subcontinent, particularly its southern end, served as both a natural link and a divider in the great sea route that connected the Mediterranean region and the Middle East with China. South India was a major and logical landfall, on whose west coast ships from Africa and Mesopotamia landed and on whose east coast westward-bound ships from China or the islands and peninsulas of Indonesia, Malaysia, or Thailand found safe harbor. Evidence from antiquity and even prehistoric times suggests that even before the most distant termini were in direct contact with one another, south India constituted a true "hinge"[1] (albeit only for shorter segments) between the separate basins of the Indian Ocean—that great "highway" for the migration of peoples, for cultural diffusion, and for economic exchange.

South India, as Stein notes (1982a), does not constitute a monolithic and undifferentiated "natural" unit, although it is conventionally identified as the Dravidian area south of the Krishna River and the watershed of its major tributary. Rather, it contains two

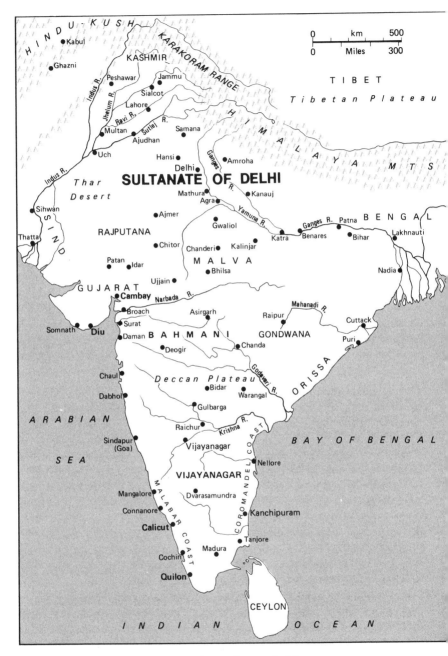

FIGURE 12. Continental India showing regions and cities.

macroecological zones: the Malabar Coast (now centered at the Indian province of Kerala), an isolated narrow coastal region along the western littoral, and, separated from Malabar by high ridges, the wider plains macroregion to the east, the land of the Tamils, whose coastal zone is referred to as Coromandel.[2] (See Figure 12.)

Most South Indianists, particularly those interested in the medieval period, have concentrated their studies on the Tamil plain since this is where a succession of "high" civilizations developed, beginning with Pallava rule in the third century A.D. (See, inter alia, Nilakanta Sastri, 1976: 101 *seq*.) The Pallavas, who had invaded from the north, were ultimately displaced by an indigenous dynasty, the Chola, who between the fifth and thirteenth centuries developed a remarkably advanced agrarian, mercantile, and industrial society. It is easy to understand why scholars have paid almost exclusive attention to this eastern region, since the social, linguistic, and cultural forms of Chola civilization "profoundly influenced people over a great portion of the southern peninsula" (Stein, 1982a: 16).

Stein is understandably reluctant to combine Malabar with this more agrarian "civilized" region, not only because the two subregions differ in terms of climate and social organization[3] but because "after the tenth century . . . [Malabar] along with the rest of Chera country (Kerala) was a region of extreme isolation from other parts of the southern peninsula." Malabar, however, cannot be ignored because of the preeminent role it played in the trade system (Stein, 1982a: 14–15). It is this role that interests us most.

It is important to recognize that both subregions of south India were involved in primitive world economies long before the thirteenth and fourteenth centuries. It is therefore necessary to glance backward to trace their linkages to systems to their west and east.

Early Links Westward to the Mediterranean

For our purposes the westernmost "circuit" of the Indian Ocean arena, still functioning with vitality in the thirteenth and fourteenth centuries, had always existed, although the traffic over that early route naturally expanded and contracted with the fortunes of the societies it linked.

Apparently, the sea trade to and from Gujarat and perhaps even the Malabar Coast was already part of a trade system connecting west and south Asia 4,000 years ago (Stein, 1982a: 18). Thus, long before the Christian era, the sea link between Mesopotamia (now Iraq) and what the Arabs referred to as "Sind" (today's Pakistan) was well established and was even beginning to stretch southward, possibly carried by the migration of northern peoples.

From the beginning, the people of the alluvial plains on which two of the world's earliest urban societies emerged—Mesopotamia between the Tigris and Euphrates Rivers that debouched into the Persian Gulf, and the valley between the branches of the Indus River whose mouth lay on the north Arabian Sea—were involved in trade, cultural contact, and perhaps even population exchange. Their trade with one another is attested to not only by the existence, on the soil, of each other's artifacts (Tibbetts, 1956: 183–184) but by excavations at important intermediate points, such as the island of Dilmun (now Bahrain), whose major function was to serve that transit.

The third riverine civilization developing in the Nile valley also seems to have maintained early sea links with other evolving centers, both at the eastern Mediterranean (Ebla north of contemporary Aleppo in present-day Syria, Byblos just north of today's Beirut, and possibly even southeastern Anatolia in present-day Turkey) and along the various coasts of the Arabian Sea: Punt (assumed to be Ethiopia), the southern littoral of the Arabian Peninsula, and perhaps even with the western edge of the Indian subcontinent, although evidence for this is more tenuous.

Certainly, by the first millennium B.C. commerce was already thriving between the Red Sea and northwest India. Control of this trade may have been captured by the Arabs of the peninsula as early as the third century before Christ, and in spite of growing Greek involvement, these sailors continued to dominate it for centuries to come (Spencer, 1983: 76; Ballard, 1984: 15–16).[4] They were often the intermediaries in the Mediterranean world's growing commercial contacts with the east.

The nature of these contacts, which remains only conjectural for earlier epochs, becomes better documented during the "classical" Hellenic and Roman periods. By then the lines from the Mediterranean to the northern and western parts of the Indian subcontinent were more deeply, albeit selectively, etched. Routes went overland and also by sea, not only via the Persian Gulf but also by way of the canal in Egypt that connected the Mediterranean and the Nile with the Red Sea.

During this phase of European exploration into the westernmost parts of the Indian Ocean arena, the Arabian Sea became a known and exploited route, and a few westerners may even have ventured into the second "circuit" that already connected southeastern India with the multiple generating units of Southeast Asia. The *Periplus of the Eurythraean Sea*, written in the first century A.D., demonstrates that navigation manuals for the sea route to India were highly refined by that time, confirming Europe's long-standing trade with the subcontinent.[5] Literary references also allude to this trade. Thus, Petronius (early first century) refers disapprovingly to the scandalous gossamer Indian cottons adorning Roman women, and Pliny (mid-first century) graphically describes the way to Indian ports through Egypt; the second century geography of Ptolemy even includes a description of the Malabar coast (Logan, reprinted 1981, I: 288–293). Christianity may have been introduced to the Malabar coast (present-day Kerala) as early as late Roman times, a factor that was later to feed Crusader rumors about the Kingdom of Prester John (Beckingham and Huntingford, 1961).

The Romans imported exotic animals, precious stones, woods and ivory, Chinese silk, spices, and even sugar, cotton and fruits from the subcontinent. But "since the Romans desired far more from India than Indians desired from Rome, the Romans had to make up the difference with precious metals" (Spencer, 1983: 77). The hoards of Roman gold coins[6] found at coastal points of the subcontinent confirm that then, as it would be later,[7] the balance of trade was overwhelmingly in India's favor (Spencer, 1983: 76–77; Richards, 1986: *passim* but particularly 31–34; Toussaint, 1966: 40).

The "fall" of Rome had serious implications for the Arab merchants whose trade underwent a sharp decline in the fifth and sixth centuries (Spencer, 1983: 79). South Arabia entered a period of economic stagnation, leaving the Persian Sassanids to keep the lines to the east open until the newly Islamized Arabs, from the

Abbasid capital in Mesopotamia, reentered the Indian Ocean trade in the eighth century. From that time until their defeat by the Portuguese in the first decade of the sixteenth century,[8] Muslim traders dominated one, two, or sometimes all three of the Indian Ocean circuits.

As recounted in Chapter 6, as early as the eighth century Arab–Persian ships were already making the complete journey from the Persian Gulf to Chinese ports on the South China Sea. This lengthy voyage, however, was never efficient, since the wind patterns dictated long port layovers in liminal places at which separate monsoon patterns met in countercyclical directions. Ports on the southwest coast of India and in the Strait of Malacca area, flanked by Sumatra and the Malay Peninsula, were such liminal points. By the tenth century the long journey was being broken at India and again at the strait, stopping places virtually dictated by the "seasons for travel," that is, the monsoons.[9]

In these locations resident colonies of foreign merchants were gradually established. (For the nature of the diaspora trade, see Curtin, 1984.) The reason was obvious. Faced with layovers of three to six months or longer, sojourners set up many of the communal institutions they needed to conduct their lives—ceremonial mosques and temples in which to pray, economic and legal institutions to govern their dealings with one another and with the indigenous inhabitants whom they occasionally converted and often married, and even whole residential quarters and bazaars in which to store transit goods and conduct transactions. The ninth century Arab historian, al-Baladhuri, for example, refers to settlements of Muslim merchants at the Indus mouth, the Malabar coast, and on Ceylon (Toussaint, 1966: 49). Goitein (1963) mentions Jewish merchant colonies not only at Malabar but on the Coromandel coast as well.

Resident factors, not used by the Italians until the fourteenth century, were thus an early feature of the Indian Ocean trade. As the scale of commercial operations expanded in the ninth century, and particularly in the tenth when Fatimid traffic from the Red Sea joined the stream of trade coming from the Persian Gulf, fewer shipowners made the complete circuit and fewer merchants accompanied their goods all the way to China. Instead, they tended to remain in their Indian colonies.

Foreign colonies of Middle Eastern merchants were established earliest on the northwestern coast of India where they blended with the local population. The Islamization of Gujarati merchants began in the first centuries of Islam. Conversions intensified at the end of the twelfth and beginning of the thirteenth centuries with the establishment of the Muslim so-called Slave or Turkish Sultanate of Delhi. Ever since Fatimid times, however, Jewish and Muslim merchants had also set up trade colonies farther south in the region called the Malabar coast.[10] By mid-thirteenth century, one of these settlements, Calicut, became the prime "colonial" port for Muslims traders in that part of south India.

Before discussing these later developments, we briefly examine the early history of the opposite littoral of south India, the Coromandel Coast, which had as ancient a role in maritime trade with Southeast Asia as the west coast had with the Middle East.

Early Links Eastward to Southeast Asia

Contacts between India and Southeast Asia apparently go much farther back in time than earlier investigators had assumed. Originally, scholars believed that China and India were the civilizing influences on Southeast Asia (even D. G. E. Hall, 1981, perpetuates this view); "natives" of the islands of Southeast Asia were viewed either as passive recipients or, at best, active imitators of the more advanced cultures and technologies introduced from the continental core regions.[11]

A new view now prevails. Spencer (1983: 67) emphasizes the importance of Wilhelm G. Solheim II's archaeological excavations in Thailand that suggest "Southeast Asians may have been the very first Asians to grind and polish stone tools, plant rice, make pottery, and cast bronze." Certainly, the results of excavations in the mid-1960s are dramatic. Solheim found evidence of the domestication of plants in Thailand as early as 10,000 B.C. and even an imprint of a grain of rice that has been carbon dated to about 3500 B.C., a thousand years before its presence has been verified in India or China. According to Solheim, Thai metallurgy began in about 4000 B.C., and fine quality bronze was already being produced by the third millennium, some 500 years before it was found in India and 1000 years before China. The long-distance outrigger was also devised by about 4,000 B.C., and this seems to have initiated major outmigrations by water. "During the third millennium B.C., in a series of distinct migrations, the boat-using peoples entered the islands of Indonesia and the Philippines and also sailed westward, reaching Madagascar around 2000 years ago" (Spencer, 1983: 69–71).

If, as Solheim suggests, Southeast Asian sailors were sailing and trading in the Indian Ocean and South China Sea by the first millennium B.C., then it seems more likely that Indian and Chinese civilizations were infused by these mobile culture carriers than that the influence was in the opposite direction (Spencer, 1983: 72). Stein (1982a) acknowledges that sea contacts via the Coromandel coast were so ancient that the basic ethnic composition of the peninsula may have been influenced by overseas migrations from Southeast Asia.

And yet, although it may have been true that these Southeast Asian mariner/traders had a "virtual monopoly on this water until the Arab traders started coming in" (Solheim as quoted in Spencer, 1983: 72), such a monopoly could not have been complete because ever since the early centuries of the Christian era, strong cultural influences have operated in the opposite direction (Stein, 1982a: 17–18).

Indian culture spread eastward along the same routes, even before Pallava times. Thus, the question of when and how the Indian Archipelago (Indonesia) was "Indianized" is, to some extent, irrelevant. The connections had, for all practical purposes, always existed. That during the early Middle Ages it should have been Indian influences, via Hinduism and Buddhism, that shaped the so-called kingdom of Srivijaya along the Strait of Malacca was merely the continuation of influences traveling back and forth along ancient waterways. (Chapter 9 discusses this in greater detail.)

Once trade began to recover in the tenth and eleventh centuries, however, economies throughout Asia expanded markedly. New powers emerged, such as the Cholas in southern India, the Khmers in Angkor, the Burmese at Pagan, the Ly in northern Vietnam, and the Sung on the Chinese mainland. "Among other results, these consolidations seem to have stimulated Asia's maritime commerce and precipitated a tremendous burst of energy among the community of international traders who traveled the navigation channels connecting eastern and western Asia" (Hall, 1980: 162).

Spencer (1983: 74, italics added) adopts the idea of an "archipelago of towns," cautioning us not to see this trade in terms of "nations." His comments are particularly apposite.

> When we speak of Indian contacts with Southeast Asia during the centuries prior to about 1000 A.D., we are referring to a diverse set of relationships whose common background consisted of a tenuous but far-flung network of maritime commerce. Although it is convenient to speak of relations between "India" and "Southeast Asia," we must remember that both realms were very diverse and did not act or interact as politically or culturally unified entities. . . . It is likely that *inhabitants of some coastal settlements in Southeast Asia had better contacts and more interests in common with other such settlements in India or south China than they had with their own hinterlands.* . . . The Indianization of Southeast Asia . . . was both preceded and paralleled by the growth of cosmopolitan port societies. . . . *In general, goods traveled farther than men; few individuals traveled across the entire arc.*

Different groups of merchants were prominent at different times, and often the same ships carried merchants from a variety of places, since the largest could accommodate several hundred persons (Spencer, 1983: 75).

Indian merchants from the Coromandel Coast were actively journeying eastward in the tenth, eleventh, and twelfth centuries. There is some evidence of interchanges between the Cholas and the rulers of Srivijaya by the eleventh century; we even have an account of a raid the Cholas made against Srivijayan ports in 1025. Twelfth-century Chinese sources recognize Chola ports as first-class trade partners and list pearls, coral, betelnuts, cardomons, and cotton products among the items imported from Coromandel. Western sources list spices, aromatics, dyeing and varnishing plants, medicinal herbs, silk, and particularly cotton (Hall, 1980: 163). These goods were carried in ships owned by Tamil merchants with "home offices" on Ceylon and the Coromandel coast (Digby, 1982: 127). Clearly, south Indian exports required a network of relations to agricultural hinterlands and inland trading towns (Hall,

1980: 164), a point we shall return to later when we discuss industrial developments and commercial practices under the Chola.

The Western Coast of India: Gujarat and Malabar
in Medieval Times

Because of the natural division of south India into two subregions
with quite different ecological bases, forms of social organization,
and international arenas for trade, it is necessary to discuss each
separately. This does not mean that there were neither cultural
linkages nor periodic political unifications. In general terms, however, the two faced opposite ways: the west coast looked to the
Middle East, a region described in Chapters 6 and 7, whereas the
east coast looked to Southeast Asia, to be discussed at greater
length in Chapter 9. We therefore begin with Gujarat and Malabar.

Gujarat

The promontory of the Gujarat peninsula on the northwest coast
of India, bordered by the Gulf of Kutch to its north and the Gulf
of Cambay to its south, had harbored ships, sailors, and merchants
since the dawn of its development. To this day, Gujaratis are noted
for their business acumen. It is likely that the small number of
Indian merchants whose presence is recorded in Egypt and possibly
even in Rome during classical times came from that region (Toussaint, 1966: 60). Other contacts were traditionally maintained with
ports in the Persian Gulf and along the Arabian littoral, since local
documents specifically refer to them. By the early days of Islam,
the ports of Cambay and Saymur had already absorbed resident
colonies of Arab merchants, some extremely wealthy, as well as
sailors from Siraf, Oman, Basra, and Baghdad, whose presence
and permanent incorporation through intermarriage Mas'udi observed in the early tenth century when he sojourned there (Chaudhuri, 1985: 98).

    The prosperity of Gujarat, sensitive to the transit trade and the
demand for the raw and finished products of its hinterlands, fluctuated with conditions in the wider system. However, these forces,

rather than operating in a single direction, often set up cross-currents of influence. Thus, Richards (1986: 1) indicates that, because of the fragmentation of power and, it might be added, ensuing impoverishment, "North India in the eighth to the twelfth centuries did not attract precious metals at the same intensity that it had in earlier periods." This was perhaps because during the ninth and tenth centuries Baghdad imported only luxury goods from India and China. By the eleventh and twelfth centuries, however, demand diversified and merchants from Baghdad and Cairo were purchasing large amounts of pepper and other spices and textiles, some destined for Europe (Richards, 1986: 2–3):

> The really major change took place after 1200. By then the carrying capacity and the trading capacity of the great maritime routes had enlarged from the norm in late antiquity. . . . By the thirteenth century true bulk commodities to meet the most basic needs had entered these great arteries of trade. Contemporary descriptions list manufactured textiles, metals, utensils, weapons; semi-processed raw materials such as raw silk, raw cotton; and extracted forest or marine products. . . . Even live horses were shipped in this trade. The most surprising change is the inclusion of bulk foodstuffs such as grains, sugar, butter, salt and dried foods.

What accounted for this thirteenth-century transformation? The great expansion in Mediterranean trade was certainly a primary factor. This global process was reinforced by more local changes as well, to which the emergence of powerful Muslim states in north India contributed significantly. The "new large scale currencies, new state tax structures, and growing populations and markets all favored enlarged flows of precious metals . . . [to India, due to] the renewed role of India in the relationships of the medieval world economy during the thirteenth, fourteenth and fifteenth centuries" (Richards, 1986; but see also Habib, 1982: 82–85).

Counterforces, however, were also at work. Thus, the Mongol conquest of Persia and Iraq by mid-thirteenth century had deflected part of the trade that formerly passed through Gujarat's harbors, since some Mediterranean traffic shifted to the Red Sea and therefore to such southern (Malabar) ports as Quilon and later Calicut. But the fact that Gujarat was absorbed into the Muslim sultanate of Delhi in 1303–1304 reinfused it with vitality, since it became

the chief importer of the luxury goods demanded by the conspicuously consuming Delhi elite (Chaudhuri, 1985: 58). Foreign merchants dominated the trade. In the early fourteenth century, Ibn
Battuta (Husain trans., 1955: 172) described Cambay, the major
port of Gujarat, as "one of the most beautiful cities as regards the
artistic architecture of its houses and . . . mosques;" these had been
constructed by "the majority of its inhabitants [who] are foreign
merchants."

Throughout the late Middle Ages, Gujarat continued to play an
important role in international shipping and commerce, gradually
gaining control over the trade in East African and Coromandel
coast ports as well. Gujarati merchants and sailors were still very
active in the Indian Ocean trade when the Portuguese made their
sudden and frightening appearance at the end of the fifteenth century. Indeed, it seems likely that the navigator who guided Vasco
da Gama from Malindi, on the East African coast, to Calicut was
a Gujarati (Gopal, 1975: 1; Tibbetts, 1981: 10).[12]

The presence of Gujaratis in East Africa was neither unusual
nor new. Cotton cloth was exported to Africa early and continued
to find its way there as late as the 1500s, since "Barbosa, the
Portuguese traveller who arrived in India some time around 1500
. . . witnessed ships from the kingdom of Cambay at the ports of
Mombasa and Malindi. . . . [and] found further that the rulers of
the island kingdoms of Zanzibar and Mafia, south of Mombasa,
were dressed in fine silk and cotton textiles, purchased in Mombasa
from Gujarati traders" (Gopal, 1975: 2). Barbosa also saw Gujarati
ships laden with textiles anchored at Aden (Gopal, 1975: 3), as
had Ibn Battuta 150 years earlier (Husain trans., 1955: xliv). When
Hormuz on the Persian Gulf was captured by the Portuguese in
1507, "the conquerors stopped the export of horses to Gujarat in
order to weaken the military might of the [Indian] Sultanate"
(Gopal, 1975: 4), since horses were, of course, the "tanks" of
medieval warfare. The close ties between Mamluk Egypt and Gujarat are further confirmed by the fact that it was their joint fleet
that the Portuguese finally routed at Diu in 1509.

Malabar—Calicut

The merchants of the Malabar coast, although perhaps of slightly
later vintage, were certainly as wealthy, powerful, astute (and

"foreign") as those of Gujarat. At least since the ninth century, Quilon in the extreme south had been an important port of call for Arab ships and, during the time when the Sung seriously took to the sea, for Chinese junks as well. It was still functioning in the 1330s when Ibn Battuta was shipwrecked nearby, although by then it was dwarfed by Calicut, its rival some distance north, which came to prominence in the mid-thirteenth century.

Accordingly to Das Gupta (1967: quotation from 4–5, italics added) Calicut's rise and fall mirrored shifts in west Asian trade routes, a point made earlier in Chapter 6.

> *Calicut* itself *was thrown up* by a mighty upheaval of Asian trade *in the middle of the thirteenth century*. Before this time the ports of the Persian Gulf had maintained a predominance in the commerce of the Arabian Sea. Vessels had usually sailed from Bussora and Hormuz to Quilon and Colombo. Quilon . . . had been the centre for the numerous junks from China. Long-range arteries of maritime trade had spanned the Asian continent as Chinese junks and Arab *dhouws* obdurately sailed to and fro between southern China and the Persian shores. This structure broke down with the collapse of the Abbasiud caliphate [*sic*] at its western end. In February 1258, the city of Baghdad was stormed by the Mongols. . . . This political collapse caused a commercial decline. The area of the Persian Gulf lost its important role in the trade of the Arabian Sea. Egypt under its vigorous Mamluk sultans assumed control, and Arab traders of Cairo . . . known as the Karimi merchants began to sail from a revived Aden to the newly established Calicut. . . . [There had been a] grave political upheaval in Malabar sometime before the turning of trade. The coast . . . had been partitioned and a vigorous young family had come into possession of a tiny strip of territory. . . .

Thus, Calicut, under the new power of the "king of the seas," Samudri Raja (later distorted to Zamorin), came to prominence in the second half of the thirteenth century when Muslim merchants coming from the Red Sea flocked to the port because the Zamorins offered them attractive trading terms in return for their political and financial support (Krishna Ayyar, 1938, for more details).[13]

Although ships sailing between the Red Sea and the Strait of Malacca occasionally docked at Sri Lanka (Ceylon, called Sarandib by Arab geographers), most stopped at the commercial complex at Calicut where Gujarati and Jewish merchants shared in the prosperous trade, although as Das Gupta (1967: 6) notes, "there is no mistaking the predominance of the Arabs especially in the carrying trade of the Arabian Sea." There is also no mistaking the dramatic effects of Calicut's sudden rise to prominence. In Das Gupta's (1967: 5–6) words:

> The prosperity of Calicut meant the decline of Quilon and the victory of the Cairo merchants over their rivals from southern China. The Arabs made Calicut their home, assisted the Samudri in his territorial expansion and drew his support for their commercial ambition. The Chinese watched their long-established trade in the Arabian Sea go down in the face of this Arab-Indian combination. "In the fifteenth century a few junks from China still reached India but most of them stopped at Malacca; Indian-owned ships covered the section between Malacca and the Indian coasts; Arab-owned ships dominated the Arabian seas . . . [With this] the long-range network of Asian trade fell into disuse, although Arab *dhouws* still made the trip from Aden to Malacca." [W. H. Moreland, as quoted by Das Gupta]

The End(?) of Arab–Indian Hegemony in the Western Indian Ocean

Throughout the medieval period, Arab ships and merchants continued to dominate the western circuit between the Persian Gulf–Red Sea and the south Indian coasts; there, they were joined by Indian ships that shared with the Chinese, dominion over the second circuit to the Strait.

During the early Sung period, Chinese ships preferred to meet Indian traders in the Strait, but from time to time China allowed Persian, Arab, Malaysian, and Indian ships to enter a few select harbors in which their transactions were closely supervised by state officials. By the late Sung and Yuan periods, however, not only did the Chinese open more ports to foreign ships but Chinese junks were aggressively foraying to Indian ports to meet Arab vessels there. The founding of the Ming dynasty in 1368 did not immediately reverse this situation (Lo, 1958). During early Ming times the Chinese continued to maintain an impressive navy, a fact demonstrated in the opening decades of the fifteenth century by the wide-ranging large fleet of Admiral Cheng Ho. Nevertheless,

Chinese withdrawal from the Indian Ocean had become permanent and dramatically complete by the mid-1430s.

This "vacuum of power," created by the disappearance of the best organized and armed navy in the entire expanse, left only the small Mamluk fleet (albeit with its Gujarati allies) standing in the way of the Portuguese intruders. When viewed from the perspective of the Mediterranean, this vacuum was certainly unusual. In the Mediterranean, a perpetual state of naval warfare existed from the ninth century onward, and commercial ships, therefore, always traveled in military convoys. That was not true in the Indian Ocean since sea warfare did not characterize commerce there. We must ask why.

In spite of the existence of at least four sea powers sharing at least portions of the continuous ocean expanse that stretched from the Arabian to the South China Seas, such trade "was essentially peaceful" (Das Gupta, 1967: 7; also Toussaint, 1966: 101). Just as trade caravans were granted a mutually beneficial immunity from plunder on land, so apparently, sea traders from a variety of provenances respected the ships of others and, indeed, often carried the goods and passengers of each other. That does not mean that "piracy" was unknown. It certainly constituted a problem in the Indian Ocean (particularly in the straits area) that required constant vigilance, punitive raids, and occasionally even pay-offs in the form of "tribute." But the ships of the various "nations" participating in the trade did not seem to view each other as threats, nor did they throw the invective of "pirate" at one another. As Chaudhuri (1985: 14) stated so well:

> before the arrival of the Portuguese . . . in 1498 there had been no organised attempt by any political power to control the sea-lanes and the long-distance trade of Asia. . . . The Indian Ocean as a whole and its different seas were not dominated by any particular nations or empires.

Merchants did not usually depend, as did the Italians, on state-armed convoys to guard their passage. Ships tended to travel together, but mostly for mutual assistance and because propitious sailing times were so strictly limited by the monsoon winds on which all, regardless of ethnicity, depended.

This system of laissez-faire and multiethnic shipping, established over long centuries of relative peace and tolerance, was clearly unprepared for an incursion by a new player following very different "rules of the game." Thus, toward the end of December 1500 when "the Portuguese captain Cabral decided to attack and seize two Muslim ships loading pepper at Calicut [then a town containing some 15,000 Muslim traders (Toussaint, 1966: 101)], he sinned against this unwritten law" (Das Gupta, 1967: 7). Das Gupta (1967: 8–9) concludes:

> The Portuguese were important not because they were violent [although they certainly were] but because they were original. They brought with them a new kind of trading which was substantially different from Asian trade. Both of course were still medieval and the newness which was Portuguese could not alter the system of production and distribution prevalent in Asia. Still there was an important difference.... [The Arab merchants of Calicut were convinced that] the Portuguese were not traders but pirates.... [T]heir apprehensions, by and large, came true. The Portuguese gradually elaborated a complex system of compulsion.

On land, they forced a series of treaties that essentially gave them the right to buy products at below market prices and at sea they instituted a violently enforced pass system that required Asian vessels to purchase a Portuguese "permit." Through their military force, the Portuguese thus caused a radical restructuring of the ports of trade throughout the Indian Ocean; this restructuring eventually undermined Calicut, albeit only gradually and incompletely.

Although its Muslim (Arab and Indian) merchant aristocracy still prospered in the early sixteenth century (Das Gupta, 1967: 11), Calicut was declining. Once the Portuguese channeled most of the trade to the ports of Cochin and Goa over which they exercised exclusive control, the remaining ports of India were reduced to secondary stature contingent on Portuguese sufferance. By the eighteenth century, an English visitor described Calicut as a modest fishing village of low leaf-thatched huts, although it was still the primary metropolis of Malabar in which remnants of the Indianized Muslim merchant community continued to exploit a dying trade (Das Gupta, 1967: 1), albeit under the heel of European hegemony.

The Organization of Southeast Indian Societies in the Middle Ages

The agrarian societies on the eastern plains—the Pallava, Chola, Pandyas, and eventually even the Vijayanagar—although neither as isolated nor as exclusively concerned with trade as their counterparts on the Malabar coast, also participated in the great revival of commerce that began in the eighth and ninth centuries. Stein (1982a: 19, italics added) tells us that

> From about the ninth century, *wealthy and prestigious associations of* [Tamil] *merchants*, trading over extensive portions of the southern peninsula and beyond, *were integrally connected with the dominant agrarian institutions*. Itinerant tradesmen . . . provided one of the means by which the scattered, advanced agrarian communities of the period were linked together.

By the eleventh century Tamil traders were organized into commercial corporations supported by the Chola state (Stein, 1982a: 20). The Chola had become more adventurous, establishing temporary control in Ceylon and the Maldives and raiding as far afield as Srivijaya, although they had "neither the tradition of, nor the apparatus suited to, the realization of state revenue through an orderly administrative system" (Stein, 1982a: 20) and were always more preoccupied with their agrarian hinterlands than their sea forays.

By the twelfth century, however, the Tamils were already losing their preeminence, as Muslim merchants from the western regions (many of them Indian) took over their roles (Stein, 1982a: 40). Interestingly, it was at this time that "spices, [and] . . . Indian and Middle Eastern silks and cottons entered Chinese ports in greater numbers" (Richards, 1986: 3). The Chola state, however, did not greatly benefit from this boom, since its interest in overseas trade seems to have come to an end some time in the thirteenth century (Stein, 1982a: 40).

As previously noted, in contrast to the freewheeling and fragmented political system of the Malabar coast, the agrarian states of southeast India, notably the Chola that lasted until 1279 (followed by an interregnum) and the Vijayanagar military feudal state that eventually succeeded it about 1350, were oriented more toward the extraction of agricultural surplus than to long-distance trade. Stein (1982a: 24–25) offers a useful explanation for the connection between terrain and Tamil political organization:

> Irrigated rice culture [as found on the Coromandel plains] permitted a high degree of routinization of cultivation practices. . . . The major tasks for the dominant people in such c⌐nditions have been to maintain control over the land and labour and extend the hydro-agricultural type of irrigation system. Where these conditions existed in south India, one found the early prominence of a powerful peasant society, of Hindu institutions and Brahmans as major recipients of agricultural surplus and of powerful regional overlordships as that of the Cholas.

This yielded a very different class structure than was found at Malabar. Although agrarian labor in the hydraulic societies of southeast India was not exactly slave, it was "bonded," that is, tied to the land (Stein, 1982a: 27, 30–31), which has given rise to interminable discussions as to whether India was feudalistic in the Middle Ages (see, for example, Mukhia, 1981; Sharma, 1965, 1985; Stein, 1985). Furthermore, unlike the situation in either north India or Malabar, the rulers were rarely part of a warrior caste.[14]

However, contrary to the system of "Oriental Despotism" posited by Wittfogel (1957) for societies dependent upon irrigation, the south Indian kingdoms were neither highly centralized nor despotic. In spite of the existence of a series of great kingships in the macroregion, centralized control over large areas was never achieved. Kings were ceremonially recognized as legitimate, but lacked imperial reach. Thus, kingship coexisted with a high degree of local autonomy vested in local assemblies of various sorts.[15] Stein (1982a: 32, 35) stresses that

> In . . . south India until the fourteenth century, . . . there is no evidence of local resources being legally and regularly transferred from local, nuclear areas of agrarian organization and production to the "state." One hears of land records, land taxes, and trade duties only at the level of the locality, or later, in the fourteenth and fifteenth centuries, at the level of clusters of localities. . . . It is only with respect to irrigation taxes that one finds systematic larger records of revenues, but these were expended locally.

Just as the government was not in full control of agricultural production, it was also unable to fully exploit the foreign trade that tied its domains to the world market. Instead, local *samayam*[16] organizations of itinerant merchants helped administer the Chola ports and "also assumed administrative control over major trade emporia of the hinterlands." Hall (1980: 165) notes that Chola ports were administered "by royal officials who, together with groups of itinerant merchants and local assemblies, controlled the activities of the foreign merchants and their contacts with the indigenous commercial networks."

Although the transit trade (albeit significantly supplemented by local pepper crops) was central to the prosperity of the Malabar region, on the Tamil plain such trade was integrated more closely with agrarian production and the processing of agricultural products. One of the crops was cotton. From an early time, the textile production associated with cotton gave some cities of the eastern region an industrial, or rather, a protoindustrial character, closer to that of Flanders than Malabar.

Textile Production in Kanchipuram

As early as the sixth century A.D., the Pallava capital of Kanchipuram (near present-day Madras) was an important urban center noted for its commercial as well as its religious functions (Mahalingam, 1969). Kenneth Hall (1980: 88–89) believes that its prominence was the result of its strategic location in one of the major cotton-producing regions of ancient South India, which led to its development as a weaving center.

Textile activity evidently continued into Chola times, even after Kanchipuram was no longer the capital city. Hall (1980: 89–90) reports:

> Cola inscriptions describe a sophisticated system of cloth production characterized by specialization: raw cotton was acquired and then redistributed to spinners who spun the threads, these were then passed along to weavers who manufactured the various qualities of cloth, then the finished cloth was retailed or wholesaled by professional merchants who specialized in cloth sales. All this activity focused upon Kancipuram.

We are still not certain how the textile industry was organized during Chola times, and Hall (1980: 115) is noticeably tentative in his exposition. He suggests that wealthy cloth merchants controlled the supply of cloth which

> may have involved a "putting out" of raw materials into the homes of spinners and weavers where the raw materials were manufactured into a finished product. In the weaving industry a group of merchants such as the *caliya-nagarattar* could well have supplied yarn to local weavers . . . [who] could have returned their finished product to the source of their raw materials . . . who then marketed the cloth. Whether a weaver received a share of the profits from the product's sale . . . is not recorded. Nor is there evidence that merchants exercised wage controls over artisans or for that matter that production standards were set or that fines were levied for poor craftsmanship.

There is some debate over the technological sophistication of Indian textile production. Irfan Habib, whose specialty is Mughul India, has been the primary proponent of the view that technology was primitive until quite late and that it advanced only through the import first of Middle Eastern and then European techniques. (See Habib, 1969, a view later revised in 1980 but also Habib, 1982.) The evidence from south India, however, reveals a different picture.

Ramaswamy (1980: 227) has demonstrated that in the south, the carding bow was employed by the sixth century A.D. and the vertical loom, apparently quite ancient, was in use by the twelfth century (Ramaswamy, 1980: 230). There is also evidence for the use of the jacquard or pattern loom from the eleventh century onward (Ramaswamy, 1980: 231) and of block printing from the twelfth century (Ramaswamy, 1980: 237). Only with respect to the late adoption of the spinning wheel was Habib's contention sustained. In the thirteenth century south Indian women were still using the spindle, since the spinning wheel was introduced into India from Turkey no earlier than the fourteenth century (Ramaswamy, 1980: 227–228). [It was not introduced into Europe until the sixteenth century (Ramaswamy, 1980: 241).] All of this suggests that "Indian loom technology was in no way inferior to that of the West or China as has so far been assumed by the majority of historians" (Ramaswamy, 1980: 231).

Although we may not understand exactly how the Chola textile industry was organized, we do know that production was at a significant scale and that, at least in Kanchipuram, weavers occupied four quarters of the city (Hall, 1980: 91). We also know that the wealth and power of the merchant class grew as the industrial base of textiles expanded.

The Merchant Class

Even before Chola times, trading towns, called *nagaram*,[17] had been established in each of the administrative districts (*nadu*) of the Pallava kingdom, in which local as well as long-distance trade could be conducted with relative freedom in return for transmitting taxes on transactions to the ruling power. This pattern continued into the Chola era. At Kanchipuram, the Chola kings maintained the same relationship with the *nagaram* (assembly of merchants) that had been established in Pallava times, giving merchants economic, administrative, and even religious control over the marketing sectors of the city in return for collecting local taxes (Hall, 1980: 93). Clearly, such autonomy was tolerated because the *nagaram* commanded "the loyalty of a vast regional commercial network" from which it generated "considerable commercially derived tax revenues for the royal treasury" (Hall, 1980: 94).

Such income depended in part on the level of textile production. The royalty profited from the taxes collected on the sale of cotton, the spinning of thread, weaving, and from fees for loom licenses. Thus, "Kancipuram's commercial activity was a direct benefit to . . . Cola monarchs." By the twelfth century such production and trade became increasingly sophisticated, as patron–client relationships gave way to more abstract ties. Producers "sold their own merchandise . . . or entered into relationships with a professional merchant class who acted as their intermediaries" (Hall, 1980: 96–97).

By the late twelfth century, international traders were making regular calls at ports on the Coromandel coast and local itinerant merchants ran a well-organized system that provided the pearls, betelnuts, spices, and cotton products demanded abroad. The Chola rulers took a positive stance toward this trade because they derived considerable financial benefits from it (Hall, 1980: 2–3). Gradually, however, they lost power to the growing strength of the merchant class who, as the Chola state decayed, "became more visible, and in some instances formed the nucleus of the development of new centers of political authority" (Hall, 1980: 4).[18]

Urbanization

As a result of the healthy position of textile manufacture and the growing international demand for this product, the thirteenth century was, in south India as in western Europe, a period of heightened urbanization. According to Stein (1982a: 36), "at no time since the Classical period of . . . Tamil . . . in the early centuries of the Christian era did urban places possess the importance they had after the thirteenth century."

But urban expansion was attributable less to long-distance trade, which was moving into the hands of Muslim traders from the west coast, than to a concentration of power within the state. One of the means used to consolidate central control was the Hindu temple, many of which were constructed in the thirteenth century (Stein, 1982a: 37). Stein (1982a: 38–39) suggests that temple construction, because it brought together so many artisans and service workers, did as much to create towns as the centralizing states that gave rise to it. This pattern was continued by the Chola's successors.

Transformations in the Mid-Fourteenth Century

As noted in the discussion of the Malabar Coast, the dates of "rise" and "fall" that prove so powerful in analyzing medieval European and, to a lesser extent, Middle Eastern subsystems, seem less relevant to the west coast of India, whose mercantile trade was tied to Egypt—the only Middle Eastern power to survive the fourteenth-century contractions precipitated by the breakup of the Mongol empire and the devastations of the Black Death.

In contrast, 1350 is a significant cutoff date for both northern and southeast India, although for different reasons. By mid-fourteenth century, two events, one in the north, and the other in the south, conspired to alter the roles these regions played in the world system. Both reduced the importance of their trade, thus contributing to the power vacuum that was developing in the Indian Ocean arena.

In the north, the Delhi empire began to break up in the second half of the fourteenth century; the final coup de grâce was administered by Tamerlane who sacked the city in 1398. The great stores of gold and silver that had accumulated through the perpetual imbalance of trade were carted off to Samarkand (Richards, 1986: 15), not to be replenished until Mughul times.

In the south, a new Hindu state, the Vijayanagar or "Abode of Victory," had emerged and conquered not only the small Muslim sultanates along the coast, but much of the former domain of the Cholas that had long been subdivided among the contending Hosaylas and Pandyas (see, inter alia, the works of Mahalingam, 1940, 1951; Dallapiccola and Lallemant, 1985; Krishnaswami Pillai, 1964). The new power, whose capital lay deep in the interior on the Deccan plateau (for recent excavations, see Fritz et al., 1985), was oriented toward neither agrarian pursuits nor international trade. For the first time in south Indian history, the region was ruled by a centralized system of military feudalism whose alien soldiers were granted the rights to the surplus they could extract from the land and from trade, in return for allegiance and troops.[19]

They seem to have done very well with the former, and along with increased agricultural production came an efflorescence of "industrial" development, particularly in textiles. During the Vijayanagar period, the organization of textile production took on many of the characteristics associated with capitalism (Ramaswamy, 1985a), complete with a merchant class that owned small factories, innovations in technology, and considerable class stratification. This was particularly evident in the temple towns, but was also found in traditional weaving villages (Ramaswamy, 1985a: 302–303).

Although much of this textile production was geared to external markets, the Vijayanagar seem to have lost control over its foreign distribution. Again, Stein (1982a: 19, italics added) states it most clearly:

Changes in the political and economic organization of south India in the fourteenth century deprived itinerant trade associations of their former functions . . . [and they] ultimately merged with localized merchant groups in the internal trade. Many of the former itinerant travellers may have become part of the Muslim trade community on the coast, taking advantage of the Muslim-dominated trade system of the Indian Ocean. *Until the fourteenth century, . . . overseas trade must be seen as the corporate extension of the south Indian domestic economy*; after the fourteenth century, an expanded, more urbanized internal south Indian economy diminished the dependence upon this older trade network and its seaward extensions. *Nor was the sea to have the same importance again until the late period of European control in south India.*

Increasingly, the trade between Coromandel and Southeast Asia was taken over by Gujarati and Malabari Muslim traders—both Arab and indigenous. This "overextension" of western basin traders into the traditionally somewhat independent circuit of the Bay of Bengal may have contributed to the growth of the potential vacuum in that area—a vacuum that the later withdrawal of the Ming was to make painfully obvious. But we reserve this story to Chapters 9 and 10.

Lessons from the Indian Case

If strategic location alone could ensure permanent hegemony, then south India—given her position as "hinge" between the eastern and western basins of the Indian Ocean, the center of the sea lane from the Mediterranean to China—should have enjoyed unrivaled dominance in the world system, both before and after the thirteenth century.

In fact, this was not the case; after the thirteenth century she played a somewhat more passive role. South India did constitute the inescapable destination for strong sea-oriented powers to her west (the Arabs) and her east (China), did, as will be seen in Chapter 9, exercise important cultural influences on the peninsular and insular sea powers of Southeast Asia, and did harbor along her coasts a set of crucial ports to which many traders came to buy locally produced or foreign products, often under the auspices and to the financial benefit of local rulers. But with the exception of the Gujaratis and some Muslim Indians intermixed with Arab or Persian stock who operated out of the Malabar and Coromandel coasts, Indians were not notably active in the sea trade itself.

Although from early times large merchant colonies of Tamil origin were well established in Ceylon (Indrapala, 1971) and on Sumatra (Nilakanta Sastri, 1932b), they are more properly understood as settlers than as itinerant seamen.

To some extent, the reason for India's somewhat passive role in the long-distance sea trade was that, throughout her history, India absorbed trade surpluses.

India (including Sri Lanka) produced products and goods much in demand in the world market . . . manufactured cotton and silk textiles, . . . dyes, tannins, spices, oil seeds and narcotics. . . . forest products such as lac, pitch, honey and ivory. . . . On the other hand, the list of major imports . . . is much shorter. Indian traders imported battle and riding horses. . . . [They also imported] spices not grown in India such as cloves, mace and nutmeg . . . from Southeast Asia. [There was] Western glassware and Chinese porcelain. . . . Metals especially copper—and certain forms of armor and weapons were imported . . . [along with] rosewater and other perfumes . . . from the Middle East. And, finally, slaves primarily from Abyssinia . . . and Circassian slaves from the Middle East. (Richards, 1986: 33–34)

But, as Richards (1986: 34) concludes, "India was self-sufficient in or indifferent to many of the heavily-traded commodities on the medieval world market." The wealth of India, the raw materials from jewels to spices, the high development of her agriculture, and the quality of her industrial output made her the object of other's desires. She sold more than she bought, although as we shall see, she was as fascinated by Southeast Asia as Europe was later to be with her. Ironically, wealth rather than poverty seemed to keep her from playing a more aggressive role in the thirteenth-century world system, a system driven more by need than satiety. Indeed, the more she was drawn into the world system that was integrating during the twelfth and thirteenth centuries, the less active she became in actually carrying that trade.

To some extent, her pivotal geographic position meant that she was always in danger of being supplanted by expansions in the sea power of those on either side of her. This seems to have occurred in the late thirteenth and early fourteenth centuries when, on the west, Muslim merchants (including Islamized Gujaratis) expanded their control of shipping to the Strait, and, on the east, the Chinese expanded their trade lanes to the subcontinent.[20] The result was a decline of sea activity at the center, as south India, particularly Tamil country under the Deccan-centered Vijayanagar, turned away from the sea to concentrate on the elaboration of large-scale agrarianism. This decline also spread to the Indianized zone at the Strait of Malacca, somewhat displaced by direct Chinese shipping.

This set the stage for a potential vacuum of power in the Indian Ocean, now monopolized by Muslims to the west and Chinese to the east. Rather than four great sea powers sharing the great expanse, by the second half of the fourteenth century only two were left. When one (the Chinese) withdrew, the zone was free to be taken, an opportunity the Portuguese later exploited. In the chapters that follow we examine in greater detail how this vacuum developed in the eastern basin of the Indian Ocean.

Notes

1. And here the term McNeill used to described Venice is even more apropos.

2. The clearest exposition of the differences between these two regions can be found in Burton Stein's chapter, "South India" (1982a) in *The Cambridge Economic History of India*, Volume I: *c.1200–c.1750* ed. by Tapan Raychaudhuri and Irfan Habib. In the section that follows I depend heavily on this work.

3. As Stein (1982a: 22–23) notes, there is a striking difference between the rich agrarian plains of the Coromandel, which require channel and tank irrigation, and the western coastal plain of Kerala in which monsoonal rains always provided sufficient moisture for two crops each year, geared to the dual monsoon cycle. This ecological contrast led to significant differences in social organization between the more centralized patriarchy of the "hydraulic" Tamil state and the smaller scale "matriarchal" (albeit protected by male warriors) agricultural society of Kerala.

4. Admiral Ballard (1984: 1) even claims that cross-sea travel most likely originated from the peninsula because its arid climate made fishing and trade a necessity not shared by other people in more favorable ecological niches; one must remain cautious, however, with respect to his purely speculative hypothesis.

5. The manual is most detailed for the west coast and there is little information for areas beyond. "Ceylon . . . was little known and seldom visited . . . [and] the Malay Archipelago, Madacascar, . . . [etc.] were still *terrae incognitae* [to the Greeks]" (Toussaint, 1966: 39).

6. There is evidence that during classical times the Coromandel coast was also involved with Roman trade, if only indirectly and perhaps overland from Malabar. Significantly, "the find-sites of the Roman coin hoards are overwhelmingly located in south India, especially in Tamil country. The best-known example of a major

Indian entrepôt for Roman goods is . . . in the heart of the Tamil country" at present-day Pondicherry, south of Madras (Spencer, 1983: 77).

7. According to Richards (1986: 10–11), precious metals destined largely for Egypt and Syria left Europe through Italian ports. "The massive . . . movement of Venetian gold ducats to Alexandria was but the most visible aspect of the continuing drain of precious metals from Europe to the Mid-East." A similar process took place at Alexandria as Egypt's trade surplus with Europe went eastward. "The Mamluk mints issued great numbers of gold ashrafis and silver dinars that circulated throughout the Indian Ocean as far as Malacca and the East African coast" (Richards, 1986: 12). "On the main eastward track . . . , ducats, ashrafi, grossi, tankas, or bullion flowed to the major ports of western India: to Cambay and its cluster of satellite ports in Gujarat; to Goa . . . , to Quilon and the Malabar ports. Galle, the principal port of Sri Lanka (Ceylon) also received these western flows . . . " (Richards, 1986: 13). Much of this excess bullion was pulled into the capitals of the Indian interior in the form of tribute and plunder. From China in the other direction came great strings of copper coins to pay for her trade deficit. "The numerous kingdoms of Southeast Asia . . . lacked a sharply-defined coinage tradition. . . . [so] gold bullion of a consistent purity assessed by weight sufficed for [their] larger transactions" (Richards, 1986: 16). "From [the region of] Malacca . . . the specie of Asia then moved to the emporia of the coast of India and Ceylon" (Richards, 1986: 18).

8. Stein (1982a: 18–19), in part because his dominant focus is on the Coromandel Coast, suggests a somewhat different periodization. He claims that the trade system tying south Indians to a wider world

> persisted from the beginning of the Christian era until perhaps the thirteenth century when two developments brought it to an end. One was the deepening Muslim control over Indian Ocean trade which favoured the commercial ascendancy of Muslim trade from western India, . . . under greater control by Muslims. Coromandel Muslims continued to participate in the Indian Ocean network, but the role of Coromandel diminished relatively after this time while that of western India grew.

9. See, inter alia, Chaudhuri, 1985: 23, 103, 107. Tomé Pires (see Cortesão, 1944), the early sixteenth-century Portuguese writer who so graphically and accurately described trade and navigation in the Indian Ocean, was not the first to notice that one simply could not traverse the entire length in a single monsoon season, although he was somewhat more accurate in explaining the reason than earlier Muslim geographers. Al-Idrisi, for example, reported that captains of the Sea of India and the Sea of China had told him that "the ebb and flow of waters occurs twice during the year; so that during the summer months, the flow of water takes place eastwards, and as against this, there is an ebb in the western part of the sea; and for the following six months, the flow takes place westwards" (Al-Idrisi, trans. by Ahmad, 1960: 35).

10. Goitein (1963: 189), who has used material from the Geniza papers to explore the role of Jewish merchant colonies in India, is the first to note that "the share of the Jewish merchants in India trade seems to have been comparatively modest."

Nonetheless, he uncovered a series of eleventh-century letters between Jewish merchants in Aden and the Malabar coast that contain references to Indian cottons and silks, Chinese porcelains and metal goods (iron and steel, brass and bronze), as well as to the more expected spices, dyes, aromatics, medicines, pearls, coconuts, and wood (Goitein, 1963: 196), demonstrating that even before the thirteenth century Asia's exports included a heavy proportion of industrial goods. Material sent from the Red Sea or Aden to the east also concentrated significantly on manufactured goods, with foodstuffs constituting only one-tenth of the items enumerated (Goitein, 1963: 197–198; see also his 1954 and 1980 articles). It should be pointed out, however, that these documents refer to a time when Jews were more prominent in Egyptian trade than they would be in late Ayyubid and Mamluk times and that he refers to a period before Calicut's Muslim merchants rose to prominence.

11. Spencer (1983: 68), indeed, accuses Indian as well as western scholars writing about the presumed influence of China and India on the "less-advanced peoples of South-East Asia of falling into the trap of European colonial attitudes, since discussions of Indian 'colonization' and 'Greater India' are in fact remarkably similar in tone to the tracts in which British authors once described Britain's alleged 'civilizing' mission in India."

12. The rumor that it was the great Arab muʿallim (master sailor), Ahmad Ibn Majid al-Najdi, author of a detailed if discursive fifteenth-century navigational manual (see Tibbetts, 1981), who led the Portuguese to the Indian Ocean is patently impossible, since he was already a very old man in 1490 when his *Kitab al-Fawaʾid* . . . was written.

13. A very similar strategy was used a century and a half later when a putative prince of the Palembang dynasty set up his rival port at Malacca and, through protection and financial inducements, gathered under his authority the merchant communities scattered throughout the Strait region.

14. The exceptions were in Kerala, where there were "warrior lineages" (Stein, 1982a: 32–33), and during the militaristic feudal period of the Vijayanagara from the mid-fourteenth century onward (see Nilakanta Sastri, 1976).

15. Indianists have emphasized the importance of self-governing bodies in villages and towns in the region during the Chola period, while at the same time insisting on the high degree of central state administration. See, for example, the various works by Nilakanta Sastri (1976, 1978, and particularly 1955) as well as Misra (1981). Stein takes them to task in his brilliant essay, "The State and the Agrarian Order in Medieval South India: A Historiographical Critique" (1975: 64–91), in which he suggests that the Chola state was neither as centralized nor as efficient as claimed, and that local self-rule, both in "secular" and Brahman villages, resulted less from ideology than from necessity.

16. By Chola times, itinerant trade was increasingly "governed by merchant fraternities of long-distance traders, called *samayam*, which represented the local marketing network within the larger system of Asian trade" (Hall, 1980: 141). "Candidates for induction swore by a code of mercantile conduct . . . which set them apart from other itinerant traders. Prosperous *samayam* members became 'merchant princes' who were allowed to follow high status life styles . . . and were

given monopoly privileges on certain goods" (Hall, 1980: 147). The *samyam* originated as "small groups of expeditionary merchants who serviced . . . isolated communities of the hinterland, . . . band[ing] together for their mutual protection. Itinerants carried their own arms, even acted like bandits" (Hall, 1980: 151). Foreign goods coming into an ordinary *nagaram* required the attention of the head of the marketplace; in contrast was the *pattana* or port, "a place officially designated as a center for the exchange of goods which arrived by boat or caravan. . . . In its South Indian context, this broad definition of 'port' was somewhat modified. During Cola times, *pattinam* was generally attached to the names of towns where international commerce was allowed, both port cities of the coast . . . and important emporia of the interior" (Hall, 1980: 142–143). It seems that local and foreign merchants in a *pattana* did not compete: local merchants handled local goods and the itinerant traders were confined to specific items of long-distance trade (Hall, 1980: 144). "While in the coastal ports . . . itinerant merchants enjoyed a special status, in the hinterland their position was more dependent on forming alliances with local institutions, [eg.] *nagaram* assemblies" (Hall, 1980: 146).

17. According to Hall (1980: 52), "a *nagaram* was a physically defined area inhabited by a group of people known as *nagarattar* [who]. . . . were members of a corporate assembly," among whom cloth and oil merchants were the most important (Hall, 1980: 53–54). The assembly of a *nagaram* seems to have been headed by a committee that employed an overseer to supervise the communal lands and a clerk and an accountant (Hall, 1980: 56). The community held land from the crown for which it paid taxes and from which it raised income (Hall, 1980: 57). "Due to the dramatic expansion of long distance trade during the Cola age, local merchants began to . . . [develop] institutional ties with itinerant merchant organizations. Such external contacts guaranteed the economic stability of local *nagaram* and . . . even allowed commercial centers to become the nucleus for the development of new centers of political authority" (Hall, 1980: 81). With their growing power the *nagaram* began to emerge from under the other local authorities and make direct revenue settlements with the Chola. In addition, during Chola times the *nagaram* even formed "their own military units from troops which were initially hired to police the local market-place and the overland trade routes" (Hall, 1980: 81). "But with the decline of Cola authority, these commercial institutions began to exert their own pressures upon their local domain and assumed independent control over local administrative responsibilities formerly shared with the agrarian institutions like the *ur* and the *nadu*" (Hall, 1980: 82).

18. Hall (1980: 2) hypothesizes that commerce was initially institutionalized via the *nagaram* to "contain the commercial penetration of foreign merchants within the region's designated market, usually the *nagaram* itself." Although this may have been the original intent, it eventually resulted in the growth of a relatively independent urban merchant–industrialist bourgeoisie, not generally found outside medieval Europe.

19. The military feudal system of the Vijayanagar empire presents some interesting parallels to the Mamluk system of Egypt. It seems to have combined a strong state exercising direct control over the cities and core agricultural areas with a system of more decentralized military "tax farming" with military chiefs (called

nayaka) assigned districts in the periphery, from which they extracted as much surplus as they could; in return for these "fiefs," they were obligated to provide a specified number of cavalry and foot-soldiers. (See, inter alia, Stein, 1982b; Krishnaswami Pillai, 1964; Mahalingam, 1940; Nilakanta Sastri and Venkataramanayya, 1946.)

20. China's technological superiority was certainly one of the reasons. Digby stresses that the "Chinese junk of the thirteenth and fourteenth centuries was technologically the most advanced and seaworthy vessel of its period," as well as the largest (Digby, 1982: 131–133).

CHAPTER

9

ᘓᘓᘓᘓᘓ

The Strait and Narrow

Whoever is lord of Malacca has his hands on the throat of
Venice.

(TOMÉ PIRES, trans. Cortesão, 1944 vol. 2: 287)

If Cambay were cut off from trading with Malacca, it could
not live.

(TOMÉ PIRES, as cited in Gopal, 1975: 8)

Palembang and Malacca Today

The plane from the "international airport" at Pekanbaru, in central
Sumatra, flies southward over an endless tropical rain forest, unbroken by roads and unscarred by settlements. The contoured plow
lines have long been left behind and there are few signs of human
life. Only a succession of rivers wind their snakelike way eastward

toward the becalmed Strait of Malacca that separates uncleared Sumatra from the lush farms and carefully cultivated rubber plantations of the Malay Peninsula. Each river widens at its mouth into a fanned estuary whose lighter color suggests a shallow unnavigable swamp. So far, the longest and widest river passed is Hari, on which medieval Jambi (current population of about 100,000) was perched.

But now, the most impressive in this sequence of rivers can be seen below. The Musi River, whose deep channel runs to the sea between the flanking swampland that forms a delta around it, looks more promising. Protected by a large island just off-shore, the river's mouth is secure, giving credence to tales from the thirteenth century that describe a chain stretched across the channel to prevent unwanted vessels from entering.

The plane lands suddenly at a clearing some 75 miles upstream on the Musi River at the provincial town of Palembang in southeast Sumatra, in which half a million Indonesian citizens lead a quiet life. They still receive some "imports" by river via very long canoes. The produce these boats deliver is unloaded by hand at river edge and laboriously carried up the shallow slope from the river to the stalls and ground display areas of the adjacent outdoor market. Machines and manufactured goods come to the primitive airport on the handful of daily planes.

It is virtually impossible to believe that from the seventh to the twelfth century Palembang was the capital of the Srivijayan "Empire"[1] and that the Prince of Palembang, deriving and maintaining his monopoly through judicious tributes and obsequious "visits" to the rulers of China, dictated the terms of passage through the Straits of Malacca and Sunda to the Indian and Arab merchant shippers who nourished the lifeline of sea-borne international trade.

On the opposite side of the Strait, in Malaysia, lies the even smaller provincial town of Malacca in which, toward the end of the fourteenth century, an exiled prince from Palembang[2] set up a rival emporium at the point at which the Malacca River debouches into the Strait. Quite far from the current shore stands the ruined gate below the elevated fortress erected by the Portuguese "conquerors." It was at this now dry point that, in the sixteenth and seventeenth centuries, Portuguese and then Dutch galleys and men-of-war docked.

The waterway has now receded, the "port area" has been filled by land whose central zone contains a grassy park, beyond which a fence blocks off the sandy beach that now preempts the spot at which ships formerly anchored off-shore. The southern filled zone already contains modern apartments, offices, restaurants, and TV shops. North of the sandy expanse is what remains of the channel of the Malacca River, narrowed in nonmonsoon season by green-gray sludge and silt. A few sailing boats, shaped like medieval *dhows*, but with old tires incongruously draped along their sides, are docked at rickety wooden piers. The go-downs (warehouses), whose steps used to lead directly to the river, now squat stranded above water level. A few small barges, square-shaped like Chinese junks, are docked farther upstream, ready to take tourists on a watertour of this dead emporium. Can this be the bustling harbor at which ships from four regions of the world system docked, each region under the auspices of its own Port Master? At Malacca, as at Palembang and Jambi, it is virtually impossible to recapture any sense of a place that played a vital role in world commerce and production.

Nothing more graphically portrays the ephemeral quality of history than a visit to the sites that dominated the world system before Europe. And nothing gives more poignant evidence of the instability of world systems than the present condition of these former "world cities."

Their dramatic decline alerts us to a relatively unusual characteristic of the region and its urbanization. One of the remarkable things about great cities is their tendency to persist through the ages, even as functions change. It is common in archaeological excavations to find layer upon layer of successive settlements. Some constant caused by locational advantage, venerated symbolic significance, or even just inertia seems to account for this persistence. And yet, the entrepôts of the Strait demonstrate little of this. Rather, one after another port rose, shone, and then flickered out, as traders moved to the next. (Singapore now holds pride of place.) What is constant is *some* entrepôt in this "gullet" of the world (as Pires called it); which one, however, was determined not by ecological but by political factors.

The ecological features are common to the region: an unruffled surface of water (even called the "lady lake") offering calm passage at a point at which seas with conflicting wind systems come together, producing a yearly cycle of sailing seasons interrupted by long windless periods; two flanking shores with low-lying coasts, behind which rise highlands covered by tropical forests; a series of rivers flowing down to the strait, at the mouths of which astute, albeit petty, political rulers could set up fort-town-ports to receive the products from upstream, to control access to their resource hinterlands, and, if conditions were right, to exchange these products for those originating elsewhere. From the highlands of the Malay Peninsula came tin, wood, and other forest products; from inland Sumatra (called by medieval Indians the "island of gold") came minerals, camphor, other resins, and trees.

The original inhabitants, some of whom clearly entered by land from Thailand and some of whom undoubtedly came by boat from the islands of Indonesia, reaped the wealth of both forest and sea. They were either fully nomadic (see Carey, 1976, on land nomads; Sopher, 1965, on sea nomads) or were engaged in shifting slash and burn agriculture. In contrast, the small entrepôts at the rivers' mouths were more likely to contain strangers following mercantile pursuits. This symbiotic relationship between inland and shore persists to this day, with the interiors containing groups of ethnically related communities and the cities of the coast containing groups that are much more ethnically diverse—primarily, in descending order, Malay, Chinese, Indian, and (now hardly any) Arab.

In this ecological setting, a stable urban hierarchy is unlikely (a point recognized by Bronson, 1977; Wheatley, 1983; Lim, 1978). There is neither a large agrarian hinterland for which a city might serve central place functions nor a markedly differentiated terrain that might give comparative advantage to some special point—for example, at the confluence of roads or rivers. Herein lies the paradox of the Strait. On the great path of world trade, the coasts of Sumatra and the Malay Peninsula form a natural and unavoidable destination; but within that area no particular stopping point is uniquely compelling.

For this chapter we have singled out two successively important medieval centers, Palembang and Malacca, but it would be erroneous to think there were no others. Indeed, points farther north—Kedah (Kalah)[3] on the Malay coast and Pasé on the Sumatran shore—could just as easily have been selected, except for the fact

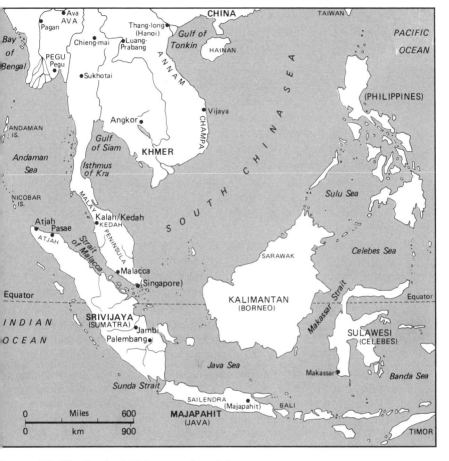

FIGURE 13. The Strait of Malacca: gullet of the sea route.

that our knowledge of them is even more deficient than it is for Palembang and Malacca. (See Figure 13.)

The Links to Outside

Just as the Strait area has always been the meeting point for the seas, so the shores of the Strait have been the meeting point for cultures. As noted in Chapter 8, the indigenous Southeast Asians played a far more original and active role in early history in the transmission of culture than is commonly recognized (MacKnight, 1986: 217). Beginning with the first millennium A.D., however, they were more likely to have been the recipients of traditions originating elsewhere.

Lying half-way between the great agrarian continental masses of India and China, the Southeast Asians were subject to cultural and religious (Hinduism and Buddhism) influences from both directions, receiving, from the fourteenth century on, their "final" transformation through Islam, now the major religion in both Sumatra–Indonesia and the Malay Peninsula. With each successive "conversion" the transformation became more deeply embedded in the social structure. Hindu institutions were adopted by the rulers but, with the exception of linguistic borrowing, barely penetrated social life, except in the expatriate communities of the international ports. Buddhist beliefs went deeper into the lower classes, but it was Islam that eventually took permanent root in the region. Indonesia is now the largest of the Islamic countries and in both Indonesia and Malaysia Islam is the dominant religion.

During the period in question, however, Indian and Chinese influences were the most important, particularly in Palembang; it was only with the conversion, in his old age, of the founder of Malacca that Islam consolidated itself throughout the region.

The Problem of Sources Revisited

It is remarkable that a region that for so long occupied the position of cross-waterway of the world should have had so little to say for itself. Despite my good intentions to examine as many indigenous documents as possible, this has proven almost impossible for the straits area. Specialist after specialist on the region bemoans the fact that our early knowledge of it comes almost exclusively from the reports of others.[4]

If contemporary local records were once kept, they were written on thin bark or bamboo slices that have long since decayed in the heat and humidity of the tropical rain forest climate. For Sumatra, before the coming of the Europeans, no residual records are available at all, with the exception of a handful of stone inscriptions. For Malaya, there is really only the *Sejarah Melayu* (the *Malay Annals*, translated first by Leyden, 1821; retranslated by C. C. Brown, 1952), but the extant manuscript (#18 Raffles) itself dates from a much later period. This document begins with the founding of Malacca, the first chapter being devoted to a dubious genealogy designed not only to legitimate the ruler's claim as inheritor of the mantle of the former empires of Srivijaya, Chola, and Sailendra (on Java) but, even more outrageously, to trace his lineage to Alexander the Great! (For evaluations of this manuscript, see, inter alia, Wolters, 1970, and Tregonning, 1962.)

There are Chinese documents and dynastic histories (carefully culled by Wang, 1958, for the pre-Sung era) that contain periodic references to the so-called Kingdom of Srivijaya and its successive capitals at Palembang and then Jambi, but these, quite unintentionally, give a particularly distorted and partial account. They make it appear that the princes of Palembang, although "rulers" of a large number of subject states, were mere "vassals" of China who periodically arrived carrying tribute in the form of royal presents. This cannot have been true, since we know that Palembang traded not only with the Chinese but with Arabs and Indians, and we understand that the Chinese term "tribute" was a euphemism for exchange during those periods when China did not encourage private trade (see Chapter 10).

Our knowledge of the importance of Buddhist learning in Palembang comes from a single seventh-century reference, the account of a Chinese scholar monk who stopped there for several months on his way to India. He reports that there were a thousand Buddhist monks in the city, but his accuracy and his motives are not above suspicion.

The final Chinese document is by a thirteenth-century harbor official, Chau Ju-Kua (trans. by Hirth and Rockhill, 1911). The author describes the places from which the foreign shippers in Zaytun (Ch'uan-chou) came. Part of his presentation, however, is taken from a source almost a century earlier whereas other parts came from interviewing the traders themselves, some of whom are clearly dissembling. Furthermore, this source dates from a period *after* the decline of Srivijaya is acknowledged to have occurred.

The tentative character of these fragmentary sources is compounded by the problem of transcribing Arabic and Chinese place names. We are still not certain where all the places mentioned in the documents were actually located and there is considerable controversy over *what* the Chinese names for specific places were. Entire articles and books (e.g., Douglas, 1949, reprinted 1980; Wheatley, 1961) have been devoted to trying to untangle the inevitable confusions arising from nomenclature in various foreign languages.

There are accounts of the Strait of Malacca area by Arab travelers and geographers who wrote between the ninth and fourteenth centuries (among them, Sulayman the Merchant as added to by Abu-Zayd al-Sirafi, presumed ninth and tenth century, Mas'udi, tenth century; al-Idrisi, twelfth century, and Ibn Battuta, the first half of the fourteenth century), but it seems that many of these writers had no direct experience with the regions they describe. By the time their accounts leave the west coast of India for Southeast Asia (if not before), they become increasingly fabulous. Only Ibn Battuta seems to have actually gone to China and back. His descriptions are "thickest" on India (where he served for many years as a Muslim judge in Delhi) and China; he has little to say about intermediate points.

South Indian documents refer in greater detail to Sumatra and Malaya, which seem to have held privileged places in the Indian imagination[5] and which, since the time of the Pallavas, had been natural outlets for Brahmanical proselytizing. The large quantity (but only in comparison to the paucity of indigenous and other sources) of Indian accounts tends to describe the "Indian Archipelago" (including Java) as overdetermined by Indian influences, a point already addressed in Chapter 8. Furthermore, it was literate Brahmans, preoccupied with religion and rituals, who created the

Sanskrit literature of the area. The more numerous resident traders from Gujarat or Coromandel failed to add their more prosaic (and for us more interesting) observations on cities and trade.

Finally, the appearance of the Portuguese in the Indian Ocean and their conquest of Malacca in 1511 produced documents of quite a different kind, empirically oriented and with an eye toward practical "application." Of these sources, the most remarkable is by Tomé Pires, whose *Suma Oriental* (trans. Cortesão, 1944) was based on his own observations in the second decade of the sixteenth century and on whatever historical background he was able to assemble on the spot. Although this constitutes a rich source on which virtually all depend, it shares with the *Travels of Marco Polo* a western perspective on "useful" information, an often unconscious selective bias, and a tendency to assume that the past was just like the present, a fact that their own presence immediately belies.

In lieu, then, of real information and sources for the Straits area in medieval times, historians have imaginatively combined and recombined the same limited number of informational scraps. Having neither the knowledge nor judgment to design yet another fictitious account, I shall try to elicit from the conflicting viewpoints of specialists—all highly expert and respected—the basic "facts" needed to describe the growth and then devolution of this part of the pre-sixteenth-century world system.

The Indian Influence on the Straits Region

The most influential scholar to have addressed the medieval history of Southeast Asia was Georges Coedès, whose *Les états hindouises d'Indochine et d'Indonésie* (original 1949, revised and translated into English 1968) established one basic orthodoxy in explaining the influence of Indian culture on the region, an orthodoxy which has been supported by self-congratulatory Indian scholars (see, for example, Nilakanta Sastri, 1949; and Majumdar, 1937–1938, 1963, who even speaks of Indian "colonies") and adopted uncritically by Toussaint (1966). They cite the incontestable evidence that Indian-style sculpture and temples are to be found throughout the southeast Asian region (at Angkor but also in Java).[6] It is the 1918 article by Coedès that first proposes the existence of a Srivijayan Empire, heavily influenced by Indian culture.

This school of thought posits the actual transplantation of south Indian settler communities to Southeast Asia some time in the fourth century. Coedès (1966: 247) argues that only such population movements could account for the fact that Indian inscriptions appear in fifth-century "Indian kingdoms on Borneo and Java." He hypothesizes that cultural influences diffused from them.[7]

A second major figure in the study of Southeast Asian trade was J. C. van Leur (1955). Part I of this collection focuses on pre-fifteenth-century trade. Van Leur divides the regions of Southeast Asia into the great rice-growing agrarian states and the sparsely populated market-trading regions, of which the Straits area was a prime example. His answer to the question of how the latter region became Indianized is at odds with the solution proposed by Coedès.

Van Leur doubts that there were early colonies of Indian settlers and argues that, even if there were, they could not have been responsible for diffusing "high culture," since they would have been comprised of traders and sailors with no knowledge of Sanskrit. Rather, he suggests that it was Brahmans who transmitted both the religion of Hinduism (and later Buddhism) and their administrative skills to the courts of local rulers whose patronage they sought. These rulers, recognizing how religious legitimation and administrative organization could be of benefit in gaining greater control over their subjects, sponsored the reproduction of these institutions in their societies. [Wheatley (1961: 185–187) concurs, as does Hall (1985: 83–93).] The evidence for this is the use, in relevant royal inscriptions, of Sanskrit rather than the vernaculars that might have been employed by lowly traders, and the artistic products associated with high culture (such as sculpture and architecture).

Adherents to this position usually trace Indian influences back at least to Pallava times (up through sixth century) and emphasize the ongoing religious interconnections between the Brahmanical culture of the Coromandel Coast and the courts of Srivijaya and Sailendra (on Java). They see the emergence of Palembang at the head of the Srivijayan empire in the seventh century as directly related to these culture-carrying Indians.

In contrast, Spencer (1983: 82) does not dismiss the role Indian merchants might have played in cultural transmission, even though it is difficult to trace. He thinks that without them, high culture could not have been transmitted.

> The eastward movement of Indian culture presupposes the movement of Indian and perhaps Malay and other mariners, merchants and adventurers along the trade routes. It was the web of maritime trade that provided the shuttle of ships across southern Asia and created the fund of navigational skills which Brahmans and other cultural emissaries had to utilize in order to carry their message across the seas.

In response to van Leur's reservations about how simple traders and adventurers could have transmitted "the esoteric, Sanskritic lore which characterized the highly ornamented court culture of the Indianized kingdoms," Spencer (1983: 83–84) reminds us that

> The movement of Indian artistic motifs, no less than that of ritual practices, . . . reflected the movement of artisans, not merely the movement of art. . . . Brahmans were as unlikely as traders to have possessed the [needed] craft skills. . . . The migration of Indian artistic styles overseas may have been a continuation abroad of the normal movement of Indian artisans to new centers of patronage.

Spencer asserts that in coastal commercial centers originating primarily in trade, such as Srivijaya, the merchant-disseminator was probably the primary force in indianizing–hinduizing Southeast Asia in the medieval period.

We know that Tamil merchants were a permanent presence along the Straits. At the height of the kingdom of Srivijaya, traders from Coromandel apparently dominated the connection, not unexpectedly, considering the active role played by the Chola in international trade before the thirteenth century. Although the Chola never had the invincible "navy" conjured up by Mookerji (1912), their fleet was certainly strong enough in the early eleventh century to make a "disciplinary" and highly destructive raid on Palembang and other entrepôts in the Srivijayan federation. As already seen in Chapter 8, however, within a century the Chola had begun to lose control over the long-distance trade passing through their ports to the Muslim merchants from western India and the Arab countries.

Not surprisingly, the role of the Gujarati merchants in the straits trade became greater after the founding of Malacca and the con-

version to Islam of its first ruler. Gopal (1975: 6) stresses that by
the fifteenth century, if not before,

> Gujarati merchants were a permanent sight in the ports of the Malay
> peninsula and Indonesian archipelago, viz. Malacca, Kedah, Bruas,
> Selangor, Mjamjam, Pase and Pedir. They were interested in taking
> with them tin, pepper and spices. However, Malacca was the point of
> convergence of Gujarati merchants and Gujarati goods in this region.

From Malacca, the Gujarati merchants went to Sumatra, Java,
Timor, Borneo, the Moluccas, and even China. The figures Pires
gives on the value and volume of Gujarat–Malacca trade are certainly impressive, and his comments on the wealth and centrality
of Cambay merchants cannot be doubted (see Gopal, 1975: 7–8).
But data from the early sixteenth century, long after the Chinese
had withdrawn from the Indian Ocean and long after the Islamization of Malacca made Gujaratis and Malaccans collusive allies,
cannot be substituted for information on earlier periods. As shall
now be seen, Chinese sources give an entirely different view, in
which Indian and Muslim influences are negligible and in which
China plays the crucial if relatively diffident role.

China and the Strait

Although China's role in international trade in the thirteenth and
fourteenth centuries is explored in greater detail in Chapter 10,
the major outlines of that role need to be presented to explain a
puzzling paradox, namely, the importance of Srivijaya in the seventh to twelfth centuries when the world system was just coming
into being, and then its virtual disappearance (at least in the documents) in the late thirteenth and early fourteenth century when
the world system reached its apex.

What at first appears to be a deviant case may actually hold the
key to the later devolution of the system. The paradox is this.
Throughout the centuries, the Strait area retained its monopoly
position along the sea trade route between China and India, and
thus, indirectly, the Arab world and Mediterranean Europe. The
value of its location indeed increased with every expansion in the

volume of trade. Yet, there is the puzzling lacuna of several centuries between the "fall" of Srivijaya and the "rise" of Malacca, not all of which can be explained by the rising power of its rival, Java. Significantly, this cycle of decline is the exact inverse of China's two centuries as an active participant in world trade.

From the time the southern Sung first took to the seas in the late twelfth century until the late fourteenth century when the Ming withdrew, the petty kingdoms of the Strait recede from recorded view. During this interval, the port towns along the Strait lost neither their physical continuity nor their locational advantage. What they appear to have lost is their "political" role as intermediaries monopolizing access to Chinese ports. The region changed from "gateway" to dependency, at the mercy of powerful core trading partners. I believe that this situation of dependency was probably the "normal" one, and that the role of gateway is really the aberration that requires explanation. We will glance briefly, then, at the former before moving on to the latter.

In spite of the importance of the Strait's entrepôts, they remained somewhat "peripheral" to the world system because industrial goods were not being produced and processed there, but in core regions such as India and China. Richards (1986: 25–26) claims that Southeast Asia was always inferior to the core areas because it neither produced nor shipped industrial goods in quantity. The southeast Asian economies, although important in the transit trade, provided only "agricultural produce and raw materials for Indian and Chinese industrial wares."

Just as neither the presence of uranium in Africa nor the strategic location of the Suez Canal in Egypt can catapult these places to core status in today's world system, so neither the desirability of its spices nor the unavoidability of its waterway could guarantee Southeast Asia core status in the thirteenth century. If the political definition of dependency is that externally generated decisions have an inordinate effect on internal events that a country is powerless to withstand, then the Strait area must be conceptualized, at least in part and in the preceding centuries, as a dependency of China.

In classical times the "center of gravity" of the Chinese population had been in the interior. What external trade existed went overland across the great silk route. This overland route declined with the fall of Rome and, from about the sixth century onward, the population of China shifted toward the southern coast. Restoration of the land route during the period of Islamic hegemony was continually threatened by the northern tribes, against whom the Great Wall had originally been built. (These threats were not eliminated until Genghis Khan conquered northern China in the opening decades of the thirteenth century.) Intermittently denied access across the steppes, China was of necessity drawn more to the sea, and a modest amount of "trade," euphemistically concealed in the institution of "tribute" from "barbarian" nations, was begun, particularly with the island countries of Southeast Asia.

The seventh century rise of Srivijaya seems to have been linked to this tribute trade. According to Wolters (1970), tribute trade placed the Chinese emperor in an aloof status vis-à-vis his "vassals" who had to prove both their legitimacy and their subordination. The representatives of Srivijaya seem to have convinced the emperors for many centuries that they had both requisite qualities, although the documentary evidence has failed to convince a number of scholars.[8] Whether or not an empire of Srivijaya ever really existed (as claimed by Coedès, 1918), Chinese documents attest to the Chinese *belief* in the existence of such an empire, which they called San-fo-Ch'i. Such documents report that Srivijaya was headquartered in Palembang and that as many as fourteen or fifteen Strait principalities were "ruled" by it. Under the guise of virtually annual "visits" by the prince of Palembang or his emissaries, considerable exchange of products went on. In one case there is a record of 38 tons of pepper being brought as a "gift"! It seems as if Srivijaya's real role was to "market" south Indian goods, as well as her own and those from the Middle East.

The euphemism of tribute trade, however, was not to go unchallenged. When, in the eighth century, Arab seamen joined their Persian precursors in making direct calls on Chinese ports, the T'ang were relatively unprepared for these different and perhaps less ceremonially sensitive entrepreneurs. At first, the new traders were confined to Canton, in which a sizable Muslim merchant community became established. As already recounted in Chapter 6, however, troubles soon developed. China's response to them was simple; she again interdicted her ports to these nonsubservient trading partners. They could go as far as the Straits area, but no farther. The representatives of Srivijaya, who ostensibly remained docile "vassals" of China, were not barred from the Chinese ports, a fact that may explain their "mysterious," if only temporary, power.

Once this policy of trade interdiction was reversed at the time of the Sung dynasty, and particularly after the so-called "Southern Sung" had retreated before the Mongol invaders, the role of the "Empire" of Srivijaya shrank. The petty principalities along the Strait were no longer indispensable as intermediaries, once Indian and particularly Arab ships were given freer, albeit supervised, access to several Chinese ports (Canton, Kinsai or Hangchow, Ch'uan-chou or Zaytun) and once Chinese ships and merchants (both "state" and "private") began to play a more active and aggressive role in the sea-borne trade. This more open trade policy continued and indeed intensified after the Mongol-ruled Yuan dynasty absorbed the lands of the southern Sung. As noted earlier, Marco Polo reported the presence of large numbers of Muslim merchants in the cities and ports of Kubilai Khan's China.

With Chinese ships sailing as far west as Quilon and Arab and (perhaps) Indian ships sailing into Chinese harbors, the route through the straits persisted, but the monopolistic powers of the Srivijayans did not. Displaced as middlemen, they were reduced to the status of pirates and strongarmers who either pillaged on the high seas or forced passing ships into the Musi River estuary to pay safe passage moneys. By this later period, Palembang had become notorious as the "den" of Chinese piracy.

This two-hundred-year period of Chinese mercantile "adventurism," which will be explored in greater detail in Chapter 10, did not last. After the Ming dynasty was set up on the ashes of the overthrown Mongol dynasty, China reverted, albeit not without debate, to her former diffidence toward trade and foreigners. The people of the straits were astute in recognizing the opportunities the presumed restoration of the tribute trade afforded to them. A revival of Srivijaya was believed to be at hand.

Wolters (1970) suggests that the lengthy genealogy introducing the *Malay Annals* is an elaborate attempt to connect the founder of Malacca (in ca. 1398) with the royal line of Palembang (as well as that of Tamil India and Sailendra Java), in an effort to legitimate Malacca as the true heir of Srivijaya, which it believed might still enjoy a favorable reputation among the Chinese. Malacca aspired to become the new "gateway" to China, the place at which merchants from all trading nations could meet but through which only a select few could pass.

Iskandar Shah [King Alexander (the Great)], the name the founder of Malacca assumed after his conversion to Islam, succeeded in attracting overseas merchants who had formerly stopped at other entrepôts. His favorable terms of trade, his low tariffs, and his well-policed waters proved irresistible. In particular, his conversion attracted Muslim traders who had previously preferred ports of call along the northeast coast of Sumatra or Kedah-Kalah farther north along the Malay coast.

Although he clearly succeeded in establishing Malacca as the primary central market, he met with less success in monopolizing the tribute trade. In the two centuries during which the Chinese had ventured out, they had clearly gained a better sense of the world; they no longer entertained illusions concerning the power of the little kingdoms along the straits.

The Arab Connections to Malacca, Palembang, and Beyond

It is from Chinese (Hui-Ch'an, 727 A.D.) and Japanese (748 A.D.) sources that we first learn of the presence of Arab and Persian sea traders in Chinese ports (Di Meglio, 1970: 108–109). Interestingly, these references predate by at least a century the earliest extant Middle Eastern source, the tales of Sulayman the Merchant (*Akhbar al-Sin wa al-Hind*, presumed 851 A.D.), which were incorporated into the tenth century text of Abu-Zayd of Siraf.

If the latter can be given credence, it demonstrates direct passage from the Persian Gulf to China, since Sulayman's itinerary describes a one-month passage from Muscat to Quilon and then through the Palk Strait just north of Ceylon, a journey of similar duration across the Bay of Bengal past the Nicobar Islands to Kalah or Kalah-Bar on the northwestern coast of the Malay Peninsula, a ten-day trip through the Strait to the Island of Tiyuma, and then finally a two-month journey, via the Indochinese peninsula, past the strait called the "Gates to China," to Canton (see, inter alia, Ferrand, 1922: 13–19). Abu-Zayd's further explication identifies the city of Kalah as "the market where the commerce in aloes, camphor, sandalwood, ivory, tin, ebony, Brazilwood and all the aromatic spices" is centralized. He notes that the "ships of Oman use this port" (Ferrand, 1922: 96).

Mas'udi, writing in the tenth century, confirms the significance of Kalah as the primary port used by Arab ships, although it must be acknowledged that his direct experience terminated at India. He draws upon Sulayman and Abu-Zayd, as well as other merchants and sailors interviewed in Siraf and elsewhere, for his description of the more eastern regions. Nevertheless, his testimony adds to earlier accounts. He notes that after the late ninth-century troubles in Canton (and the subsequent barring of Arab traders from that port), Kalah, an imposing town with high walls and many gardens, assumed increased importance as it became the intermediary point of meeting for Muslim and Chinese ships (see, inter alia, Shboul, 1979: 162; Di Meglio, 1970: 109). Buzurg's *'Aja'ib al-Hind* also mentions Kalah and its commercial dealings with Arabs (Di Meglio, 1970: 112), and the twelfth-century geography of al-Idrisi, admittedly "second hand," identifies Kalah as the final destination for Arab ships arriving from Ceylon and the Nicobar Islands (trans. by Ahmad, 1960: 34).

Although Palembang also became a port of call for Arab ships at that time, it is interesting to note how few Arab references to it there are. The term *Zabaj*, often used in contradistinction to Kalah, seems to refer to Sumatra, Srivijaya, or Palembang, but according to Di Meglio (1970: 113), the term most often used for Srivijaya was Maharaja [*sic*], whose capital was Sribuza, which she identifies as Palembang. Buzurg described Sribuza (Srivijaya) as possessing a magnificent wide and secure bay,[9] streets lined with shops (800 money changers on their special street!), and favorable taxes.

Arab and Persian geographers of the late twelfth and thirteenth centuries, such as Yaqut, Qazwini, and Ibn Sa'id, also refer to the straits area, but they tend to substitute descriptions taken from earlier works, already cited, for direct observations. They do add

Java to the account, reflecting the increased importance of that power, which had outstripped Srivijaya in wealth and commercial activity by the late twelfth century. By the thirteenth century, the Java-based kingdom of Majapahit controlled northeast Sumatra and parts of the Malay Peninsula, finally eclipsing Srivijaya in the mid-fourteenth century (Di Meglio, 1970: 114–115).

Just before that time, in 1345–1346, Ibn Battuta traveled from the west coast of India (stopping in ports such as Cambay, Calicut, and Quilon and leaving us some first hand observations) to China. However, in contrast to the numerous descriptions available for India and China, he supplies little information on the relative importance of the various trading communities in the straits and the Indian archipelago. Some scholars have suggested that the lack of attention he pays to these intermediate places is symptomatic of their reduced importance as trading states. This may be correct; however, his transit through the Strait seems to have been rapid and his port calls few.

Reflecting his interests as a Muslim functionary, Ibn Battuta devotes considerable attention to the spread of Islam in the region. From him we know of the conversions to Islam of the rulers of Pasé and Perak in northeastern Sumatra and in the towns along the northern coast of Java (Di Meglio, 1970: 116–117). Archaeological and inscriptional finds confirm that from the last third of the thirteenth century Islam had been making considerable progress in these regions.

Even more than in the case of earlier "Indianization," such religious and cultural conversions seem to have been the work of Muslim merchants and sailors, although it is not known how many of these Muslim merchants were actually from the Middle East. Given the diaspora trade that had long characterized the zone, resident "ethnic" communities of Arabs and Muslim Indians (mostly from Gujarat) had long dotted the ports along the coasts. They intermarried with local families, employed workers and accumulated clients, and institutionalized within their wealthy and high status communities the honest business practices and charitable social services associated with the faith, thereby attracting converts.

Among these were a number of the rulers whose conversions may possibly have been linked to a more utilitarian purpose: a means of attracting Muslim merchants in a period of declining power for the petty princedoms. The most notable of these rulers was the founder of Malacca, which in the fifteenth century totally eclipsed the rival ports. Although Malacca's founding postdates the period being examined in this book, it cannot be ignored, since, as already noted, the periodization so suited to the Mediterranean world does not coincide neatly with that of the Indian Ocean trade. Particularly in tracing the implantation and spread of Islam in the entire region of Southeast Asia, the story clearly cannot be stopped midstream.

Perhaps the best way to convey the central role played by the port of Malacca in fifteenth-century international trade, before the Portuguese conquered it in 1511 and shaped it to their own ends, is to describe the organization of its port activities. There were four Harbor Masters, each of whom handled incoming and out-going boats, collected duties on their merchandise, and provided go-downs (warehouses and landing docks) for the storage of their goods and lodgings for their owners. Each was responsible to the local minister of finance for the good conduct and creditworthiness of the traders under his jurisdiction. Why were there four? Obviously, because the trade (and the diversity of merchant shippers) was so great that no single official could handle it all.

Each of the large regions from which the international traders came fell under the jurisdiction of its special harbor master. One was concerned exclusively with ships coming from the Middle East, Persia, India, and Ceylon, the second with ships from Sumatra and other points along the straits—the "local" trade. The third dealt with ships coming from the closer islands, such as Java, Borneo, and Makasser, and the final harbor master with traders from Siam (Thailand), Cambodia, Ryu Kyu, Brunei, and, most important, China. No single other fact can quite capture the "shape" of the world system by the fifteenth century than this cast of characters, no one of which was dominant and all of whom had to put into port along the Strait.

This soon changed. By the sixteenth century, the port maintained its dominance—but under the new naval power of Portugal which, for a brief moment at least, had made itself the master of the Indian Ocean and the straits that led to China. Although Portugal would be challenged by the Dutch and then the British, none of the European intruders would be effectively challenged by the system it had preempted. China, the only power that could have resisted European hegemony, had withdrawn from the contest some seventy years earlier.

Chapter 10 analyzes the sources of China's power and her puzzling unwillingness or inability to use it. Before addressing this central issue, however, it is necessary to assess what our examination of the Straits region has taught us about the pre-European world system.

Lessons from the Straits

Comprador states that serve as gateways or interchange points for others are fully dependent upon the industrial production and commercial interests of the regions that use them. Their rise and fall cannot be independently generated, regardless of their local resources or strategic location.

The existence of locally produced assets (even aromatics, spices, and precious metals, much valued in the thirteenth century) by no means guarantees a market; it only makes one possible. The difference between something that exists in or on the ground (a potential resource) and something that can be defined as a real resource, is the extraction that is stimulated by "envaluation." The latter is a market phenomenon. Dependent regions are those that cannot or do not develop and use their own resources but provide them to others. That is why the Oil States of today remain "dependencies."

In that sense, the area of the Straits constituted a natural dependency in the world system of the thirteenth and fourteenth centuries. The resources of the region—minerals such as tin, copper, and particularly gold, and organic products such as wood, fruits, spices, nuts, resins, camphor, and other aromatic or medicinal items—were relatively abundant locally, requiring only the application of labor for their extraction. Such labor, applied with considerable skill by the indigenous populations of the interior,[10] was highly responsive to the level of demand expressed in the port towns along the coast. When demand was high, natural products were redefined as resources for export; when demand fell off, the population reverted to a subsistence economy. The crucial fact, however, was that demand came essentially from outside. It was the rising demand for products of all kinds, generated in the rapidly reticulating world system of the twelfth century and later, that converted the area of the Straits from a modest dependency of China to a set of comprador communities.

There is no denying that the "natural" role of the ports along the Strait was that of comprador (or "agent" for trade), a role that is both politically contingent and economically unstable. For example, the region's two best examples in today's world system— Singapore and Hong Kong—both owe their "miracle" status to their "extraterritoriality." Singapore is a "free" port in which a wide variety of trading partners exchange externally produced goods free of oppressive restrictions and taxes, store their wealth safely, and switch their capital at will from one trading circuit to another. Singapore most closely resembles its predecessor, Malacca. Hong Kong is a similar "free trade" zone whose chief function is to serve as a "gateway" to China, which, until recently, restricted the access of foreign traders and, even today, channels it through international ports such as Shanghai and Canton. Hong Kong's prosperity is thus completely tied to her privileged access to an otherwise restricted market. In this, it bears considerable resemblance to Palembang or Jambi, whose importance derived from their special relationship to the tribute trade preferred by pre-Sung dynasties.

It is easy to understand why such positions are politically fragile. Being the chief international port along a waterway all must frequent depends not only on geographic advantage but on the ability of that port to attract a variety of different foreign merchant firms by assuring security of person and goods and freedom of action. Most importantly, the entrepôt must "guarantee" that other traders will be using the same interchange. Clearly, not all these variables are within the control of the port itself.

This chapter began with a description of the present much-decayed state of fabled Malacca, which was for centuries the unrivaled international port along the Strait. The decline of Malacca illustrates the politically contingent character of its existence. Under the Portuguese the port retained its former importance, even though many Muslim traders switched their port preference to Atjah. Once the British established their rule in the area, however, they decided to build up ports at the defensible ends of the Strait; the construction of first-rank ports at Penang and Singapore condemned neglected Malacca to her present oblivion.[11] These two rival ports were inherited by the newly independent state of Malaysia in the 1960s when both came under a common policy of control. Singapore's final hegemony was achieved only after that island seceded from the Malaysian confederation to set up an independent comprador state.

The example of Hong Kong similarly provides insight into the demise of the so-called empire of Srivijaya, which, as seen, achieved its greatest glory when it enjoyed privileged access to a China otherwise closed to outsiders. The future of Hong Kong has now been determined. Within a relatively short period of time, Great Britain's lease on this extraterritorially governed enclave will run out and the port will revert to Chinese administration. The consequences of this expected loss of its "special relationship" with Chinese markets are already being seen in the massive divesting and expatriation of local and foreign capital and the relocation (scuttling?) of traders and their companies to Europe, the United States, and Canada. On the other hand, foreign interests are beginning to forge more direct ties with the Chinese economy to replace those formerly mediated by the comprador city-state. A similar phenomenon may have accounted for the collapse of Srivijaya. It is interesting to speculate on what Hong Kong will look like fifty years hence, although it is unlikely that it will revert to Palembang's backwoods state.

What are the implications of these facts for the growth and decline of the thirteenth-century world system? It is clear that the area of the Strait was a relatively passive force in both phases of the cycle. Its status was derived almost totally from what went on in the rest of the system, which at best it could facilitate, but never cause or prevent. Only during periods when the truly hegemonic powers of the system "permitted" it, could the small principalities along the Strait assume an ostensibly active role in channeling world trade.

Even then, their activities were distinctly local in their ramifications. City-state could compete with city-state for a share in the transit market. Undisciplined entrepreneurs—the sea nomads whose *prahus* could dart, without warning, from the numberless rocky forested islands that dot the zone—could occasionally raise the protective rent on transit or cause ships to deflect passage through the Sunda Strait or even across the Thai peninsula at the Kra Isthmus. But the "gullet" of the world could only obstruct trade or let it pass easily and profitably; it could not generate it.

The small kingdoms along the passage never became naval powers in their own right. Although Nooteboom (1950–1951) argues to the contrary, during the period under examination most shipping went on Arab and Indian vessels coming from the west and on Chinese junks coming from the northeast. Whenever the Chinese moved aggressively outward, the intermediary ports paradoxically became more prosperous but less important. Whenever the Chinese pulled back from the western circuit or, even worse, interdicted direct passage of foreign ships into their harbors, the ports in the straits flourished, but only because Chinese vessels took up the easternmost circuit slack by meeting their trading partners at Palembang, Kedah, or, later, Malacca. Once the Chinese withdrew from that circuit in the fifteenth century, however, a vacuum was created. When Europe filled that defenseless vacuum in the sixteenth century, the "old" world system of the thirteenth century became the embryo of the "modern" system that still shapes our world today, albeit with declining power.

Notes

1. There is considerable controversy over whether Palembang was the "head" of anything that might be called an "empire" (see, in particular, note 8).

2. Again, this point has been most cogently refuted by Wolters (1970), who suggests that the genealogy contained in the *Malay Annals* (English trans., 1821 seq., Raffles ms. 18) is not to be taken as "true." But of this, more later.

3. Scholars even disagree about the location of this port to which the Arabic sources make constant reference. Although there is a present-day province in Malaysia called Kedah, and many believe that the port was in that general area, some scholars (Wheatley, 1961) place it farther north near the Isthmus of Kra in Thailand.

4. Although virtually all historians indicate the frustrating lack of indigenous written documentation, few have pointed as clearly as Alastair Lamb (in Wang, 1964: 100–101) to a way out of the difficulties. Lamb notes that only "a careful synthesis of . . . archaeological, anthropological and linguistic evidence," that is, the study of inscriptions and non-Malayan texts, can yield the answers needed.

However, in assembling all three types of evidence, it is necessary to be cautious, discounting for distortions.

> The history derived from the texts is . . . a history in search of a country. The scholarly literature on the location of place names from Chinese, Arabic and Indian sources . . . is very extensive. . . . [but] surprisingly inconclusive and speculative. The history derived from archaeological investigation . . . is quite precise . . . but it does not give us anything very substantial in the way of names and dates. . . . We can trace the rise and fall of settlements. We can see the measure of influence from China and India. We cannot, however, find out with certainty what the settlements were called. (in Wang, 1964: 101)

5. As Spencer (1983: 80–81) so astutely notes, "Indian views of Southeast Asia in ancient times are woven into the colorful fabric of religious lore. . . . [which] provides a means of delineating ancient India's geographical horizons." The Golden Island of the epics refers to Southeast Asia. "The island of Sumatra was most consistently described as an island of gold. Local products . . . were the chief attractions: gold, silver, gems, camphor. . . . [so we know that] Indians were [probably] frequenting Southeast Asia in search of wealth even before there was a substantial trade with China."

6. The absence of Indian-style monumental temples in the region of Palembang and Jambi, however, is disappointing. It has led some scholars to suggest that "Indianization" of southeast Asian architecture followed a somewhat different route. Instead of moving episodically across water, Indian material culture may have spread overland to the Indochina region (Champa, Vietnam) and then down through Thailand and the Malay Peninsula before diffusing to eastern Java (i.e., at Borobudur). Even in these cases there seems to have been no wholesale "implantation" of foreign forms but rather the gradual incorporation, or indigenization, of models whose ultimate provenance was the Indian subcontinent. Nooteboom (1950–1951: 125) presents fascinating evidence for such indigenization based upon his technical studies of boats. Examining the carved frieze of the Borobudur Temple, he concludes that the boats depicted are complicated double outriggers (capable of moving frontward and back); these were native to Java but were never used in Indian shipping.

The paucity of Indian-style monuments in the vicinity of today's Palembang is far from conclusive proof that there was no such capital; the terrain itself would dictate against great monuments. William Marsden's classic history of Sumatra, written toward the end of the eighteenth century (3rd ed. 1811, reprinted 1966: 361), describes Palembang as situated in "a flat marshy tract" and extending eight miles along both banks of the river and adjacent creeks. "The buildings . . . being all of wood or bamboos, standing on posts, and mostly covered with thatch of palm-leaves" were supplemented by "a great number of floating habitations, mostly shops . . . almost all communication . . . [is by] boats." Archaeological remains, under those circumstances, are distinctly unlikely.

7. Nooteboom (1950–1951), as much a Sumatran "nationalist" as Coedès is an Indian admirer, has argued forcefully that the presence of Indian influences in Sumatra and Java should not be attributed to Indian colonization but to diffusion,

the effect of Srivijayan shipping itself (Nooteboom, 1950–1951: 127). He points to a continuous record of Sumatran navigation (canoes on rivers, double outriggers on the open sea) from prehistoric times and stresses the active role Sumatran boats played in medieval passages to India (Nooteboom, 1950–1951: 119–123).

8. Whether or not an actual "empire" of Srivijaya ever existed is a remarkably moot point in history. Wang (1958), Coedès (1918, 1968), and of course Nilakanta Sastri (1949) assume its existence, as does Hall (1985), although he differs with the former on how it ran. Spencer (1983), on the other hand, shares the skepticism of some, including myself, who believe it may have been a "front." The most damaging information comes from the disappointing results of an extensive archaeological excavation in 1974 in the vicinity of Palembang; virtually no artifacts were found that dated from the period of presumed Srivijayan hegemony. Either Srivijaya was a hoax (or a figment of Coedès' and Ferrand's imagination) or its capital, Palembang, lay elsewhere. It should be noted that Wolters wrote his book on the fall of Srivijaya before these excavations, which makes his otherwise excellent source less than definitive, whereas Hall (1985) participated in the excavations and wrote his book after them.

9. This reference to a bay makes the description suspect, particularly if Palembang's present location is the same as her original one. It may be that there was a city called Palembang, known to the Arabs as Sribuza, but that it was somewhere else! Hall (1985) falls back on this position.

10. The example of camphor demonstrates how much skill such extraction required; it was not simply a matter of picking nuts and berries. Camphor is a calcified resin created in the interior of a tree by a disease, and its presence is not obvious from outside. Although Marsden (1811, reprinted 1966) suggested that locating camphor-containing trees involved a great deal of trial and error and excessive cutting, in fact there was considerable native knowledge regarding the location of these precious objects. Similarly, although gold dust was sometimes sifted in streams, in other parts of Sumatra large nuggets of gold were mined, which indicated considerable skill in prospecting.

11. Admittedly, there were other reasons underlying the British decision. With the development of deep-draught steam vessels, Malacca's port facilities were no longer very efficient; lighterage was required to relay goods and passengers between the larger ships anchored off-shore and the shallow port that could not accommodate them. Only massive investments could have "saved" Malacca as a port.

10

꽃꽃꽃꽃꽃

All the Silks of China

The most extensive, populous, and technologically advanced region of the medieval world was China. Its impressive strength had accumulated over the course of its long history of state organization, intellectual sophistication, and efficient peasant production. During the Sung dynasty period (960 until 1234 in the north, continuing to 1276 in the south), in spite of successive "barbarian" threats from the northern fringes that eventually culminated in Mongol conquest and rule of the entire country under the Yuan dynasty (1276–1368), China may have reached her highest level of premodern achievement. This was reflected in her enormous population. Official figures from the People's Republic suggest that China had at least 73 million inhabitants by 1190; Ho (1970: 52) estimates that in the thirteenth century, just prior to the Mongol invasion, China's population in the areas under Chin and Sung rule may have been a hundred million. A global inspection of the world system in the thirteenth century would, with little hesitation, have led to a prediction of continued growth and expanding Chinese power.

In this chapter we explore economic developments in China

during the Sung and Yuan periods, looking both at her internal production and commerce and at her linkages to the other subsystems with which she was in increasing contact: the Arab world that played an important albeit secondary role, the Indian and south Asian worlds that were part of the semiperiphery, and Europe, which had only recently begun to move into the larger arena from her former peripheral status. The chapter concludes with a description of the events that precipitated the reversal of China's position and that thus led to the demise of the world system that had been developing in the thirteenth and fourteenth centuries or, rather, to its reshaping into "the" Eurocentered modern world system.

China's Participation in International Trade

The literature generated both in China and abroad gives the impression that the Chinese were "not interested in" trade, that they tolerated it only as a form of tribute, and that they were relatively passive recipients rather than active seekers of commercial gain. As seen in Chapter 9, scholars of the Srivijayan "empire" have sometimes tried to explain the special role that confederation played between the seventh and twelfth centuries by citing the exclusionary trade policies of the Chinese emperors.

This impression, however, is created almost entirely by a literal interpretation of official Chinese documents, such as the government-commissioned histories of successive dynasties or the chronicles of the court. These documents follow highly stylized and conventional forms and are intended to project an image of the emperors as benign and diffident practitioners of Confucian virtue and noblesse oblige. They must, therefore, be interpreted with caution, which Wolters (1970) obviously has failed to do.

Upon closer examination, it is apparent that much more trade went on than official documents reveal, and that tribute trade, the only type referred to in dynastic documents, was only the tip of an iceberg of unrecorded "private" trade. According to Wang (1970: 215), it was only a myth, albeit one "fostered by Chinese officialdom and perpetuated in official writings," that maritime trade was of little interest to the Chinese. He stresses that there were actually two levels of maritime trade that must be investigated separately: the "public" (or tribute) trade conducted directly by the emperor's court, and the "private" trade that, although ignored in the official documents, almost always exceeded the former in bulk and value (Wang, 1970: 216).

Even this distinction, however, is not entirely adequate. It creates the illusion that the two types of trade and the participants engaged in them were discrete. Given the close connection between the state (court) and civil society in medieval China, however, such segregation was patently impossible. In addition to handling the "tribute" trade, state officials, including emissaries, seem to have traded on their own, with the knowledge if not full approval of the court; furthermore, the rulers, either in their personal menages or through the state apparatus, seem to have engaged in considerable production and exchange. The existence of royal workshops, for which slaves provided the productive power, had been as common in Han China as in Byzantium, and they were later described in Yuan China by Marco Polo and Ibn Battuta (English trans., 1929: 291, 294–295).[1] The government monopoly over the production and marketing of salt placed the state in an important regulatory role that paralleled, on a much larger scale, the salt monopoly in Venice. The backing of the state was a *sine qua non* for the monetary system that, from T'ang times if not earlier, made sophisticated use of credit and even paper currency.

In the last analysis, however, the amount of "private" trade (particularly foreign maritime trade) that was tolerated was contingent upon state policy, which sometimes inhibited it by enforcing stringent controls on the visits of foreign merchants and which always attempted to supervise it through regulations on their admission, travel, and transactions. Foreign trade in China, therefore, was neither a monolithic entity nor was it unvarying.

Just as there was slippage between the Confucian "ideal" of disdain for commerce and the reality of active engagement, there was also considerable variation in the practice of trade over time. There was no unchanging and inflexible Chinese "attitude" toward commerce, Max Weber's (1951 trans.) contentions notwithstanding. Rather, the amount of "capitalistic" production and trade (Balazs, 1964: 34–54) fluctuated as conditions altered or as Chinese views changed. Relatively long periods of "expansiveness" seem to have alternated with periods of defensive withdrawal, quite independent of the religious ideology that remained relatively constant. (It may be worth noting that, even in the absence of a Confucian "ethic," there has been a series of twentieth-century alternations between the opening and closing and then reopening of China to the world that have earlier precedents.)

Wang (1970: 219–220) divides the long stretch of premodern Chinese history into four phases during which different realities and policies of external trade prevailed. The first of these was prior to the fifth century A.D., when maritime trade was as yet insignificant. During this period, population was concentrated in the northern region of the country whose connections to the sparsely settled southern coasts were still at a very primitive level. What external trade there was went overland across the Silk Road.

The second period, between the fifth and eighth centuries, saw significant migrations that increased the population of the south,[2] as well as improvements in agriculture and communications. In agriculture, the draining of the Yangtse River valley swamps and advances in techniques of wet rice cultivation expanded the frontier. In communications, the construction of the Grand Canal between the Yellow and Yangtse Rivers reduced the cost of internal transport and integrated the southern periphery with the core economic and political center of the north. During these centuries, while the northern overland route lay relatively dormant, internal markets were being developed and the ground was being prepared for a marked expansion in maritime trade from southern ports (Wang, 1970: 220–221).

During the third period, roughly from the ninth century to the last third of the fourteenth century, China experienced a remarkable expansionary phase of her economic development. As was the case in Europe, a virtual revolution in agriculture underlay the new prosperity and long-distance trade and industry intensified it. Whereas Europe's heightened productivity came from better ploughs and draught-animal harnesses, in south China it came from hydraulics: "the dam, the sluice-gate, the noria . . . and the treadle water pump" (Elvin, 1973: 128). Elvin claims that by the thirteenth century, China had "the most sophisticated agriculture in the world, India being the only conceivable rival" (Elvin, 1973: 129). This "take-off" was sustained, even though Turkic and Mongolian tribes continued to threaten her northern frontiers and eventually overran portions and then the whole of her expanse.

During the ninth and tenth centuries the population increased, particularly on the southern coastal plain where rapid urbanization, stimulated by industrial developments and growing maritime trade, propelled the society forward. During the rule of the Southern Sung (1127–1276), Chinese agricultural productivity, industrial technology, and commercial and financial sophistication underwent significant transformations that, in spite of (or perhaps even stimulated by) the occupation of large portions of her territory by militaristic nomads from the northern frontier, led to active integration of China with world markets.

When the Mongols conquered first the northern lands of the Chins/Juchens (ca. 1233) and eventually the territory formerly ruled by the Southern Sung (1276), they actively adopted and even developed further the technological and social inventions of the high culture they ruled but to which they always felt inferior (Wang, 1970: 221–222). Although Kubilai Khan held court at Peking in the north, China's center of economic and demographic gravity had decisively moved southward. By the end of the thirteenth century, southern China may have contained some 85 to 90 percent of the country's population (Kracke, 1954–55: population estimate from 480).

The twelfth through early fourteenth centuries were, in some ways, an aberration in Chinese trade, since during that period there was very little in the way of "treaty" or public trade. On the other hand, there was a virtual explosion of "private" trade (Wang, 1970: 217), which will be described later in this chapter.

The fourth and final period came after the fall of the Yuan dynasty and its replacement by the indigenous Ming in 1368. According to Wang (1970: 222–223), by that time

> the Chinese had achieved almost all the preconditions for a flourishing trade both within and outside the empire. . . . [T]here was demand for maritime trade, there was the surplus wealth for investment and risk-taking, there were credit and financial institutions albeit still lacking in security, there were the technical skills for seafaring and there was political stability.

In addition, there was a sizable navy, consisting of both government and private ships that were the largest and most seaworthy in the world. According to Lo (1958: 150), toward the end of the fourteenth century the Ming navy consisted of some 3500 ocean-going ships, including over 1700 warships and 400 armed transports for grain. No naval force in the world at that time came close to this formidable armada.

At first, such strength was exploited. After a brief period of disarray, precipitated by plagues and civil war, the Ming made "a bid for maritime dominance of Asian water . . . [which met] with unprecedented successes."[3] In July 1405, Admiral Cheng Ho headed an impressive navy of 62 giant ships sent to "call upon" the kings of the Indian Ocean as an emissary for the Ming (Pelliot, 1933: 275). Within two years he had visited Java, Calicut, Atjah (in Sumatra), and Palembang, then under a Chinese governor. Setting out on his second voyage in 1408 with a fleet of 48 ships (Pelliot, 1933: 277, 281, 283), he spent the next three years visiting, among others, Champa, Malacca, and Ceylon, but, as in his first voyage, his navy did not proceed beyond India (Pelliot, 1933: 290). Five other missions followed between the end of 1412 and 1430, each requiring several years. Official visits (and exchange of "trib-ute") were made to virtually every major port of Java, India, Sumatra, and Borneo, as well as the East African coast (Malindi and Mogadishu) and the Arabian Sea–Persian Gulf area, where Cheng Ho made port calls at Aden and Hormuz (Pelliot, 1933: *passim*). Indeed, Cheng Ho visited every important point within the three circuits of the Indian Ocean. China seemed to be on the verge of assuming a hegemonic role over the entire system.

Instead, these visits abruptly ended. The Ming withdrew their fleet, restricted maritime trade, and terminated relations with for-eign powers. "So sharp was the shift in policy after 1435 that *no one since has seriously regarded China as a sea power*" (Wang, 1970: 223, italics added; but see also Lo, 1958, and the end of this chapter for a different interpretation).

The question that has perplexed—indeed caused despair among—serious scholars for at least the past one hundred years is why, given China's position of supremacy at the time, she did not take the final steps to become the truly hegemonic power in the world system that had reached a level of integration not to be matched for another three centuries. Grousset (1942: 318), perhaps the best Asian scholar of the last generation, posed the hypothetical question that has plagued everyone investigating the period "before European hegemony," namely, what would the destiny of Asia (and we might add, the world) have been if European navigators, approaching the Indies and Malaya, had found a Chinese thalassocracy established there?

Although this is an illicit question, it does capture the issue. In the late fourteenth and early fifteenth centuries, China had everything needed to establish her rule over the Indian Ocean—from her coasts to the Persian Gulf. Close to exercising domination over a significant portion of the globe and enjoying a technological advantage not only in peaceful production but in naval and military might as well (Toussaint, 1966; McNeill, 1982: Chapter 2), why did she turn her back, withdraw her fleet, and thus leave an enormous vacuum of power that Muslim merchantmen, unbacked by state sea power, were totally unprepared to fill, but which their European counterparts would be more than willing and able to—after a hiatus of some 70 years?

It is this conundrum—so crucial to the rise and fall of the thirteenth-century world system—that constitutes the major focus of this chapter. Before we can address it, we must first demonstrate that China had the capacity, if not the will, to become the world's hegemonic power. If by the fourteenth century she had already been surpassed by industrial, military, transport, and economic institutional developments in Europe, it could be argued that the outcome would have been the same, even if China had not withdrawn from the contest. Her fleet would have met, and succumbed to, the superior power of a rising Europe. In the sections that follow we intend to demonstrate that such a self-serving proposition is untrue.

Technological Sophistication

In the past, before western scholars had sufficient information about China's achievements in science and technology, it was commonly argued that Europe's eventual triumph in the world arena was the result of her unique scientific and technological inventiveness, and, conversely, that Orientals, although perhaps "clever," had never been able to sustain a scientific revolution. The voluminous investigations of Needham (inter alia, 1954–85, 1970, 1981) have more than corrected this error. We now have much fuller documentation on Chinese contributions to medicine and physiology, physics, and mathematics, as well as their more practical applications in technology.

According to Sivin (1982: 105–106), Needham did not go far enough; he stopped short of admitting that, by Sung times, China had had a true scientific "revolution," a position strongly argued by Chinese scholars (e.g., Li et al., 1982; although Chang, 1957, dissents). Whether or not the term "scientific revolution" is justified, there can be no doubt that in late medieval times the level of Chinese technical competence far exceeded the Middle East, which, in turn, had outstripped Europe for many centuries. Space permits only a few examples here: paper and printing, iron and steel, weaponry (including guns, cannons, and bombs), shipbuilding and navigational techniques, as well as two primary manufactured exports, silk and porcelain.

Paper

According to Tsien (in Li et al., 1982: 459):

> paper was invented in China before the Christian era, adopted for writing at the beginning of the 1st century A.D., and manufactured with new and fresh fibres from the early 2nd century.... Woodblock printing was first employed ... around 700 A.D. and moveable type in the middle of the 11th century.

Some time in the ninth century, the Arabs learned the process of paper making from the Chinese and later transmitted that precious knowledge to "westerners." Braudel (1973: 295) suggests that the first European paper mills appeared in twelfth-century Spain but that the Italians did not begin to produce paper until the fourteenth century; Cipolla (1976: 206), basing his remarks on a 1953 article by Irigoin, however, claims that by the second half of the thirteenth century the court in Byzantium no longer bought its paper from the Arabs but from Italy. (For more details, see T. F. Carter, 1925, revised 1955.) But in any case, China's edge was significant.

Iron and Steel

Even more impressive than paper manufacture were Chinese advances in siderurgy, which were several hundred years in advance of Europe's. From at least the eighth century onward, coal was being mined[4] in northern China and used in furnaces that produced high-quality iron and even steel "either by means of the co-fusion of pig iron and wrought iron, or by direct decarbonization in a cold oxidizing blast" (Elvin, 1973: 86; see also Needham, "Iron and Steel Production in Ancient and Medieval China," 1956 lecture reproduced in Needham, 1970: 107–112, and the works of Hartwell, 1962, 1966, 1967).

Hartwell's (1967) estimates of the scale of iron production are truly staggering. By his calculations, the tonnage of coal burned annually in the eleventh century for iron production alone in northern China was "roughly equivalent to 70 percent of the total amount of coal annually used by all metal workers in Great Britain at the beginning of the eighteenth century" (Hartwell, 1967: 122).[5] By the end of the eleventh century the Sung were minting iron coins and making many metal products as well. According to Hartwell (1967: 122–123):

> 7,000 workers were engaged in actually mining the ore and fuel, and operating the furnaces, forges, and refining hearths . . . [while] others were engaged in transporting the raw materials from the mines to the iron works.
>
> The scale of production at individual establishments was unprecedented . . . and probably was not equalled anywhere in the world until the Industrial Revolution of the nineteenth century.

If we add to the workers engaged in direct ore extraction and processing those workers who fabricated tools and weaponry, there can be no doubt as to the high level of China's industrial development.

To some extent, such technological advances proved to be their undoing. Elvin (1973: 18, 84–87) suggests that the invading Chin not only adopted the methods of metallurgy from northern China but passed them along to the Mongols who learned to tip their arrows with metal; this significantly improved their military might and gave them the power to defeat not only Russia but eventually both the Chin and the Southern Sung.

In any case, the invasion of the north by these nomadic groups precipitated a decline in the amount of iron produced in that region. Hartwell suggests that demographic and institutional changes both played a part in this retrenchment, which had begun to show up by the middle of the thirteenth century. During Chin times, the population of the northern iron-producing region had remained roughly constant and, with it, the level of production and demand. But during the period of Mongol rule, there was a precipitous drop in population as people fled south or were deported to provide labor elsewhere. Between 1234, when it came under Mongol rule, and 1330, the population of the province of Honan dropped by 86 percent (Hartwell, 1967: 151), clear evidence that coal and iron were not the only casualties of the invasion.

Hartwell (1967: 150–151) considers institutional changes equally culpable, however. He notes that

> By the middle of the thirteenth century, the independent entrepreneur of the Northern Sung had been replaced by the appanage [benefice], free by unfree labor, and the expanding mass market . . . by the fixed and limited demands of the appanage in key iron producing centers. . . . During the reign of Qubilai (1260–1294), salaried officials representing the central government gradually replaced the appanage holders. . . . But independent management was not restored, and the continued use of unfree labor and the lack of free markets remained characteristic features of the North China iron industry until after the fall of the Yuan (1368).

The "golden age" of iron and steel production thus ended with the northern Sung period; although the Southern Sung may have had knowledge of the techniques they were too far from large coal deposits to make a large-scale siderurgical industry cost-efficient. The Mongols, however, could not afford to abandon iron and steel making since metals, in combination with gunpowder, were a significant part of the armory of their war machine.

Weaponry and the Navy

The Chinese evidently stumbled upon the explosive character of gunpowder around 650 A.D., although the first reference to it does not appear before a mid-ninth century science text. By the early tenth century gunpowder is mentioned as the ignition for a flame-throwing weapon, and by about 1000 A.D. "the practice of using gunpowder in simple bombs and grenades was coming into use" (Needham, "The Epic of Gunpowder and Firearms," reprinted 1981: 30–31). The illustrations in Needham (1981: 36–38) and Skoljar (1971: 136) leave little doubt that the Chinese used gunpowder for more than fireworks displays.

Chinese artisans working under the Chin transformed the relatively mild gunpowder known to the Sung into a true explosive first employed in 1221; a further innovation in 1272–1273 combined the standard Muslim mechanical stone thrower with an explosive projectile (Elvin, 1973: 88). By the early fourteenth century, if not before, a device that is unmistakably a canon for lobbing bombs was in use (see the illustration of it in Needham, reprinted 1981: 31), and Lo (1955) tells us that ships of the Yuan navy were regularly equipped with this device.

The "gun" proper also appeared about this time. It was a logical extension of the Chin's earlier "fire spurting lances," which shot gunpowder out of rolled paper, and the improved version that the Southern Sung had used in 1259 to defend themselves from the Mongols, which shot pellets from a bamboo barrel. By the fourteenth century, the Mongols were equipped with a true metal-barreled gun capable of shooting explosive pellets (Elvin, 1973: 89). When the Ming eventually inherited the disintegrating Yuan empire in the latter part of the fourteenth century, the use of firearms in warfare was fully characteristic (Elvin, 1973: 92).

It is therefore difficult to countenance a view of Chinese technology as either stagnant or devoted to frivolous ends; it was "dead" serious. Had it not been dismantled, the Chinese navy would have proved a formidable enemy capable of rendering Portuguese ships and guns powerless.

Nor were Chinese ships and navigational techniques in any way inferior to those of the Europeans. As noted in Chapter 4, the compass originated in China and then diffused to the Arabs and Italians. The first clear reference to the use of the magnetic needle in Chinese navigation appears in a sea manual written around 900 A.D., and, by the eleventh and twelfth centuries, floating compasses were in common use on Chinese ships (Needham, 1960 lecture on "The Chinese Contribution to the Development of the Mariner's Compass," reprinted 1970: particularly 243–244) as was the wind-rose (Teixeira da Mota, 1964: 60). And throughout Sung and Yuan times, Chinese ships were larger and more seaworthy than those of any other nation. They were certainly the match of Europe, as the work of Lo demonstrates.

Consumer Goods for International Trade

High technological competence also characterized the two Chinese products that were most in demand in the world market, silk and porcelain. The most important of these in earliest times was raw silk, over which the Chinese had a monopoly.[6] Silk continued to be delivered to the luxury markets of the Middle East and Europe even during periods of retrenchment, but the Chinese monopoly was broken in the sixth century when silk cocoons were smuggled out of China by Syrians who began a modest production of their own. By the medieval period, however, porcelain had displaced silk as China's primary export (Hudson, 1970: 160). Shards of Chinese ceramic ware are to be found in large quantities all along the coastal edges of the Indian Ocean and its extensions, including East Africa.

To some extent, the substitution (or rather supplementation) of porcelain for silk reflects geopolitical changes within China and changes in the methods of transport to foreign markets. Silk was an ideal product to carry overland since it had high value and low weight and bulk. Once the reorganization of Chinese space had occurred, with the concentration of population and power along the southeastern coast, shipping became the major means of transport, which made it possible (and indeed necessary) to fill maritime vessels with bulkier goods. A twelfth-century Chinese source (*P'ing-chou-k'o-t'an* by Chu Yu, as cited by Hudson, 1970: 160) describes how merchants divided up space on ships, "each getting a share and sleeping on top of his goods by night." Most of the cargo consisted of pottery.

Chinese porcelain was of fine quality and its designs were attractive, but pottery-making was virtually universal and designs could be, and indeed were, copied. Why then was Chinese porcelain in such high demand? The answer seems to lie beyond the issue of demand; it probably had to do with ballast. China's imports were relatively bulky specialty items, but her exports were high value low bulk. Ships could not return from China without ballast, which crockery provided. (See, inter alia, Chaudhuri, 1985: 53, on this point.) The "balance of payments" over time and space can virtually be traced by the global distribution of Chinese pottery from various dynastic periods.

That was not the case with respect to silk production, in which the Southern Sung excelled. It is interesting to compare the technology and organization of sericulture and silk spinning and weaving with the other textile industries more common in the rest of the world system of the time—woolens in Europe, linen (and cotton) in Egypt and Syria, and fine cotton in India—and it is hard to resist a technologically deterministic explanation for variations in the nature of industrialization in these places. To produce any type of natural textile, a symbiotic relationship must exist between agriculturalists and industrial workers, between rural and urban areas; that is a constant. And yet variations in the raw material itself determine where the work will be done and by whom.

In the production of woolen cloth, the demand for grazing land comes into competition with land for agriculture, thus displacing farmers whose labor is made available for processing the wool—women largely spinning and men predominantly fulling, dyeing, and weaving. Wool is easily transportable in its raw state, which permits a separation between where it is raised and where it is transformed into cloth. As noted in Chapter 3, in the thirteenth and early fourteenth centuries, English-raised wool fed the looms of Flanders.

Cotton and linen follow a different course. With these, agricultural land remains under cultivation and crops require intensive labor. Furthermore, to preserve the soil, fiber crops must be rotated with legumes, which means that there is neither a division of labor between cotton and flax growers and ordinary farmers nor any displacement of labor from the land. The raw materials may be transported for further refining or, since they are bulky, may receive preliminary processing and cleaning before being shipped to spinners and weavers. Furthermore, there are often byproducts that can undergo simple industrial treatment on the site (cotton seeds, for example, can be pressed for their oil), which leads to a certain amount of rural "industrialization."

The production of silk is very different (see Figure 14). It is far more complex and involves a larger set of rural workers whose

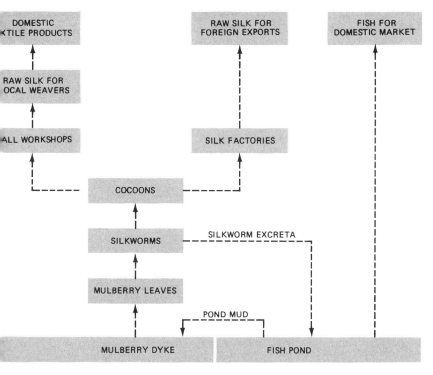

FIGURE 14. System of silk production (based on So).

daily proximity is essential. "Agro-urban" settlements are a natural consequence. I have not been able to find any descriptions of the technology of silk production in southern China in the Middle Ages, but it was probably not very different from that described in great detail in So's (1986) book on the south China silk district in the nineteenth and early twentieth centuries. So (1986: 86; 87 for quotation) stresses that in the complex symbiotic system of silk production (see Figure 14), the peasant family constituted the basic unit of labor.

The father and son in a peasant household would start planting seedlings on the polder as early as January. In the following winter, they would cut the newly grown mulberry plant to about one foot above the ground and cover . . . [it] with fertile fish pond mud. In the meantime, the mother and daughter would be busy buying silkworm egg sheets and watching the hatching of silkworms. In the coming spring, the daughter would pick the fresh mulberry leaves and feed them to the newly born silkworms. The worms would eat graciously, grow quickly, and demand more and more mulberry leaves on an increasing scale. The father and son meanwhile would clean the daily silkworm refuse and prepare the worms for their "sleeps." After five sleeps or rests, a full-grown silkworm would have spun and covered itself with silk thread and formed a cocoon. The whole family would then be busy with the silk-reeling process.

Note that the process requires the labor of men and women co-operating over a long time. Note also that it carries a built-in risk that the supply of mulberry leaves will fail to keep pace with the exponentially-expanding appetites of the worms.[7] Furthermore, the care of the worms as well as the reeling of the silk threads calls for a very tender touch. Controlled temperature, subdued light, gentle handling, and a hushed environment (especially during their "sleeps") are essential for the hatching and growth of the delicate worms. Once the cocoons are ready, they must be plunged into hot water and, since the filament from a single cocoon is too thin to wind, "the fibers from four to eighteen cocoons are collected and passed together through an agate guide or ring, and then wound on to a slowly revolving wheel" (So, 1986: 101). To obtain a continuous thread, one must add new pieces to the reel accurately; great skill is required to produce thread of uniform width. Women performed this taxing work and in general played a more prominent role in sericulture than their counterparts in wool and cotton textile production.

It is clear that this extended labor process was not easily transferred to "factories," nor was it easily amenable to labor-saving devices. If the technology of the Chinese textile industry lagged behind textile production in other places, it may have been due more to the dictates of the material than to any lack of technical inventiveness.

Business Practices and Institutions

Not only was China technologically advanced in production, but she was not lacking in social inventiveness either. Virtually all the institutions required to facilitate state and private capitalism were in place by Sung and Yuan times. Three such institutions are basic: a system that organizes production and distribution, a system of money and credit that facilitates investments and accounts, and a system for regulating imports and exports. We take each of these up in turn.

Production and Distribution

Kato begins his discussion on the Hang (association of merchants) in China with the following remark: "It is a well-known fact that in China there are associations of merchants resembling, in some degree, the guilds of the middle ages in Europe, formed around buildings called 'hui-kuan' . . . " (1936: 45), which have clear precedents in T'ang and Sung times (Kato, 1936: 46). At those early times, the term "hang" referred both to the association and to the street "consisting of shops dealing in the same goods or engaged in the same trade" (Kato, 1936: 46). The parallels with the Middle Eastern bazaar and with the guilds of medieval Europe are striking.

The variety of guilds in medieval China was impressive. Gernet lists only a sample of those found in the Southern Sung capital of Hangchow: jewellers, gilders, gluemakers, art and antique dealers, sellers of crabs, olives, honey, or ginger, doctors, soothsayers, scavengers, bootmakers, bath keepers, and, as in medieval towns throughout the world, the money changers, who dealt "in precious metals, salt-exchange bills[8] and other kinds of promissory notes. They displayed, piled up on their stalls, articles in gold and silver and also copper coins" (Gernet, English trans. 1962: 87). As Gernet notes (1962: 88), the guilds not only served to regulate their internal affairs but, as they did in the Middle East, to represent the trade vis-à-vis the government.

> One of the principal advantages of forming trade guilds was that they provided merchants and artisans with a means of regulating their relations with the State. It was to the heads of the guilds that government authorities applied when making requisitions of any kind, whether of goods from shops or of artisans from the workshops. In this way, official intermediaries ensured that fair prices and fair wages were paid.

Kato (1936: 62–63) is less sanguine but probably more realistic when he notes that the government often paid below market prices for the goods it requisitioned and, in addition, set a high price for the goods it forced the merchants to buy from the government. I suspect that the transition from the independent merchant class described by Gernet to the greater control and exploitation over it by the government described by Kato coincided with the transition from Sung to Yuan rule. (The same transition occurred in Egypt between Fatimid and Mamluk times, and for a similar reason—military rule by strangers.)

It must be admitted, however, that an independent and powerful bourgeoisie was not likely to develop in a society in which merchants were not accorded as much honor as government functionaries and in which a centralized state set the terms for money and credit. Merchants may have been "indispensable intermediaries in converting agricultural surplus into disposable state income," as Chaudhuri (1985: 11) claims, and the state elite may have depended upon merchants to create a market and to centralize tax collection (Chaudhuri, 1985: 16), but when paper money backed by the state became the approved currency, the chances for amassing capital in opposition to or independent of the state machinery became difficult.

Paper Money and Credit

In Europe and the Middle East, governments issued metal coins whose value was determined by weight and whose exchange rate depended on accepted ratios between silver and gold (and possibly lesser metals). In China, copper constituted the preferred coin, but it was only one form of currency. Although the value of official metallic coins can be manipulated by a government (by diluting its valued content with baser metals), it cannot be fully controlled; exterior trade could move metals in and out of countries and merchants engaged in overseas trade could always amass fortunes elsewhere. Under these conditions, "paper money" originated in the promissory notes issued by long-distance traders for their own convenience.

The situation was quite different in China, in which paper money was, in ways, much closer to our "legal tender" than to the medieval bills of exchange elsewhere. That is because it developed out of government transactions rather than merchant agreements. Elvin (1973: 155), depending heavily on Yang (1952: 51–53), summarizes the early development as follows:

Bills for the transfer and exchange of cash and commodities had been known since T'ang times. The earliest of all were probably the "food tickets" of the divisional militia.... In the eighth century, the T'ang government developed the so-called "flying cash" system on the basis of the complementary north–south flows of money arising from the tax system on the one hand and the tea trade on the other. Merchants could pay in money at the capital and receive a certificate from the government which, when presented at any provincial treasury, entitled the bearer to draw an equivalent sum.... The Sung dynasty operated an essentially similar system under the name of "money of convenience."

The major group who found convenience in this method were the merchants who, during Sung times, became extremely powerful. The only problem, however, was that money moved in only one direction, from the capital to the provinces.

True paper money, introduced in Szechuan at the beginning of the eleventh century to solve an entirely different problem of exchange, eventually provided a solution to this dilemma (Yang, 1952: 156–157). Originally, combines of rich merchants printed and backed their own paper currencies, but chances for fraud abounded. At first, the government tried to stop the abuses, but then decided to print its own script. The state monopoly over money, which existed between about 1000 and 1400, not only furnished businessmen with "a convenient means of exchange," but produced a healthy profit for the government (Yang, 1952: 9). Elvin (1973: 159) explains:

Like the merchants' notes which they replaced, early government notes were normally issued against the deposit of money by members of the public.... For them to become exactly like present-day paper money a few further developments were necessary. The state had to issue notes directly ... without waiting for public demand, ... [validity had to have no time limit, and a] cash reserve had to be set up representing a proportion of the value.... All of these ... seem to have come about fairly rapidly.

Paper money was adopted in north China by the end of the eleventh century and in the Chin and Southern Sung territories it was in regular use by the twelfth century, although it still coexisted with metal coins.

The Mongol conquerors adopted the system (making money!)

with alacrity, but went one step farther. To ensure the value of its paper money, it forbade the use of silver and gold in business transactions; by 1280, only paper was accepted for trade. "Notes were convertible into gold and silver" only for use in manufacture; they [precious metals] could not circulate (Yang, 1952: 63–64).

That the Yuan achieved considerable success in enforcing this difficult proscription is attested to by foreign visitors. Thus, at the end of the thirteenth century, Marco Polo could write that the ordinary money in Cathay was a piece of cotton paper stamped with Mangu's (Möngke) seal. Foreign traders had to exchange their gold and silver for it. The system remained in force throughout Mongol rule. Balducci Pegolotti (Yule trans., *Cathay and the Way Thither*, Vol. II, 1937: 294) advises the Italian merchant readers of his early fourteenth-century manual that "The lord of Cathay takes your silver for his treasury and gives you yellow paper, stamped with the lord's seal, called balishi, and everyone accepts it when you buy silk, etc."[9]

This is confirmed by Ibn Battuta who, writing about the 1340s, says (1929 trans.: 283) that foreigners could not use gold and silver in commerce but only "pieces of paper, each the size of the palm of the hand, and stamped with the sultan's seal. . . . If anyone goes to the bazaar with a silver dirham or a dinar, intending to buy something, no one will accept it." According to Ibn Battuta (1929 trans.: 286), Muslim traders/travelers never touched money.

When a Muhammadan merchant enters any town in China, he is given a choice between staying with some specified merchant among the Muslims domiciled there, or going to a hostelry. If he chooses to stay with the merchant, his money is taken into custody and put in the charge of the resident merchant. The latter then pays from it all his expenses with honesty and charity. When the visitor wishes to depart, his money is examined, and if any of it is found to be missing, the resident merchant . . . is obliged to make good the deficit. If the visitor chooses to go to a hostelry, his property is deposited under the charge of the keeper. . . . [who] buys for him whatever he desires and presents him with an account.

There were several important consequences of the adoption of paper money (universal credit) and the insistence that it be used even by foreign merchants. First, by increasing the velocity of money, it stimulated economic growth (for China, see Elvin, 1973: 146; for Europe, see Goldstone, 1984). Second, by requiring everyone to use the same currency, the state was able to regulate the foreign exchange rate and thus become the indispensable intermediary between foreign and local merchants.

The Control of the Foreign Sea Trade

Overland trade continued throughout the periods under discussion and was largely in the hands of Uighur and Muslim traders. The sea trade was another matter. Foreign ships were confined to a limited number of ports in which they could be supervised and controlled. Canton (referred to in Arabic documents as Khanfu) was the first of these ports, in use as early as T'ang times and almost always the most important. Even in T'ang times, before paper money supplanted coinage, the Chinese carefully controlled visitors to that port. Sulayman the Merchant (Ferrand trans., 1922: 54) describes docking in Canton in the mid-ninth century:

> When the sailors arrive by sea to China, the Chinese seize their goods and lock them up in warehouses. They protect them for six months from the time of their arrival to when the last ships of that monsoon season arrive. The Chinese impose a custom duty of 30% [of the goods] on all imported merchandise and return the rest to the merchant who owns it.

It can only be presumed that the confiscated goods entered both the domestic economy of the emperor and the profitable trade of the custom's officials. So much for the distinction between "private" and "tribute" trade! It must be acknowledged, however, that this was a period during which Chinese ships were also going out; Arab documents confirm their appearance in the harbors of Siraf, Basra, and Oman, which means that, in the interests of reciprocity, the Chinese had to treat foreign merchants fairly.

By the time of the Southern Sung and later the Yuan, two other "treaty" ports began to outstrip Canton: the port that served the city of Hangchow (Kinsai), the capital city of the Southern Sung,[10] which by all accounts was the world's largest city, and Ch'uan-chou (in Fukien), which Italians and Arabs called Zaytun, and which both Marco Polo and Ibn Battuta considered the greatest port in the world.[11]

We are particularly fortunate to have not one but two documents, written by or about Chinese individuals (one of Muslim origin) who served in the early and late thirteenth century as superintendents of foreign merchant ships docking in Zaytun (Ch'uan-chou) in Fukien Province. These provide a remarkably detailed picture of the trade—where the ships came from, what they carried, and how their goods were taxed and their activities controlled.

The first of these documents, the *Chu-fan-chi*, was written about 1225 by Chau Ju-Kua, superintendent for merchant shipping in the province of Fukien. Unfortunately, his work also incorporates material from an 1178 source (translators' introduction, Hirth and Rockhill, 1911), which makes it difficult to treat it as a precise description of the early thirteenth century. The document attempts to describe the lands of the "barbarians" and identifies the products imported into China from them. It therefore allows us to determine what parts of the "West" were known to China in the thirteenth century and to gain some sense of the wide variety of items involved in external trade. No scholar of thirteenth-century Asian trade can ignore this fertile, although often inaccurate and sometimes confusing, source.[12]

For our purposes, the second source is more interesting, since it details how foreign traders were actually handled. P'u Shou-keng, superintendent of the trading ships' office in Ch'uan-chou (Zaytun), was the last Sung incumbent of that office and collaborated with the Mongol invaders in 1280 (see English trans. from the Japanese by Kuwabara, 1928 and 1935). His surname P'u (=Abu) indicates that he was a descendent of one the members of the numerous resident communities of the Ta-Shih[13] in Chinese ports (Kuwabara, 1935: 2–3) and, by virtue of his office, he was a very wealthy man. As Kuwabara (1935: 36–37) explains:

> From the T'ang era, when foreign trade-ships entered a Chinese port, the traders had to pay not only customs duty . . . but also make some presents of foreign goods to the court. . . . Besides these presents . . . the traders had to make some bribes to local officers, including the superintendent, under the pretence [sic] of showing samples. . . . [T]he government sent officials to examine the cargoes. . . . After the in-

spection . . . there was held a banquet to console the officials for their troubles, to whom once again they had to make presents. . . . All these might rather be called matter-of-fact perquisites of Chinese officials. However, some of the most avaricious would . . . compel the traders to sell their goods below their proper prices, and make profit from [re]selling them.

So much for the separation of public from private trade. It was easy to become rich if you were the superintendent of shipping!

One did not gain this lucrative post easily, however. P'u Shou-keng was no mere government appointee; he owed his position to the naval exploits of ships under his direction, which had subdued the pirates in the harbor. This suggests that by the time of the decline of the Southern Sung, alternate forms of power had developed (sea as well as land war lords). P'u Shou-keng eventually used his naval strength to aid the Mongols when they invaded the territory of the Southern Sung, and, for his cooperation, was awarded high honors and made the grand military commander of the province (Kuwabara, 1935: 38–40).

P'u Shou-keng was not an isolated case. Muslim communities were powerful in the Yuan state (recall in Chapter 5 Marco Polo's description of the Muslim governor, Ahmad, in Khanbalik), and all descriptions of the major port cities of China include references to entire quarters that they occupied. To give some sense of the organization of trade cities in medieval China, we examine the city of Hangchow.[14] Perhaps no abstract discussion can convey as clear a sense of the remarkable achievements of thirteenth-century China as the picture Gernet has reconstructed of this city of a million inhabitants that was, until nineteenth-century London, the world's largest city.

Hangchow in the Thirteenth Century

Built between the shores of an enormous artificial lake (West Lake) and the banks of the Che River leading to the sea, the city of Hangchow and its suburbs covered an area of some seven to eight square miles. It was surrounded by walls pierced by "five gateways through which canals passed, and by thirteen monumental gates at which terminated the great thoroughfares" (Gernet, 1962: 26).

By the thirteenth century, the suburban zone outside the walls was even more extensive than the walled city itself. The city, adapting the "pivot of the four quarters" (Wheatley, 1971) to its elongated site, was planned so that the major "imperial way" traversed the city from north to south with the remaining streets intersecting it at right angles (Gernet, 1962: 27).

Within the built-up area, densities varied widely. The southern hill region contained the imperial palace, around which were the residential zones of the rich—the high officials and "the merchants who had made their fortune in the maritime trade" (Gernet, 1962: 32). The houses of the poor offered a shocking contrast. Residents were crowded into narrow-fronted houses of three to five storeys with shops or workshops on the ground floor. The interiors of these superblocks were honeycombed by narrow alleys and passageways and an elaborate system of fire fighting was developed to control the frequent outbreaks in these inaccessible points. In these alleyways, all goods had to be carried by hand, whereas on the paved Imperial Way, three miles long and 180 feet wide(!), there were carriages drawn by tiny horses or by men (Gernet, 1962: 40–41). As in Venice, canals played a major part in transport, from the Grand Canal that brought in distant goods to the smaller local canals that ran between neighborhoods.

There were at least ten markets in the city as well as the fish market near the lake and the wholesale market outside the city. Merchants were therefore numerous and rich. They entertained guests at the many tea houses and restaurants of the city (where ordering from hundreds of selections was done by number, a pattern maintained in Chinese restaurants to this day) or hired boats and musicians to cruise on West Lake (Gernet, 1962: 51–55). Given the new expansion into international trade, many of the richest merchants and ship owners were not natives of the city but had come from Canton or the Yangtse area. Gernet (1962: 82) suggests that their presence reflected "the embryo of a 'national market' " that was then developing.

With the unification under the Yuan, that embryo developed into a fully integrated system unifying the northern and southern regions of the country and connecting the hitherto separated land (over Central Asia) and sea (through the Indian Ocean) axes. Chinese merchants and shippers dealt with resident foreign counterparts. One entire quarter of the city housed foreign, mostly Muslim, traders. In the early fourteenth century Hangchow grew even larger, as a result of this infusion from abroad.

According to Ibn Battuta (1929 trans.: 293–297), who visited Hangchow in the 1340s, it was still "the largest [city] on the face of the earth." He reports that it took many days to traverse the six cities that made it up; each city had its own wall and all six were surrounded by another wall.

In the first city [clearly the outer ring] are the quarters of the city guards and their commander . . . twelve thousand men. . . . [W]e entered the second city through . . . the Jews' Gate. In this city live the Jews, Christians, and the sun-worshipping Turks [Zoroastrians]. . . . On the third day we entered the third city, and this is inhabited by the Muslims. Theirs is a fine city, and their bazaars are arranged just as they are in Islamic countries; they have mosques in it and muezzins—we heard them calling the noon prayer as we entered. . . . The numbers of Muslims in this city is very large. . . . [T]here is a fourth city, which is the seat of government. . . . No one resides in this city, except the sultan's slaves and servants. . . . On the following day we entered the fifth and largest city, which is inhabited by the . . . [Chinese common folk]. Its bazaars are good and contain very skilful artificers. . . . [The next day we crossed the Boatman's Gate to the sixth city] which lies on the banks of the great river [and] is inhabited by seamen, fishermen, caulkers, and carpenters, along with archers and footsoldiers. . . .

It seems hard to believe that so remarkable a city should not have become the core of a world system—but it did not. Today, Hangchow has about as many people as it had in the thirteenth and fourteenth centuries, but it is now only a provincial capital, dwarfed by Peking and Shanghai.

Among the causes of its stagnation were the Ming's partial withdrawal from that system after 1368 and their complete abandonment of sea trade after 1433. The Ming came to power in 1368, but the seeds of their rebellion against the Yuan had been sown before mid-fourteenth century. It will be recalled from Chapter 5 that the Black Death probably erupted first in China and that this considerably undermined the ability of the Mongol rulers to sustain their imperial reach. It is not without significance that Chu Yuan-Chang, one of the founders of the Ming dynasty, was orphaned in 1344 when he lost both parents and two brothers in an outbreak that may have been bubonic plague. History is clearer on the famines that followed the plague, and these events certainly intensified the revolt against the Mongol rulers who were perceived as both corrupt and unfair (Chan, 1982: 6–7). The restoration of indigenous Chinese rule under the Ming had several consequences, one of which was an eventual withdrawal from foreign contacts.

Why China Withdrew

As noted earlier, scholars have speculated broadly on the reasons for the Ming withdrawal, their explanations ranging from the purely ideological–religious to, less commonly, social structural. Those who take the former position stress the significance of the Confucian ethic, which demeaned worldly striving and commercial/ industrial gain and placed "moral example" above the legal protection of property. Institutional historians supplement this explanation by emphasizing the social bifurcation of the Chinese elite into, on the one hand, a bureaucratic or Mandarin class, which controlled the state apparatus but did not engage in business, and, on the other, a wealthy merchant class, which had no access to state power. Unlike their European counterparts, therefore, not only could they not use the state to advance their interests, but they were subject to periodic and apparently capricious reversals of fortune that undermined their position in civil society. In both explanations, change tends to be minimized, which makes them less robust in accounting for the cycles of economic activity and policy that have been described.

To account for change, there would have to have been enormous fluctuations over time in the hold of Confucianism over the Chinese "imagination" or in the power of the Mandarin class to translate its ideology into practice. Although certainly there was some degree of oscillation in both of these, it does not appear to have been sufficient to account for all of the variance. It cannot account for the total supplanting of tribute (public) trade by private trade during the Southern Sung period, although it might partially account for the support of trade and industry during the Yuan dynasty. This provides a partial hint.

In spite of more than a century of rule and the clear respect the

Mongol conquerors displayed toward the superior Chinese culture (which they expressed in concrete ways by adopting the religion and utilizing the indigenous administrative apparatus), the Mongols remained, in the last analysis, an alien force within the country. The Yuan dynasty, of course, did not "invent" the systems of private trade and government finance that, in the late thirteenth and early fourteenth centuries, proved so conducive to the expansion of industry at home and maritime trade abroad. Rather, they adopted and expanded patterns that were already part of Sung China's stance toward the world system (Schurmann, 1956: *passim.*). Nevertheless, these preexistent patterns came to be identified with Mongol rule, and therefore were called into question by the restorers of Chinese autonomy, the Ming.

Perhaps to disassociate themselves from their Mongol predecessors who had "shamelessly" permitted unbridled "commerce," the Ming sought to reestablish symbols of authenticity from the past that could dramatize the Chinese-ness of the new order and validate its legitimacy. Confucianism, which demeaned crass moneymaking, and the older form of tribute trade were two such symbols, as we shall see.[15]

Nevertheless, during the early phase of Ming rule (1368–1403), although the sea trade declined, this did not seem to be the result of any abrupt reversal of policy. Rather, the temporary hiatus could easily be attributed to the competing demands on the new dynasty, which now had to consolidate its rule over an enormous land mass that had just suffered the devastations caused by epidemics, a grueling if "successful" war of rebellion against the Mongol rulers, and the widespread disruptions associated with these two not unrelated forces. It is not necessary to seek "policy" answers to the question of why commerce was inhibited during the early Ming period. In this first phase of Ming rule, there were real rather than symbolic reasons for a decline in shipping. Indeed, those changes had facilitated their rebellion.

The Black Death in China

It is a moot point whether the epidemics that wracked large portions of China between 1350 and 1369 were caused by the same bubonic infection that was simultaneously decimating populations in Central Asia and the Mediterranean world or whether they were attributable to some other type of disease. (See Figure 7 above, which shows the congruence of epidemic and trade routes.) However, William McNeill believes it extremely likely that a virulent outbreak of the Black Death also occurred in China in these years. The appendix to McNeill's *Plagues and Peoples* (1976: 259–269) lists all the references Joseph Cha could find to epidemics in China between 243 B.C. and 1911 A.D. by year and place of occurrence. During medieval times, there is only one protracted period during which high mortalities from epidemics are reported in a large number of places, and that is in the fourteenth century.

If Cha's data are accurate and relatively complete, it appears that early in the fourteenth century Hopei became a focus of infection for the first time in several hundred years, since epidemics were reported there in 1313, 1321, 1323, and 1331; in the latter year it is estimated that nine-tenths of Hopei's population died, which suggests that an entirely new type of infection had entered China. Within fifteen years of the catastrophic loss of population in Hopei (that is, by 1345–1346), epidemics appeared in Fukien (where the port of Zaytun was located) and in coastal Shantung to the north of Fukien. By 1351–1352 epidemics were reported in Shansi, Hopei, and Kiangsi, in 1353 in Hupeh, Kiangsi, Shansi, and Suiyan, in 1354 in Shansi, Hupeh, Hopei, Kiansi, Hunan, Kwangtung, and Kwangsi, in 1356 in Honan, in 1357 in Shantung, in 1358 in Shansi and Hopei, in 1359 in Shensi, Shantung, and Kwangtung, in 1360 in Chekiang, Kiansu, and Anhui, in 1362 in Chekiang, and in 1369 in Fukien again, where corpses lay in piles on the roads. After that date, the frequency of epidemics seems to have declined somewhat and there is no evidence of their spread to new areas.

On the basis of this evidence, McNeill hypothesizes that Mongol horsemen introduced the plague to Hopei (1976: 143), from which it spread throughout much of China, particularly China south of the Yangtse River.[16] Thus weakened, the Mongols were unable to maintain their Yuan dynasty and were forced to retreat to Mongolia and Central Asia, leaving a devastated China to the Ming who succeeded them in 1368.

Partly for symbolic reasons (Peking had always been the "real" Chinese capital), but perhaps also for practical reasons as well (conditions in the south were particularly bad), the Ming redirected their attention to north China, seeking to build up the economic base around Peking. It will be recalled that Peking's external economy had traditionally been linked to the state of communications across Asia. Central Asia, however, remained in the hands of the Mongols and, by the turn of the fifteenth century, was under the rule of Tamerlane. The land link from north China to Europe, which had declined precipitously in mid-fourteenth century, was now completely blocked.

Why China Withdrew Revisited

In the early decades of the fifteenth century, after order had been restored and the major effects of the Black Death had begun to dissipate, China once again sought to expand her power. Since the Mongols controlled the land route, the Ming returned to the only path open—the sea. At that time the Chinese resumed naval expansion, investing heavily in new ships. Trade does not seem to have been the only or even primary purpose this enlarged navy was intended to serve. Two other goals were also sought—one symbolic, the other military. Both were directed toward increasing China's power in the world.

Ships were definitely used to enhance China's symbolic power at this time. The journeys of the enormous "treasure ships" (each carrying a crew of 500, according to Lo, 1958: 151) under Admiral Cheng Ho were not designed for commercial purposes, although some court supporters hoped that they would lead to further trade. Rather, the impressive show of force that paraded around the Indian Ocean during the first three decades of the fifteenth century was intended to signal the "barbarian nations" that China had reassumed her rightful place in the firmament of nations—had once again become the "Middle Kingdom" of the world. Having established this, her ships returned home to await their homage (and some "tribute trade").

That outcome, however, was not to be, a fact related to the second naval purpose, namely, military conquest. In 1407, using her powerful warships, the Ming invaded and conquered Annam province. Later, however, her fleet was defeated there in 1420, which signaled the "beginning of a series of set-backs which resulted in the evacuation of Tonkin in 1428" (Lo, 1958: 151–152).

The Chinese had to choose between strengthening their naval forces for a decisive victory or retreating. Economic difficulties at home forced the second alternative.

By mid-fifteenth century, the Ming were facing a grave economic crisis (Lo, 1958: 155); revenues dropped and the currency became shaky. There was no money to sustain the powerful fleet. Pirates (mostly Japanese) harassed Chinese ships and the tribute trade faltered as fewer and fewer nations participated. As Lo (1958: 157–158) states:

> Symptoms of the naval decline were apparent. In foreign policy and in strategic outlook, there was a change from offensive to defensive, from advance to withdrawal. The expansive characteristic of the early Ming navy had been demonstrated forcefully by the voyages of the "treasure ships" . . . and the victorious campaign in Annam. . . . But, afterwards, the strategic policy changed. The advance bases in Fukien were withdrawn. . . . (1436–49) and the Shen-chia-men base . . . was withdrawn in 1452. . . . Warships, no longer sent out to sea on patrols, were anchored in ports where they rotted from neglect.

During the latter part of the fifteenth century, well over half of the existing ships in the Ming navy were scrapped and no new ones were built (Lo, 1958: 158). Lo is unequivocal, then, in attributing the "mysterious" withdrawal of the Ming navy from the Indian Ocean to the not so mysterious economic collapse of China by mid-fifteenth century.

China's Economic Collapse

If Lo's contention is correct, then the real question is not why China withdrew from the sea but, rather, why China experienced an economic collapse in the fifteenth century that forced her to scuttle her navy. Even when historians of China abandon the "change of philosophy" argument and examine economic factors, they still tend to look primarily at internal causes—pointing to rampant corruption, political factions, "bad government," and a growing gap between revenues and expenditures under the later Ming dynasty. Although these explanations cannot be discounted entirely, they have to be placed in the context of the rise and fall of the world system traced in this book.

Could the economic difficulties experienced by China have been caused, at least in part, by the fact that the world system had collapsed around it? This is a line of reasoning worth exploring. It is our hypothesis that the foundations of that system had begun to erode early in the fourteenth century, that they were precipitously weakened by the epidemic deaths in the mid- and latter-fourteenth century, and that they were finally undermined completely by the collapse of the Mongol "empire" that, although it allowed the Ming to come to power, also cut China off from its Central Asian hinterland. Thus, what is viewed in Chinese history as a restoration of a legitimate dynasty must be viewed in world system perspective as the final fragmentation of the larger circuit of thirteenth-century world trade in which China had played such an important role. Although a full discussion of this theory is reserved for Chapter 11, in which we examine the multiple sources of the system's demise, we might recapitulate the particular factors that affected the Chinese case. Let us review the sequence of China's rise to understand the foundations on which it rested.

During the classical period, when Peking had been the capital and court center, China's dominant connection to the rest of the world was overland via Central Asia. Even after the southeast coast was better populated and that region integrated with the northern core, maritime trade remained a decidedly secondary activity. With the decline in T'ang strength, however, the state became increasingly dependent upon foreign troops (largely Uighur, see Chapter 5) for its northern defense and a system comparable to the war lords seems to have developed in the north. "[B]y the ninth century, these local military governors, who were often foreigners, dominated their regions and did not permit interference from the central government" (Rossabi, 1983: 5). When the T'ang dynasty finally collapsed in 907, the country fragmented into fifteen "kingdoms," ten in the south under Chinese rule and five in the north under rulers of foreign origin. Peking, however, remained the primary capital, albeit under foreign influence. But even then, a new group of Mongolians, the Khitans (Chins), began testing the frontiers.

By 960 the Sung dynasty had reunited a "lesser" empire consisting of south China and much of the north, but that latter region remained under threat from the Chins, with whom the Sung were forced to sign a humiliating treaty in 1005, agreeing to pay an annual tribute in return for peace on the northern (now considerably contracted) border. Neither tribute nor conciliation could protect the Sung indefinitely, however. When their alliance with the invading Juchens against the Chin backfired, they regrouped in the south, setting up Hangchow as their provisional capital. Their defeat may have desensitized them to the new threat posed by Genghis Khan's forces, which were overrunning the territory of their northern enemies.

By then, the Southern Sung had already developed a powerful navy and were able to supplement it by requisitioning the large fleets of Chinese merchant shippers (Elvin, 1973: 90). It will be recalled that the "birth" of commercial shipping in China via the Indian Ocean occurred only after the massive populating of southeast China and the development of a communication system between north China (with its capital at Peking) and south China. However, commercial shipping became the major external economic base of China only when the Southern Sung were literally forced, as a result of the occupation of the north by Turkic and Mongol peoples, to withdraw south of the Yangtse River.

In spite of their navy, the Sung were eventually defeated by the Mongols, not only on land but, surprisingly, on the sea as well. Although the Yuan fleet made use of the vessels and sailors it had captured and Yuan shipping more than took the place of Sung, in the Chinese empire reunited under the Yuan, Peking resumed its role as capital and as imperial residence. Even though the southern ports continued to monopolize the sea trade, the true control center of the empire had again moved north.

After the Mongol invasion and the final unification by 1279 of north and south China under the Yuan dynasty, China's internal and largely agrarian economic base was supplemented by two systems of external trade that operated synergistically. One was the reactivated "silk route" across Central Asia that terminated at Peking; the other was the Indian Ocean sea trade that terminated in Canton, Zaytun, and, to a lesser extent, Hangchow. Thus, China constituted a crucial link between the land and sea trades and, in her domain of influence at least, became a formidable power in an increasingly integrated world system. This "full functioning" resulted in an extremely prosperous, although unequally distributed, economy.

The Ming inherited all of China, but in a vastly changed geopolitical situation. Although since Sung times the center of Chinese population, production, and trade had been in the south, by mid-fourteenth century that region had been devastated by epidemics. Furthermore, Peking, the symbol of Chinese identity and legitimacy, lay in the north. The Ming, for both practical and symbolic reasons, regrouped in the north, but by then the north had been deprived of its natural outlet. The overland route that formerly terminated in Peking was closed by Tamerlane.

The southern sea route, however, still functioned. One last effort was made to reactivate it, but by then it was too late. Trade in the Indian Ocean was also in decline. Cheng Ho's journeys did not yield the desired results. Not only did the navy "not pay" but, in the new retreatism, the ports, far from the capital, were now judged to be infested with foreigners and their "inauthentic" commercial pursuits. The result was a Chinese withdrawal that concentrated on rebuilding the agrarian base and internal production and marketing. The aberration of some two hundred years of southern port centrality to the economy ended, and with it, the chance for world hegemony.

Lessons from the Chinese Case

China's geographic position in the thirteenth century world system was crucial because it linked the northern overland route with the equally if not more important Indian Ocean sea route. When both of these pathways of trade were fully functioning, and particularly when China was unified and could therefore serve as a "frictionless exchange medium" to connect them, the circuit of world trade was complete. Indeed, it was only when this circle was completed in the thirteenth and early fourteenth centuries that one could speak of a premodern "world system."

As was true in other subregions of that world system, the economic health of China rested primarily on her own ontogenic developments in political organization, technological inventiveness and skill, and commercial sophistication—that is, her ability to harness her local resources. But another part of her economic vitality—a fairly large part by the thirteenth and early fourteenth centuries—came from her ability to extract surplus from the external system. When the external system underwent retrenchment and fragmentation, it was inevitable that all parts formerly linked to it would experience difficulties, including China.

In this and the preceding chapters we have tried to outline the cycles of growth and decline that virtually every member of the "archipelago of towns" making up the international trade system underwent between about 1200 and 1350. The remarkable degree of congruence (admittedly with deviations we have attempted to explain) between these cycles suggests that they were not independent of one another. We have certainly seen in each case how the rise in the cycle was clearly related to greater integration with the rest of the world. What has not been stressed sufficiently is the extent to which "delinking" led to declines in all these places. This topic is addressed in greater detail in Chapter 11.

Notes

1. Ibn Battuta describes the quarters of slaves in at least two of the cities he visited in the 1340s. In Qanjanfu he notes that the "sultan's slaves" live in the second walled city just outside the governor's citadel (1929 trans.: 291) and in Hangchow, "the biggest city I have ever seen on the face of the earth" (1929 trans.: 292), he describes slaves as occupying the innermost area of the citadel (Ibn Battuta 1929 trans.: 294–295).

> The citadel lies in the center of this city [Hangchow]. . . . Within it are arcades, in which workmen sit making rich garments and weapons . . . sixteen hundred master-workmen there, each with three or four apprentices working under him. They are all without exception the slaves of the Qan . . . they have chains on their feet . . . [and] may not go beyond the gate. . . . Their custom is that after one of them has served for ten years, he is freed of his chains. . . . When he reaches the age of fifty he is exempted from work and maintained.

We should note, however, that slavery was not common between Han and Yuan times, although certain forms of forced labor undoubtedly persisted.

2. Massive population migrations, often planned and executed under state direction, have been a recurring feature in Chinese history, since "the state repeatedly used migration as a means to effect popular relief, political and social integration,

economic development, and control of the rich and powerful" (Lee, 1978: 21). Lee illustrates his points with examples taken from over three thousand years of Chinese history.

3. It must be admitted that considerable controversy exists over the significance of the seven "shows of power" of the Chinese fleet that, under Admiral Cheng Ho, probed the entire ocean expanse from China to Hormuz between 1405 and 1435. Some scholars suggest that these forays were in no way related to a bid for commercial hegemony but signaled a symbolic return to the Confucian ideal of tribute due to the emperor from lesser peoples. At best, the ambiguity of their purpose may be related to ambivalence or at least divided opinions within the court as to the future direction of policy. (Schurmann, 1956: 114–115, recounts an earlier split in the Yuan government over a similar issue.) It may be that when the voyages were undertaken, no clear decision had been reached as to their ultimate aim.

4. Elvin (1973: 85) suggests that it was the deforestation in the north during T'ang times that forced the conversion to coal furnaces.

5. And what is even more sobering is the realization that Marco Polo was totally unfamiliar with the black chunks he saw in China and was confused as to their use. He knew only that they were used to heat homes and bath water! Here is all he (1958 trans.: 130) has to say about it.

> Let me tell you next of the stones that burn like logs. It is a fact that throughout the province of Cathay there is a sort of black stone, which is dug out of veins in the hillsides. . . . These stones keep a fire going better than wood . . . [and] give out great heat. . . . It is true that they also have plenty of firewood. But . . . [people take baths and] every man of rank or means has his own bathroom in his house. . . . So these stones, being very plentiful and very cheap, effect a great saving of wood.

6. By 1000 B.C. China was producing silk. "One of the earliest surviving specimens . . . was found in a tomb that dates from c. 350 B.C." (Loewe, 1971: 169).

7. So (1986: 88–89) cites the work of Howard and Buswell for the following dramatic figures: 8 catties of leaves are required per eggsheet in the first stage of life; this increases to 70 catties per sheet in stage 3 and, in the final phase (the last three days before spinning their cocoons), demand shoots up to 2,000 catties! It is not surprising to learn that entrepreneurial capitalism and financial speculation focused not on the production of worms but on mulberry leaf "futures."

8. Salt was a government monopoly in China even during preimperial times and was used to raise revenue. "The T'ang and Sung in particular turned to salt monopoly revenue . . . during their greatest financial and military crises" because, given its limited areas of production, it "was susceptible to bureaucratic management" (Worthy, 1975: 101–102). Early in the twelfth century the Sung salt administration was centralized; one of the primary producing areas was Hangchow Bay (Worthy, 1975: 105). "Merchants wishing to purchase salt produced [there] . . . first had to buy their vouchers at [one of] . . . the Monopoly Bureau offices. . . . Merchants would take their vouchers to the appropriate distribution center" and wait their turn, sometimes for months, during which their vouchers might be devalued. Once given their salt, "the merchants were given an accompanying permit . . . which

proved that the salt . . . was legally acquired." But in spite of all these bureaucratic controls, there seems to have been considerable illicit traffic that undermined the government monopoly (Worthy, 1975: 134–139). During Yuan times, other items in addition to salt (liquor, tea, etc.) became governmental monopolies (Schurmann, 1956: 146–212).

9. The government monopoly over currency was lost in Ming times when, in spite of attempts to police counterfeiting to keep paper money strong, silver and gold came back into circulation (Yang, 1952: 66).

10. "Hang-chou was known to the Westerners of the Middle Ages by the names of Khinsai, Khinzai, Khanzai, etc. . . . [which] was thought . . . to be a transliteration of King-sze . . . or Capital, which had been corrupted by the foreigners into Khinsai" (Kuwabara, 1928: note 21, p. 21), although Kuwabara actually believes it to be a corruption of Hing-tsai (1928: 24).

11. Ch'uan-chou seems to have been as old a port as Canton, even though the first Arab records mention only the latter. By the end of the tenth century, both ports were considered "foreign trade" ports and, in the twelfth century, they were the only two in which foreign ships were permitted to dock (translators' introduction to Chau Ju-Kua, *Chu-fan-chi*, 1911: 18–19, 22). Later, Hangchow and several other ports were opened to foreign traders.

12. Wheatley (1959: 5–140) has combed this document thoroughly. Original material is found in Hirth and Rockhill (1911: 195 *seq*).

13. Ta-Shih was the Chinese name for western Asia and for Arabs and Persians from there. Although they were still considered "barbarians" by the Chinese, their high culture and superiority to other barbarians was acknowledged. Chinese documents stress that most of the foreign trade was in the hands of these foreigners and that they maintained sizable self-ruled quarters in most Chinese cities of note. See, inter alia, Enoki (1954).

14. Zaytun would have been the best city to select. Unfortunately, however, I was unable to find more than isolated and scattered descriptions of it, almost exclusively in Chinese sources. Jin Xiaochang, a Chinese historian at the New School, prepared at my suggestion a research paper on Zaytun during the Sung and Yuan dynasties. According to his estimates, Zaytun had, at its Yuan peak, a a population of some 400,000-500,000. Of even greater significance, his research provides strong documentary evidence that Chinese shipping expanded in the thirteenth century. Comparing Zaytun's "ports of call" mentioned in three primary sources [*Yun-lu man-chao* (1206), *Chu-fan-chi* (1230s), and *Dao-yi-zhi-lue* (1302)] he finds that their number increased from 32 (1206 source) to 48 (1230 source) to 78 (1302 source). See Jin Xiaochang, "Quan-zho and its Hinterland During the Sung and Yuan Dynasties" (unpublished paper, New School for Social Research: 1988).

15. Wang (1970: 223) suggests a somewhat different explanation. He hypothesizes that Confucian attitudes "did not interfere [with maritime trade] at early periods, partly because they were not so dominant as they became after 1368 but also partly because the maritime trade had not reached a point where its further growth would have challenged the accepted view of the Confucian state." I find this both too simple and nonfalsifiable. The question to be asked is why it was perceived as a threat at that particular moment. I believe that my hypothesis offers a plausible, albeit equally untestable, answer to that question.

16. It is unlikely that the plague spread from the interior to ports, as McNeill suggests. Rather, the initial outbreak at Hopei may have been an independent event. If it was, then the plague is first found simultaneously in 1345 in two of the foreign ports and, only later, inland. I am grateful to Jin Xiaochang for mapping Cha's data for me.

Restructuring the Thirteenth-Century World System

The purpose of this concluding chapter is not only to synthesize our findings from the thirteenth century but to address a question of far wider significance, namely, why world systems fail. Since we believe that many of the same variables operate, albeit in reverse ways, in both the organizing and disorganizing phases of a cycle, the explanation for why world systems fail will be drawn, at least in part, from an understanding of how they are forged.

The Thirteenth-Century World System Synthesized

This book has traced the rise, from the end of the twelfth century, of an incipient world system that, at its peak in the opening decades of the fourteenth century, involved a vast region stretching between northwest Europe and China. Although it was not a *global* system, since it did not include the still-isolated continental masses of the Americas and Australia, it represented a substantially larger system than the world had previously known. It had newly integrated an impressive set of interlinked subsystems in Europe, the Middle East (including the northern portion of Africa), and Asia (coastal and steppe zones).

Although, naturally, this system was extremely *uneven*, integrating into the network only an archipelago of "world cities" elevated above a sea of relatively isolated rural areas and open stretches, such spottiness was not unique to the thirteenth century. Unevenness in itself does not invalidate the existence of an overarching system. Indeed, it is debatable whether the discrepancy between world city and hinterland in the thirteenth century was nearly as great as the gap that separates Tokyo or New York from rural Togo in today's world system.

Even though, when compared to the contemporary epoch, the thirteenth-century system of international trade and the production associated with it could not be described as either large scale or technologically advanced, we have tried to demonstrate in the preceding chapters that it was substantially more complex in organization, greater in volume, and more sophisticated in execution, than anything the world had previously known. Nor was it basically inferior to what it would be in the sixteenth century.

Sophistication was evident in the technology of shipping and navigation, the social organization of production and marketing, and the institutional arrangements for conducting business, such as partnerships, mechanisms for pooling capital, and techniques for monetization and exchange. Thus, it is important to recognize that no simple, deterministic explanation can account for Europe's later hegemony. Explanations that concentrate on the special technological, cultural, psychological, or even economic characteristics of European society are not sufficient, since they tend to ignore the contextual changes in the preexistent system.

First, no enormous advances occurred in the sixteenth century in the all-important area of sea transport. Although European vessels were considerably better than they had been, they were still not superior to the Chinese ships Admiral Cheng Ho had paraded through the Indian Ocean in the early fifteenth century. Indeed, the threshold of true integration by sea was not attained until much later. Not until the development of the steamship in the nineteenth century did the shape of the world system dramatically alter.

Nor was there any quantum leap in the area of social invention (the organization of production, the financing of capital investment, the instruments of money and credit) in the sixteenth century. There, too, the rule is one of continuities and gradual advances through diffusion and elaboration, rather than decisive breakthroughs. To consider Arab commerce deficient because in the thirteenth century it did not have modern banks, or Chinese paper legal tender deficient because it lacked a gold standard, is illicit and anachronistic, since such institutions gradually grew in Europe as development continued. It is just as credible to propose that the primitive institutions of money and credit that existed in the nonwestern world in the thirteenth century would undoubtedly have continued to evolve, had that part of the world remained important to world trade. Failure to develop more sophisticated business techniques was a symptom of the demotion of the nonwestern world's power, not a cause of it.

Finally, given this earlier incipient world system in which no unity prevailed in culture, religion, or economic institutional arrangements, it is difficult to accept a purely "cultural" explanation for dominance. No particular culture seems to have had a monopoly over either technological or social inventiveness. Neither a unique syndrome of psychology, a special economic form of organizing production and exchange, nor any particular set of religious beliefs or values was needed to succeed in the thirteenth century. The fact that the "West won" in the sixteenth century, whereas the earlier system aborted, cannot be used to argue convincingly that *only* the institutions and culture of the West *could have succeeded*.[1]

Indeed, what is noteworthy in the world system of the thirteenth century is that a wide variety of cultural systems coexisted and cooperated, and that societies organized very differently from those in the west dominated the system. Christianity, Buddhism, Confucianism, Islam, Zoroastrianism, and numerous other smaller sects often dismissed as "pagan" all seem to have permitted and indeed facilitated lively commerce, production, exchange, risk taking, and the like. And among these, Christianity played a relatively insignificant role.

Similarly, a variety of economic systems coexisted in the thirteenth century—from "near" private capitalism, albeit supported by state power, to "near" state production, albeit assisted by private merchants. Furthermore, these variations were not particularly congruent with either geographic region or religious domain. The organization of textile production in Kanchipuram was not unlike that in Flanders, whereas in China and Egypt larger scale coordination was more typical. The state built boats for trade in both Venice and China, whereas elsewhere (and even at different times in Genoa, China, and Egypt) private vessels were comandeered when the state needed them.

Nor were the underlying bases for economic activities uniform. Participating in the world system of the thirteenth century were (1) large agrarian societies such as India and China that covered subcontinents in expanse, in which industrial production was oriented mainly but not exclusively to the processing of agricultural raw materials; (2) small city-state ports such as Venice, Aden, Palembang, and Malacca, whose functions are best described as compradorial; (3) places as diverse as south India, Champagne, Samarkand, the Levant, and ports along the Persian Gulf, whose importance was enhanced by their strategic location at points where pathways between flanking trading partners met; and (4) places that contained valued raw materials unavailable elsewhere (fine-quality wool in England, camphor in Sumatra, frankincense and myrrh on the Arabian Peninsula, spices in the Indian archipelago, jewels in Ceylon, ivory and ostrich feathers in Africa, and even military slaves in eastern Europe). These resources did not *account* for the world system; they were *products* of it.

The economic vitality of these areas was the result, at least in part, of the system in which they participated. All these units were not only trading with one another and handling the transit trade of others, but had begun to reorganize parts of their internal economies to meet the exigencies of a world market. Production of certain fiber crops fed a growing demand for textiles abroad; increased acreage to graze sheep similarly supplied wool to spinners and weavers producing for export; an enlarged metallurgical sector satisfied burgeoning outside demands for weapons; and specialization in prospecting for camphor and precious metals or in growing pepper or other spices followed from export demands. These developments were all the result of the world system that, by the end of the thirteenth century, had made prosperity pandemic. The results of that effusive period of economic growth are reflected in the increased size of cities participating in it (see Figure 15 for sample cases).

Yet, some fifty years later, the system began to unravel and, by the late fifteenth century, only small parts of it retained their former vigor. The cycle was coming to an end. Why? To say that economic expansions and contractions tend to be cyclical is no answer. It seems mystical to talk of Kondratieff (45–55 years) or other regularly recurring economic cycles as if they were forces in their own right, rather than more or less useful observational or measurement artifacts. It is true that a period of some hundred years of "rise" and fifty years of "fall" has been selected for study, but to some extent that was only for convenience. The cycle fits Europe best—and not by any accident. In fact, the limiting years were originally selected because of their congruence with a known fluctuation in European history. As seen, however, even in western Europe the beginning point varies from place to place, and the upturn, depending on the focus, could well have been placed earlier or later. The downturn point is less arbitrary, since it coincides with the demographically disastrous Black Death that most European historians agree set in motion deep structural changes on the continent.

The Middle Eastern cycle, however, would exhibit far different temporal "borders," if that region were being studied alone rather than in relationship to a world system that included northern Europe. The beginning of growing strength in the Middle East region comes as early as the eighth century, although the terminal phase varies from one subarea to another. After the eighth- to tenth-century "peak," which favored both Baghdad and Cairo, the histories of these two imperial centers diverge. Indeed, the high points of Egyptian medieval history are almost inverse images of Iraq's stagnation. Nor, in spite of the demographic decimations caused by the Black Death, did Egypt experience the marked decline that so many other portions of the world system did in the latter four-

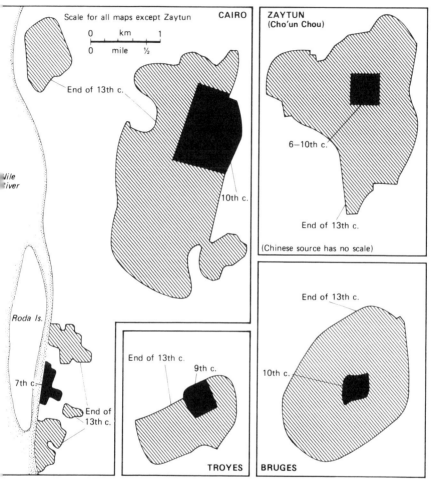

FIGURE 15. The growth of selected cities between the ninth/tenth and the end of the thirteenth century.

teenth century. As shown, the trade monopoly Venice and Cairo achieved through their uneasy and ambivalent alliance insulated both from the retrenchments engulfing their rivals. Cairo's final decline did not come until *after* the Portuguese circumnavigated Africa a century and a half later. The Ottoman conquest of Egypt in 1516 did not cause but merely confirmed this loss of position.

Farther east, the cycles were also not neatly synchronized. On the west coast of India, whose fate was linked so closely to the Middle East, the longer upswing phase of the cycle paralleled the cycle in Egypt to which it was causally linked. In contrast, the increasing passivity, if not decline, on the east coast of India began before the fourteenth century and closely corresponded to the declining importance of the Srivijayan city-states, in turn linked to Chinese aggressiveness; the Chinese actively bypassed both the straits traders and the ports on the Coromandel coast, going directly to Quilon.

Across the northern steppelands, the cycle of integration and fragmentation was tied to changes in the empire established by the tribal confederation referred to as "the Mongols." The expanding phase came early in the thirteenth century, with maximum consolidation achieved by the early fourteenth century. In contrast, fragmentation and territorial losses (including China) characterized the second half of the fourteenth century. As earlier contended, the periodicity in this region had an inordinate effect on the cycles of other participants in the thirteenth-century world system.

China had her own cycle of development that began somewhat earlier—certainly by the eleventh- and twelfth-century Sung dynasty—and that did not finally retrench until the mid-fifteenth century. That cycle reached its apogee under the Yuan dynasty when the southern region (with its port outlets to the Indian Ocean trade) was fully united with the northern zone (with its caravan links across Central Asia). When both of these lines to the world system were open, China flourished; when they closed, China declined, and, with her, the rest of the world system as it had been organized in the thirteenth century.

Given this variability, one must not reify "cycles." Rather, the theory we have been setting forth suggests that *when there was a period of congruence among the upward cycles of related regions,* these cycles moved synergistically. Upturns were the result, at least in part, of the linkages each region managed to forge with other parts of the world system, and feedbacks from that system, in turn, intensified local development.

The same was true in reverse. When separate regions experienced setbacks, either from unique or common underlying causes, the overall direction of the change vector was deflected. And just *because* the regions had become so interlinked, declines in one inevitably contributed to declines elsewhere, particularly in contiguous parts that formed "trading partnerships."

One of the most important systemic changes that occurred at mid-fourteenth century, of course, was the significant drop in population that occurred simultaneously and not independently in many parts of the world, as a result of the pandemic of the Bubonic Plague and/or other epidemics that ravaged much of the system. Although responses to these population declines varied from place to place (in some regions recovery was rapid, in others, recovery was slow or never occurred), two consequences were fairly universal. One was a reemphasis on agricultural production, which absorbed a higher proportion of the smaller population than it had even decades before. The other was a drop in the rate of urbanization. Both were symptoms of the fact that participants were no longer able to generate the surpluses characteristic of the thirteenth century. Thus, there was also a drop, albeit temporary, in the overall volume and value of trade, particularly long-distance trade.

The second systemic change was geopolitical. In the course of the thirteenth century, the geopolitical medium through which merchants and their goods circulated had become increasingly frictionless and continuous. The simultaneous operation of two different routes across Central Asia (a southern and a northern) and two different routes between the Middle East and Asia via the Indian Ocean (the Red Sea and the Persian Gulf) meant that any blockages developing at specific synapses of the circulatory system could be bypassed. This flexibility not only kept the monopoly protection rent that guarders of individual routes exacted from passing traders within "bearable" limits, but it guaranteed that goods would go through, in spite of localized disturbances.

By the middle of the fourteenth century, however, the admittedly fractious unity of the Central Asian empire assembled by

Genghis Khan and then bequeathed to multiple successors was in disarray. This eventually closed the Central Asian route that had earlier provided an alternative to the sea route. Finally, when the Mongols, severely weakened by the Black Death (or some other disastrous epidemic), "lost" China in 1368, the world lost the key link that had connected the overland route, terminating at Peking, with the sea routes through the Indian Ocean and South China Sea, terminating at the ports of southeast China. The repercussions of this disjunction at the eastern end of the world system were felt throughout the trading world.

During the late fourteenth and fifteenth centuries, the link between Europe and Asia, via the Mediterranean and the Indian Ocean, was sustained by the Venetian–Egyptian marriage of convenience. Indeed, the sea route they controlled gained additional strength because competing pathways were essentially closed. However, the south and southeast Asian systems to which this narrowed line connected were already in decline.

Internal developments in south and southeast Asia reduced the number of powers active in that system. In south India, the western coastal ports continued to play an important role in trade, but the east coast, ruled by the mountain-based Vijayanagar, became even more passive in the sea trade. There was an overextension of the trading circuit of Middle Eastern and western Indian traders and shippers into the Bay of Bengal circuit that had formerly constituted the natural sphere of Coromandel activity.

The slack created by the declining activities of Coromandel traders was belatedly and only partially taken up by the principalities along the strait, most notably Malacca. These principalities never had a truly independent base of power, however. Their vitality was the result of the motivation for trade on the part of India, on the one side, and China, on the other. Only during periods in which direct contact between the two giants was actively blocked by embargos or was passively reduced by declines in the shipping fleets at either end, did the straits region play, almost by default, a more active role. The limited independent power of the principalities of the strait was clearly demonstrated by the fact that they declined when overall trade diminished. This occurred in two phases, at least with respect to China.

When the Ming first came to power in China, their interest in trade was temporarily inhibited by a preoccupation with more pressing concerns and possibly, by a "change in philosophy." In the opening decades of the fifteenth century (1403–1430), there was a revival of interest in external contacts, but it was both ambivalent and, as seen, aborted. The withdrawal of the Chinese fleet after 1435, coupled with the overextension into the two easternmost circuits of the Indian Ocean trade of the Arab and Gujarati Indian merchants, neither protected by a strong navy, left a vacuum of power in the Indian Ocean. Eventually, this vacuum was filled— first by the Portuguese, then by the Dutch, and finally by the British.

Of crucial importance is the fact that the "Fall of the East" preceded the "Rise of the West," and it was this devolution of the preexisting system that facilitated Europe's easy conquest. It would be wrong, therefore, to view the "Rise of the West" as either a simple "takeover" of a prior functioning system or an event whose outcome was attributable exclusively to the internal characteristics of European society. Rather, two paradoxical forces were at work.

First, pathways and routes developed by the thirteenth century were later "conquered" and adapted by a succession of European powers. Europe did not need to *invent* the system, since the basic groundwork was already in place by the thirteenth century when Europe was still only a peripheral and recent participant. In this sense, the rise of the west was facilitated by the preexisting world economy that it restructured.

It must be recognized, however, that the "takeover" of that system was certainly not according to the old rules. The old world system that was deeply penetrated by Portuguese intruders in the early sixteenth century offered little resistance. Why? In part, it could not, since it was already at a low (albeit possibly temporary) point of organization. Perhaps it had adapted so completely to the coexistence of multiple trading partners that it was unprepared for players interested in short-term plunder rather than long-term exchange. More than anything else, then, it was the new European approach to trade-cum-plunder that caused a basic transformation in the world system that had developed and persisted over some five centuries.[2]

In the earlier system, although there were certainly rivalries and no small amount of interregional conflict, the overall pattern of

trade involved a large number of players whose power was relatively equal. No single participant in the thirteenth- and early
fourteenth-century world system dominated the whole, and most
participants (with the possible exception of the Mongols) benefited
from coexistence and mutual tolerance. Individual rulers did jealously seek to control the terms of trade and the "foreign traders"
in their own ports and inland centers, but the ambition to dominate
the entire system seemed beyond their needs and aspirations (and
probably capacities). The change in the "rules of the game" introduced by the European newcomers in the sixteenth century,
therefore, caught the older players off guard.

The new rules were being imposed not only on the old world
but, with even greater vigor, on the new. In this connection it is
important to note that the European shift to the Atlantic had begun
even before the closing decade of the fifteenth century when the
voyages of Columbus and Vasco da Gama signaled a decisive break
with the past. Although these journeys were sponsored by Atlantic
rim monarchs of the Iberian peninsula, the groundwork for them
had been laid by Genoa, from which Columbus originated.

Recall that the two rival sea powers, Venice and Genoa, had
very different geographic "natural" advantages. Venice, on Italy's
east coast, had easiest access to the eastern Mediterranean. Furthermore, her transalpine connections to the North Sea ran
through (today's) Austria and Germany. She was thus poorly situated to exploit the Atlantic. In contrast, Genoa, on the west coast
of the Italian boot, had a freer hand in the western Mediterranean,
particularly after her Muslim North African rivals had been defeated after the middle of the thirteenth century, when Christian
Spain "reconquered" Andalusia, which decreased the hazards of
passage via Gibraltar. This permitted her expansion into the Atlantic, a "middle sea" that in the sixteenth century began to usurp
the Mediterranean's key role. Thus, although Venice ostensibly
defeated Genoa in their centuries-long rivalry, it was Genoa's "solution" to the eastern trade question that eventually triumphed in
the next world system.

Recall that Genoese galleys had begun to enter the Atlantic by
the late thirteenth and early fourteenth centuries to bypass a no
longer hospitable or profitable land passage through France; the
growth of Genoese Atlantic shipping was in inverse relation to the

decline of the Champagne fairs, no longer "free" and no longer easily reached by the Flemish cloth merchants. Thus, Genoa's move into the Atlantic was primarily motivated by changes that were occurring within the local European subsystem, rather than in the "world system," and was at first directed only toward Europe.

Nevertheless, it eventually led to the total transformation of the larger system. It is not that the European navigators, by sailing down the coast of Africa or even westward to the Americas, "discovered" new routes. In the medieval period Arab navigators already knew the route around Africa and there is at least some evidence that landfalls in the Americas had, from time to time, been made by earlier sailors from the Middle East. But Middle Eastern traders did not need this circuitous route since they controlled the shorter one.

It was not until Venice consolidated her relations with Egypt, the state that guarded that shorter route, that her rivals—at first only Genoa but later also the naval powers on the Atlantic rim—sought alternative paths to the east. Eventually they found them, and this, more than any institutional or motivational characteristics of European culture, changed world history.

Although this consequence perhaps falls outside the scope of this book, it is impossible to ignore it entirely. What decisively transformed the shape of the "modern" world system was not so much the Portuguese takeover of the "old world" but the Spanish incorporation of the "new world" (as Chaunu, 1983, clearly illustrates). This geographic reorientation displaced the center of world gravity in a decisive manner and, if Marx's contention is accepted (see note 2), provided, through primitive accumulation, the windfalls of wealth that eventually were spun into industrial gold. This, perhaps, is why European scholars have in the last analysis been fixated on the sixteenth century.

Why Spain and Portugal, which first reaped the windfall of the new world, proved incapable of harnessing that wealth is an entirely different question and one that Weber's thesis on the Protestant Ethic addresses in compelling fashion. In contrast, his works on the comparative religious ethics of Confucianism, Hinduism, Taoism and Islam seem to be somewhat off the mark. Although he makes a telling case for Protestant versus Catholic, the evidence from the thirteenth- and fourteenth-century economies of China, India, and the Arab world seems to cast doubt on his view that eastern cultures provided an inhospitable environment for merchant-accumulators and industrial developers. As seen, these figures were very much present in the thirteenth-century world; what they lacked were free resources.

With respect to European development, it is important to recognize that it was not until several centuries later that the new globalized system incorporating the Americas yielded its full return and catapulted Europe to world hegmony. By that time, eastern trade had revived, but under a new hegemonic system that at first was exercised by proxies (the state-supported European trading companies) but eventually by strong states themselves. But that is an entirely different story.

The Restructuring of Systems

Two points should now be obvious: first, the principles of organization of world systems can have considerable variability; and second, world systems are dynamic and therefore undergo periodic restructuring.

The Variability of Structures

As Wallerstein (1974) has convincingly argued, the "modern" world system that emerged in the centuries following the sixteenth gradually became organized hierarchically according to different modes of production (capitalist, semifeudal, and precapitalist) that were roughly coterminous with a specific geographic distribution: a capitalist *core hegemon* located in northwest Europe, an agrarian semiperiphery geographically concentrated in eastern and southern Europe, and a periphery, located everywhere else. Yet this pattern of organization is not the only one conceivable for a world system.

As shown, the world system of the thirteenth century was organized on very different principles. Rather than a single hegemon, there were a number of coexisting "core" powers that, via both conflictual and cooperative relations,[3] became increasingly integrated over the course of the thirteenth and the first half of the fourteenth century. Since the system *was not hierarchical*, in the sense that no single hegemon dictated the terms of production and trade to others, no geographic entity could be said to be located at *the* center. Rather, cores, semiperipheries, and peripheries (and undoubtedly some intermediate categories as well) were found at a number of places around the globe. The Arabo-Persian imperial centers constituted one such core, surrounded by their semiperipheries and in contact with their peripheries through single-stranded reaches. The control centers of the Mongol empire constituted another "core," particularly when, over time, the dominant Mongol group coalesced with China. The towns of developing western Europe (Flanders, France, and Italy) had begun to form a third "core" region, organizing their hinterlands and handling the latter's relations to the outside world. In addition, there were "subimperial powers," such as the Delhi Sultanate in the north and trader societies in coastal India and the ports of Southeast Asia; these served as gateways and enclaves to connect their respective regions with world production and commerce. The term semiperiphery does not seem very appropriate when applied to them.

The reason it is important to recognize the variability of system-organizational principles is that, by definition, living systems are dynamic. They *reorganize* as the principles change. Just as older social formations live on within societies whose dominant mode of production is undergoing transformation, so too, when a given system of organization breaks up, the old parts are generally incorporated into the new, even though they may have different structural relationships.

Restructuring

Today, analysts use the term "restructuring" to refer to the ongoing reorganization of the world system that has been occurring in dramatic fashion in the past half century (following World War II). The concept, however, has wider applicability when it is recognized that restructuring has taken place several times before. Just as the particular modern world system generated in the sixteenth century was preceded by a thirteenth-century system with very different characteristics, so the thirteenth-century system had its precursor in classical times.

Some two thousand years ago, an earlier incipient world system existed which involved almost all the regions (except northern Europe) participating in the thirteenth-century system. Geographically, its shape was very similar to the thirteenth-century one, although politically it was structured more along imperial lines, and economically its parts were much less well integrated. Whitmore (1977: 141), focusing on Southeast Asia, has summarized it as follows:

> With the zenith of the Roman Empire on the west, the Han Empire in the east, and the growth of commerce in India, the international trade route worked itself, via a series of links, through Southeast Asia towards China. Coming from the Mediterranean, this route went to the west coast of India, around to the east coast, and across the Bay of Bengal to the Malay Peninsula. . . . The commercial importance of Southeast Asia at this time lay predominantly in the fact that it sat astride this maritime route to and from China.

He had only to add the great "Silk Road" across Central Asia, also functioning at that same time, to reproduce the circuit that was completed again in the thirteenth century.

But note the earlier system's different structure: two imperial powers at opposite ends of the system in only extremely limited and indirect contact with one another, and multiple and fragmented intervening places unable to sustain the system, once the great powers declined. That system also "failed" after the fall of Rome and the loss of Han unity, only to be restructured eventually through the "rise" of the Islamic world and its growing extentions to the east. It was this reorganization that eventually culminated in the thirteenth-century world system traced in this book.

If we assume that *restructuring*, rather than *substitution*, is what happens when world systems succeed one another, albeit after intervening periods of disorganization, then failure cannot refer to the parts themselves but only to the declining efficacy and functioning of the ways in which they were formerly connected. In saying that the thirteenth-century world system failed, we mean that the system itself devolved. Its devolution was both caused by and a sign of the "decline" in its constituent parts, with multiple feedback loops.

Thus, the cliché "rise and fall," which has been indiscriminately applied to nations,[4] empires,[5] civilizations,[6] and now world systems, is too imprecise. In the course of history, some nations, or at least groups within them, have gained relative power vis-à-vis others and have occasionally succeeded in setting the terms of their interactions with subordinates, whether by means of direct rule (empires), indirect supervision (what we today term neocolonialism), or through unequal influence on the internal policies of others (hegemony). When this happens, it is called a "rise." Conversely, the loss of an advantageous position is referred to as a "decline," even if there is no real deterioration in absolute level of life.[7] The rise and fall of empires is judged by different criteria. Empires are considered to rise when their geographic span of control widens and, conversely, to decline when those boundaries contract. Even more complex is the idea of the rise and fall of whole civilizations, in which the cultural content as well as its expanse is judged as alternately "high" or "decadent."

World systems do not rise and fall in the same way that nations, empires, or civilizations do. Rather, they rise when integration increases and they decline when connections along older pathways decay. It would be sophmoric to suggest that the world returns to the status quo ante when the vigor of a given dynamic of integration dissipates, however. Rather, the old parts live on and become the materials out of which restructuring develops, just as the earlier system inherited not a *tabula rasa* but a set of partially organized subsystems. By definition, such restructuring is said to occur when *players who were formerly peripheral* begin to occupy more powerful positions in the system and when *geographic zones formerly marginal to intense interactions* become foci and even control centers of such interchanges. (If the players and zones remain constant, there is no restructuring, no matter how greatly activities in the system fluctuate, as long as they do not disappear.)

From earliest times, the geographically central "core regions" through which the continental mass of Europe and Asia was integrated were Central Asia and the Indian Ocean, to which the Mediterranean was eventually appended. These cores persisted through the classical and thirteenth-century world systems. A decisive reorganization of this pattern did not occur until the sixteenth century, when northern Europe moved out into the Atlantic, leaving the Mediterranean a backwater that Ottoman power was unable to reverse (Braudel, 1972).

A similar change now seems to be taking place, as the Pacific supplants the Atlantic as the zone of expansion and dynamism in a world system that has been almost totally globalized. If we are to understand this present trend in restructuring, we will need a better theory of systemic change than the one usually invoked to explain the "Rise of the West" and, by default, the "Fall of the East." The next section outlines some of the assumptions of such a theory.

A Theory of Systemic Change

First, neither the formation of systems nor their devolution/restructuring can be explained causally by referring to discrete variables, no matter how robust. This is particularly true when variables such as national character are invoked. Rather than being conceptualized as the result of "independent" causes affecting "dependent" ones, systemic changes should rather be viewed as shifts in the direction and configuration of central trends (or vectors).[8] Such vectoral outcomes result from the cumulative effect of multiple shifts in smaller vectors, some of which are independent of one another but many of which derive from interrelated or systemic causes. In a system, it is the *connections* between the parts that must be studied. When these strengthen and reticulate, the system may be said to "rise;" when they fray, the system declines, although it may later undergo reorganization and revitalization.

Second, successive systems reorganize in a somewhat cumulative fashion, the lines and connections laid down in prior epochs tending to persist even though their significance and roles in the new system may be altered. Given cumulative technological change, which offers at least the potential to increase the range and speed of interactions, systems tend to expand and become more integrated, unless major catastrophes interfere.[9]

Third, no system is fully integrated and therefore none can be completely controlled, even by the most powerful participants. The traditional "same cause yields same effect" logic that underlies positivist social science seems sadly ill-equipped to deal with systemic change. Instead, the theories of chaos (recently described by Gleick)[10] may be more pertinent. In world systems, as in weather systems, small localized conditions may interact with adjacent ones to create outcomes that might not otherwise have occurred, and large disturbances sometimes flutter to an end while minor ones may occasionally amplify wildly, depending upon what is happening in the rest of the system.

The fourth assumption is that changes have causes but only in context. The very same acts have different consequences when they occur at different times and when the surrounding system is structured differently. The Vikings reached the New World without reorganizing the old one. The Arabs sailed around Africa without making the Atlantic a core. Chinese science (including gunpowder) was there, but failed to make China hegemonic. The examples could be multiplied.

And finally, a theory of systemic change should be able to account for system decay as well as system growth. This, however, is not as easy as it sounds. In tracing the development, expansion, and greater connectivity of a system, there is a natural tendency to concentrate selectively on those things that increase "systemness." No such natural principle of selection, however, is available to scholars trying to analyze the decline of a system. It is thus easier to account for positive changes than for negative ones.[11]

Future World Systems

The question with which we would like to conclude is whether the Eurocentered "modern" world system that was built on the ruins of the thirteenth-century world system is likely to persist—or whether we have already entered a phase of further restructuring that will eventually be considered at least as dramatic and significant as the one that occurred in the sixteenth century. Much of the literature dealing with world systems seems to treat European hegemony as the end of the story. But from the vantage point of our analysis of a preexisting system, it is possible to speculate on the impermanence of all systems.

One of the striking characteristics of the "modern" world system, as it evolved to the period following the Second World War, was the undisputed hegemonic power of the United States. Rather than marking the beginning of a new phase, however, this appears to represent the end of an old one. The destruction, in that conflict, of so many parts of Europe created a vacuum of power not unlike that brought about by the Black Death in the fourteenth century. It seems to have been a watershed moment between systems.

Since that time we have witnessed the development of a variety of new players and a displacement of the center of a global system from the Atlantic to the Pacific Ocean, much as the transition to the sixteenth-century world system was marked by a displacement from the Mediterranean to the Atlantic. The rise of Japan to world core status, certified by her incorporation into the Trilateral Commission, is one of the most striking elements of the current restructuring. The return to the world system of China, that formerly inward-oriented giant with a quarter of the world's population, is a second notable change. Related to these trends has been the rapid development of the so-called "miracle" economies of Asia (the NICs, that is, Newly Industrializing Countries)—South Korea, Taiwan, Singapore, etc.—that have now begun to organize production in their own peripheries. In contrast, many of the former colonies of Europe in Africa and the Middle East, after gaining their independence in the wake of World War II, have actually been demoted in the world system; some even seem to have "fallen out" of the system entirely. Nor has the world become uniformly "capitalist," as socialism has spread from eastern Europe to parts of the third world.

In the face of this reorganization of the geopolitics of the world, the United States has attempted to retain its earlier hegemony by two strategies: one has been militarily, either directly or through regional surrogates; the second has been through the globalization of capital, a phenomenon not unrelated to the arms trade.

Both strategies may be meeting with declining success. Direct force of arms has resulted in an unrelieved series of real defeats, whereas indirect military ventures have succeeded chiefly in miring region after region in local conflicts in which the goal seems to be the perpetuation rather than the resolution of conflict. Although this serves to reduce the number of players in the world system, it does not eliminate all contenders and competitors. The United States has sought to build coalitions with the remaining powers through international finance. This has led, however, to such a level of international indebtedness that constant and further expansion seems impossible.

It may be that the old advantages that underlay the hegemony of the West are dissipating. In the thirteenth century, a variety of protocapitalist systems coexisted in various parts of the world, none with sufficient power to outstrip the others. With the development of western capitalism, coupled with the primitive accumulation made possible by the "discovery" and conquest of the "New World," one part of the world system forged ahead of the rest and, by the late nineteenth century *Age of Empire* (Hobsbawm, 1987), had fully consolidated the gains derived from unequal development.

In the latter part of the twentieth century, the old "core" is attempting to preserve by economic means the privileges it forfeited through decolonization. But that attempt has become increasingly unsuccessful. The impact of restructuring has fallen more and more on the old hegemons—Great Britain first and now the United States. Since multiple powers now share the spoils and there has been a greater convergence among economic systems (the Soviet Union has Perestroika, socialist countries "privatize," whereas the western powers increasingly plan their economies), no single player has a spectacular advantage.

The system may now be so unstable that any global shock can precipitate a radical transformation in it. The era of European/western hegemony may be superseded by a new form of world conquest, but that is hard to imagine. Rather, it seems more likely that there will be a return to the relative balance of multiple centers exhibited in the thirteenth-century world system. But that would require a shift to different rules of the game, or at least an end to the rules Europe introduced in the sixteenth century.[12]

Under the new conditions of the twenty-first century, in which the world system will have become truly global, the ability of nations to live in peaceful coexistence becomes even more imperative than it was in earlier times. In the thirteenth century there were many zones of subsistence untouched by the cores, and, even among the great powers, withdrawal from the system was a viable option. Neither of these conditions applies in today's world. Perhaps we have much to learn from studying the thirteenth-century world system, organized so differently than our own.

Notes

1. Although Eurocentric historians and social scientists have been tempted to attribute Europe's sixteenth-century success to the unique genius of, alternatively, European "culture" or "capitalism" in its pure form, this book casts doubt on these explanations.

2. It is necessary to call attention to a major inconsistency in Marx that I believe accounts for his indecision as to the origins of modern capitalism in Europe. (See our discussion in Chapter 1.) In the *Communist Manifesto*, and in some of the explications of the transition from feudalism to capitalism authored by Engels, it is argued that capitalism developed out of the internal contradictions *within Europe* between new material forces of production of bourgeois origin and the "fetters" of the older feudal social relations of production (property relations)—a phenomenon clearly evident by the thirteenth century. In Marx's later writings, particularly in *Das Kapital*, a very different analysis of the rise of modern European capitalism appears. In his discussions of the role of primitive accumulation, Marx clearly argues that the impetus to modern capitalism sprang from the *international arena* in which crude expropriation of wealth (resources and labor) through brute force yielded a quantum jump in the capital available for investment in European production. In this analysis, the role of the state is clearly brought out. Obviously, it was not until the sixteenth century that European "conquests" made such primitive accumulation possible.

3. Georg Simmel is credited with the brilliant insight that conflict, too, is a form of interaction. See his essay on "Conflict."

4. See, for example, Mancur Olson (1982).

5. Including, most recently, Robert Gilpin (1987), David Calleo (1987), and Paul Kennedy (1987).

6. Of which, among many, are Spengler's *The Decline of the West* (originally published 1926) and Toynbee's *A Study of History* (1947–1957).

7. The entire debate generated by the eighth chapter of Paul Kennedy's recent work (1987) seems to revolve around this distinction. For the terms of this popular debate, see, inter alia, the series of articles that appeared in the Magazine section of the *New York Times* in 1988.

8. In a paper delivered at the 1987 meetings of the American Sociological Association, Polish sociologist Stefan Nowak (1987: particularly 27–33) came close to expressing my theory of "vectors," although his analysis was a bit too positivist for my taste.

9. As World War II did in the twentieth century.

10. See James Gleick (1987). I have oversimplified here a most promising theoretical development.

11. In a letter Immanuel Wallerstein wrote to me when I was in the early stages of this project, he cautioned me that decline would be harder to analyze than rise. I must admit he was right, but the difficulty is built into the problem. I have done the best I could.

12. After selecting the title for my book I came accross its antonym, *After Hegemony* (Keohane, 1984), which conveys this point explicitly.

Bibliography

A Guide to the Bibliographic Guide

The form adopted for this bibliography is a compromise between the needs of readers and researchers. Readers would ideally like to find a single bibliography arranged in strict alphabetic order by author's name, so that when a work is cited in the text the full bibliographic information can be readily found. Specialized researchers, on the other hand, are more likely to want the references grouped by country or region. The principles of organization I have adopted will satisfy neither completely. In general, theoretical works and those dealing with the world (to which references are made almost exclusively in Chapters 1 and 11) have been placed in the first section, together with works that refer to Europe as a whole or to more than one subregion of Europe. These are followed by citations to works dealing with the Champagne fairs (relevant to Chapter 2), Flanders (Chapter 3) and, finally, Italy (Chapter 4). The second major section of the bibliography covers the Middle East region. Some general works have been placed with the subsection on the Mongols (Chapter 5) but most of the references relevant to Chapters 6 and 7 appear in the subsection entitled the Arab World. The third major portion of the bibliography deals with regions east of the Arab World. General sources have been placed with the subsection on India (relevant to Chapter 8), followed by subsections on Southeast Asia (Chapter 9) and China (Chapter 10). Given the nature of the literature, it has not always been possible to abide by these general principles of classification.

General and Europe

Abu-Lughod, Janet. 1987–88. "The Shape of the World System in the Thirteenth Century," plus comments, *Studies in Comparative International Development* 22 (Winter): 3–53.

Anderson, Perry. 1974a. *Lineages of the Absolutist State*. London: NLB.

Anderson, Perry. 1974b, reprinted 1978. *Passages from Antiquity to Feudalism*. London: Verso.

Bairoch, P. 1982. "Urbanisation and Economic Development in the Western World: Some Provisional Conclusions of an Empirical Study," pp. 61–75 in *Patterns of European Urbanisation since 1500*. ed. by H. Schmal. London: Croom Helm.

Baratier, Edouard. 1970. "L'activité des occidentaux en orient au moyen âge," pp. 333–341 in *Sociétés et compagnies de commerce en orient et dans l'Océan Indien*. Paris: S.E.V.P.E.N.

Barraclough, Geoffrey, ed. 1978. *The Times Atlas of World History*. Maplewood, New Jersey: Hammond.

Barzun, Jacques and Henry Graff. 1957. *The Modern Researcher*. New York: Harcourt Brace.

Bernard, J. 1972. "Trade and Finance in the Middle Ages. 900–1500," pp. 274–338 in Volume I of *The Fontana Economic History of Europe*. London: Collins.

Bloch, Marc. 1961. *Feudal Society*. Chicago: University of Chicago Press.

Braudel, Fernand. 1972. *The Mediterranean and the Mediterranean World in the Age of Philip II*. 2 volumes. Trans. by Sian Reynolds. New York: Harper & Row.

Braudel, Fernand. 1973. *Capitalism and Material Life: 1400–1800*. Vol. I. London: Weidenfeld and Nicholson.

Braudel, Fernand. 1977. *Afterthoughts on Material Civilization and Capitalism*. Trans. by P. M. Ranum. Baltimore: The Johns Hopkins University Press.

Braudel, Fernand. 1980. *On History*. Trans. by Sarah Matthews. Chicago: University of Chicago Press.

Braudel, Fernand. 1982–1984. *Civilization & Capitalism, 15th–18th Century*. Trans. by Sian Reynolds. 3 volumes. 1982. Vol. I. *The Structures of Everyday Life*; 1983. Vol. II. *The Wheels of Commerce*; 1984. Vol. III. *The Perspective of the World*. London: Collins; New York: Harper & Row.

Braudel, Fernand. 1985. *La dynamique du capitalisme*. Paris: Arthaud.

Brenner, Robert. 1977. "The Origins of Capitalist Development: A Critique of Neo-Smithian Marxism," *New Left Review* 104 (July–August): 25–92.

Calleo, David. 1987. *Beyond American Hegemony: The Future of the Western Alliance*. New York: Basic Books.

Calvino, Italo. 1974. *Invisible Cities*. Trans. by W. Weaver. New York and London: Harcourt Brace Jovanovich.

Cambridge Economic History of Europe. 1952. Vol. II. *Trade and Industry in the Middle Ages*. ed. by M. M. Postan and E. E. Rich. Cambridge: Cambridge University Press.

Carus-Wilson, E. M. 1941. "An Industrial Revolution of the Thirteenth Century," *Economic History Review* 11: 41–60.

Cave, R. C. and H. H. Coulson, eds. 1936. *A Source Book for Medieval Economic History*. Milwaukee: The Bruce Publishing Co.

Chase-Dunn, Christopher. 1989. *Global Formation: Structures of the World Economy*. New York: Basil Blackwell, in press.

Chaunu, Pierre. 1969, second ed. 1983. *L'expansion européenne du XIIIe au XVe siècle*. Paris: Presses Universitaires de France. English translation of the first edition is available under the title *European Expansion in the Later Middle Ages*. 1979. Trans. by Katherine Bertram. Amsterdam: North-Holland Publishing Company.

Chevalier, Bernard. 1969. *L'occident de 1280 à 1492*. Paris: A. Colin.

Cheyney, Edward P. 1936. *The Dawn of a New Era, 1250–1453*. New York: Harper & Brothers.

Chirot, Daniel. 1985. "The Rise of the West," *American Sociological Review* 50: 181–195.

Cipolla, C. M. 1956. *Money, Prices, and Civilization in the Mediterranean World, Fifth to Seventeenth Century*. Princeton: Princeton University Press.

Cipolla, C. M. 1976. *Before the Industrial Revolution: European Society and Economy, 1000–1700*. New York: Norton.

Colloques Internationaux d'Histoire Maritime, Sixième colloque, held in Venice in 1962. 1970. *Méditerranée et Océan Indien*. Paris: S.E.V.P.E.N.

Cox, Oliver. 1959. *The Foundations of Capitalism*. New York: Philosophical Library.

Curtin, Philip D. 1984. *Cross-Cultural Trade in World History*. Cambridge: Cambridge University Press.

de Rachewiltz, Igor. 1971. *Papal Envoys to the Great Khans*. London: Faber & Faber.

de Vries, Jan. 1984. *European Urbanization 1500–1800*. Cambridge, Massachusetts: Harvard University Press.

Deyon, P. 1979. "L'enjeu des discussions autour du concept de 'protoindustrialisation,' " *Revue de Nord* 61: 9–15.

Dobb, Maurice. 1947, reprinted 1984. *Studies in the Development of Capitalism*. New York: International Publishers.

Doehaerd, Renée. 1978. *The Early Middle Ages in the West: Economy and Society*. Trans. by W. G. Deakin. Amsterdam: North-Holland Publishing Company.

Doehaerd, Renée. 1984. *Oeconomica Mediaevalia*. Brussels: V.U.B., Centrum voor Sociale Structuren. Collection of older essays.

Dollinger, P. 1964. *La hanse (XII–XVIIe siècles)*. Paris. English translation is available under the title *The German Hansa*. 1970. Trans. by D. S. Ault and S. H. Steinberg. Stanford: Stanford University Press.

Duby, Georges. 1976. *Rural Economy and Country Life in the Medieval West*. Columbus: University of South Carolina Press.

Ekholm, Kajsa. 1980. "On the Limitations of Civilization: The Structure and Dynamics of Global Systems," *Dialectical Anthropology* 5 (July): 155–166.

Ennen, Edith. 1956. "Les différents types de formation des villes européennes," *Le Moyen Age*, Série 4, Vol. 2.

Ennen, Edith. 1979. *The Medieval Town*. Trans. by Natalie Fryde. Amsterdam: North-Holland Publishing Company.

Espinas, Georges. 1931. "Histoire urbaine, direction de recherches et resultats," *Annales: Economies. Sociétés. Civilisations*. First series, 3: 394–427.

Espinas, Georges. 1933–1949. *Les origines du capitalisme*. 4 volumes. Lille: E. Raoust.

Fontana Economic History of Europe. 1969–1982. 6 volumes. London: Fontana.

Fourquin, G. 1969. *Histoire économique de l'occident médiéval*. Paris: Presses Universitaires de France.

Friedmann, John and Goetz Wolff. 1982. "World City Formation," *International Journal of Urban and Regional Research* 6: 309–343.

Ganshof, F. 1943. *Etude sur le développement des villes entre Loire et Rhin au moyen âge*. Paris: Presses Universitaires de France. Also Brussels: Editions de la Librairie Encyclopédique.

Ganshof, François. 1953. *Le moyen âge*. Paris: Hachette.

Genicot, L. 1964. "On the Evidence of Growth of Population from the 11th to the 13th Century," *Change in Medieval Society*. ed. by Sylvia Thrupp. New York: Appleton-Century Crofts.

Genicot, L. 1968, second ed. 1984. *Le XIIIe siècle européen*. Paris: Presses Universitaires de France.

Genicot, L. 1973. "Les grandes villes de l'occident en 1300," pp. 199–219 in *Mélanges E. Perroy*. Paris: Presses Universitaires de France.

Gilpin, Robert. 1987. *The Political Economy of International Relations*. Princeton: Princeton University Press.

Gimpel, Jean. 1975. *La révolution industrielle du moyen âge*. Paris: Editions du Seuil.

Gleick, James. 1987. *Chaos: Making a New Science*. New York: Viking Press.

Goldstone, J. 1984. "Urbanization and Inflation in England, 1500–1650," *American Journal of Sociology* 89: 1122–1160.

Gottfried, Robert. 1983. *The Black Death: Natural and Human Disaster in Medieval Europe*. New York: Macmillan.

Gutkind, Erwin. 1964–1967. *International History of City Development*. New York: Macmillan. Several volumes deal with European cities.

Havinghurst, Alfred. 1958. *The Pirenne Thesis. Analysis, Criticism and Revision*. Boston: D. C. Heath and Co.

Heer, Friedrich. 1962. *The Medieval World: Europe, 1100–1350*. Trans. from the German by Janet Sondheimer. Cleveland: World Publishing Co.

Hobsbawm, Eric. 1987. *The Age of Empire: 1875–1914*. New York: Pantheon Books.

Hodges, Richard and David Whitehouse. 1983. *Mohammed, Charlemagne and the Origins of Europe: Archaeology and the Pirenne Thesis*. Ithaca: Cornell University Press.

Hohenberg, Paul and Lynn H. Lees. 1985. *The Making of Urban Europe, 1100–1950*. Cambridge, Massachusetts: Harvard University Press. Part I deals with the eleventh to fourteenth centuries.

Joinville and Villehardoun. Chronicles of the Crusades. Original 1963, reprinted 1985. Trans. with an introduction by M. R. B. Shaw. New York: Dorset Press.

Jones, E. L. 1981, second ed. 1987. *The European Miracle*. Cambridge: Cambridge University Press.

Kennedy, Paul. 1987. *The Rise and Fall of the Great Powers: Economic Change and Military Conflict from 1500 to 2000*. New York: Random House.

Keohane, Robert. 1984. *After Hegemony: Cooperation and Discord in the World Political Economy*. Princeton: Princeton University Press.

Kraus, Henry. 1979. *Gold was the Mortar: The Economics of Cathedral Building*. London: Routledge and Kegan Paul.

Krey, A. C. 1958 reprint of original 1921. *The First Crusade, the Accounts of Eye-Witnesses and Participants*. Gloucester, Massachusetts: P. Smith.

Kuhn, Thomas. 1962. *The Structure of Scientific Revolutions*. Chicago: University of Chicago Press.

Latouche, Robert. 1961. *The Birth of Western Economy: Economic Aspects of the Dark Ages*. Trans. by E. M. Wilkinson. London: Methuen.

Lavedan, Pierre and Jeanne Hugueney. 1974. *L'urbanisme au moyen âge*. Geneva: E. Droz.

Le Goff, Jacques. Original 1956, now in 6th ed. 1980. *Marchands et banquiers du moyen âge*. Paris: Presses Universitaires de France.

Levenson, Joseph, ed. 1967. *European Expansion and the Counter-example of Asia*. Englewood Cliffs, New Jersey: Prentice-Hall.

Lewis, Archibald. 1970. *The Islamic World and the West, A.D. 622–1492*. New York: John Wiley.

Lewis, Archibald. 1978. *The Sea and Medieval Civilisations, Collected Studies*. London: Variorum Reprints.

Lloyd, T. H. 1982. *Alien Merchants in England in the High Middle Ages*. New York: St. Martin's Press.

Lopez, R. S. 1949. "Du marché temporaire à la colonie permanente: l'évolution de la politique commerciale au moyen âge," *Annales: Economies. Sociétés. Civilisations*. Second Series 4: 389–405.

Lopez, Robert S. 1955. "East and West in the Early Middle Ages: Economic Relations," pp. 113–164 in *Congresso (X) Internazionale de Scienze Storiche, Relations* (Florence) III.

Lopez, Robert S. 1970. "Les méthodes commerciales des marchands occidentaux en Asie du XI au XIV siècle," pp. 343–348 in *Sociétés et compagnies de commerce en orient et dans l'Océan Indien*. Paris: S.E.V.P.E.N.

Lopez, Robert S. 1976. *The Commercial Revolution of the Middle Ages, 950–1350*. Cambridge: Cambridge University Press.

Lopez, R. S. and H. A. Miskimin. 1962. "The Economic Depression of the Renaissance," *The Economic History Review*, Second Series, XIV: 397–407.

Lopez, Robert S. and Irving Raymond, eds. 1967. *Medieval Trade in the Mediterranean World*. New York: Norton.

Lyon, Bryce Dale, ed. 1964. *The High Middle Ages, 1000–1300*. New York: The Free Press of Glencoe.

Maalouf, Amin. 1984. *The Crusades through Arab Eyes*. Trans. by Jon Rothschild. London: Al Saqi Books.

Mann, Michael. 1986. *The Sources of Social Power*, Vol. I. Cambridge: Cambridge University Press.

Marx, Karl. *Corpus* but especially the *Grundrisse*.

Marx, Karl. 1964. *Grundrisse*. Excerpts trans. by Jack Cohen, edited and with an introduction by Eric Hobsbawm under the title, *Pre-capitalist Economic Formations*. New York: International Publishers.

McEvedy, Colin. 1961. *The Penguin Atlas of Medieval History*. Hammondsworth: Penguin Books.

McNeill, William Hardy. 1963. *The Rise of the West: A History of the Human Community*. Chicago: University of Chicago Press.

McNeill, William Hardy. 1976. *Plagues and Peoples*. Garden City, New Jersey: Anchor Books.

Mélanges d'histoire du moyen âge: dédiés à la mémoire de Louis Halphen. 1951. Paris: Presses Universitaires de France.

Mendels, F. 1972. "Proto-industrialization: The First Phase of the Industrialization Process," *Journal of Economic History* 32: 241–261.

Miskimin, Harry A. 1969. *The Economy of Early Renaissance Europe, 1300–1460*. Englewood Cliffs, New Jersey: Doubleday.

Miskimin, Harry, David Herlihy, and A. L. Udovitch, eds. 1977. *The Medieval City*. New Haven: Yale University Press.

Mollat, Michèl, ed. 1962. *Les sources de l'histoire maritime en Europe du moyen âge au XVIIIe siècle*. 4th Colloque Internationale d'Histoire Maritime. Paris: S.E.V.P.E.N.

Mollat, Michèl. 1977a. *Etudes sur l'économie et la société de l'occident médiéval, XIIe–XVe siècle*. London: Variorum Reprints.

Mollat, Michèl. 1977b. *Etudes d'histoire maritime, 1938–1975*. Turin: Bottega d'Erasmo. A collection of earlier published essays.

Mollat, Michèl. 1984. *Explorateurs du XIIIe au XVI siècle*. Paris: J. C. Lattes.

Mols, R. S. J. 1954. *Introduction à la démographie historique des villes d'Europe du XIVe au XVIIIe siècles*. 2 volumes. Gembloux: J. Ducolot.

Morgan, D. O., ed. 1982. *Medieval Historical Writing in the Christian and Islamic Worlds*. London: School of Oriental and African Studies, University of London.

Mundy, John and Peter Riesenberg. Reprinted 1979. *The Medieval Town*. Huntington, New York: Robert E. Krieger Publishing.

Nowak, Stefan. 1987. "Comparative Studies and Social Theory." Mimeo. paper, delivered at Annual Meeting of the American Sociological Association, Chicago.

Olson, Mancur. 1982. *The Rise and Decline of Nations: Economic Growth, Stagflation and Social Rigidities*. New Haven: Yale University Press.

Packard, Sidney. 1962. "The Process of Historical Revision: New Viewpoints in Medieval European History." Northampton, Massachusetts: Smith College.

Pirenne, Henri. 1898. "Villes, marchés et marchands au moyen âge," *Revue Historique* LXLII.

Pirenne, Henri. 1925. *Medieval Cities*. Princeton: Princeton University Press. Republished Garden City, New Jersey: Doubleday, 1956.

Pirenne, Henri. 1939. *Mohammed and Charlemagne*. Translated from the 10th edition in French. London: Allen and Unwin.

Pirenne, Henri. 1956. *A History of Europe: From the Invasions to the XVIth Century*. Trans. by Bernard Miall. New York: University Books.

Polanyi, Karl, C. M. Arensberg, and H. W. Pearson, eds. 1957. *Trade and Market in the Early Empires: Economies in History and Theory*. Glencoe, Illinois: The Free Press.

Postan, M. M. 1928. "Credit in Medieval Trade," *Economic History Review* I: 234–261.

Postan, M. M. and E. E. Rich, eds. 1952. *Trade and Industry in the Middle Ages*. Vol. II of the *Cambridge Economic History of Europe*. Cambridge: Cambridge University Press.

Postan, M. M. and Edward Miller, eds. 1963. *Economic Organisation and Policies in the Middle Ages*. Vol. III of the *Cambridge Economic History of Europe*. Cambridge: Cambridge University Press.

Power, Eileen. 1924 original, reprinted 1963. *Medieval People*. New York: Barnes & Noble.

Power, Eileen. 1941. *The Wool Trade in English Medieval History*. Oxford: Oxford University Press.

Renouard, Yves. 1948. "Conséquences et intérêts démographiques de la peste noir de 1248," *Population* 3: 454–466.

Renouard, Yves. 1951. "Les voies de communication entre pays de la Méditerranée et pays de l'Atlantique au moyen âge. Problèmes et hypothèses," pp. 587–594 in *Mélanges d'histoire du moyen âge, dédiés à la mémoire de Louis Halphen*. Paris: Presses Universitaires de France.

Reynolds, Robert. 1961. *Europe Emerges: Transition toward an Industrial World-Wide Society, 600–1750*. Madison: University of Wisconsin Press.

Richard, Jean. 1976. *Orient et occident au moyen âge: Contact et relations (XIIe–XVe siècle)*. London: Variorum Reprints.

Rorig, Fritz. 1967 English trans. *The Medieval Town*. London: B. T. Batsford.

Rosecrance, Richard. 1986. *The Rise of the Trading State: Commerce and Conquest in the Modern World*. New York: Basic Books.

Runciman, W. G. 1983. "Capitalism without Classes: The Case of Classical Rome," *British Journal of Sociology* 34: 157–181.

Russell, J. C. 1972. *Medieval Regions and Their Cities*. Bloomington, Indiana: University of Indiana Press.

Schneider, Jane. 1977. "Was There a Pre-capitalist World-System?" *Peasant Studies* 6: 20–27.

Simmel, Georg. Original essays 1904 and 1922. English trans. 1955. *Conflict and the Web of Group Affiliations*. Trans. by Kurt H. Wolff and Reinhard Bendix. New York: The Free Press.

Sjoberg, Gideon. 1960. *The Pre-Industrial City, Past and Present*. Glencoe, Illinois: The Free Press.

Sombart, W. 1975. *Krieg und Kapitalismus*. New York: Arno Press.

Sombart, Werner. *Der Moderne Kapitalismus*, various editions.

Southern, R. W. Original 1962, reprinted 1980. *Western Views of Islam in the Middle Ages*. Cambridge, Massachusetts: Harvard University Press.

Spengler, Oswald. 1926–28 original. *The Decline of the West*. New York: Knopf.

Tawney, R. H. 1926. *Religion and the Rise of Capitalism: A Historical Study*. New York: Harcourt Brace.

Taylor, John C. 1979. *From Modernization to Modes of Production*. Atlantic Highlands, New Jersey: Humanities Press.

Thrupp, Sylvia. 1977. "Comparisons of Cultures in the Middle Ages: Western Standards as Applied to Muslim Civilization in the Twelfth and Thirteenth Centuries," pp. 67–88 in *Society and History: Essays by Sylvia Thrupp*. ed. by R. Grew and N. Steneck. Ann Arbor: University of Michigan Press.

Tillion, Germaine. 1983. *The Republic of Cousins: Women's Oppression in Mediterranean Society*. English trans. of *Harem et les cousins*. London: Al Saqi Books.

Tilly, Charles. 1981. *As Sociology Meets History*. New York: Academic Press.

Toynbee, Arnold J. 1947–1957. *A Study of History*. 10 volumes. New York and London: Oxford University Press.

Unger, Richard William. 1980. *The Ship in the Medieval Economy, 600–1600*. London: Croom Helm.

Usher, A. P. 1943. *The Early History of Deposit Banking in Mediterranean Europe*. Cambridge, Massachusetts: Harvard University Press.

van der Wee, H. 1975–76. "Reflections on the Development of the Urban

Economy in Western Europe during the Late Middle Ages and Early Modern Times," *Urbanism Past and Present* I: 9–14.

van Houtte, J. A. 1977. *Essays on Medieval and Early Modern Economy and Society*. Leuven: University Press. Reprints of previously published articles in the languages in which they appeared.

Wallerstein, Immanuel. 1974. *The Modern World-System* I. New York: Academic Press.

Wallerstein, Immanuel. 1979a. *The Modern World-System* II. New York: Academic Press.

Wallerstein, Immanuel. 1979b. *The Capitalist World Economy: Essays*. New York: Cambridge University Press.

Wallerstein, Immanuel. 1983. *Historical Capitalism*. London: Verso Editions.

Weber, Max. Original 1904–05, English trans. 1958. *The Protestant Ethic and the Spirit of Capitalism*. New York: Charles Scribner's Sons.

Weber, Max. 1958a. *The City*. Trans. by Don Martindale and Gertrud Neuwirth. Glencoe, Illinois: The Free Press.

Weber, Max. 1958b, reissued 1967. *The Religion of India: The Sociology of Hinduism and Buddhism*. Trans. by Hans Gerth and Don Martindale. Glencoe, Illinois: The Free Press.

Weber, Max. 1968. Sections on "Premodern Capitalism" and "Modern Capitalism," trans. by Frank Knight, pp. 129–165 in *Max Weber on Charisma and Institution Building*. ed. by S. N. Eisenstadt. Chicago: University of Chicago Press.

Weber, Max. 1978. *Economy and Society*. 2 volumes. New York: Bedminster Press.

Weber, Max. 1981 reprint. *General Economic History*. New Brunswick, New Jersey: Transaction Books.

White, Lynn, Jr. 1962. *Medieval Technology and Social Change*. Oxford: Clarendon Press.

Wolf, Eric. 1982. *Europe and the People without History*. Berkeley: University of California Press.

France

Alengry, Charles. 1915. *Les foires de Champagne. (Etude d'histoire économique.)* Paris: Libraire Arthur Rousseau. The bibliography in this work is extremely inaccurate and the rest of the book is untrustworthy.

Baldwin, John W. 1986. *The Government of Philip Augustus*. Berkeley: University of California Press.

Barel, Yves. 1975, 1977. *La ville médiévale: Système social—système ur-*

bain [on the city of Montpellier]. Grenoble: Presses Universitaires de France.

Bautier, R. H. 1942–3. "Les registres des foires de Champagne," *Bulletin Philologique et Historique de C.T.H.S.*: 157–185.

Bautier, R. H. 1945. "Marchands siènnois et 'draps d'Outremont' aux foires de Champagne," *Annuaire-Bulletin de la Société de l'Histoire de France*: 87–107.

Bautier, R. H. 1953. "Les foires de Champagne, recherches sur une évolution historique," *Recueils de la Société Jean Bodin* (Brussels) V: 97–147.

Bautier, R. H. 1958. "L'exercice de la juridiction gracieuse en Champagne du milieu du XIIIe s. à la fin du XVe," *Bibliothèque de l'Ecole des Chartes* 116: 29–106.

Bautier, R. H. 1960. "Recherches sur les routes de l'Europe médiévale, I. De la Méditerranée à Paris et des foires de Champagne par le Massif Centrale," *Bulletin Philologique et Historique du C.T.H.S.*: 90–143.

Bautier, R. H. 1966/issued 1970. "Les relations économiques des Occidentaux avec les pays d'Orient au moyen âge: Points de vue et documents," pp. 263–331 in *Actes du VIIIe Colloque International d'Histoire Maritime*. Beirut, 1966. Issued under the title *Sociétés et compagnies de commerce en orient et dans l'Océan Indien*. Paris: S.E.V.P.E.N.

Benton, John F. 1976. "The Accounts of Cepperello da Prato for the Tax on *Nouveaux Acquêts* in the Bailliage of Troyes," pp. 111–135, 453–457 in *Order and Innovation in the Middle Ages: Essays in Honor of Joseph R. Strayer*. ed. by William C. Jordan et al. Princeton: Princeton University Press.

Bibolet, Françoise. n.d. "Les institutions municipale de Troyes aux XIV et XVe siècles." In Troyes Municipal Library.

Bibolet, Françoise. 1945. "Le rôle de la guerre de cent ans dans le développement des libertés municipales à Troyes," in *Mémoires de la Société Académique d'Agricultures, des Sciences, Arts et Belles-Lettres du Département de l'Aube* XCIX: 1939–1942. Published late at Troyes.

Bibolet, Françoise. 1957. "Le développement urbain des villes de foires de Champagne au moyen âge," *La Vie en Champagne* (June).

Bibolet, Françoise. 1964–66. "La Bibliothèque de Chanoines de Troyes: leurs manuscrits du XIIe au XVIe s.," pp. 139–177 in *Mémoires de la Société Académique d'Agricultures, des Sciences, Arts et*

Belles-Lettres du Departement de l'Aube CIV. In Troyes Municipal Library.

Bibolet, Françoise. 1966. "Troyes et Provins," in *La Vie en Champagne* (May).

Bibolet, Françoise. 1970. "Les métiers à Troyes aux XIVe et XVe siècles," in *Actes du 95° Congrès National de Sociétés Savantes.* Reims. Published by Bibliothèque Nationale. In Troyes Municipal Library.

Bourquelot, Félix. 1865. *Etudes sur les foires de Champagne, sur la nature, l'entendue et les règles du commerce qui s'y faisait aux XIIe, XIIIe et XIVe siècles. Mémoires presentés par divers savants à l'Académie des Inscriptions et Belles-Lettres,* Deuxième Série, Tome V. 2 volumes. Paris: L'Imprimerie Imperiale.

Bourquelot, Félix. Original, 1839–40, reprinted 1976. *Histoire de Provins.* Original Paris: Allouard; reprinted Marseille: Laffitte Reprints.

Boutiot, T. 1870–1880, reprinted 1977. *Histoire de la ville de Troyes et de la Champagne méridionale.* Troyes: Dufey-Robert, and Paris: Aug. Aubry, 1870–1880. In 5 Volumes. 1870. Vol. I; 1872. Vol. II; 1873. Vol. III; 1874. Vol. IV; and 1880. Vol. V (an index prepared posthumously by his son, Henry Boutiot). This book has been reissued 1977 in 5 volumes. Brussels: Editions Culture et Civilisation.

Carré, Gustave. 1880. *Aperçu historique sur la ville de Troyes.* Troyes: E. Caffe. In Troyes Municipal Library.

Carré, Gustave. 1881. *Histoire populaire de Troyes et du département de l'Aube.* Troyes: L. Lacroix.

Chapin, Elizabeth. 1937. *Les villes de foires de Champagne des origines au debut du XIVe siècle.* Paris: H. Champion.

Coornaert, Emile. 1957. "Caractères et mouvement des foires internationales au moyen âge et au XVI siècle," in *Studi in onore di Armando Sapori,* Vol. I. Pages 357–363 deal with the Champagne fairs. Milan: Istituto Editoriale Cisalpino.

Corrard de Breban. 1977. *Les rues de Troyes, anciennes et modernes.* Marseille: Laffitte Reprints.

Crozet, René. 1933. *Histoire de Champagne.* Paris: Boivin.

Desportes, Pierre. 1979. *Reims et les Rémois aux XIIIe et XIVe siècles.* Paris: Picard.

Doehaerd, Renée. 1939. "Un conflit entre les gardes des foires de Champagne et le comte de Hainaut, 1302," *Annales du Cercle Archéologie de Mons* 56: 171–184.

Dollinger, Pierre, P. Wolff, and S. Guenée, eds. 1967. *Bibliographie d'histoire des villes de France*. No. 282 of Histoire de France bibliographies. Paris: C. Klincksieck.

Dubois, Henri. 1976. *Les foires de Châlon et le commerce dans la vallée de la Saône à la fin du moyen âge (vers 1280–vers 1430)*. Paris: Publications de la Sorbonne, Imprimerie Nationale.

Dubois, Henri. 1982. "Le commerce et les foires au temps de Philippe Auguste," pp. 689 seq. in *Colloques Internationaux du Centre National de la Recherche Scientifique*, No. 602.

Duby, Georges, ed. 1980. *Histoire de la France urbaine*. Paris: Editions du Seuil. Volume II is on *La Ville médiévale des Carolingiens à la Renaissance*.

Evergates, Theodore. 1974. "The Aristocracy of Champagne in the Mid-Thirteenth Century: A Quantitative Description," *Journal of Interdisciplinary History* V: 1–18.

Evergates, Theodore. 1975. *Feudal Society in the Bailliage of Troyes under the Counts of Champagne, 1152–1284*. Baltimore: The Johns Hopkins University Press.

Finot, Jules. 1894. *Etude historique sur les relations commerciales entre la France et la Flandre au moyen âge*. Paris: Alphonse Picard.

The First Crusade. The Chronicle of Fulcher of Chartres and Other Source Materials. 1971. Edited and translated by Edward Peters. Philadelphia: University of Pennsylvania Press.

Gallais, Pierre and Yves-Jean Riou eds. 1966. *Mélanges offerts à René Crozet*. Poitiers: Société d'Etudes Médiévales.

Ganshof, F. I. 1948. *Etude sur le développement des villes entre Loire et Rhin au moyen âge*. Paris: Presses Universitaires de France.

Gies, Joseph and Frances Gies. 1969. *Life in a Medieval City* [Troyes in 1250 A.D.]. New York: Harper Colophon.

Higounet, Ch., J. B. Marquette, and Ph. Wolff. 1982. *Atlas historique des villes de France*. 3 volumes. Paris: Editions de Centre National de la Recherche Scientifique.

Kleinclausz, A. Original 1939–1952, reprinted 1978. *Histoire de Lyon*. 3 volumes. Marseille: Laffitte Reprints.

Lalore, C. 1883. "Ce sont les coutumes des foires de Champagne," *Annales de l'Aube*. In Troyes Municipal Library.

Laurent, Henri. 1932. "Droits des foires et droits urbains aux XIIIe et XIVe siècles," *Revue Historique de Droit Français et Etranger*, 4e série, Tome XI: 600–710.

Laurent, Henri. 1934. "Choix de documents inédits pour servir à l'histoire de l'expansion commerciale des Pays-Bas en France au moyen âge," *Bulletin Comm. Royale d'Histoire*: 335–416.

Laurent, Henri. 1935. *Un grand commerce d'exportation au moyen âge:*

la draperie des Pays-Bas en France et dans les pays méditerranéens (XIIe–XVe siècle). Liège-Paris: Librairie E. Droz.

Lefèvre, André. 1868–69. "Les finances de la Champagne au XIIIe et XIVe siècles," in *Bibliothèque de l'Ecole des Chartes*, 4e série, IV and V.

Lestocquoy, Jean. 1952b. *Patriciens du moyen âge: Les dynasties bourgeoises d'Arras du XIe au XVe siècle*. In *Mémoires de la Commission Départementale des Monuments Historiques du Pas-de-Calais*, Tome V, fasc. 1.

Longnon, A. 1901–1914. *Documents relatifs au Comte de Champagne et de Brie (1172–1361)*. 3 volumes. Paris. Part of *Documents inédits sur l'histoire de France*.

Mesqui, Jean. 1979. *Provins. La fortification d'une ville au moyen âge*. Paris-Geneva: Bibliothèque de la Société Française d'Archéologie.

Mikesell, Marvin W. 1961. *Northern Morocco: A Cultural Geography*. Berkeley: University of California Publications in Geography #14.

Portejoie, Paulette. 1956. *L'ancien coutumier de Champagne (XIIIe siècle)*. Poitiers: Imprimerie P. Oudin.

Postan, M. 1952. "The Trade of Medieval Europe: The North," in *Cambridge Economic History of Europe* II. Cambridge: Cambridge University Press.

Renouard, Yves. 1963. "Les voies de communication entre la France et le Piedmont au moyen âge," *Bollettino Storico-Bibliografico Subalpino*: 233–256. In Marciana Library, Venice.

Roserot, Alphonse. 1883. "Les origines des municipalités de Troyes," in *Mémoires de la Société Académique de l'Aube* 47: 291–303.

Roserot, Alphonse [under direction of]. Reprinted 1977. *Dictionnaire historique de la Champagne méridionale (Aube) des origines à 1790*. Published originally in Langres in the 1940s. This has been reissued, Marseille: Laffitte Reprints. 4 volumes: I is A–D; II is E–Q; III is R–Y; and IV is Plates.

Sayous, André-Emile. 1929. "Le commerce de Marseille avec la Syrie au milieu du XIII siècle," *Revue des Etudes Historiques* XCV: 391–408.

Sayous, André-Emile. 1932. "Les opérations des banquiers en Italie et aux foires de Champagne pendant le XIIIe siècle," *Revue Historique* CLXX: 1–31.

Vallet de Viriville, A. 1841. *Les archives historiques du département de l'Aube et de l'ancien diocèse de Troyes, capitale de la Champagne, depuis le VIIe siècle jusqu'à 1790*. Troyes Municipal Library.

Flanders

Beyers, Frans. n.d. "De familie ʿvander Beurse' in de oorsprong van de handelsbeurzen." Offprint in Municipal Library at Bruges.

Bigwood, G. 1921. *Le régime juridique et économique du commerce de l'argent dans la Belgique du moyen âge.* Brussels, 2 volumes. Académie Royale de Belgique, *Mémoirs*, Tome XIV, 2ème série.

Blockmans, V. 1939. "Eenige nieuwe gegevens over de Gentsche draperie: 1120–1213," pp. 195–260 in *Handelingen van de Koninkl. Commissie voor Geschiedenis*, CIV, 3/4. Brussels. University of Ghent Library.

Blockmans, W. 1983. "Vers une société urbanisée," in *Histoire de Flandre.* ed. by R. Doehaerd. Brussels: La Renaissance du Livre.

Blockmans, W., I. de Meyer, J. Mertens, G. Pauwelyn, and W. Vanderpijpen. 1971. *Studiën betreffende de sociale strukturen te Brugge, Kortrijk en Gent in de 14de en 15de eeuw.* Gent: Rijksuniversiteit.

Bogaerts, P. and Deljoutte, V. 1846. *Notice historique sur les impôts communaux de Bruges depuis leur origines jusqu'en 1294.* Brussels: Em. Devroyé et Cie. In Bruges Municipal Library.

Bruges: City of Art. 1984. Bruges: Gidsenbond Brugge.

Brulez, W. and J. Craeybeckx. 1974. "Les escales au carrefour des Pays-Bas (Bruges et Anvers) 14e–16e siècles," *Receuils de la Société Jean Bodin* 32: 417–474.

Carlier, J. J. 1861–1872. "Origine des foires et des marchés en Flandre," *Annales du Comité Flamand en France* VI: 127–139.

Carson, Patricia and Gaby Danhieux. 1972. *Ghent: A Town for All Seasons.* Ghent: E. Story-Scientia.

de Roover, Raymond. 1948. *Money, Banking and Credit in Medieval Bruges: Italian Merchant-Bankers, Lombards and Money-Changers, A Study in the Origins of Banking.* Cambridge, Massachusetts: Mediaeval Academy of America.

de Roover, Raymond. 1963. "The Organisation of Trade," in *Cambridge Economic History of Europe*, Vol. III. Cambridge: Cambridge University Press.

de Roover, Raymond. 1968. *The Bruges Money Market around 1400.* Brussels: Verhandelingen van de Koninklijke Vlaamse Academie.

de Smet, J. 1933. "L'effectif des milices brugeoises et la population de la ville en 1340," *Revue Belge de Philologie et d'Histoire* XII: 631–636.

Doehaerd, Renée. 1946. *L'expansion économique belge au moyen âge.*

Brussels: La Renaissance du Livre. Reprinted in her *Oeconomica Mediaevalia*.

Doehaerd, Renée. 1983a. "Un berceau d'une région," pp. 15–41 in *Histoire de Flandre*. Brussels: La Renaissance du Livre.

Doehaerd, Renée, ed. 1983b. *Histoire de Flandre: des origines à nos jours*. Brussels: La Renaissance du Livre.

Duclos, Adolphe. 1910. *Bruges: histoire et souvenirs*. Bruges: K. van de Vyvere-Petyt.

Dumont, Jacques. n.d. *Bruges et la mer*. Brussels: Editions Charles Dessart.

Dusauchoit, R. 1978. *Bruges: Portrait d'une ville*. Bruges.

Espinas, Georges. 1923. *La draperie dans la Flandre française au moyen âge*. 2 volumes. Paris: August Picard.

Espinas, G. and Henri Pirenne. 1906–1923. *Recueil de documents relatifs à l'histoire de l'industrie drapière en Flandre*. 4 volumes. Brussels: Publications of La Commission Royale d'Histoire. Additions in 1929 *Bulletin de la Commission Royale d'Histoire* XCIII.

Ferrier de Tourettes, A. 1836. *Description historique, et topographique de la ville de Bruges*. Brussels: Louis Hauman. In Municipal Library at Bruges.

Ferrier de Tourettes, A. 1841. *Description historique, et topographique de Gand*. Brussels: Hauman et cie. In New York Public Library.

Finot, Jules. 1894. *Etude historique sur les relations commerciales entre la France et la Flandre au moyen âge*. Paris: Alphonse Picard.

Fris, Victor. 1913. *Histoire de Gand depuis les origines jusqu'en 1913*. Second edition with a preface by Henri Pirenne. Gand: G. de Tavernier.

Ganshof, François L. n.d. *Pages d'Histoire* on Bruges: 99–106. In Bruges library.

Ganshof, François L. 1949. *La Flandre sous les premiers comtes*. Brussels: La Renaissance du Livre.

Gerneke, C. and F. Siravo. 1980. "Early Industrialization in Gand," *Storia della Città* 17: 57–78.

Gilliat-Smith, Ernest. 1909. *The Story of Bruges*. London: J. M. Dent.

Gilliodts-Van Severen, Louis. n.d. *Bruges: ancien et modern*. In Municipal Library at Bruges.

Gilliodts-Van Severen, Louis. 1881. "Glossaire flamand-latin du 13e siècle," *Bulletin de la Commission Royale d'Histoire*, Série 4, Tome 9: 169–208.

Gilliodts-Van Severen, Louis. Various dates. *Inventaire des archives de la ville de Bruges*. In Municipal Library at Bruges.

Haëpke, R. 1908. *Brügge: Entwicklung zum mittelalterlichen Weltmarkt.* Berlin: K. Curtius.

Hymans, Henri Simon. 1906. *Gand et Tournai.* Paris: H. Laurens.

Lestocquoy, J. 1952a. *Aux origines de la bourgeoisie: les villes de Flandre et d'Italie sous le gouvernement des patriciens, XIe–XVe siècles.* Paris: Presses Universitaires de France.

Letts, Malcolm. 1924. *Bruges and Its Past.* Bruges: C. Beyaert.

Manuscrits datés conservés en Belgique. Tome I, *819–1400.* 1968. Brussels-Gent: E. Story-Scientia. In Municipal Library at Bruges.

Maréchal, Joseph. n.d. "Bruges: Métropole de l'occident," *Internationales Jahrbuch fur Geschichts-und Geographie-Unterricht* Band XIII: 150 *seq.* In Municipal Library at Bruges.

Maréchal, Joseph. 1953. "La colonie espagnole de Bruges du 14e au 16e siècle," *Revue du Nord* 35: 5–40.

Moore, Ellen Wedemeyer. 1985. *The Fairs of Medieval England.* Toronto: The Pontifical Institute of Medieval Studies.

Nicholas, David. 1971. *Town and Countryside: Social, Economic and Political Tensions in Fourteenth-Century Flanders.* Bruges: "De Tempel."

Nicholas, David. 1978. "Structures du peuplement, fonctions urbaines et formation du capital dans la Flandre médiévale, *Annales: Economies. Sociétés. Civilisations.* 33: 501–527.

Nicholas, David. 1979. "The English Trade at Bruges in the Last Years of Edward III," *Journal of Medieval History* 5.

Nicholas, David. 1985. *The Domestic Life in a Medieval City: Women, Children and the Family in Fourteenth-Century Ghent.* Lincoln, Nebraska: University of Nebraska Press.

Nicholas, David. 1988. *The Van Arteveldes of Ghent.* Ithaca: Cornell University Press.

Panorama van Brugge Geschiedschrijving Sedert Duclos (1910). Gedsenbond van Brugge en West-Vlaanderen. 1972. A detailed bibliography on Bruges, and indispensable.

Pilon, Edmond. 1939. *Bruges.* Paris: H. Laurens.

Pirenne, Henri. n.d. "Coup d'oeil sur l'histoire de Gand," preface extract of *Gand.* Vander Haeghen. Extract in University of Ghent library.

Pirenne, Henri. 1895. "La chancellerie et les notaires des comtes de Flandre avant le XIIIe siècle," in *Mélanges Havet.* Paris: Leroux.

Pirenne, Henri. 1897. *Documents relatifs à l'histoire de Flandre pendant la première moitié du XIVe siècle. Commission Royale d'Histoire.* 5m série, Tome 7, No. 124. Brussels: Hayez.

Pirenne, Henri. 1899. "La Hanse Flamande de Londres," *Bulletin de l'Académie Royale de Belgique*. 3m série, Tome 37, 2me partie, No. 1: 65–108.

Pirenne, Henri. 1911. "Le plus ancien règlement de la draperie brugeoisie," *Bulletin de la Commission Royale d'Histoire de Belgique* 80.

Pirenne, Henri. 1929. *Histoire de Belgique*. 7 volumes, 1902–1932. I have used the fifth edition. Vol. I. *Des origines au commencement du XIVe siècle*. Brussels: Maurice Lamertin.

Robinson, Wilfrid. 1899. *Bruges: An Historical Sketch*. Bruges: L. de Plancke.

Saint Génois, Baron Jules de. 1846. *Les voyageurs Belges du XIIIe au XVIIe siècle*. Volume I. Brussels: A. Jamar. Examined at Royal Geographical Society of Egypt. (Preface dated at Gand.)

Vander Haegen, Victor. n.d. *Inventaire des archives de la ville de Gand*. In New York Public Library.

van der Wee, H. 1975. "Structural Changes and Specialization in the Industry of the Southern Netherlands, 1100–1600," *Economic History Review*, Second Series, Vol. 28, No. 2: 203–221.

Vanhoutryve, André. 1972. *Bibliografie van de geschiedenis van Brugge. Handzome, Utigaven Familia et Patria*. In Municipal Library at Bruges.

van Houtte, J.-A. 1943. *Esquisse d'une histoire économique de la Belgique*. Louvain: Editions Universitas.

van Houtte, J.-A. 1952. "Bruges et Anvers, marchés 'nationaux' ou 'internationaux' du XIV au XVIe siècle," *Revue de Nord* 34: 89–109.

van Houtte, J.-A. 1953. "Les foires dans Belgique ancienne," *Recueils de la Société Jean Bodin* V: 175–207.

van Houtte, J.-A. 1966. "The Rise and Decline of the Market of Bruges," *Economic History Review*, Second Series 19: 29–47. Reprinted in *Essays on Medieval and Early Modern Economy*, pp. 249–274.

van Houtte, J.-A. 1967. *Bruges: Essai d'histoire urbaine*. Brussels: La Renaissance du Livre.

van Houtte, J.-A. 1977. *Essays on Medieval and Early Modern Economy and Society*. Leuven: Leuven University Press. Collection of previously published articles.

van Houtte, J.-A. 1982. *De Geschiedenis van Brugge*. Bruges: Lanoo/Tielt/Bussum.

van Werveke, Hans. 1943. *Jacques van Artevelde*. Brussels: La Renaissance du Livre.

van Werveke, Hans. 1944. *Bruges et Anvers; Huit siècles de commerce flamand*. Brussels: Editions de la Librairie Encyclopédique. The Flemish version of this book was published in 1941.

van Werveke, Hans. 1946. *Gand. Esquisse d'histoire sociale.* Brussels: La Renaissance du Livre.

van Werveke, Hans. 1955. "Les villes Belges: Histoire des institutions économiques et sociales," *Recueils de la Société Jean Bodin.* Vol. VII, *La Ville.*

Vercauteren, F. 1950–51. "Documents pour servir à l'histoire des financiers lombards en Belgique," *Bulletin de l'Institut Historique Belge de Rome.*

Verhulst, A. 1960. "Les origines et l'histoire ancienne de la ville de Bruges (IXe–XIIe siècles)," *Le Moyen Age* 66: 37–63.

Verhulst A. 1977. "An Aspect of the Question of Continuity between Antiquity and Middle Ages: The Origin of Flemish Cities between the North Sea and the Schelde," *Journal of Medieval History* 3: 175–206.

Vlaminick, Alphonse de. 1891. "Les origines de la ville de Gand," in *Académie Royale d'Histoire de Belgique.* Mémoire Couronnés. Brussels.

Willems, J. F. 1839. "De la population de quelques villes belges au moyen âge," *Bulletin Académie Royale de Belgique* VI: 162–169.

Italy

Balducci Pegolotti, Francesco de. Latin edition issued in 1936. *La Pratica della Mercatura.* A document of the early fourteenth century. ed. by A. Evans. Cambridge, Massachusetts: The Mediaeval Academy of America. An abridged English version is in Volume II *Cathay and the Way Thither*, 1924, revised 1937. ed. and trans. by H. Yule. Published by the Hakluyt Society.

Benvenuti, Gino. 1977. *Storia della Repubblica di Genova.* Milan: Mursia.

Bettini, Sergio. 1978. *Venezia. Nascita di una città.* Milan: Electa. A history of Venice from its origins to the XIIIth century.

Borsari, Silvano. 1963. *Il dominio veneziano a Creta nel XIII secolo.* Naples: F. Fiorentino.

Braunstein, Philippe. 1967. "Le commerce du fer à Venise au XVe siècle," *Studi Veneziana* VIII (1966): 267–302.

Braunstein, Philippe and Robert Delort. 1971. *Venise: Portrait historique d'une cité.* Paris: Editions du Seuil.

Brion, Marcel. 1962. *Venice: The Masque of Italy.* Trans. by Neil Mann. London: Elek Books.

Brun, R. 1930. "A Fourteenth Century Merchant in Italy," *Journal of Economic and Business History* II: 451–466.

Brunello, Franco. 1981. *Arti e mestieri a Venezia nel Medioevo e nel Rinascimento*. Vicenza: N. Pozza.

Byrne, E. H. 1916. "Commercial Contracts of the Genoese in the Syrian Trade of the 12th Century," *Quarterly Journal of Economics* XXXI: 127–170.

Byrne, E. H. 1919–20. "Genoese Trade with Syria in the 12th Century," *American Historical Review* XXV: 191–219.

Byrne, E. H. 1930. *Genoese Shipping in the Twelfth and Thirteenth Centuries*. Cambridge, Massachusetts: Mediaeval Academy of America.

Cessi, Roberto. 1942a. *Documenti relativi alla storia di Venezia anteriori al Mille*. Vol I, Secolo V–IX; Vol. II, Secolo IX–X. Padua: Gregoriana Editrice.

Cessi, Roberto. 1942b. "Venezia e l'Oriente," pp. 315–343 in *Problemi storici e orientamenti storigrafici . . .* Como. In Marciana Library, Venice.

Cessi, Roberto. 1964. *Un millennio di storia Veneziana*. Venice: Casa di Resparmio sotto gli auspici dell' Ateneo Veneto.

Cessi, Roberto, 1968. *Storia della Repubblica di Venezia*. 2 volumes. Milan-Messina: G. Principato. A new revised and expanded one volume edition was published in 1981. Florence: Giunti Martello.

Cessi, Roberto. 1985. *Venezia nel duecento: tra oriente e occidente*. Venice: Deputazione Editrice.

Chiaudano, Mario. 1970. "Mercanti genovesi nel secolo XII," pp. 123–146 in *Richerche storiche ed economiche in memoria di Corrado Barbagallo*, Vol. II. Naples. In Marciana Library, Venice.

Chivellari, Domenica. 1982. *Venezia*. Milan: Electra.

La Civiltà Veneziana del secolo di Marco Polo. Conferenze di R. Bacchelli, A. Monteverdi, R. S. Lopez, Y. Renouard, O. Demos. 1955. Venice: Centro di Cultura e Civiltà della Fondazione Giorgio Cini.

Commune di Genova. 1983. *Navigazione e Carte Nautiche nei secolo XIII–XVI*. Genoa: Sagep Editrice.

Cracco, Georgio. 1967. *Societa e stato nel medioevo veneziano (secolo XII–XIV)*. Florence: L. S. Olschki.

Delogu, Paolo et al. 1980. *Longobardi e Bizantini*. Turin: U.T.E.T.

De Negri, Teofilo Ossian. 1974. *Storia di Genova*. Milan: A. Martello.

Doehaerd, Renée, ed. 1941, 1952, 1969. *Les relations commerciales entre Gênes, la Belgique et l'Outremont, d'après les archives notariales génois*. 1941. Volume I: XIIIe et XIVe siècles. Brussels and Rome: Palais des Académies. 1969. Vol. II: 1320–1400. ed. by Leone Liagre de Sturler. Brussels and Rome. 1952. Vol. III: 1400–1440. ed. by R. Doehaerd and C. Kerremans.

Edler, Florence. 1934. *Glossary of Medieval Terms of Business: Italian Series 1200–1600*. Cambridge, Massachusetts: Mediaeval Academy of America.

Fugagnollo, Ugo. 1974. *Bisanzio e l'Oriente a Venezia*. Trieste: LINT.

Gênes et l'Outre-mer. 1973, 1980. Tome I, 1973. *Les actes de Caffa du notaire Lamberto di Sambuceto 1289–1290*. ed. by Michèl Balard. Tome II, 1980. *Les actes de Kilia du notaire Antonio di Ponzo 1360*. ed. by Michèl Balard. La Haye: Mouton. Paris: Ecole Pratique des Hautes Etudes, Sorbonne. See also under Balard in Middle East section.

Goy, Richard. 1985. *Chioggia and the Villages of the Venetian Lagoon: Studies in Urban History*. Cambridge: Cambridge University Press.

Hazlitt, W. Carew. 1915. *The Venetian Republic: Its Rise, Its Growth, and Its Fall, A.D. 421–1797*. 2 volumes. London: Adam and Charles Black. Volume I covers A.D. 409–1457.

Headlam, Cecil. 1908. *Venetia and Northern Italy, Being the Story of Venice, Lombardy and Emilia*. London: J. M. Dent.

Heers, Jacques. 1961. *Gênes au XVe siècle*. Paris: S.E.V.P.E.N.

Heers, Jacques. 1962. "Urbanisme et structure sociale à Gênes au moyen âge," pp. 369–412 in Vol. I of *Studi in onore di Amintore Fanfani*. Milan: Istituto Editoriale Cisalpino.

Heers, Jacques. 1977. *Family Clans in the Middle Ages: A Study of Political and Social Structures in Urban Areas*. Trans. by Barry Herbert. Amsterdam: North-Holland Publishing Company.

Heers, Jacques. 1979. *Société et économie à Gênes (XIVe—XVe siècles)*. London: Variorum Reprints.

Herlihy, David. 1985. *Medieval Households*. Cambridge, Massachusetts: Harvard University Press.

Herlihy, David and Christiane Klapisch-Zuber. 1985. *Tuscans and Their Families: A Study of the Florentine Catasto of 1427*. Trans. from the French. New Haven: Yale University Press.

Hocquet, Jean-Claude. 1979, 1982. *Le sel et la fortune de Venise*. 2 volumes. Vol. I, 1979. *Production et monopole*; Vol. II, 1982. *Voiliers et commerce en Méditerranée, 1200–1650*. Second ed. Lille: Hocquet.

Hrochova, Vera. 1967–8. "Le commerce vénitien et les changements dans l'importance des centres de commerce en Grèce du 13e au 15e siècles," *Studi Veneziana . . .* (Florence) IX: 3–34.

Hughes, D. O. 1975. "Urban Growth and Family Structure in Medieval Genoa," *Past and Present* 66: 3–28.

Hyde, John Kenneth. 1973, reissued 1983. *Society and Politics in Medieval Italy: The Evolution of the Civil Life. 1000–1350.* London: Macmillan, Basingstoke.

Kedar, B. Z. 1976. *Merchants in Crisis: Genoese and Venetian Men of Affairs and the Fourteenth-Century Depression.* New Haven: Yale University Press.

Kreuger, Hilmar C. 1957. "Genoese Merchants, Their Partnerships and Investments, 1155 to 1164," pp. 255–272 in *Studi in onore di Armando Sapori*, Vol. I. Milan: Istituto Editoriale Cisalpino.

Lane, Frederic C. 1944. "Family Partnerships and Joint Ventures in the Venetian Republic," *Journal of Economic History* IV: 178–196.

Lane, Frederic C. 1957. "Fleets and Fairs: The Functions of the Venetian Muda," pp. 649–663 in *Studi in onore di Armando Sapori*, Vol. I. Milan: Istituto Editoriale Cisalpino.

Lane, Frederic C. 1963. "Recent Studies on the Economic History of Venice," *Journal of Economic History* XXII, No. 3: 212–224.

Lane, Frederic C. 1966. *Venice and History: The Collected Papers of Frederic C. Lane.* ed. by a committee of colleagues and former students. Baltimore: The Johns Hopkins University Press.

Lane, Frederic C. 1973. *Venice: A Maritime Republic.* Baltimore: The Johns Hopkins University Press.

Lane, Frederic C. and Reinhold Mueller. 1985. *Money and Banking in Medieval and Renaissance Venice*, Vol. I. Baltimore: The Johns Hopkins University Press.

Longworth, Philip. 1974. *The Rise and Fall of Venice.* London: Constable.

Lopez, Robert. 1937. "Aux origines du capitalism génois," in *Annales d'Histoire Economique et Sociale.* In Marciana Library, Venice.

Lopez, Roberto. 1955. "Venezia e le grande linee dell'espansione commerciale del secolo XIII," *Civiltà veneziana del secolo di Marco Polo*: 37–82. Florence: In Marciana Library, Venice.

Lopez, Roberto. 1956. *La prima crisi della banca di Genova (1250–1259).* Milan: Università L. Bocconi.

Lopez, Roberto. 1957. "I primi cento anni di storia documentata della banci di Genova," *Studi in onore di Armando Sapori*, Vol. I: 215–253. Milan: Istituto Editoriale Cisalpino.

Lopez, Robert S. 1964. "Market Expansion: The Case of Genoa," *Journal of Economic History* XXIV: 445–464.

Lopez, Robert S. 1970. "Venice and Genoa: Two Styles, One Success," *Diogenes* 71: 39–47.

Lopez, Robert S. 1975. *Su e giù per la storia di Genova*. Genoa: Università di Genova, Istituto di Paleografia e Storia Medievale.

Luchaire, Julien. 1954. *Les sociétés italiennes du XIIIe au XVe siècle*. Paris: A. Colin.

Luzzatto, Gino. 1954. *Studi di storia econòmica veneziana*. Padua: CEDAM.

Luzzatto, Gino. 1961. *An Economic History of Italy from the Fall of the Roman Empire to 1600*. Trans. by Philip Jones. London: Routledge & Kegan Paul. New York: Barnes & Noble.

Martines, Lauro, ed. 1972. *Violence and Civil Disorder in Italian Cities, 1200–1500*. Berkeley: University of California Press.

McNeill, William. 1974. *Venice: The Hinge of Europe, 1081–1797*. Chicago: University of Chicago Press.

Miozzi, Eugenio. 1957–1969. *Venezia nei secoli*. 4 volumes. Vols. I and II: La Città; Vol. III: La Laguna; Vol. IV: Il Salvamento. Venice: Casa Editrice Libeccio.

Morozzo della Rocca, A. Lombardo. 1940. *Documenti del commercio veneziano nel secoli XI-XIII*. 2 volumes. Rome: Istituto Storico Italiana. In Marciana Library, Venice.

Mueller, Reinhold C. 1977. *The Procuratori di San Marco and the Venetian Credit Market: A Study of the Development of Credit and Banking in the Trecento*. Baltimore and New York: Arno Press.

Musso, Gian Giacomo. 1975. *Navigazione e commercio genovese con il Levante nei documenti dell' Archivio di stato de Genova (Secolo XIV–XV)*. Rome: Pubblicazioni degli archivi de Stato, No. 84.

Norwich, John Julius. 1982. *A History of Venice*. London: Penguin Books. Distributed in New York: Knopf-Random House. This is a reissue in one volume of *Venice: The Rise to Empire*. Volume I, 1977. *Venice: The Greatness and the Fall*. Volume II, 1981. London: Allen Lane.

Origo, Iris. 1957. *The Merchant of Prato: Francesco di Marco Datini, 1335–1410*. New York: Knopf.

Pirenne, Henri. 1933–4. "La fin du commerce des Syriens en Occident," *L'Annuaire de l'Institut de Philologie et d'Histoire Orientales* II: 677–687.

Queller, Donald E. 1986. *The Venetian Patriciate: Reality vs. Myth*. Urbana: University of Illinois Press.

Renouard, Yves. 1962. "Routes, étapes, et vitesses de marche de France à Rome au XIIIe et au XIVe siècles d'après les itinéraires d'Endes Rigaud (1254) et de Barthélemy Bonis (1350)," *Studi in onore di Amintore Fanfani* III: 403–428. Milan.

Renouard, Yves. 1966. *Italia e Francia nel commercio medievale*. Rome: Le Edizioni del Lavoro (Lecce, ITES).

Renouard, Yves. 1968. *Les hommes d'affaires italiens du moyen âge*, 2nd edition. Paris: Armand Colin.

Renouard, Yves. 1969. *Les villes d'Italie, de la fin du Xe siècle au début du XIV siècle*. New edition by Philippe Braunstein. 2 volumes. Paris: S.E.D.E.S. (Société d'Edition d'Enseignement Supérieur). Pp. 79–146 of Vol. I on Venice; pp. 228–258 on Genoa.

Reynolds, R. L. 1931. "Genoese Trade in the Late Twelfth Century, Particularly in Cloth from the Fairs of Champagne," *Journal of Economics and Business History* III: 362–381.

Reynolds, R. L. 1945. "In Search of a Business Class in Thirteenth Century Genoa," *Journal of Economic History* Supplement 5: 1–19.

Runciman, Steven. 1952. "Byzantine Trade and Industry," *Cambridge Economic History of Europe*, Vol. II: 86–118. Cambridge: Cambridge University Press.

Sapori, A. 1952. *Le marchand italien au moyen âge*. Paris. A. Colin. 1970. *The Italian Merchant in the Middle Ages*. Trans. by Patricia Ann Kennen. New York: Norton.

Sayous, A. E. 1929. "Les transformations commerciales dans l'Italie médiévale," *Annales d'Histoire Economique et Sociale* I: 161–176.

Sayous, A. E. 1931. "Der Moderne Kapitalismus de Werner Sombart, et Gênes aux XIIe et XIIIe siècles," *Revue d'Histoire Economique et Sociale* XIX: 427–444.

Sayous, A. E. 1932. "Les opérations des banquiers en Italie et aux foires de Champagne pendant le XIIIe siècle," *Revue Historique* CLXX: 1–31.

Sayous, A. E. 1933. "L'origine de la lettre de change. Les procédés de crédit et de paiement dans les pays crétiens de la Méditerranée occidentale entre le milieu du XIIe et celui du XIIIe siècle," *Revue Historique de Droit Français et Etranger*, 4me Série, Tome XII: 60–112.

Sismondi de Sismonde, J.-C.-L. 1906 reprint. *History of the Italian Republics in the Middle Ages*. London: Longmans Green. Published originally in 1807–1815.

Strayer, Joseph. 1969. "Italian Bankers and Philip the Fair," *Economy, Society, and Government in Medieval Italy: Essays in Memory of Robert L. Reynolds*. ed. by David Herlihy: 113–121. Kent, Ohio: Kent State University Press.

Studi in onore di Armando Sapori. 1957. 3 volumes. Milan: Istituto Editoriale Cisalpino.

Thiriet, Freddy. 1969, 4th edition. *Histoire de Venise*. Paris: Presses Universitaires de France.

Thrupp, Sylvia. 1977. *Society and History: Essays by Sylvia Thrupp*. ed. by Raymond Grew and Nicholas Steneck. Ann Arbor: University of Michigan Press.

Villehardouin, Geoffroi de. 1972 reissue. *La Conquête de Constantinople*. Paris: Firmon-Didot.

Waley, Daniel Philip. 1973. *The Italian City-Republics*. New York: McGraw-Hill.

Yver, G. 1903. *Le commerce et les marchands dans l'Italie méridionale aux XIIIe et XIVe siècles*. Paris: A. Fontemoing. Republished 1968. New York: B. Franklin.

Middle East

General and Mongols

al-Narshakhi, Muhammad ibn Jafar. 1954. *The History of Bukhara*. Trans. by R. N. Frye. Cambridge, Massachusetts: Mediaeval Academy of America.

Balard, Michèl, ed. *Gênes et l'Outre-mer*. 2 volumes. Tome I. 1973. *Les Actes de Caffa du notaire Lamberto di Sambuceto 1289–1290*. Paris: Ecole des Hautes Etudes en Sciences Sociales. Tome II. 1980. *Actes de Kilia du notaire Antonio di Ponzo 1360*. Paris: Ecole des Hautes Etudes en Sciences Sociales.

Barfield, Thomas J. 1990. *The Perilous Frontier: Nomadic Empires and China*. Oxford: Basil Blackwell.

Barthold, V. V. 1928. *Turkestan Down to the Mongol Invasion*. Second edition translated from the original Russian and revised by the author with the assistance of H. A. R. Gibb. London: Luzac and Co.

Blunt, W. 1973. *The Golden Road to Samarkand*. London: Hamish Hamilton.

Bouvat, Lucien. 1927. *L'Empire Mongol, 2e phase*. Histoire du Monde, VIII/3. Paris: Edition de Boccard.

Boyle, John Andrew, trans. 1958. ʿAta Malik Juvaini. *The History of the World Conqueror*. 2 volumes. Cambridge, Massachusetts: Harvard University Press. Covers Mongol dynasties from Genghis Khan through Möngke (1251–1259).

Boyle, John Andrew, ed. 1968. *The Cambridge History of Iran*, Vol. V.

The Seljuk and Mongol Periods. Cambridge: Cambridge University Press.

Boyle, John Andrew, trans. 1971. *The Successors of Genghis Khan*. Translated from the Persian of Rashid al-Din Tabib. New York: Columbia University Press. Covers the period down to the reign of Möngke's great nephew Temur Oljeitu (1294–1307).

Boyle, John Andrew. 1977. *The Mongol World Empire, 1206–1370*. London: Variorum Reprints.

Brent, Peter Ludwig. 1976. *The Mongol World Empire: Genghis Khan: His Triumph and His Legacy*. London: Weidenfeld and Nicolson.

Bretschneider, Emilii V. Reprinted 1910. *Mediaeval Researches from Eastern Asiatic Sources: Fragments towards the Knowledge of the Geography and History of Central and Western Asia from the 13th to the 17th Century*. 2 volumes. London: K. Paul, Trench and Trübner. For Volume I, see Bretschneider (1875, 1876). Vol. II consists of Part III, a lengthy explanation of a Mongol-Chinese medieval map of Central and Western Asia; and Part IV, material on the 15th and 16th centuries (not relevant here).

Bretschneider, E. V. 1875. *Notes on Chinese Mediaeval Travellers to the West*. Shanghai: American Presbyterian Mission Press. This is Part I of Vol. I of *Mediaeval Researches*. It translates Chinese primary documents from 1219, 1220–1221, 1221–1224, and 1259. The last is an account of Hulegu's expedition to western Asia in 1253–1259.

Bretschneider, E. V. 1876. *Notices of the Mediaeval Geography and History of Central and Western Asia Drawn from Chinese and Mongol Writings, and Compared with the Observations of Western Authors in the Middle Ages*. London: Trübner and Co. This is Part II of Vol. I of *Mediaeval Researches*. It translates Chinese documents about the "Mohammedans" and descriptions of expeditions by the Mongols to the west.

Chambers, James. 1985. *The Devil's Horsemen: The Mongol Invasion of Europe*. New York: Atheneum Press.

Charlesworth, Martin. 1924. *Trade Routes and Commerce of the Roman Empire*. Cambridge: Cambridge University Press.

Charol, Michael. 1961, revised 4th imprint. *The Mongol Empire, Its Rise and Legacy*, by Michael Prawdin (pseud.). Trans. by Eden and Cedar Paul. London: Allen & Unwin.

Cleaves, Francis W., trans. 1982. *The Secret History of the Mongols*, Part I. Cambridge, Massachusetts: Harvard University Press.

Commeaux, Charles. 1972. *La vie quotidienne chez les Mongols de la conquête (XIIIe siècle)*. Paris: Hachette.

Dawson, Christopher H., ed. 1955, reprinted 1980. *The Mongol Mission*. New York: AMS Press.

de Rachewiltz, Igor. 1971. *Papal Envoys to the Great Khans*. London: Faber & Faber.

d'Ohsson, C. 1834–35. *Histoire des Mongols depuis Tchinguiz-khan jusqu'à Timour Bey ou Tamerlan*. 4 volumes. The Hague and Amsterdam: Les Frères van Cleef.

Grigor of Akanc' (13th century writer). 1954. *History of the Nation of Archers (the Mongols)*. The Armenian text edited with an English translation and notes by Robert P. Blake and Richard N. Frye. Cambridge, Massachusetts: Harvard-Yenching Institute.

Grousset, René. 1939, reprinted 1948. *L'Empire des steppes: Attila, Genghis-Khan, Tamerlan*. Paris: Payot.

Grousset, René. 1941. *L'Empire Mongol. Ire phase*. Histoire du Monde VIII/3. Paris: Edition de Boccard.

Grousset, René. 1967. *Conqueror of the World*. English trans. by D. Sinor and M. MacKellar. London: Oliver and Boyd.

Guzman, G. 1968. "Simon of Saint-Quentin and the Dominican Mission to the Mongols, 1245–1248." Doctoral Dissertation, Department of History, University of Cincinnati.

Haenisch, Erich, trans. 1941, second edition in 1948. *Die Geheime Geschichte der Mongolen: Aus einer mongolischen Neiderschrift des Jahres 1240 von der Insel Kode'e im Keluren-Fluss*. [The Secret History of the Mongols.] Translated and annotated for the first time. Leipzig: Otto Harrassowitz.

Hodgson, Marshall. 1974. *The Venture of Islam*, Vol. II. *The Expansion of Islam in the Middle Periods*. Chicago: University of Chicago Press.

Joveyni, ʿAlāʾ al-Dīn ʿAtā Malek (1226–1283). 1912–1937. *Taʾrikh-i-Jahān-gushā of ʿAlāʾ ud-Dīn ʿAtā Malik-i-Juwaynī* (composed in 1260), 3 volumes. ed. by Mirza Muhammad ibn ʿAbduʾl-Wahhāb-i-l-Qazwini. London: Luzac & Co. See Boyle (1958) for English translation.

Kwanten, Luc. 1979. *Imperial Nomads: A History of Central Asia, 500–1500*. Philadelphia: University of Pennsylvania Press.

Lach, D. F. 1965. *Asia in the Making of Europe*, Vol. I. Chicago: University of Chicago Press.

Latham, Ronald, trans. 1958. *The Travels of Marco Polo*. London: The Folio Society.

Lombard, M. 1950. "Caffa et la fin de la route mongole," *Annales: Economies. Sociétés. Civilisations*. 5: 100–103.

Lombard, M. 1975. *The Golden Age of Islam*. Trans. by Joan Spencer. Amsterdam: North-Holland Publishing Company.

Lopez, Robert. 1943. "European Merchants in the Medieval Indies: The Evidence of Commercial Documents," *The Journal of Economic History* 3: 164–184.

Martin, H. D. 1950. *The Rise of Chingis Khan and His Conquest of North China*. Baltimore: The Johns Hopkins University Press.

Morgan, D. O. 1982. "Persian Historians and the Mongols," pp. 109–124 in *Medieval Historical Writing in the Christian and Islamic Worlds*. ed. by D. O. Morgan. London: School of Oriental and African Studies.

Morgan, David. 1986. *The Mongols*. Oxford: Basil Blackwell.

Olschki, Leonardo. 1943. *Marco Polo's Precursors*. Baltimore: The Johns Hopkins University Press.

Pelliot, Paul. 1950. *Notes sur l'histoire de la horde d'or*. Paris: Adrien-Maisonneuve.

Pelliot, Paul and L. Hambiss, trans. 1951. *Histoire des campagnes de Genghis Khan*. Leiden: E. J. Brill. A Chinese history compiled during the reign of Kubilai Khan.

Petech, L. 1962. "Les marchands italiens dans l'empire mongol," *Journal Asiatique* CCL, No. 4: 549–574.

Polo, Marco. *Travels*, various editions. See Latham (1958) and Yule, Hakluyt.

Power, Eileen. 1926. "The Opening of Land Routes to Cathay," in *Travel and Travellers of the Middle Ages*. ed. by Arthur P. Newton. London: K. Paul, Trench, Trübner & Co.

Rashid-ad-din [Tabib]. 1836, reprinted 1968. *Jami* at-Tawārikh* [Universal History]. Trans. from original Persian into French by Marc Etienne Quatremère under the title *Histoire des mongols en la Perse, écrité en persan par Raschideldin*. Vol. I only. "Collection Orientale: Histoire des Mongols" I. Amsterdam: Oriental Press.

Rashid al-Din Tabib (1247–1318). 1971. *The Successors of Genghis Khan*. New York: Columbia University Press. See Boyle (1971).

Rockhill, William W. 1900. *The Journey of William of Rubruck to the Eastern Parts of the World, 1253–55, as narrated by himself, with two accounts of the early journal of John of Pian de Carpine*. Translated from the Latin and edited by W. W. Rockhill. London: Hakluyt Society, Series 2, Vol. IV, No. 304.

Saunders, J. J. 1971. *The History of the Mongol Conquests*. London: Routledge and Kegan Paul.

Spuler, Bertold. 1965. *Goldene Horde: Die Mongolen in Russland 1223–1502*. Wiesbaden: Otto Harrassowitz.

Spuler, Bertold. 1972. *History of the Mongols, Based on Eastern and Western Accounts of the Thirteenth and Fourteenth Centuries.* Trans. from the German by Stuart and Helga Drummond. Berkeley: University of California Press.

Steensgaard, Niels. 1973. *Carracks, Caravans and Companies: The Structural Crisis in the European–Asian Trade in the Early 17th Century.* Lund: Studentliteratur.

Waley, A. 1963. *The Secret History of the Mongols and Other Pieces.* London: Allen and Unwin.

Warmington, E. H. 1928. *The Commerce between the Roman Empire and India.* Cambridge: Cambridge University Press.

Wellard, James. 1977. *Samarkand and Beyond: A History of Desert Caravans.* London: Constable.

Yuan-ch'ao pi-shih. *The Secret History of the Mongols.* Vol I. 1982. Trans. from the Chinese by Francis W. Cleaves. Cambridge, Massachusetts: Harvard-Yenching Institute. (See Cleaves, 1982.) There is also a French version: *Histoire secrète des Mongols. Restitution du texte mongol et traduction française des Chapitres I à VI.* 1949. Paris: Libraire d'Amerique et d'Orient. Posthumously published works of Paul Pelliot.

Yule, Sir Henry, trans. and ed. 1913, 1924, 1925, and 1926. *Cathay and the Way Thither, Being a Collection of Medieval Notices of China.* New edition revised throughout in light of the recent discoveries by Henri Cordier. 4 volumes. London: Hakluyt Society, Series 2, Volumes 33, 37, 38, and 41. Includes translations from Marco Polo, Balducci Pegolotti, Odoric de Pordenone, etc.

Arab World

Abu-Lughod, Janet. 1971. *Cairo: 1001 Years of the City Victorious.* Princeton: Princeton University Press.

Ahmad ibn Mājid al-Najdi. 1981. *Kitāb al-Fawāʾid fi usūl al-bahr waʾl-qawāʾid.* Trans. and ed. with a lengthy introduction by G. R. Tibbetts. London: Royal Asiatic Society of Great Britain and Ireland. (See Tibbetts, 1981.)

Akhbar as-Sin wa l-Hind, Relation de la Chine et de l'Inde rédigée en 851 (anonymous). 1948. Texte etabli, traduit et commenté par Jean Sauvaget. Paris: Belles Lettres. See also earlier translations by Reinaud and by Ferrand.

al-Maqrizi. *Al-Mawaʿiz wa al-iʿtibar fi dhikr al-khitat wa al-ʿathar.* 2 volumes. A. H. 1270. Bulaq.

al-Masʿudi (d. 956). 1861–77. *Muruj al-Dhahab wa Maʿadin al-Jauhar.* Arabic text and French translation in C. Barbier de Meynard and Pavet de Courteille, under the title *Les Prairies d'or*. 9 volumes. Paris.

al-Muqaddasi (d. 1000). *Ahsan al-Taqasim fi Marifat al-Aqalim*. Arabic text in de Goeje, Vol. III. English trans. by G. S. A. Ranking and R. F. Azoo. Calcutta, 1897–1910. Partial French trans. by André Miguel. Damascus: Institut Français de Damas, 1963.

al-Yuqubi, Ahmad ibn Abi Yaqub (d. 897). 1937. *Les Pays*. Trans. of *Kitab al-Buldan* by Gaston Wiet. Cairo.

Ashton, Sir Leigh. 1933–34. "China and Egypt," *Transactions of the Oriental Ceramic Society*: 62–72.

Ashtor, Eliyahu. 1956, reprinted 1978. "The Karimi Merchants," *Journal of the Royal Asiatic Society*: 45–56. Reprinted in his *Studies on the Levantine Trade in the Middle Ages*.

Ashtor, Eliyahu. 1974, reprinted 1978. "The Venetian Supremacy in Levantine Trade: Monopoly or Pre-Colonialism?" *Journal of Economic History* (Rome) III: 5–53. Reprinted in his *Studies on the Levantine Trade in the Middle Ages*.

Ashtor, Eliyahu. 1976. *A Social and Economic History of the Near East in the Middle Ages*. Berkeley: University of California Press.

Ashtor, Eliyahu. 1976, reprinted 1978. "The Venetian Cotton Trade in Syria in the Later Middle Ages." Reprinted pp. 675–715 in his *Studies on the Levantine Trade in the Middle Ages*.

Ashtor, Eliyahu. 1978. *Studies on the Levantine Trade in the Middle Ages*. London: Variorum Reprints. Collection of French and English essays reprinted from various journals, 1956–1977.

Ashtor, Eliyahu. 1981. "Levantine Sugar Industry in the Late Middle Ages: A Case of Technological Decline," pp. 91–132 in *The Islamic Middle East, 700–1900: Studies in Economic and Social History*. ed. by Abraham L. Udovitch. Princeton: Darwin Press.

Ashtor, Eliyahu. 1983. *Levant Trade in the Later Middle Ages*. Princeton: Princeton University Press. Primarily on Italian merchants and Mideast trade.

Aubin, J. 1953. "Les Princes d'Ormuz du XIIIe au XVe siècle," *Journal Archéologie* 241: 80–146.

Aubin, J. 1959. "La ruine de Siraf et les routes du Golfe Persique aux XIe et XIIe siècles," *Cahiers de Civilisation Médiévale* X–XIII (July–September): 187–199.

Aubin, J. 1964. "Y a-t-il interruption du commerce par mer entre le Golfe Persique et l'Inde du XIe au XIVe siècles?" pp. 165–173 in *Océan Indien et Méditerranée*. Sixième Colloque d'Histoire Maritime. ed. by Lourenço Marques. Paris: S.E.V.P.E.N.

Ayalon, David. 1956. *Gunpowder and Firearms in the Mamluk Kingdom: A Challenge to a Medieval Society*. London: Vallentine, Mitchell.

Bowen, Richard le Baron. 1949. *Arab Dhows of Eastern Arabia*. Rehoboth, Massachusetts: Privately printed.

Bowen, Richard le Baron. 1951. "The Dhow Sailor," reprinted from *The American Neptune* XI (July).

Brummett, Palmira. 1987. "Venetian/Ottoman Relations." Ph.D. Thesis, University of Chicago. Chapter II is entitled "The Transformation of Venetian Diplomatic Policy Prior to the Conquest of Cairo (1503–1517)."

Cahen, Claude. 1964–65. "Douanes et commerce dans les ports méditerranéens de l'Egypte médiévale d'après le Minhadj d'al-Makhzumi." Offprint by Brill, Leiden. Originally appeared in *Journal of the Economic and Social History of the Orient* 8, Part 3 (November 1964).

Cahen, Claude. 1970. "Le commerce musulman dans l'Océan Indien au moyen âge," pp. 179–189 in *Sociétés et compagnies de commerce en orient et dans l'Océan Indien*. Paris: S.E.V.P.E.N.

Cambridge Economic History series on the Middle East.

Chittick, H. Neville. 1974. *Kilwa: An Islamic Trading City on the East African Coast*. 2 volumes. Nairobi: British Institute in Eastern Africa.

Cook, M. A., ed. 1970. *Studies in the Economic History of the Middle East From the Rise of Islam to the Present Day*. Oxford: Oxford University Press.

Depping, G. B. 1830. *Histoire du commerce entre le Levant et l'Europe depuis les croisades jusqu'à la fondation des colonies d'Amerique*. 2 volumes. Paris: L'Imprimerie Royale.

Dols, Michael. 1981. "The General Mortality of the Black Death in the Mamluk Empire," pp. 397–428 in *The Islamic Middle East, 700–1900: Studies in Economic and Social History*. ed. by Abraham L. Udovitch. Princeton: Darwin Press.

Ehrenkreutz, Andrew. 1981. "Strategic Implications of the Slave Trade between Genoa and Mamluk Egypt in the Second Half of the Thirteenth Century," pp. 335–345 in *The Islamic Middle East: 700–1900: Studies in Economic and Social History*. ed. by Abraham Udovitch. Princeton: Darwin Press.

El-Messiri, Sawsan. 1980. "Class and Community in an Egyptian Textile Town." Ph.D. dissertation, University of Hull (on Mehalla al-Kubra, Egypt).

Encyclopedia of Islam II. 1970. Economy, Society, Institutions. Leiden: E. J. Brill.

Ferrand, Gabriel. 1913 and 1914. *Relations de voyages et textes géographiques arabes, persans et turks relatifs à l'Extrême-Orient du VIIIe au XVIIe siècles.* 2 volumes. Paris: Ernest Leroux.

Ferrand, Gabriel. 1921–28. *Instructions nautiques et routiers Arabes et Portugais des XVe et XVI siècles.* Reproduits, traduits and annotés par G. Ferrand. 6 volumes. Paris: Librairie Orientaliste Paul Geuthner.

Ferrand, Gabriel, trans. and ed. 1922. *Voyage du marchand arabe Sulayman en Inde et en Chine redigé en 851, suivi de remarques par Abû-Zaid Hasan (vers 916).* Paris: Editions Bossard. Volume VII of *Les Classiques de l'Orient.*

Fischel, W. J. 1958. "The Spice Trade in Mamluk Egypt," *Journal of the Economic and Social History of the Orient* 1: 157–174.

Goitein, Solomon. 1957. "The Rise of the Near Eastern Bourgeoisie in Early Islamic Times," *Journal of World History* III: 583–604.

Goitein, Solomon. 1958. "New Light on the Beginnings of the Karimi Merchants," *Journal of the Economic and Social History of the Orient* 1: 175–184.

Goitein, Solomon. 1961. "The Main Industries of the Mediterranean as Reflected in the Records of the Cairo Geniza," *Journal of the Economic and Social History of the Orient* 4: 168–197.

Goitein, Solomon. 1964a. "Artisans en Méditerrannée orientale aux haut moyen âge." *Annales* XIX: 847–868.

Goitein, Solomon. 1964b. *Jews and Arabs: Their Contacts through the Ages.* New York: Schocken Books.

Goitein, Solomon. 1966a. *Studies in Islamic History and Institutions.* Leiden: E. J. Brill.

Goitein, Solomon. 1966b. "The Mentality of the Middle Class in Medieval Islam," pp. 242–254 in *Studies in Islamic History and Institutions.* Leiden: E. J. Brill.

Goitein, Solomon. 1967. *A Mediterranean Society: The Jewish Communities of the Arab World as Portrayed in the Documents of the Cairo Geniza.* Volume I, *Economic Foundations,* of particular significance. Berkeley and Los Angeles: University of California Press. See also subsequent 3 volumes published to 1983. Vol. II on the *Community*; Vol. III on *The Family*; Vol. IV on *Daily Life.* Berkeley and Los Angeles: University of California Press.

Goitein, Solomon. 1980. "From Aden to India: Specimens of the Correspondence of India Traders of the Twelfth Century," *Journal of the Economic and Social History of the Orient* XXII: 43–66.

Groom, N. St. J. 1981. *Frankincense and Myrrh: A Study of the Arab Incense Trade.* London: Longman.

Haarmon, Ulrich. 1984. "The Sons of Mamluks in Late Medieval Egypt," pp. 141–168 in *Land Tenure and Social Transformation in the Middle East*. ed. by Tarif Khalidi. Beirut: American University of Beirut Press.

Hamdan, Gamal. 1962. "The Pattern of Medieval Urbanism in the Arab World," *Geography* (Sheffield) XLVII, No. 215, Part 2 (April) 121–134.

Heyd, W. 1878–1879. *Geschichte des Levantehandels im Mittelalter*. 2 vols. Stuttgart: J. G. Cotta.

Heyd, W. 1885–1886. *Histoire du commerce du Levant au moyen âge*. French translation by Furcy-Raynaud. In 2 volumes of which Vol. I is most relevant. Leipzig: Otto Harrassowitz. This was reissued in Amsterdam in 1983 by A. M. Hakkert. The French translation is very inaccurate; it is better to use the original German.

Hilal, Adil Ismail Muhammad. 1983. "Sultan al-Mansur Qalawun's Policy with the Latin States of Syria 1279–90, and the Fall of Acre." Cairo: American University in Cairo, Department of History. Typed thesis.

Holt, P. M. 1982. "Three Biographies of al-Zahir Baybars," pp. 19–29 in *Medieval Historical Writing in the Christian and Islamic Worlds*. ed. by D. O. Morgan. London: School of Oriental and African Studies.

Hourani, George F. 1951. *Arab Seafaring in the Indian Ocean in Ancient and Early Medieval Times*. Princeton: Princeton University Press.

Hudud al-ʿAlam. "The Regions of the World;"a Persian Geography 372 A.H.–982 A.D. (anonymous). 1937. Translated and explained by V. Minorsky. 1937. Oxford: Oxford University Press. Also E. J. W. Memorial New Series XI, with preface by V. V. Barthold. ed. by C. E. Bosworth. 2nd ed. 1970. London: Luzac.

Humphreys, R. Stephen. 1977. *From Saladin to the Mongols: The Ayyubids of Damascus, 1193–1260*. Albany: The State University of New York Press.

Ibn al-Balkhi (1104–1117). 1912. "Description of the Province of Fars in Persia at the Beginning of the Fourteenth Century," *Journal of the Royal Asiatic Society*: 1–30, 311–339, 865–889.

Ibn Battuta (died 1377). *The Travels of Ibn Battuta, A.D. 1325–1354*. English trans. by Sir H. A. R. Gibb. Full edition in 4 volumes. 1958–71. Cambridge: Cambridge University Press for the Hakluyt Society. See also *Voyages d'Ibn Batoutah*. 1854–1874. Arabic text accompanied by a French translation by C. Defrémery and

Dr. B. R. Sanguinetti. 5 volumes. Paris: Imprimerie Nationale. An English translation of the sections dealing with India, the Maldive Islands, and Ceylon is available by A. Mahdi Husain. 1955. Baroda: Oriental Institute.

Ibn Battuta. Eng. trans. of selections. 1919. *Travels in Asia and Africa, 1325–1354*. Trans. by H. A. R. Gibb. London: G. Routledge & Sons. Reissued 1969. New York: A.M. Kelley.

Ibn Hawqal, Abu al-Qasim Muhammad. *Kitab Surat al-ʿArd*. French trans. by J. H. Kramers and Gaston Wiet. 1864. *Configuration de la terre*. Paris: Maison Neuve & Larose.

Ibn Hawqal (d. 988). 1800. *The Oriental Geography of Ebn Haukal, an Arabian Traveller of the Tenth Century*. Trans. by William Ouseley. London: Wilson & Co.

Ibn Iyas. 1945. *Histoire des mamlouks circassiens*. Trans. by Gaston Wiet. Cairo: Imprimerie de l'Institut Français d'Archéologie Orientale.

Ibn Iyas (1448–ca.1524). 1955. *Journal d'un bourgeois du Caire: Chronique d'Ibn Iyâs*. Traduit et annoté par Gaston Wiet. Paris: A. Colin.

Ibn Jubayr, Travels of. 1952. Trans. by J. C. Broadhurst. London: Jonathan Cape.

Issawi, Charles. 1970. "The Decline of Middle Eastern Trade, 1100–1850," pp. 245–266 in *Islam and the Trade of Asia: A Colloquium*. ed. by D. S. Richards. Philadelphia: University of Pennsylvania Press.

Jacoby, David. 1977. "L'expansion occidentale dans le Levant: les Vénetiens à Acre dans la seconde moitié du treizième siècle," *The Journal of Medieval History* 3: 225–264. Reprinted in Jacoby (1979).

Jacoby, David. 1979. *Recherches sur la Méditerranée orientale du XIIe au XVe siècles. Peuples, sociétés, économies*. London: Variorum Reprints.

Kuwabara, J. 1928, 1935. "P'u shou-keng. . . . A General Sketch of the Trade of the Arabs in China during the T'ang and Sung Eras," *Memoirs of the Research Department of the Toyo Bunko* II: 1–79; VII: 1–104.

Labib, Subhi. 1965. *Handelsgeschichte Ägyptens im Spätmittelalter (1171–1517)*. Wiesbaden: F. Steiner.

Labib, Subhi. 1970. "Les marchands Karimis en Orient et sur l'Océan Indien," pp. 209–214 in *Sociétés et compagnies de commerce en orient et dans l'Océan Indien*. Paris: S.E.V.P.E.N.

Lamb, A. 1964. "A Visit to Siraf, an Ancient Port of the Persian Gulf," *Journal of the Malayan Branch of the Royal Asiatic Society* XXXVII: 1–19.

Lambton, A. 1962. "The Merchant in Medieval Islam," pp. 121–130 in *A Locust's Leg, Studies in Honour of S. H Taqizadeh*. London: Percy Lund, Humphries & Co.

Lapidus, Ira M. 1967. *Muslim Cities in the Later Middle Ages*. [Aleppo, Damascus, some Cairo.] Cambridge, Massachusetts: Harvard University Press. Second edition Cambridge University Press, 1984.

Le Lannous, Maurice. 1970. "Les grandes voies de relations entre l'Orient et l'Occident," pp. 21–28 in *Sociétés et compagnies de commerce en orient et dans l'Océan Indien*. Paris: S.E.V.P.E.N.

Lewis, Bernard. 1948–50. "The Fatimids and the Route to India," *IFM*, XI.

Lopez, R. S., Harry Miskimin, and Abraham Udovitch. 1970. "England to Egypt, 1350–1500: Long-Term Trends and Long-Distance Trade," pp. 93–128 in *Studies in the Economic History of the Middle East*. ed. by M. A. Cook. London: Oxford University Press.

Marques, Lourenço, ed. 1964. *Océan Indien et Méditerranée*. Sixième Colloque d'Histoire Maritime. Paris: S.E.V.P.E.N.

Martin, Esmond Bradley. 1978. *Cargoes of the East: the Ports, Trade and Culture of the Arabian Seas and Western Indian Ocean*. London: Elm Tree Books.

Minorsky, M. V. 1951. "Géographes et voyageurs musulmans," *Bulletin de la Société Royale de Géographie d'Egypte* XXIV: 19–46.

Mollat, M. 1971. "Les relations de l'Afrique de l'Est avec Asie," *Cahiers d'Histoire Mondiale* XIII, No. 2 (Neuchatel): 291–316.

Morley, J. A. E. 1949. "The Arabs and the Eastern Trade," *Journal of the Malayan Branch of the Royal Asiatic Society* XII: 143–175.

Pauty, E. 1951. "Villes spontanées et villes crées en Islam," *Annales de l'Institut d'Etudes Orientales* IX (Algiers): 52–75.

Petry, Carl F. 1981. *The Civilian Elite of Cairo in the Later Middle Ages*. Princeton: Princeton University Press.

Pirenne, Jacqueline. 1970. "Le développement de la navigation Egypte-Inde dans l'antiquité," pp. 101–119 in *Sociétés et compagnies de commerce en orient et dans l'Océan Indien*. Paris: S.E.V.P.E.N.

Prawer, J. 1951. "The *Assise de teneure* and the *Assise de vente*; a Study of Landed Property in the Latin Kingdom," *The Economic History Review*, 2nd series IV: 77–87.

Rabie, Hassanein M. 1972. *The Financial System of Egypt A. H. 564–741, A.D. 1169–1341*. London: Oxford University Press.

Reinaud, J. T. 1845. *Relation des voyages faits par les Arabes et les Persans dans l'Inde et à la Chine dans le IXe siècle de l'ère Chrétienne*.

Arabic text and French trans. of Hasan ibn Yazid Abu-Zayd al-Sirafi. Paris: Imprimerie Royale. 2 volumes: Tome I, Introduction (pp. i–clxxx) and translation; Tome II, Arabic text. See also Ferrand and Sauvaget.

Richard, Jean. 1976. "Colonies marchandes privilegiées et marché seigneurial: La fonde d'Acre et ses 'droitures'," reprinted in his *Orient et Occident au moyen âge: contact et relations (XIIe–XVes)*. London: Variorum Reprints.

Richards, D. S. ed. 1970. *Islam and the Trade of Asia: A Colloquium*. Philadelphia: University of Pennsylvania Press.

Richards, D.S. 1982. "Ibn Athir and the Later Parts of the *Kamil*: A Study in Aims and Methods," pp. 76–108 in *Medieval Historical Writing in the Christian and Islamic Worlds*. ed. by D.O. Morgan. London: School of Oriental and African Studies.

Rodinson, Maxime. Original 1966, English trans. 1974. *Islam and Capitalism*. London: Allen Lane.

Sauvaget, Jean. 1934. "Esquisse d'une histoire de la ville de Damas," *Revue d'Etudes Islamiques*: 421–480.

Sauvaget, Jean. 1940. "Sur d'anciennes instructions nautiques arabes pour les mers de l'Indes," *Journal Asiatique*: 11–20.

Sauvaget, Jean. 1941. *Alep: Essai sur le développement d'une grande ville syrienne*. Text and Atlas in 2 volumes. Paris: Paul Geuthner.

Sauvaget, Jean., ed. and trans. 1948. *Akhbar as-Sin wa l'Hind, Relation de la Chine et de l'Inde*. Paris: Belles Lettres.

Sauvaget, Jean, ed. 1949. *La Chronique de Damas d'al-Jazari, Années 689–698 H*. Paris: H. Champion.

Scanlon, George. 1970. "Egypt and China: Trade and Imitation," pp. 81–95 in *Islam and the Trade of Asia: A Colloquium*. ed. by D. S. Richards. Philadelphia: University of Pennsylvania Press.

Serjeant, R. B. 1963. *The Portuguese off the South Arabian Coast*. Oxford: The Clarendon Press.

Shboul, Ahmad M. H. 1979. *Al-Masʿudi and His World; a Muslim Humanist and His Interest in Non-Muslims*. London: Ithaca Press.

Stern, S. M. 1967. "Ramisht of Siraf, A Merchant Millionaire of the Twelfth Century," *Journal of the Royal Asiatic Society*: 10–14.

Teixeira da Mota, A. 1964. "Méthodes de navigation et cartographie nautique dans l'Océan Indien avant le XVI siècle," pp. 49–90 in *Océan Indien et Méditerranée*. Sixième Colloque International d'Histoire Maritime. Paris: S.E.V.P.E.N.

Tibbetts, G. R. 1981. Trans. and ed. with lengthy introduction. *Arab Navigation in the Indian Ocean before the Coming of the Portuguese. The Kitab al-fawaʾid fi usul al-bahr wa'l-qawaʾid of Ah-*

mad B. Majid al-Najdi. London: Royal Asiatic Society of Great Britain and Ireland.

Toussaint, Auguste. 1966. *A History of the Indian Ocean.* London: Routledge and Kegan Paul.

Tyan, Emile. 1960. *Histoire de l'organisation judiciare en pays d'Islam.* 2nd ed. rev. Leiden: E. J. Brill.

Udovitch, Abraham. 1967. "Credit as a Means of Investment in Medieval Islamic Trade," *Journal of African and Oriental Studies* 80: 260–264.

Udovitch, Abraham. 1970a. *Partnership and Profit in Medieval Islam.* Princeton: Princeton University Press.

Udovitch, Abraham. 1970b. "Commercial Techniques in Early Medieval Islamic Trade," pp. 37–62 in *Islam and the Trade of Asia: A Colloquium.* ed. by D. S. Richards. Philadelphia: University of Pennsylvania Press.

Udovitch, Abraham. 1979, reprinted 1981. "Bankers without Banks: Commerce, Banking and Society in the Islamic World of the Middle Ages," pp. 255–273 in *The Dawn of Modern Banking.* New Haven: Yale University Press. Reprinted Princeton: Program in Near Eastern Studies.

Udovitch, Abraham, ed. 1981. *The Islamic Middle East, 700–1900: Studies in Economic and Social History.* Princeton: Darwin Press.

Udovitch, Abraham. 1985. "Islamic Law and the Social Context of Exchange in the Medieval Middle East," *History and Anthropology* I (England): 445–464.

Watson, Andrew M. 1981. "A Medieval Green Revolution: New Crops and Farming Techniques in the Early Islamic World," pp. 29–58 in *The Islamic Middle East, 700–1900: Studies in Economic and Social History.* ed. by Abraham Udovitch. Princeton: Darwin Press.

Weissman, Keith. 1986. Lecture at University of Chicago. Unpublished.

Wiet, Gaston. 1955. "Les marchands d'épices sous les sultans mamlouks," *Cahiers d'Histoire Egyptienne,* série VII, fasc. 2 (May): 81–147.

Wiet, Gaston. 1964. *Cairo: City of Art and Commerce.* Norman: University of Oklahoma Press.

Wiet, Gaston. 1971. *Baghdad: Metropolis of the Abbasid Caliphate.* Trans. by Seymour Feiler. Norman: University of Oklahoma Press.

Ziadeh, Nicola A. 1953. *Urban Life in Syria under the Early Mamluks.* Beirut: American Press.

Ziadeh, Nicola A. 1964. *Damascus Under the Mamluks.* Norman: University of Oklahoma Press.

Asia

General and India

Abulfeda (1273–1331). 1957. "Abu l-Fida's Description of India (Hind and Sind)," trans. by S. Maqbul Ahmad and Muhammad Muzaffer Andarabi. *Medieval India Quarterly* II: 147–170. Selections from *Taqwin al-Buldan* of Abu al-Fida.

al-Idrisi. 1960. *India and the Neighbouring Territories in the Kitab Nuzhat al-Mushtaq fi-Khiteraq al-ʿAfaq of al-Sharif al-Idrisi*. Trans. and commentary by S. Maqbul Ahmad, with a forward by V. Minorsky. Leiden: E. J. Brill.

Anstey, V. 1952. *The Economic Development of India*. London and New York: Longmans, Green and Co.

Appadorai, A. 1936. *Economic Conditions in Southern India (A.D. 1000–1500)*. 2 volumes. Madras: University of Madras.

Arasaratnam, Sinnappah. 1986. *Merchants, Companies, and Commerce on the Coromandel Coast, 1650–1740*. Delhi: Oxford University Press.

Attman, Artur. 1981. *The Bullion Flow between Europe and the East, 1000–1750*. Goteborg: Kungl. Veternskaps-Och Vitterhessamhallet.

Ballard, George A. 1984. *Rulers of the Indian Ocean*. New York-Delhi: Neeraj Publishing House.

Barbosa, Duarte, 1867, reprinted 1970. *A Description of the Coasts of East Africa and Malabar*. ed. and trans. by Henry J. Stavely. Originally published Hakluyt Society, First Series No. 11; reprinted London.

Bartholomew, J. G. 1913. *A Literary and Historical Atlas of Asia*. London: J. M. Dent & Sons.

Bastin, John Sturgus. 1961. "The Changing Balance of the Southeast Asian Pepper Trade," *Essays on Indonesian and Malayan History* I: 19–52. Singapore: Eastern Universities Press.

Bayly, C.A. 1985. "State and Economy in India over Seven Hundred Years," *Economic History Review*, Second Series 38, No. 4: 583–596.

Beckingham, C. F. and G. W. B. Huntingford, editors [of Francisco Alvares]. 1961. *The Prester John of the Indies*. London: Cambridge University Press, Hakluyt Society. 2 volumes.

Bhattacharya, Bimalendu. 1979. *Urban Developments in India Since Prehistoric Times*. Delhi: Shree Publishing House.

Bhattacharya, S. and R. Thapar, eds. 1986. *Situating Indian History*. Delhi: Oxford University Press.

Byers, T. J. and H. Mukhia, eds. 1985. *Feudalism and Non-European Societies*. London: Frank Cass.

The Cambridge Economic History of India. 1982. Vol. I. *c. 1200–c. 1750*. ed. by T. Raychaudhuri and Irfan Habib. Cambridge: Cambridge University Press. See the chapters by Simon Digby and Burton Stein.

Chaudhuri, K. N. 1985. *Trade and Civilisation in the Indian Ocean: An Economic History from the Rise of Islam to 1750*. Cambridge: Cambridge University Press.

Cortesão, A., ed. 1944. *The Suma Oriental of Tomé Pires*. 2 volumes. London: The Hakluyt Society.

Dallapiccola, A. L. and S. Z. Lallemant, eds. 1985. *Vijayanagara: City and Empire—New Currents of Research*. Stuttgart: Steiner Verlag.

Das Gupta, Ashin. 1967. *Malabar in Asian Trade: 1740–1800*. Cambridge: Cambridge University Press. Includes section on earlier period.

Digby, Simon. 1982. "The Maritime Trade of India," pp. 125–159 in *The Cambridge Economic History of India*, Vol. 1. ed. by T. Raychaudhuri and Irfan Habib. Cambridge: Cambridge University Press.

Elliot, Henry M. and John Dowson. Original 1867–1877, reprinted 1969. *The History of India, as Told by Its Own Historians*. 8 volumes. Allahabad: Kitab Mahal.

Fritz, John M., George Mitchell, and M. S. Nagaraja Rao. 1985. *Where Kings and Gods Meet*. Tucson: University of Arizona Press.

Goitein, S. D. 1954. "From the Mediterranean to India: Documents on the Trade to India, South Arabia, and East Africa from the Eleventh and Twelfth Centuries," *Speculum* XXIX: 181–197.

Goitein, S. D. 1963. "Letters and Documents on the India Trade in Medieval Times," *Islamic Culture* 37, No. 3: 188–205.

Gopal, Surendra. 1975. *Commerce and Crafts in Gujarat: A Study in the Impact of European Expansion on Precapitalist Economy*. New Delhi: People's Publishing House.

Grewel, J. S. and Indu Banga, eds. 1981. *Studies in Urban History*. Amritsar: Guru Nanak Deo University.

Habib, Irfan. 1976. "Notes on the Indian Textile Industry in the Seventeenth Century," *S. C. Sarkar Felicitation Volume*. New Delhi.

Habib, Irfan. 1980. "The Technology and Economy of Mughal India," *The Indian Economic and Social History Review* XVII: 1–34.

Habib, Irfan. 1982. "Northern India Under the Sultanate," pp. 45–101 in *The Cambridge Economic History of India*, Vol. 1. ed. by T.

Raychaudhuri and Irfan Habib. Cambridge: Cambridge University Press.

Hall, D. G. E. 1981. *A History of South-East Asia*, 4th ed. London: The Macmillan Press.

Hall, Kenneth. 1978. "International Trade and Foreign Diplomacy in Early Medieval South India," *Journal of the Economic and Social History of the Orient* XXI: 75–98.

Hall, Kenneth R. 1980. *Trade and Statecraft in the Age of the Colas*. New Delhi: Abhinav Publications.

Heitzman, E. J. 1985. "Gifts of Power, Temples, Politics and the Economy in Medieval South India." Ph.D. dissertation, University of Pennsylvania.

Husayn Nainar. 1942. *Arab Geographers' Knowledge of South India*. Madras: University of Madras.

Ibn Battuta. 1955. *The Rehla of Ibn Battuta (India, Maldive Islands and Ceylon)*. Trans. with comments by A. Mahdi Husain. Baroda: Oriental Institute.

Indrapala, K. 1971. "South Indian Mercantile Communities in Ceylon, circa 950–1250," *The Ceylon Journal of Historical and Social Studies*, New Series 1, No. 2: 101–113.

Karashima, N. 1984. *South Indian History and Society: Studies from Inscriptions, 850–1800*. Delhi: Oxford University Press.

Krishna Ayyar, K. V. 1938. *The Zamorins of Calicut, From Earliest Times Down to A.D. 1806*. Calicut: Norman Printing Bureau.

Krishna Ayyar, K. V. 1966. *A Short History of Kerala*. Ernakulum: Pai & Co.

Krishnaswami Pillai, A. 1964. *The Tamil Country under Vijayanagaru*. Annamalai Historical Series No. 20. Annamalainagar: Annamalai University.

Loewe, Michael. 1971. "Spices and Silk: Aspects of World Trade in the First Seven Centuries of the Christian Era," *Journal of the Royal Asiatic Society of Great Britain and Ireland*, No. 2: 166–179.

Logan, William. Reprinted 1981. *Malabar*. 2 volumes. Trivandrum: Charithram Publications.

Mahalingam, T. V. 1940. *Administration and Social Life under Vijayanagar*. Madras: University of Madras.

Mahalingam, T. V. 1951. *Economic Life in the Vijayanagar Empire*. Madras: University of Madras.

Mahalingam, T. V. 1969. *Kancipuram in Early South Indian History*. New York & Madras: Asia Publishing House.

Miller, J. Innes. 1969. *The Spice Trade of the Roman Empire, 29 B.C.– A.D. 641*. Oxford: The Clarendon Press.

Mines, Mattison. 1984. *The Warrior Merchants: Textiles, Trade and Territory in South India*. Cambridge: Cambridge University Press. (Deals with contemporary period but there are precedents.)

Misra, S. C. 1981. "Some Aspects of the Self-Administering Institutions in Medieval Indian Towns," pp. 80–90 in *Studies in Urban History*. ed. by J. S. Grewel and Indu Banaga. Amritsar: Guru Nanak Deo University.

Mookerji, R. K. 1912, 2nd ed. 1962. *Indian Shipping: A History of the Sea-Borne Trade and Maritime Activity of the Indians from the Earliest Times*. 2nd edition. Allahabad: Kitab Mahal.

Mukhia, H. 1981. "Was There Feudalism in Indian History?" *Journal of Peasant Studies* VIII: 273–310.

Natkiel, Richard and Antony Preston. c. 1986. *The Weidenfeld Atlas of Maritime History*. London: Weidenfeld and Nicolson.

Nilakanta Sastri, K. A. A. 1932a. *Studies in Cola History and Administration*. Madras: University of Madras.

Nilakanta Sastri. K. 1932b. "A Tamil Merchant-Guild in Sumatra," pp. 314–327 in *Tijdschrift voor Indische Taal-. Land-. und Volkenkunde*.

Nilakanta Sastri, K. A. A. 1938. "The Beginnings of Intercourse between India and China," *Indian Historical Quarterly* 14: 380–387.

Nilankanta Sastri, K. A. A. 1955. *The Colas*. 2nd edition. Madras: University of Madras.

Nilakanta Sastri, K. A. A. 1976. fourth rev. ed. *A History of South India from Prehistoric Times to the Fall of Vijayanagar*. Madras and London: Oxford University Press.

Nilakanta Sastri, K. A. A. 1978. *South India and South-East Asia: Studies in Their History and Culture*. Mysore: Geetha Book House.

Nilakanta Sastri, K. A. A. and N. Venkataramanayya, eds. 1946. *Further Sources of Vijayanagara History*. 3 volumes. Madras: University of Madras.

Palat, Ravi Arvind. 1983. "The Vijayanagara Empire: Reintegration of the Agrarian Order of Medieval South India, 1336–1565." Unpublished paper presented to Conference on the Early State and After, Montreal, revised version in *Early State Dynamics*. ed. by J. J. M. Claessen and P. van de Velde. Leiden: E. J. Brill, in press.

Palat, Ravi Arvind. 1986. "From World-Empire to World Economy: Changing Forms of Territorial Integration and Political Domination in Medieval South India." Presented to the Conference on South Asia and World Capitalism at Tufts University. Unpublished paper available from Suny-Binghamton: Fernand Braudel Center.

Pillay, K. K. 1963. *South India and Ceylon*. Madras: University of Madras.

Pillay, K. K. 1969. *A Social History of the Tamils*. Madras: University of Madras.

Poujade, Jean. 1946. *La route des Indes et ses navires*. Paris: Payot.

Ramaswamy, Vijaya. 1980. "Notes on the Textile Technology in Medieval India with Special Reference to South India," *Indian Economic and Social History Review* XVII, 2: 227–241.

Ramaswamy, Vijaya. 1985a. "The Genesis and Historical Role of the Masterweavers in South Indian Textile Production," *Journal of the Economic and Social History of the Orient* XXVIII: 294–325.

Ramaswamy, Vijaya. 1985b. *Textiles and Weaving in Medieval South India*. Delhi: Oxford University Press.

Raychaudhuri, Tapan and Irfan Habib, eds. 1982. *The Cambridge Economic History of India*. Volume I: *c. 1200–c. 1750*. Cambridge: Cambridge University Press.

Richard, Jean. 1968. "European Voyages in the Indian Ocean and the Caspian Sea," *Iran: Journal of Persian Studies* VI: 45–52.

Richards, John, ed. 1983. *Precious Metals in the Later Medieval and Early Modern Worlds*. Durham, North Carolina: Duke University Press.

Richards, John F. 1986 unpublished. "Precious Metals and India's Role in the Medieval World Economy." Paper presented to the Conference on South Asia and World Capitalism, Tufts University.

Rockhill, W. W. 1913–1915. "Notes on the Relations and Trade of China with the Eastern Archipelago and the Coasts of the Indian Ocean during the Fourteenth Century," in *T'oung Pao* (Leiden). Part I in Vol. XIV (1913), pp. 473–476; Vol. XV (1914), pp. 419–447; Vol. XVI (1915), pp. 61–159, 234–271, 374–392, 435–467, 604–626.

Sastry, K. R. R. 1925. *South Indian Guilds*. Madras: Indian Publishing House.

Schwartzberg, Joseph E., ed. 1978. *A Historical Atlas of South Asia*. Chicago: University of Chicago Press.

Sharma, R. S. 1965. *Indian Feudalism: c. 300–1200*. Calcutta: University of Calcutta.

Sharma, R. S. 1985. "How Feudal was Indian Feudalism?" *Journal of Peasant Studies* XII: 19–43.

Singaravelu, S. 1966. *Social Life of the Tamils: The Classical Period*. Kuala Lumpur: University of Malaya.

Singh, M. P. 1985. *Town, Market, Mint and Port in the Mughal Empire 1556–1707: An Administrative-cum-Economic Study*. New Delhi: Adam Publishers.

Spencer, George W. 1983. *The Politics of Expansion: the Chola Conquest of Sri Lanka and Sri Vijaya*. Madras: New Era Press.

Stein, Burton. 1960. "The Economic Function of a Medieval South Indian Temple," *Journal of Asian Studies* 9, No. 2: 163–176.

Stein, Burton. 1965. "Coromandel Trade in Medieval India," pp. 47–62 in *Merchants and Scholars: Essays in the History of Exploration and Trade*. ed. by John Parker. Minneapolis: University of Minnesota Press.

Stein, Burton. 1969. "Integration of the Agrarian System of South India," pp. 173–215 in *Land Control and Social Structure in Indian History*. ed. by R. E. Frykenberg. Madison: University of Wisconsin Press.

Stein, Burton, ed. 1975. *Essays on South India*. Asian Studies Program, Hawaii: The University Press of Hawaii. See, in particular, his essay, "The State and the Agrarian Order in Medieval South India: A Historiographical Critique," pp. 64–91.

Stein, Burton. 1980. *Peasant State and Society in Medieval South India*. Delhi, Oxford: Oxford University Press.

Stein, Burton. 1982a. "South India," pp. 14–42 in *The Cambridge Economic History of India*, Vol. I. ed. by T. Raychaudhuri and Irfan Habib. Cambridge: Cambridge University Press.

Stein, Burton. 1982b. "Vijayanagara c. 1350–1564," pp. 102–124 in *The Cambridge Economic History of India*, Vol. I. ed. by T. Raychaudhuri and Irfan Habib. Cambridge: Cambridge University Press.

Stein, Burton. 1985. "Politics, Peasants and the Deconstruction of Feudalism in Medieval India," *Journal of Peasant Studies* XII: 54–86.

Sundaram, K. 1968. *Studies in Economic and Social Conditions of Medieval Andhra, A.D. 1000–1600*. Madras: Triveni Publishers.

Tibbetts, G. R. 1956. "Pre-Islamic Arabia and South-East Asia," *Journal of the Malayan Branch of the Royal Asiatic Society* XXIX: 182–208.

Venkatarama Ayyar, K. R. 1947. "Medieval Trade, Craft, and Merchant Guilds in South India," *Journal of Indian History* 25: 271–280.

Verma, H. C. 1978. *Medieval Routes to India: Baghdad to Delhi: A Study of Trade and Military Routes*. Calcutta: Naya Prokash.

Wijetunga, W. M. K. 1966. "South Indian Corporate Commercial Organizations in South and Southeast Asia," *First International Conference Seminar of Tamil Studies*: 494–508. Kuala Lumpur: University of Malaya Press.

Wittfogel, Karl. 1957. *Oriental Despotism: A Comparative Study of Total Power*. New Haven: Yale University Press.

Zaki, Muhammad. 1981. *Arab Accounts of India during the Fourteenth Century*. New Delhi: Munshiram Manohartel Publishers.

Strait of Malacca

Bartholomew, J. G. 1913. *A Literary and Historical Atlas of Asia*. London: J. M. Dent & Sons.

Bastin, John and Harry J. Benda. 1968. *A Short History of Modern South East Asia*. Kuala Lumpur: Federal Publications.

Bastin, John S., R. O. Winstedt, and Roelof Roolvink, eds. 1964. *Malayan and Indonesian Studies: Essays Presented to Sir Richard Winstedt on His Eighty-Fifth Birthday*. Oxford: The Clarendon Press.

Berg, Lodewijk Willem Christian van den. 1887. *Hadthramut and the Arab Colonies in the Indian Archipelago*. Partial English trans. by C. W. H. Sealy. Bombay: Government Central Press. Part II includes material on Arab immigrant groups in Sumatra but for the nineteenth century only.

Braddell, Sir Roland. Reprinted 1970. *A Study of Ancient Times in the Malay Peninsula*. Kuala Lumpur: Malayan Branch of the Royal Asiatic Society Reprint.

Bronson, Bennet. 1977. "Exchange at the Upstream and Downstream Ends: Notes toward a Functional Model of the Coastal States in Southeast Asia," pp. 39–52 in *Economic Exchange and Social Interaction in Southeast Asia*. ed. by Karl L. Hutterer. Ann Arbor: Michigan Papers on South and Southeast Asia, No. 13.

Brown, C. C., trans. 1952. "Sejarah Melayu or 'Malay Annals,' " *Journal of the Malayan Branch of the Royal Asiatic Society* XXV, Parts 2 and 3: 6–276.

Carey, Iskandar. 1976. *Orang Asli: The Aboriginal Tribes of Peninsular Malaysia*. Kuala Lumpur: Oxford University Press.

Coedès, G. 1918. "Le royaume de Crivijaya," *Bulletin de l'Ecole Française d'Extrême-Orient* (Hanoi and Paris) XVIII, No. 6: 1–36.

Coedès, G. 1968. *The Indianized States of Southeast Asia*. ed. by W. F. Vella and trans. by S. B. Cowing. Honolulu: East-West Center. Translation of *Les états hindouises d'Indochine et d'Indonésie*. Paris: Edition de Boccard, 1964 (first edition 1949).

Coedès, G. 1966, reissued 1983. English trans. *The Making of South East Asia*. Berkeley: University of California Press paper reissue.

Cordier, Henri. 1912–32. *Bibliothèca Indosinica*. In *Etudes Asiatiques*.

Publications de l'Ecole Française d'Extrême-Orient. 4 volumes and index. Paris: Imprimerie Nationale, E. Leroux.

Cortesão, A., ed. 1944. *The Suma Oriental of Tomé Pires.* 2 volumes. London: The Hakluyt Society.

Cowan, C. D., ed. 1964. *The Economic Development of South East Asia: Studies in Economic History and Political Economy.* London: Allen & Unwin.

Crawfurd, John. 1820. *History of the Indian Archipelago.* 3 volumes. Edinburgh: Archibald Constable.

Crawfurd, J. 1856, reissued 1971. *A Descriptive Dictionary of the Indian Islands and Adjacent Countries.* Originally London. Reissued Kuala Lumpur and New York: Oxford University Press.

Di Meglio, R. R. 1970. "Arab Trade with Indonesia and the Malay Peninsula from the 8th to the 16th Century," pp. 105–136 in *Islam and the Trade of Asia: A Colloquium.* ed. by D. S. Richards. Philadelphia: University of Pennsylvania Press.

Douglas, F. W. 1949, reprinted 1980. "Notes on the Historical Geography of Malaya. Sidelights on the Malay Annals," pp. 459–515 in *A Study of Ancient Times in the Malay Peninsula.* ed. by R. Braddell. Kuala Lumpur: Malayan Branch of the Royal Asiatic Society Reprint.

Ferrand, G. 1922. "L'empire sumatranais de crivijaya," *Journal Asiatique* (Paris) XX (July–September): 1–104; (October–December): 161–246.

Hall, D. G. E. 1961. *Historians of South East Asia.* London: Oxford University Press.

Hall, D. G. E. 1964, reissued 1968. *A History of South-East Asia.* London and New York: St. Martin's Press.

Hall, Kenneth R. 1985. *Maritime Trade and State Development in Early Southeast Asia.* Honolulu: University of Hawaii Press.

Heard, Nigel. 1968. *The Dominance of the East.* London: Blandford Press.

Hutterer, Karl L., ed. 1977. *Economic Exchange and Social Interaction in Southeast Asia. Perspectives from Prehistory and Ethnography.* Ann Arbor: University of Michigan Papers on South and Southeast Asia, No. 13.

Lach, D. F. 1965–1977. *Asia in the Making of Europe.* Starts with Vol I, Book I. Chicago: University of Chicago Press, 1965. Several not relevant. Vol. II, Book I, *The Visual Arts.* 1970; Book II, *The Literary Arts.* 1977. Most important for our purposes is Vol. II, Book III, *The Scholarly Disciplines.* 1977.

Lim, Heng Kow. 1978. *The Evolution of the Urban System in Malaya.* Kuala Lumpur: Penerbit Universiti Malaya.

MacKnight, C. C. 1986. "Changing Perspectives in Island Southeast Asia," pp. 215–227 in *Southeast Asia in the 9th to 14th Centuries*. ed. by David G. Marr and A. C. Milner. Singapore: Chong Moh.

Majumdar, R. C. 1937–38. *Hindu Colonies in the Far East*. 2 volumes. Lahore: The Punjab Sanskrit Book Depot. 2nd ed. 1963. Calcutta: Firma K. L. Kuknopadhyay.

Majumdar, R. C. 1963. *Ancient Indian Colonization in South-East Asia*. Baroda: B. J. Sandesara.

Marr, David G. and A. C. Milner, eds. 1986. *Southeast Asia in the 9th to 14th Centuries*. Singapore Institute of Southeast Asian Studies and the Research School of Pacific Studies, Australian National University. Singapore: Chong Moh.

Marsden, William. 3rd ed. 1811, reprinted 1966. *A History of Sumatra*. Kuala Lumpur: Oxford University Press.

McCloud, Donald G. 1986. *System and Process in Southeast Asia: The Evolution of a Region*. Boulder, Colorado: Westview Press.

Meilink-Roelofsz, M. A. P. 1970. "Trade and Islam in the Malay–Indonesian Archipelago Prior to the Arrival of the Europeans," pp. 137–157 in *Islam and the Trade of Asia: A Colloquium*. ed. by D. S. Richards. Philadelphia: University of Pennsylvania Press.

Nilakanta Sastri, K. A. 1940. "Sri Vijaya," *Bulletin de l'Ecole Française d'Extrême-Orient* XL: 239–313.

Nilakanta Sastri, K. A. 1949. *History of Sri Vijaya*. Madras: University of Madras Press.

Nilakanta Sastri, K. A. 1978. *South India and South-East Asia: Studies in Their History and Culture*. Mysore: Geetha Book House.

Nooteboom, C. 1950–1951. "Sumatra en de zeevaart op de Indische Oceaan," pp. 119–127 in *Indonesië, vierdejaargang 1950–1951*. S'Gravenhage: van Hoeve.

Pigeaud, T. G. T., ed. 1960–63. *Java in the Fourteenth Century. A Study in Cultural History . . . 1365 A.D.* 3rd edition in 5 volumes. The Hague: M. Nijhoff.

Pires, Tomé. See Cortesão (1944).

Sandu, Kernial Singh and Paul Wheatley. 1983. *Melaka: The Transformation of a Malay Capital c. 1400–1980*. 2 volumes. Kuala Lumpur: Oxford University Press for the Institute of Southeast Asian Studies.

Simkin, C. G. F. 1968. *The Traditional Trade of Asia*. London: Oxford University Press.

Sopher, David E. 1965. *The Sea Nomads. A Study Based on the Literature of the Maritime Boat People of Southeast Asia.* Memoirs of the National Museum, Singapore, No. 5. Printed by Lim Bian Han.

Tibbetts, G. R. 1956a. "The Malay Peninsula as Known to the Arab Geographers," *Journal of Tropical Geography* IX: 21–60.

Tibbetts, G. R. 1956b. "Pre-Islamic Arabia and South East Asia," *Journal of the Malayan Branch of the Royal Asiatic Society* XXIX: 182–208.

Tibbetts, G. R. 1957. "Early Muslim Traders in South East Asia," *Journal of the Malayan Branch of the Royal Asiatic Society* XXX: 1–45.

Tregonning, K. G. 1962. *Malaysian Historical Sources.* Singapore: Department of History, University of Singapore.

van Leur, J. C. 1955. "On Early Asian Trade," *Indonesian Trade and Society: Essays in Asian Social and Economic History.* The Hague-Bandung.

Wang, Gungwu, ed. 1964. *Malaysia: A Survey.* London: Pall Mall Press and also Praeger.

Wheatley, Paul. 1961. *The Golden Khersonese: Studies in the Historical Geography of the Malay Peninsula before A.D. 1500.* Kuala Lumpur: University of Malaya Press.

Wheatley, Paul. 1983. *Nagara and Commandery: Origins of the Southeast Asian Urban Traditions.* Chicago: University of Chicago Geography Department.

Whitmore, John K. 1977. "The Opening of Southeast Asia, Trading Patterns through the Centuries," pp. 139–153 in *Economic Exchange and Social Interaction in Southeast Asia. Perspectives from Prehistory and Ethnography.* ed. by Karl L. Hutterer. Ann Arbor: University of Michigan Papers on South and Southeast Asia, No. 13.

Winstedt, R. O. 1917. "The Advent of Muhammadanism in the Malay Peninsula and Archipelago," *Journal of the Straits Branch of the Royal Asiatic Society* 77: 171–175.

Winstedt, R. O. 1935. "A History of Malaya," *Journal of the Malayan Branch of the Royal Asiatic Society* XIII: 1–210. Second edition, Singapore, 1962.

Winstedt, R. O. 1948. *Malaya and its History.* London: Hutchinson's University Library.

Winstedt, R. O. 1982. *A History of Malaya,* revised and enlarged. Kuala Lumpur: Marican and Sons. (See Winstedt, 1935.)

Wolters, O. W. 1967. *Early Indonesian Commerce: A Study of the Origins of Srivijaya.* Ithaca: Cornell University Press.

Wolters, O. W. 1970. *The Fall of Srivijaya in Malay History.* Ithaca: Cornell University Press.

Wolters, O. W. 1975. "Landfall on the Palembang Coast in Medieval Times," *Indonesia* 20: 1–57.

China

Allsen, Thomas, 1983. "The Yuan Dynasty and the Uighurs of Turfan in the 13th Century," pp. 243–280 in *China among Equals: The Middle Kingdom and Its Neighbors, 10th–14th Centuries*. ed. by Morris Rossabi. Berkeley: University of California Press.

Aubin, F., ed. 1970–1980. *Etudes Song. In mémoriam Etienne Balazs*. This is a serial publication of articles. Série: Histoire et Institutions. Paris: Mouton & Cie. and Ecole des Hautes Etudes.

Balazs, E. 1964a. "The Birth of Capitalism in China," pp. 34–54 in *Chinese Civilization and Bureaucracy: Variations on a Theme*. Trans. by H. M. Wright. New Haven and London: Yale University Press.

Balazs, E. 1964b. *Chinese Civilization and Bureaucracy: Variations on a Theme*. Trans. by H. M. Wright. New Haven and London: Yale University Press.

Balazs, E. 1976. "Une carte des centres commerciaux de la Chine à la fin du 11e siècle," pp. 275–280 in *Etudes Song. In mémoriam Etienne Balazs*. ed. by F. Aubin. Paris: Mouton.

Bulletin of Sung and Yuan Studies. Annual to 1981; continues as *Sung Studies Newsletter*.

Carter, T. F. 1925, 2nd ed. 1955. *The Invention of Printing in China and its Spread Westward*. Second edition revised by L. C. Goodrich. New York: Ronald Press Co.

Chan, Albert. 1982. *The Glory and Fall of the Ming Dynasty*. Norman: University of Oklahoma Press.

Chang, Fu-jui. 1962. *Les fonctionnaires des Song: index de titres*. Paris: Mouton.

Chang, Wing-tsit. 1957. "Neo-Confucianism and Chinese Scientific Thought," in *Philosophy East and West* 6. An attempt to explain the failure of China to develop modern science.

Chau, Ju-Kua. 1911. *Chau Ju-Kua: Chu-fan-chi [His Work on the Chinese and Arab Trade in the Twelfth and Thirteenth Centuries]*. Translated from the Chinese by Friedrich Hirth and W. W. Rockhill. St. Petersburg: Printing Office of the Imperial Academy of Sciences.

Chou, Chin-chêng. 1974. *An Economic History of China*. Trans. by Edward Kaplan. Bellingham: Program in East Asian Studies, Western Washington State College.

Dawson, Raymond S. 1972, 1976. *Imperial China*. London: Hutchinson. Also Harmondsworth: Penguin.

de Rachewiltz, Igor. 1983. "Turks in China under the Mongols: A Preliminary Investigation of Turco-Mongol Relations in the 13th and 14th Centuries," pp. 281–310 in *China among Equals: The Middle Kingdom and its Neighbors, 10th–14th Centuries*. ed. by Morris Rossabi. Berkeley: University of California Press.

Di Meglio, R. R. 1965. "Il commercio arabo con la Cina dal X secolo all'avvento dei Mongoli," *Annali Istituto Universitari Orientale di Napoli*: 89–95.

Duyvendak, J. J. L. 1949. *China's Discovery of Africa*. London: A. Probsthain.

Elvin, Mark. 1973. *The Pattern of the Chinese Past*. Stanford: Stanford University Press.

Enoki, Kazuo. 1954. "Some Remarks on the Country of Ta-Sh'ih as Known to the Chinese Under the Sung," *Asia Major* IV, 1, New Series: 1–19.

Fairbank, John K. 1957. *Chinese Thought and Institutions*. Chicago: University of Chicago Press.

Fairbank, J. et al. 1973. *East Asia: Tradition and Transformation*. Boston: Houghton Mifflin.

Filesi, Teobaldo. 1972. *China and Africa in the Middle Ages*. Trans. by David Morison. London: Frank Cass in association with the Central Asian Research Centre. Published originally in Italian in 1962.

Gernet, Jacques. 1962. *Daily Life in China on the Eve of the Mongol Invasion, 1250–1276* [Hangchow, China]. Trans. by H. M. Wright. London: Allen & Unwin.

Grousset, René. 1942. *Histoire de la Chine*. (Paris) 1952 English trans. *The Rise and Splendour of the Chinese Empire*. London: G. Bles.

Haeger, John W., ed. 1975. *Crisis and Prosperity in Sung China*. Tucson: University of Arizona Press.

Hartwell, Robert. 1962. "A Revolution in the Chinese Iron and Coal Industries during the Northern Sung, 960–1126 A.D.," *Journal of Asian Studies* XXI: 153–162.

Hartwell, Robert. 1966. "Markets, Technology, and the Structure of Enterprise in the Development of the Eleventh-Century Chinese Iron and Steel Industry," *Journal of Economic History* XXVI: 29–58.

Hartwell, Robert. 1967. "A Cycle of Economic Change in Imperial China:

Coal and Iron in Northeast China, 750–1350," *Journal of the Social and Economic History of the Orient* X: 102–159.

Hartwell, Robert. 1982. "Demographic, Political, and Social Transformations of China, 750–1550," *Harvard Journal of Asiatic Studies* XXXXII: 365–442.

Hermann, Albert. 1966. *An Historical Atlas of China*. Chicago: Aldine Publishing Co.

Hervouet, Yves. 1969. *Bibliographie des travaux en langues occidentales sur les Song parus de 1946 à 1965*. Bordeaux: Université de Bordeaux.

Hirth, Friedrich and W. W. Rockhill, eds. and trans. 1911. *Chau Ju-Kua*. St. Petersburg: Printing Office of the Imperial Academy of Sciences. See Chau (1911).

Ho, Ping-ti. 1970. "An Estimate of the Total Population of Sung-Chin China," pp. 34–54 in *Etudes Song. In mémoriam Etienne Balazs*, Sér. 1, No. 1. ed. by F. Aubin. Paris: Mouton & Cie. and Ecole des Hautes Etudes.

Hsiao, Chi-ching. 1978. *The Military Establishment of the Yuan Dynasty*. Cambridge, Massachusetts: Harvard University Press.

Hsieh, Chiao-min. 1973. *Atlas of China*. ed. by Christopher Salter. New York: McGraw-Hill.

Hucker, Charles O. 1975. *China's Imperial Past: An Introduction to Chinese History and Culture*. Stanford: Stanford University Press.

Hucker, Charles O. 1978. *China to 1850: A Short History*. Stanford: Stanford University Press.

Hudson, G. F. 1970. "The Medieval Trade of China," pp. 159–168 in *Islam and the Trade of Asia: A Colloquium*. ed. by D. S. Richards. Philadelphia: University of Pennsylvania Press.

Ibn Battuta. 1929. *Travels in Asia and Africa, 1325–1354. Selections*. Trans. by H. A. R. Gibb. Paper reprint 1983. London: Routledge and Kegan Paul.

Kahle, Paul. 1956. "Chinese Porcelain in the Lands of Islam." In *Opera Minora*. Leiden, 1956. Also *Transactions of the Oriental Ceramic Society* (1940–41): 27–46. London: The Society.

Kato, Shigeshi. 1936. "On the Hang or the Association of Merchants in China," *Memoirs of the Research Department of the Toyo Bunko* VIII: 45–83.

Kracke, Edward, Jr. 1954–55. "Sung Society: Change within Tradition," *Far Eastern Quarterly* XIV: 479–488.

Kuwabara, J. 1928 (Part I) and 1935 (Part II). "P'u Shou-keng. . . . A

General Sketch of the Trade of the Arabs in China during the T'ang and Sung Eras," *Memoirs of the Research Department of the Toyo Bunko* II, Part I, 1–79; *Memoirs of the Research Department of the Toyo Bunko* VII: Part II, 1–104.

Langlois, John J., ed. 1981. *China Under Mongol Rule.* Princeton: Princeton University Press.

Lee, James. 1978. "Migration and Expansion in Chinese History," pp. 20–47 in *Human Migration, Patterns and Policies.* ed. by W. H. McNeill and R. Adams. Bloomington: University of Indiana Press.

Lee, Mabel Ping-hua. 1921. *The Economic History of China, with Special Reference to Agriculture.* New York: Columbia University Press.

Li, Dun Jen. 1978. *The Ageless Chinese: A History.* New York: Scribner.

Li Guohao, Zheng Mengwen, and Cao Tiangin, eds. 1982. *Explorations in the History of Science and Technology in China.* Shanghai: Shanghai Chinese Classics Publishing House.

Liu, James T. C. and Peter J. Golas, eds. 1969. *Problems in Asian Civilizations: Change in Sung China: Innovation or Renovation?* Lexington, Massachusetts: D. C. Heath.

Lo, Jung-Pang. 1955. "The Emergence of China as a Sea Power during the Late Sung and Early Yuan Periods," *Far Eastern Quarterly* XIV: 489–503.

Lo, Jung-Pang. 1957. "China as a Sea Power, 1127–1368." Ph.D. Dissertation, University of California, Berkeley.

Lo, Jung-Pang. 1958. "The Decline of the Early Ming Navy," *Oriens Extrêmus* V: 149–168.

Lo, Jung-Pang. 1969. "Maritime Commerce and its Relation to the Sung Navy," *Journal of the Economic and Social History of the Orient* XII: 57–101.

Lo, Jung-Pang. 1970. "Chinese Shipping and East-West Trade from the Tenth to the Fourteenth Century," pp. 167–174 in *Sociétés et compagnies de commerce en orient et dans l'Océan Indien.* Paris: S.E.V.P.E.N.

Lopez, R. S. 1952. "China Silk in Europe in the Yuan Period," *Journal of the American Oriental Society* 72: 72–76.

Ma, Laurence J. C. 1971. *Commercial Development and Urban Change in Sung China (960–1279).* Ann Arbor: University of Michigan Press.

McKnight, Brian E. 1971. *Village and Bureaucracy in Southern Sung China.* Chicago: University of Chicago Press.

McNeill, William H. 1982. *The Pursuit of Power: Technology, Armed*

Force, and Society Since A.D. 1000. Chicago: University of Chicago Press.

Milton, Joyce. 1970. *Tradition and Revolt: Imperial China, Islands of the Rising Sun.* New York: HBJ Press.

Morton, William S. 1980. *China: Its History and Culture.* New York: Lippincott and Crowell.

Needham, Joseph. 1954–85. *Science and Civilisation in China.* 6 volumes. Cambridge: Cambridge University Press.

Needham, Joseph. 1970. *Clerks and Craftsmen in China and the West: Lectures and Addresses on the History of Science and Technology.* Cambridge: Cambridge University Press.

Needham, Joseph. 1981. *Science in Traditional China: A Comparative Perspective.* Collection of papers and lectures. Hong Kong and Cambridge, Massachusetts: Harvard University Press.

Pelliot, Paul. 1933. "Les grands voyages maritimes Chinois au debut du XVe siècle," *T'oung Pao* XXX: 235–455.

Reischauer, E. O. 1940–41. "Notes on T'ang Dynasty Sea Routes," *Harvard Journal of Asiatic Studies* V: 142–164.

Rockhill, W. W. 1913–1915. "Notes on the Relations and Trade of China with the Eastern Archipelago and the Coast of the Indian Ocean during the Fourteenth Century." in *T'oung Pao* (Leiden). Vol. XIV (1913), pp. 473–476; Vol. XV (1914), pp. 419–47; Vol. XVI (1915), pp. 61–159, 234–271, 374–392, 435–467, 604–626.

Rodzinski, Witold. 1979–1983. *A History of China.* 2 volumes. Oxford and New York: Pergamon Press.

Rodzinski, Witold. 1984. *The Walled Kingdom: A History of China from Antiquity to the Present.* New York: Free Press.

Rossabi, Morris, ed. 1983. *China among Equals: The Middle Kingdom and Its Neighbors, 10th–14th Centuries.* Berkeley: University of California Press.

Sadao, Aoyama. 1976. "Le développement des transports fluxiaux sous les Sung," pp. 281–294 in *Etudes Song*, Sér. I, Histoire et Institutions. Trans. into French from the Japanese by F. Aubin. Paris: Mouton.

Salmon, C. and D. Lombard. 1979. "Un vaisseau du XIIIème s. retrouvé avec sa cargaison dans la rade de Zaitun," *Archipelago* XVIII: 57–67.

Schurmann, H. F. 1956. *Economic Structure of the Yüan Dynasty: Translation of Chapters 93 and 94 of the Yüan shih.* Cambridge, Massachusetts: Harvard University Press.

Sellman, Roger R. 1954. *An Outline Atlas of Eastern History.* London: E. Arnold. Also includes India, Southeastern Asia.

Shiba, Yoshinobu. 1970. *Commerce and Society in Sung China*. Trans. by Mark Elvin. Ann Arbor, Michigan: Center for Chinese Studies, University of Michigan.

Shiba, Yoshinobu. 1983. "Sung Foreign Trade: Its Scope and Organization," pp. 89–115 in *China among Equals: The Middle Kingdom and Its Neighbors, 10th–14th Centuries*. ed. by M. Rossabi. Berkeley: University of California Press.

Sivin, N. 1982. "Why the Scientific Revolution Did Not Take Place in China—or Didn't It?" pp. 89–106 in *Explorations in the History and Technology in China. Compiled in Honor of the 80th Birthday of J. Needham*. ed. by Li et al. Shanghai: Shanghai Chinese Classics Publishing House.

Skinner, G. William, ed. 1977. *The City in Late Imperial China*. Stanford: Stanford University Press.

Skoljar, Sergei A. 1971. "L'artillérie de jet à l'époque sung," pp. 119–141 in *Etudes Song. In mémoriam Etienne Balazs*, Sér. 1, No. 2. ed. by F. Aubin. Paris: Mouton.

So, Alvin. 1986. *The South China Silk District*. Albany, N.Y.: State University of New York Press.

Sung Studies Newsletter. 1970–1977. Ithaca, N.Y.

Tsien, Tsuen-hsuin. 1982. "Why Paper and Printing were Invented First in China and Used Later in Europe," pp. 459–469 in *Explorations in the History of Science and Technology in China: Compiled in Honor of the 80th Birthday of Joseph Needham*. ed. by Li et al. Shanghai: Shanghai Chinese Classics Publishing House.

Wang, Gungwu. 1958. "The Nanhai Trade: A Study of the Early History of Chinese Trade in the South China Sea," *Journal of the Malayan Branch of the Royal Asiatic Society* XXXI, Part 2: 1–135.

Wang, Gungwu. 1970. " 'Public' and 'Private' Overseas Trade in Chinese History," pp. 215–225 in *Sociétés et compagnies de commerce en orient et dans l'Océan Indien*. ed. by M. Mollat. Paris: S.E.V.P.E.N.

Weber, Max. 1951, reissued 1968. *The Religion of China: Confucianism and Taoism*. Trans. by Hans Gerth. Glencoe, Illinois: The Free Press.

Wheatley, Paul. 1959. "Geographical Notes on Some Commodities Involved in Sung Maritime Trade," *Journal of the Malayan Branch of the Royal Asiatic Society* XXXII (2): 5–140.

Wheatley, Paul. 1971. *The Pivot of the Four Quarters: A Preliminary Enquiry into the Origins and Character of the Ancient Chinese City*. Edinburgh: Edinburgh University Press.

Wilbur, C. Martin. 1943. "Industrial Slavery in China during the Former

Han Dynasty (206 B.C.–A.D. 25)," *The Journal of Economic History* III: 56–69.

Wilkinson, Endymion. 1973. *The History of Imperial China: A Research Guide*. Cambridge, Massachusetts: Harvard University Press.

Wilson, A. A., S. L. Greenblatt, and R. W. Wilson, eds. 1983. *Methodological Issues in Chinese Studies*. New York: Praeger.

Worthy, Edmund. 1975. "Regional Control in the Southern Sung Salt Administration," pp. 101–141 in *Crisis and Prosperity in Sung China*. ed. by John Haeger. Tucson: University of Arizona Press.

Yang, Lien-chêng. 1952. *Money and Credit in China: A Short History*. Cambridge, Massachusetts: Harvard University Press.

Yang, Lien-chêng. 1969. *Excursions in Sinology*. Cambridge, Massachusetts: Harvard University Press.

Index